ZAPOTEC STONEWORKERS

The Dynamics of Rural Simple Commodity Production in Modern Mexican Capitalism

Scott Cook
The University of Connecticut

UNIVERSITY
PRESS OF
AMERICA

Library of Congress Catalog Card Number: 81-40584

Dedicated to

the <u>Metateros</u> in the Oaxaca Valley
and to My Parents in the Ohio Valley

Metatero cutting a block (trozo) of stone
with a crowbar (barreta) in the Mesa Grande
quarry, San Sebastian Teitipac.

ACKNOWLEDGMENTS

The field work upon which this monograph is based was conducted in the Valley of Oaxaca, Mexico during a continuous period of residence from July 1966 through July 1968 and for shorter periods in 1970, 1972, and in 1977-1979. Preliminary field work in the municipio of San Sebastian Teitipac was conducted during the summer of 1965 when I was a participant in the Tri-Institutional Field Training Program sponsored in Oaxaca by the Department of Anthropology of Stanford University. Financial support during 1965 and 1966/67 was provided by a PHS Predoctoral Fellowship and Supplementary Research grant administered by the Department of Anthropology of The University of Pittsburgh, and during 1967/68 by the National Science Foundation through the Oaxaca Markets Study Project, Department of Anthropology, University of California at Los Angeles, with Ralph L. Beals as principal investigator. Funding for research during the summer of 1970 was provided by the Latin American Studies Center at Michigan State University; subsequent funding was provided by the Graduate Research Foundation at The University of Connecticut (1972, 1977), by the Social Science Research Council (summer and fall, 1978), and by the National Science Foundation (BNS-78-13948) (1979).

I owe a debt of gratitude to several persons in Mexico who, over the years, have been instrumental in authorizing and facilitating my research in their country. I am especially grateful in this regard to Fernando Camara of the Instituto Nacional de Antropología e Historia and to Rodolfo Stavenhagen and Alejandro Guzman of the Dirección General de Culturas Populares in Mexico City, to Lorenzo Gamio and Manuel Esparza, successive directors of the Centro Regional of I.N.A.H. in Oaxaca, and to various officials in the state government of Oaxaca, especially to Lic. Osvaldo Garcia Criollo and Ing. Fernando Avila Nava who, in recent years served as successive directors of the Dirección General de Desarrollo Económico. I also wish to express my gratitude to the authorities and many residents of San Sebastian Teitipac, San Juan Teitipac, Tlacolula de Matamoros, and Magdalena Ocotlán who were tolerant,

v

cooperative, and hospitable toward this inquisitive
'gringo' as he observed their activities, interrupted
their routines, and asked many bothersome questions
about matters that were sometimes personal or sensitive.
A special debt of thanks goes to Wenceslao Gutierrez
and his family, Luis Gutierrez, and Filomeno Gabriel
in San Sebastian Teitipac, to Efren and Rosendo Carranza
in San Juan Teitipac, to Armando Carranza, Emilio
Alvarado, and Inocencio Morales in Tlacolula de
Matamoros, and to Atanasio Hernandez in Magdalena
Ocotlán for indispensable assistance and hospitality
in their respective communities.

Cecil R. Welte in Oaxaca City generously provided
me with work space and access to library and other resources in his Oficina De Estudios De Humanidad Del
Valle de Oaxaca; he also made available his surveying
and cartographic skills when they were needed during the
project, and was a constant source of stimulating commentary on my research and on Oaxaca studies in general.
Ralph L. Beals provided guidance and encouragement at
various stages during my work with his project in
1967-68, and the late Edward E. LeClair, Jr. was an
incisive and provocative critic of theoretical and analytical aspects of my earlier research, and was kind
enough to make a detailed commentary on several chapters
of an early draft of the present manuscript.

The faculty and students of the Department of
Anthropology at The University of Connecticut--especially
those who participate in the Comparative Studies in
Economy and Society program--have, over the past decade,
provided me with an important critical perspective from
which to judge the direction and relevance of my work
in Oaxaca. I also wish to express my appreciation to
my parents and to my wife Hilda and our children, all
of whom have inevitably been drawn into my Oaxaca research and who have endured this involvement over the
years with patience, understanding and interest.

Last, but not least, I wish to thank The University of Connecticut Research Foundation for providing
the funds and personnel, a series of cooperative and
persevering typists, which have made possible the production of this typescript; and also the Publications
Department at the University, and especially Ray
Blanchette, for drafting the figures. Needless to say,
I am especially grateful to the University Press of
America for its willingness to publish this monograph;
it came through where a host of others feared to tread.

". . . son los de este pueblo, muy oficiosos,
y solícitos en la mercancía, y trajino a
otras provincias, y los que no tienen caudal
para tanto, tienen hornos de cal y de cántaros
de barro, canteras de piedra, de que hacen
los metates, o molinos ordinarios de maíz,
y de todo proveen a la ciudad, con grande
abundancia . . ."

". . . these people are very industrious,
and solicitous of commodities which they
transport to other provinces, and those
who lack the wealth for such, have kilns
for lime and for clay pitchers, quarries
for stone, from which they make metates, or
ordinary corn grindstones, and they provision the city with everything in great
abundance . . ."

Fray Francisco de Burgoa (Geográfica
Descripcion I:416), 17th Century Spanish
chronicler referring to the 'Valley Zapotec.

TABLE OF CONTENTS

xii

LIST OF FIGURES

LIST OF TABLES

LIST OF PHOTOGRAPHS

Metateros working together to move a large slab of stone which has been blasted loose from its bed (Magdalena Ocotlan).

xix

CHAPTER I. INTRODUCTION

The Problem

This is a study of a rural craft industry in the
'Central Valleys' region of the state of Oaxaca,
Mexico, that produces <u>metates</u> or grindstones to supply
a traditional regional demand which, like its object
commodities, is a pre-capitalist survival.[1] Even
though the Oaxaca economy has long functioned within
the orbit of national and international capital,
certain of its production and exchange sectors, namely,
those involving the manufacture of products for auto-
consumption and of commodities like metates for use in
present-artisan households, have incorporated and
continue to incorporate elements suggestive of a non-
capitalist form of commodity economy. Together with
my attempt throughout this monograph to convey to the
reader a complete and accurate picture of the objective
and subjective life-conditions of the metate producers
(i.e., the <u>metateros</u>), I will also identify, describe,
and analyze the ways in which this type of small
industry plays a dynamic role in local and regional
economic life.[2]

While the study includes a detailed analysis
of the community matrix within which the <u>metateros</u>
live and work as an essential prelude to an intensive
examination of all aspects of the internal structure
and dynamics of their industry (which, incidentally,
I assume to be representative of non-capitalist craft
production by male workers in the region), it also
examines the position of the industry and of its
communities in the regional economy. Finally, in the
concluding chapter, I will present some tentative
findings from my continuing research on small-scale,
labor-intensive industries in the 'Central Valleys' so
as to document in a preliminary way the dynamics of
rural simple commodity production in Oaxaca today, and
to trace some of its relationships with the surrounding
capitalist matrix.[3]

It is appropriate here to briefly clarify what
is meant by the concept of simple (or small) commodity
production and to emphasize the contradictory nature of

1

the historical process it represents. On the one hand, the concept assumes a domestic production regime, operating with non-waged family labor-power, in which the direct producers own or control the principal means of production and produce essentially for auto-consumption. These conditions imply an anti-capitalist dynamic that pulls direct producers away from labor and other commodity markets, which are predicated upon a separation of production from consumption and of direct producers from the means of production, and toward domestic units striving for reproductive viability through production for own-use. On the other hand, simple commodity production implies some degree of production for exchange by domestic units and, consequently, the necessary involvement of direct producers in exchange or marketing relationships. This, in turn, implies a potential for expanded reproduction or for the accumulation of exchange value and the consequent expansion of the commodity producing capacity of the domestic unit as an enterprise. It is presumably this aspect of small commodity production which had led students of Middle America to follow Sol Tax in labelling it as "penny capitalism" (1953) or students of European economic history to consider it as a sort of transitional form between feudalism and capitalism (cf. Sweezy, Dobb, et.al., 1967; Dobb 1963 and 1976). Small commodity production does, in essence, embody certain necessary elements for becoming capitalist, yet it need not develop in this direction-- especially when it is subsumed in a capitalist social formation and has structural limitations imposed upon its accumulative potential (or where more advanced capitalist forms have preempted its development in specific lines of production). Small commodity production may thrive in the latter situation not only because it serves as a kind of refuge for direct producers whose labor-power is either not in demand or is the object of seasonal or irregular demand by capitalist enterprises but also because it provides an arena for labor-intensive forms of capital accumulation and serves as a training ground for would-be or incipient capitalists. Its trajectory, then, is clearly linked to the dynamic of accumulation in the advanced capitalist sector and to its role as a sort of pioneer of capitalism in both agricultural and industrial spheres of labor-intensive, capital-scarce types of production; but it also contains an anti-capitalist tendency rooted in the propensity of its component units to produce for autoconsumption with non-waged, family labor-power (cf. Cook 1978:293-310; Palerm 1980:199-224).[4]

2

The problem of capitalist/noncapitalist relations, as well as the concept of simple commodity production, are products and concerns of the Marxist tradition. Although this tradition was not explicitly or systematically employed, either theoretically or methodologically, during the most intensive period of my research on the metate industry (1966-1968), it has assumed an increasing operational importance in my subsequent work. What, the reader may justifiably ask, are some of the reasons for this trend?

Perhaps the most comprehensive explanation lies in my progressive disenchantment with the theoretical and analytical limitations of the two approaches prevailing in economic anthropology during the 1960s. I have explained elsewhere precisely how, in my judgment, historical materialism presents a viable approach for resolving certain fundamental contradictions generated by the 'formalist-substantivist' controversy that bisected economic anthropology during this period (Cook 1969 and 1974; cf. Semenov 1974:226 for a commentary on the insertion of Marxism into this controversy in my 1969 article). I should emphasize in retrospect that this changing theoretical posture was, in fact, developing in counterpoint to my attempt to deal with a series of concrete analytical problems in my Oaxaca research.

Some limitations of the two prevailing approaches, which became increasingly apparent to me during the course of my continuing research on the metate industry, can be briefly summarized as follows: (1) a tendency to reduce so-called 'explanations' of complex processes involving inter-related and contradictory variables to mere descriptions of a series of isolated events or activities; (2) a tendency to seek meaning or explanation of economic process exclusively at the level of empirically observable behavior and a concomitant failure to develop any coherent theoretical or conceptual framework for penetrating the level of 'appearances' (i.e., observable economic conduct) to expose underlying social dynamics grounded in relations of production; (3) a pervasive focus on atomistic individual agents as units of analysis and explanation, even to the extreme of viewing social structure as simply the patterned configuration of individual behaviors with no methodology for viewing individual agents as personifications of social categories or as representatives of particular sets of socioeconomic relations and interests; and (4) an almost completely 'circulationist' view of the economy which reduces it

3

to exchange and distribution activities while simultaneously disregarding or minimizing the forces and relations of production so that, for example, commodities are taken as givens and exchange/distribution relations are viewed as synonymous with economic relations rather than being considered within a broader matrix of social production. In Chapters 2, 7, and 8 I will present examples of the application of Marxist concepts and analysis which overcome these limitations in the orthodox economic anthropological approaches. These examples should by no means be construed to imply that I arbitrarily reject all non-Marxist approaches as useless or that I advocate a personalized version of the Marxist tradition as a ready-made, problem-free alternative mode of analysis and explanation. On the contrary, in several subsequent chapters I also employ non-Marxist concepts and reasoning and, in Chapters 7 and 8, I identify and discuss some of the difficulties encountered in my limited effort to systematically apply selected elements of Marxist theory.

My posture towards the Marxist tradition has been and remains one of proceeding with caution, pragmatism and flexibility, of avoiding sectarian controversy and focusing principally on that central current of Marxism which is firmly but not slavishly grounded in the Marx-Engels-Lenin corpus. I am skeptical of new, fashionable yet often arrogant and usually pedantic 'theoretical readings' of the mainstream corpus but try to understand them as reflecting the necessarily changing character of Marxist thought. I have yet to encounter any viable alternative to the premise that the production of knowledge is a process which must proceed through a dialectical interplay between subject and object, theory and fact, thought and experience, reality as represented conceptually and reality as perceived empirically (Cook 1974:806-808).

There is little doubt that among social and economic anthropologists the methodological balance has swung decidedly in favor of those who advocate 'macro' as opposed to 'micro' analysis, and that accordingly the preferrred unit of investigation has shifted away from the local community toward the regional, national, or international system. There is, however, substantial disagreement about how this strategy can or should be most effectively operationalized. Indeed, there is no uniformity of scholarly opinion as to how the objectified social totality (i.e., the 'social formation,' 'total society' or 'social system') ought to be conceptualized, and even less as to which dimension or part of such a heuristic entity ought to serve as the strategic point of departure for inquiry. For the most part I find myself in agreement with the arguments of those scholars who have laid down the theoretical and analytical ground-work for this shift in focus; but I reject a concomitant tendency to deemphasize or eliminate micro-empirical inquiry as either incompatible with the macro-approach or as tantamount to empiricism. I strongly agree with W. Kula's perceptive observation that ". . . the most fruitful macroanalytic research will never make microanalytic research superfluous" (1976:45), and I would further propose that the central problematic in contemporary social scientific inquiry hinges on the analysis of the dialectic between macroprocess and microprocess in concrete situations with concepts formulated on the basis of logic and experience. Moreover, if our attempt is to approximate the social reality lived daily by direct producers in regional economies then we must employ a method which assigns a high priority to collecting data from these people themselves and which does not restrict itself to a combination of abstruse a priori concepts and abstract a posteriori inferences from national censuses.

My position on these issues should not be accepted uncritically; during the course of reading sub-sequent chapters of the monograph the reader will be able to form independent, critical judgments regarding my selective use of Marxist and non-Marxist approaches and of my admittedly eclectic, empirical orientation. I make no prior claims as to the definitiveness of my interpretations or applications of these approaches, and it is the reader's duty to determine the degree of success or failure with which I have proceeded. It should be kept in mind that my overriding concern in conducting this study has been analytical: to contribute to the process of producing valid knowledge about craft production in a regional economy of Mexico; theoretical issues have been considered only to the extent necessary to promote the achievement of this analytical goal. I ask that the monograph be evaluated from this point of departure.

The Structure of Society and Economy
in Oaxaca Today

Developing in Oaxaca during the Spanish colonial
period and entering the 20th century historical stream
essentially intact was an underdeveloped capitalist
socioeconomic formation encompassing the following
rural institutional components: (1) a village-based
social system in which constituent households were
interrelated through a civil-religious hierarchy
comprising a series of ranked and age-graded posts or
'cargos'; (2) a fiesta or ceremonial cycle in which
sponsorship of a saint's cult celebrations (mayordomías)
and wedding celebrations (fandangos) was often obligatory and prestigeful in proportion to its cost; (3)
obligatory communal labor service (tequio) for the
performance of work on village projects (e.g., irrigation canals, communal field cultivation and harvest,
construction of public buildings); (4) an institutionalized mechanism of reciprocal exchange known as
guelaguetza which involves the circulation of goods and
services; (5) inter-community production specialization
and the concomitant importance of artisans and traders;
(6) a cyclical or rotating marketplace organization to
facilitate inter-community trade; and (7) a peasant-
Indian labor force conditioned to exploitative work
arrangements (wage labor or various kinds of rent) and
involved in production for exchange as well as for use--
with profit-oriented production controlled by members
of a petty or middle bourgeoisie and subsistence-
oriented production controlled primarily by independent
households (cf. Spores 1965; Taylor 1972; Hamnett 1971;
Mendieta y Nuñez et. al., 1949; Carrasco 1951; Wolf
1967; Chance 1978).

Today, the peasant-artisan villagers of Oaxaca
make their living by working the land (basic crops are
maize, beans and squash with a wide variety of other
subsistence and cash crops also cultivated), by animal
husbandry (cattle, sheep, goats, pigs, poultry), and by
producing a wide variety of artisan products (e.g.,
pottery, baskets, sarapes and other woven goods,
metates, rope, leather and wood products). Wage labor,
often involving temporary seasonal migration out of
the local village, has provided an important supplementary source of cash income for Oaxaca peasant households for several decades but is becoming increasingly
important in recent years (e.g., construction work in
urban areas). Agricultural technology remains simple
with the ox-drawn plow, the machete, the hoe (coa),
the crowbar (barreta), and the sickle (hoz) making up

the basic tool kit; a wide range of other tools and
equipment (including tractors and water pumps) is
available but their ownership and use is restricted
due to the scarcity (unequal distribution) of money
capital and credit. Both channel and pot irrigation
(which are pre-columbian in origin) are widely practiced
but agricultural production still depends heavily on
rainfall and unirrigated (temporal) lands; rainfall is
seasonal with the rainy season beginning in April and
lasting through September or October each year (cf.
Flannery et. al., 1967; Kirkby 1973; Lees 1973).
Cultivation tends to be limited to fields lying
outside the habitation area of the nucleated settlements according to the "infield-outfield" pattern of
land use (Wolf 1966:21), although there is cultivation
of garden plots within or near residence lots in most
villages. Permanent cultivation occurs only in the
presence of irrigation, and irrigated lands yield two
crops annually (consult Kirkby 1973 for more detailed
information on agricultural practices in Oaxaca).

The 'Central Valleys' region is, as we've seen,
characterized by a wide-spread reliance on seasonal
agriculture but there are zones in which irrigation
is significant (Kirkby 1973; Lees 1973) and these are
multiplying constantly through the impact of government-
sponsored projects.[5] As demonstrated in a study of the
Mezquital Valley (Hidalgo) by Medina and Quezada (1975),
craft production in rural Mexico is more prevalent in
areas with little or no irrigation. Likewise, my
recent research in the 'Central Valleys' region
indicates that the inter-district variation in the
incidence of craft production is significantly
associated with the differential distribution of
irrigation agriculture between districts. Thus, the
district with the highest proportion (21.7%) of first
class arable lands (i.e., those classified as de riego
and de humedad) is Etla which has a low incidence of
craft production; the district with the lowest
proportion of first class lands is Ocotlan which,
along with Tlacolula (5.28%--1st class), has the
highest incidence of craft production in the region.
On the other hand, Zimatlan, which has the lowest
incidence of craft production, has a percentage of
first class lands (5.41%) which is only slightly above
that of Tlacolula (and well below that of Etla) but
has the highest average of capital invested per
agricultural production unit of 5 hectares or less
(2nd highest per units of 5 hectares or more), as well
as the highest average value of reported agricultural
sales (see Appendix 2). Given the excellent work that

has already been done on the relationship between physiographic zones and land use (including case studies of costs and yields for different types of agriculture, e.g., Flannery, et. al., 1967; Kirkby 1973), and considering the improvements which are being made in census format and procedures, it is likely that future research will be able to establish clearer and more precise relationships between agriculture and craft production at the district level, as well as to make more definitive inter-district comparisons.

The proposition that a close linkage exists between agricultural and craft production in the Mexican rural economy has been documented in many case studies of local (e.g., Nash 1961; Diaz 1966; Cook 1970; Novelo 1976; Contreras 1976) and regional (e.g., Medina and Quezada 1975; Littlefield 1976; Guzman 1977) scope. There are several ways in which this linkage is expressed concretely but these can usually be reduced to the same prime cause: unequal distribution of arable land in the countryside and low fertility-productivity of land which is cultivated by peasant-artisans. As this study of the metateros will show, craft work in the Oaxaca countryside is often performed by landless or land poor households whose low agricultural productivity obliges them to produce craft commodities in order to acquire cash to purchase agricultural or other products essential to the maintenance and reproduction of their domestic units. The variability of demand for agricultural labor is also a relevant factor, especially given the prevalence of rainfall or seasonal (temporal) agriculture and the fact that there is a dry-season reduction in the demand for agricultural labor.

Whether we examine the contemporary economy of the 'Central Valleys' region from the perspective of circulation (i.e., the destination of products into use- or exchange-value circuits) or from that of the "social existence-form of labour power" (Takahashi 1967:31), we can classify it as a dependent mercantile capitalist formation, emancipated from colonial-tributary relations, but subjected to the hegemony of industrial capital and its state monopoly structure (cf. Leal 1975), which contains an important sector of small commodity production. It is not possible to estimate the proportion of total output in this economy which is produced for exchange, but it is clear that most artisan products and a substantial volume of agricultural products flow directly into commodity circuits. This is consistent with the regional division of labor in which many rural settlements have agricultural or craft product specializations whose origins can, in a significant number of them, be traced to the prehispanic or colonial periods (see Taylor 1972 and Chance 1978 for specific examples).

In this regional economy a significant proportion of the total peasant-artisan population (ca. 100,000 in 1970--see Appendix I) owns or directly controls the essential means of production and retains disposal rights over the bulk of the commodities they produce. Yet there is also significant inequality in the ownership of the means of production within and between communities, and many direct producers are dependent upon others for access to these means. These dependency relations generate a process through which a portion of the total product of those rural direct producers without necessary means of production (e.g., land, ox teams) is appropriated by the owners of such means (e.g., as rent in kind, rent in labor, money rent), most of whom are also direct producers but of a different socioeconomic stratum. There is also a substantial incidence of incipient or small-scale industrial capitalist enterprise (e.g., trapiches or cane-grinding mills which produce panela or caked brown sugar, mescal distilleries, textile manufactories) and capitalist relations are also evident in the agricultural, construction, and service sectors of the regional economy. While many direct producers are temporarily or partially involved in these capitalist relations of production as wage-laborers, it still appears that relations based on producer control of the means of production, reinforced by private ownership or usufruct, predominate.

Despite the differentiation of the rural population into socioeconomic strata (see Chapters 2 and 8 below), which is associated with wealth and productivity differences among domestic units, direct producers of all strata are necessarily involved, even if in differing degrees or indirectly, in labor processes geared toward the provisioning of the unit's reproductive requirements. The total income of the typical peasant-artisan domestic unit (PADU) in Oaxaca (this applies to all metatero units) is allocated between different essential functions as follows (see Beals 1975:86-101, 326-340; Wolf 1966): (1) fund of necessary consumption or the "subsistence budget"; (2) ceremonial fund or the "public and festive budget"; (3) fund for the replacement and expansion of the means of production or the "operational budget"; and (4) transfers to the interior (e.g., to the wealthiest peasants or other rural bourgeoisie) or to the exterior (e.g., via product, money, or labor markets) (see Szkely 1977:52 et. passim). In the process of provisioning these funds most PADUs, which ideally are neither wage-paying nor profit-seeking, produce commodities for potential consumers outside of the producing unit (and, as is the case with the metatero units, outside of the local community or region). Thus, to be a peasant-artisan in Oaxaca implies some degree of necessary involvement in producing for other-use and of consuming commodities not produced by one's own domestic unit. This process may be represented as the circuit C - M - C (commodity - money - commodity).

In the division of labor and specialization of the 'Central Valleys' region (see Figure 1), the metate industry includes only four of approximately two hundred local industrial units, allocated among some twenty-four discrete branches of production in 87 separate municipalities (personal survey). A tabulation of data from the 1970 General Population Census (DGE 1972) and from the V Agricultural-Livestock Census (DGE 1975) at the district level for the entire region (see Appendixes 1 and 2) indicates that approximately 8% of the regional EAP works primarily in "industries of transformation" (which includes most craft industries like the metate industry).[6] A large but undetermined number (perhaps a majority) of small producers in the region work only seasonally or irregularly in non-agricultural occupations and, consequently, are classified for census purposes as 'peasant agriculturists.' Unfortunately the available census data do not enable us to estimate the proportion of the EAP in agriculture which fits into the category of disguised part-time artisans. Our data do indicate that the domestic form which prevails among the metateros also predominates in nearly all branches of production surveyed in the region. Unlike other craft industries which produce commodities destined for urban or tourist markets, however, the domestic form in the metate industry has remained relatively independent of control by merchant capital.[7]

It is beyond the scope of this monograph to deal with the history of the division of labor in the region. Yet one important point should be made in this regard: to emphasize the general organizational continuity of the regional economy, conceived in cultural ecological terms as I have done elsewhere (Cook 1968:Ch.1; cf. Cook and Diskin, eds. 1976:Ch.1),

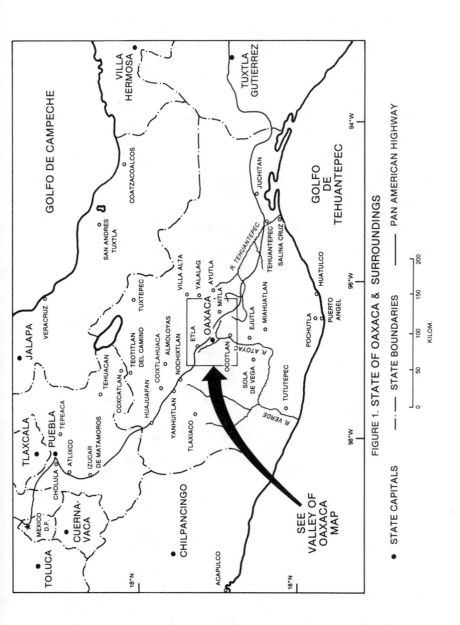

FIGURE 1. STATE OF OAXACA & SURROUNDINGS

● STATE CAPITALS   —··— STATE BOUNDARIES   ——— PAN AMERICAN HIGHWAY

11

tends to downplay the discontinuities which have surfaced over the centuries as the political economic structure has been transformed (e.g., from the dominance of tributary relations to dominance by merchant capital— see Hamnett 1971). Also, it tends to gloss over the extent, frequency, and rationale of changes in production specializations at the community and regional levels. The case of Magdalena Ocotlan, which will be looked at more closely in Chapter 2, is illustrative. This settlement entered the 20th century with no production of metates or of embroidered products for the market. Yet today, many Magdalena households regularly produce both types of products for sale [metate production was introduced during the first decade of this century, whereas embroidery was introduced during the 1970s]. It is likely that such changes have been widespread and frequent, across space and time, in settlements throughout the region. Eric Wolf, writing in general terms about rural Latin America, offered one plausible explanation for such changes as follows:

> While striving to guarantee its members some basic livelihood within the confines of the community, the lack of resources and the very need to sustain the system of religion and power economically force the community to enter the outside market. Any imposition of taxes, any increase in expenditures relative to the productive capacity of the community, or the internal growth of the population on a limited amount of land, must result in compensatory economic reactions in the field of production. These may be wage labor, or the development of some specialization which has competitive advantages within the marginal economy of such communities (1955:458).

As a point of departure for analysis it is useful to assume that the metate industry in the Teitipac villages and in Magdalena express "compensatory economic reactions," and the same assumption is applicable to many of the occupations within the inter-settlement division of labor in the region. It is my hope that the discussion and analysis in ensuing chapters will provide the means for rigorously evaluating this proposition.

A well documented feature of the regional
economy is its cyclical marketing organization in which
a series of marketplaces (plazas) operate on a rotating
basis on separate days of the week and in different
locales (Malinowski and De la Fuente 1957; Cook and
Diskin in 1976). It is clear that prior to the arrival
of the Spanish in the region there were daily markets
in the most important settlements which facilitated
the exchange of agricultural and artisan products
(Mendieta y Nuñez et. al., 1949:xviii), and it is
reasonable to suppose that the emergence of Antequera
(Oaxaca City) as a control center of the colonial trade
in cochineal dyestuff and cotton products (Dahlgren
1963; Hamnett 1971) reinforced the growth of its
marketplace in the regional marketing system. Today,
Oaxaca City is the hub of the regional marketing
system which is maintained through a network of mutually
interdependent settlements. Towns and villages of the
'Central Valleys' provide agricultural and artisan
products, as well as labor services, to the city; and
they are consumers of the goods and services which the
city produces or distributes (as a distribution center
for products manufactured in the national or international industrial economy or for agricultural produce
from other regions of Mexico), [cf. Eric Wolf 1967:302].

The typical village ties into this organization
through the marketplace in Oaxaca City where trade is
conducted daily (though Saturday is the principal
trading day or dia de plaza) and through the marketplace in a district headquarters town or cabecera
(i.e., Etla, Tlacolula, Ocotlan, Zimatlan, Zaachila,
Ejutla, Miahuatlan) where market is held on a particular
day of the week on a rotating basis. Many villagers,
as buyers and sellers, commute daily or weekly between
their home village and either Oaxaca City or their
district town to transact business. By no means all
of the external trade of the typical village, however,
is channeled through the formal city or town marketplaces. A significant yet undetermined volume of
trade bypasses the plaza system through a direct
village-to-village circuit; trading may also occur
between villagers and town- or city-based merchants.
These local and regional market transactions, whether
marketplace-mediated or not, are conducted within a
formal institutional framework which either fosters or
legitimizes competitiveness, the 'free' circulation
of products and people, private proprietorship,
contractual relations, and fixed or negotiated pricing.
This institutional framework is a ubiquitous feature
of capitalism which is dominant in Mexico and Oaxaca

and, it must be emphasized, that these institutions are
compatible with small commodity production (cf. Beals
1967; Diskin 1969; Waterbury 1970; Cook and Diskin
1976).[8]

The Contradictions of Development
in Contemporary Oaxaca

The current situation in the historical process
of social reproduction in Oaxaca is mirrored in a series
of contradictory characterizations of its rural population as either 'peasants' or 'rural proletarians';
'proletarians with land' or 'semi-proletarians'; small
commodity producers or producers of products for auto-
consumption; producers for exchange or producers for
own-use; exploiters (rural bourgeoisie) or exploited
(peasant-artisans, jornaleros, peones, mozos, operarios,
etc.); experiencing 'depeasantization' through wage-
labor or 'repeasantization' through the recuperation or
restitution of lands; migrating, circulating, or
migrating in reverse; that they valorize their labor-
power or that they don't valorize it; that they
produce a surplus or that they produce below their
subsistence needs; and so on. In actuality none of
these characterizations is completely true and none is
completely false. All of them reflect a contradictory
reality generated by the interplay between capitalist
and simple commodity forms of production and circulation. I hope to demonstrate in this study some of the
specific ways in which small production is subsumed to
capitalist production or, expressed differently, the
extent to which and how it does or does not facilitate
the reproduction of capitalist production relations or
the accumulation of capital. In other words, this is
a case study designed to determine if and to what
degree one craft industry has been or is being sub-
verted, subsumed or, perhaps, even "refunctionalized"
by predatory capitalist forms (Szekely 1977:57); only
the latter process is compatible with an expansion of
small production or with the so-called 'repeasantization' of the countryside.

With few exceptions the literature about Oaxaca
has failed to recognize, much less examine, the
theoretical and analytical implications of these
contradictory forces and processes. The problem of
the destiny of capitalism in Oaxaca has not been clearly
posed or has been posed partially, euphemistically, or
incorrectly through the use of concepts like 'dual

14

economy,' 'plural society' or 'refuge region' or of such conceptual dichotomies like 'traditional-modern,' 'folk-urban,' 'open-closed,' 'subsistence-exchange' or 'market-nonmarket.' Indeed, a scrutiny of the existing literature yields no comprehensive, systematic study departing from the assumption that the corporate village is no longer a viable minimal unit of social reproduction (i.e., "operating unit"--Adams 1970:48) in most, if not all regions of Oaxaca and has been replaced in that role by the 'town-_plaza_ + multivillage' (or an equivalent) system (cf. Cook and Diskin, eds. 1976:260). In summary, then we have only a superficial, embryonic understanding of the nature and consequences of capitalist relations and development for rural life in Oaxaca.[9]

Consequently, this monograph--especially in Chapter 8 which incorporates selected preliminary findings from ongoing research on a wide range of small industries--will attempt to systematize and clarify our thinking about the effects upon peasant-artisan domestic units (PADUs) of their multiple and variable relationships with both small commodity and capitalist forms of production and circulation. On the one hand, it appears that the dynamics of regional capitalist accumulation pull the peasant-artisan in different directions simultaneously: toward the capitalist enterprise as a wage-laborer or back to the land as an interest- or rent-paying _minifundista_ trying to become a petty capitalist 'farmer'--perhaps as a consequence of the contradictions within the capitalist sector itself (e.g., merchant vs. industrial capital, private sector vs. public sector capital, metropolitan vs. provincial capital). On the other hand, it may be that under certain conditions the pull of capitalism in Oaxaca, though dominant in the long-run, is weaker in the short-run than the dynamic of the small commodity form which pulls the peasant-artisan away from the labor market and into the process of use- and exchange-value production to provision his/her domestic unit. As will be documented in subsequent chapters, this is the case among the _metateros_. However, in other regional industries, what appears _prima facie_ to be small commodity production proves upon closer analysis to be disguised capitalist production (e.g., as is the case with needlework and weaving outworkers to be discussed below) or, at least, production which has the latent function of assuring the reproduction of peasant-artisan labor-power for seasonal or part-time employment by capitalist enterprises (e.g., as is the case with the palm-weaving industry in San Lorenzo

Albarradas where the women of the typical PADU make
petates and tenates for sale in the Tlacolula or Ayutla
marketplaces while many of their men work seasonally
outside the village as wage-laborers in industries like
mescal production, construction, and mining). I will
examine these and similar cases in a subsequent
publication.

On the Contemporary Significance
of 'Zapotec'

One remaining issue which merits mention and
clarification in this overview of the region is that
of the contemporary significance of 'Zapotec.' More
specifically, in what sense are the metateros,
whose economic activities are the focus of this study,
'Zapotec,' and how is their status in this regard
diagnostic of that of other peasant-artisans in the
'Central valleys' region? The least complicated of
possible responses to this question is as follows:
the metateros are Zapotec to the degree that they are
carriers of cultural elements, primarily linguistic in
nature, which were dominant among the precolonial
indigenous peoples who preceded them, at least as far
back as 2000 years ago, as occupiers and transformers
of the regional habitat (see Whitecotton 1977:chs. 2,3,
& 4 for a detailed analysis of the precolonial Zapotec).
From the Spanish Conquest to the present these cultural
elements, which were always changing artifacts of ongoing social process, have lost their dominance and
integrity, and survive into the last quarter of the
20th century as irreversibly deformed and disarticulated
behavioral traits. These latter are dispersed throughout the region among peasant-artisan communities which,
as objects of social, political, and economic forces
beyond their control, collectively comprise one section
of the 'living museum' of rural Oaxaca. Whitecotton,
in his recent work of synthesis in Zapotec studies,
summarizes this colonial experience succinctly:

By the end of the Spanish Colonial
period, the Zapotecs had been reduced
to a peasantry, or, more properly, to
communities of peasants. Little that
was distinctively Zapotec remained of
their culture and society; instead,
the rural Indian peasant culture of
central and southern Oaxaca was a

16

conglomeration of things pre-Spanish
and of things Spanish. While Zapotec
languages continued to be spoken,
rural Zapotecs identified mostly with
a community and very little with a
Zapotec ethnic group. As today, it
is probable that one first was a
member of a town . . . and second a
member of a region. . . . Zapotec
ethnicity, on a larger level, was of
little consequence, as there were
(and are) few, if any, social forms
that gave it unity (1977:219).

Today all of the metateros speak a Zapotec
dialect and it remains their preferred medium of speech
within the village; but all of them also speak Spanish,
and do so not only outside the village but, to an
increasing degree, within the village, especially in
conversing with their younger children who are taught
only Spanish in school. They are, in effect, a
bilingual people--although Zapotec is strictly a
spoken language with all written communication being
conducted in Spanish. The metateros of the two
Teitipac villages speak the same dialect of Zapotec
which is somewhat different from, though not to the
degree of precluding communication, the dialect spoken
by the metateros of Magdalena Ocotlan (see Whitecotton
1977:12-15 for a summary of the basic features of the
Zapotec language).

The regional picture is that Zapotec predominates among 98.5% of the indigenous language
speakers but that 90.5% of the region's inhabitants
also speak Spanish (68% speak only Spanish whereas
22.5% are bilingual in Spanish and Zapotec). As
expected, the highest proportion of monolingual
Spanish speakers is found in the Centro district.
Of the Zapotec speakers, 30% are monolingual and they
are concentrated, somewhat surprisingly, in the districts of Tlacolula and Ocotlan. My field experience
in the metate-producing and other villages in these
districts suggests that most of the monolingual
Zapotec speakers are elderly women of 60+ years of age
(see Nolasco 1972:151).

To summarize this discussion of the status of
'Zapotec' the following points are crucial: (1)
Zapotec remains a viable language, though its area of
use is socially circumscribed, and it shares the role

17

of a regional vehicle of communication with Spanish
which is the dominant language among the regional
population; (2) it is largely disarticulated with a
wider cultural system or ensemble of cultural traditions,
and has little social or political significance
regionally or nationally--except to the degree that it
is employed manipulatively, for ideological purposes,
by non-Zapotec members of the bourgeoisie and/or by the
state apparatus. Again to quote Whitecotton:

> Although Zapotec is a viable language,
> it remains primarily a situational
> language spoken mostly in the home and
> the village. But Spanish also is used
> in every village, and also as the
> language of discourse among those from
> different villages or regions, as the
> lingua franca of trade. . . . As a
> result, Zapotec had tended to fragment
> into linguistic entities which do not
> necessarily correspond with cultural
> entities. . . . To many Zapotec
> speakers, pueblo or regional affilia-
> tions are much more important than is
> the commonality of speaking Zapotec.
> In short, Zapotec is used in specific
> social contexts; speaking Zapotec . . .
> does not constitute an overriding or
> unidimensional attribute denoting a
> distinctive cultural pattern (op. cit.,
> pp. 14-15).

And yet, in retrospect, the persistence of Zapotec as
a medium for intraregional communication remains
striking, and evokes the possibility that it dovetails
with a rationale embodied in the dialectics of regional
historical process. The outsider and non-speaker who
regularly interacts with the inhabitants of different
rural communities throughout the region cannot help
but ponder the possibility that a substantial corpus of
significant knowledge about regional life lies hidden
behind the Zapotec barrier.

A Final Note to the Reader

It is within the institutional and cultural
framework outlined above that the activities of village-

based producers and marketers like the <u>metateros</u> must be examined. While they are members of domestic groups in corporate communities of long settlement, their production and exchange activities often subject them to forces and relations whose locus lies beyond the local community or region. In the final chapter I will make a preliminary attempt to explain how and why this is so and to provide documentation of it. But, until that distant destination is reached, the reader will be asked to accept it as a fundamental axiom as I limit the inquiry to a description, analysis and explanation of how one group of rural direct producers, with a specialized role in the regional division of labor, copes with a complex tangle of sub-regional forces and relations which impinge upon the reproduction of their labor-power and of the structure of their socioeconomic life.

There is one additional comment I want to make in concluding the introduction, namely, that throughout this monograph I have allowed the <u>metateros</u> to speak for themselves so that the reader may come to appreciate, as I have, their astuteness, directness, doggedness, and most of all, their humanity. In all candor, I must admit that there have been many occasions during the long process of struggle with this manuscript when I have become alienated from the results of my work simply because the many sensitive, sensible, industrious, and good-humored people I had come to know and respect over the years in rural Oaxaca were absent. They had been unintentionally victimized by the sterile, impersonal analysis and tortued discourse which we social scientists seem bound to practice. This has been both a source of profound frustration to me as a humanist and of stimulating challenge as a scientist——how to keep the human subjects of my inquiry present as individuals and not to allow them to be homogenized and dehumanized into lifeless abstractions or speechless categories. You, the readers, like the <u>metateros</u>, have no one to blame but the author if I fail to achieve a balance between human and scientific expression in this monograph. All I can say in my own defense to both groups is that I have tried my best to achieve it.

FOOTNOTES

[1] The industry is dispersed among four agrarian communities: San Sebastian Teitipac, San Juan Teitipac, Tlacolula de Matamoros, and Magdalena Ocotlan. The metate, along with its companion mano, is an important utensil in the kitchen of the typical peasant household of Oaxaca and other areas of Mesoamerica, though for many it is no longer as indispensable as it was prior to the introduction and spead of mechanical corngrinding mills (molinos de nixtamal). Nevertheless, as a utilitarian implement the metate is still used regularly by the peasant housewife to grind (or re-grind) nixtamal (maize softened by being soaked in a lime/water solution) for the preparation of dough (masa) to bake tortillas, and also to grind other grains, seeds, spices, and vegetable foods. As Malinowski and De La Fuente (1957:154) pointed out, the metate is the most important durable consumer good sold in the modern Mexican marketplace that has its origins in the prehispanic economy. It is produced, exchanged and utilized almost exclusively by peasants.

[2] The 'Central Valleys' region is one of the traditionally recognized yet loosely defined regional divisions in the state (see Welte 1976). It can be delimited precisely in hydrographic and topographic terms and can be defined to encompass an area which is economically integrated through an inter-community division of labor that provides the basis for a seven-day periodic marketplace or plaza system (Malinowski and De La Fuente 1957; Beals 1975; Cook and Diskin, eds., 1976). The region so delimited and defined includes a large portion of the territorial jurisdictions of nine political-administrative 'districts' (Centro, Ejutla, Miahuatlan, Ocotlan, Solo de Vega, Tlacolula, Zaachila, Etla and Zimatlan), and has a total of 142 municipios (municipalities) or 26% of the state total of 541. According to the 1970 Census (DGE 1972), the region had 549,560 inhabitants (27.3% of the state total) and an economically active population (EAP) or 102,812 (19.7% of the state's EAP), of whom about 71% are agriculturists; the region has a population density of 56.08 persons/km^2 and a total surface area of 16,234 km^2 (17.2% of Oaxaca's total

area). See Moguel 1979 for a survey of the various
attempts to 'regionalize' Oaxaca.

The 'Valley of Oaxaca,' as the core or heartland
of the 'Central Valleys' region, lies approximately
350 miles south of Mexico City in the southern highlands
of Mexico, between 16°40' - 17°20' and 96°15' - 96°55'
W. The Y-shaped valley has Oaxaca City (1980 population ca. 200,000) at its center, with the towns of
Tlacolula and Mitla in its eastern arm; Zaachila,
Zimatlan, Ocotlan and Ayoquesco in its southern arm;
and Etla in its northern arm (see Figure 1; also Cook
and Diskin 1976 part 1, section 1). There are a total
of 256 separate populated places in the Valley with a
total population (1970 census) of 348,000 inhabitants.
The Valley is drained by two rivers: the upper Rio
Atoyac, flowing from north to south, and its tributary,
the Rio Salado or Tlacolula, flowing westward to join
the Atoyac near Oaxaca City. Additional geographical-
ecological features of the Valley have been concisely
described by W. Sanders as follows:

The Valley of Oaxaca covers a total
area of 3,375 km^2. Of this total,
700 km^2 is valley bottom or alluvium.
A transverse profile of the valley
reveals four major ecological zones:
the contemporary floodplain of the
river (a narrow, relatively minor
zone); a higher floodplain that lies
above it and is the major area of
the alluvium and key agricultural
resource of the valley; the gently
sloping piedmont; and the steep slopes
of the surrounding mountains. The
elevation of the valley floor is
between 1500 and 1600m, and the annual
rainfall varies between 500 and 800
mm (1972:143).

The altitude of the Valley is ". . . just high
enough to eliminate the disadvantages of the tropical
climate proper to the geographical location, without
giving it the rigor that characterizes the high
mountains" (Schmieder 1930:1). The mean annual
temperature of 68°F. combined with the mean annual
rainfall of approximately 23 inches (570 mm) makes for
a moderate semiarid climate in which the basic contrast
is between the rainy season which typically begins in

21

April or May and lasts to September or October, and the
dry season from November through March. Most of the
rain is a result of local convectional air currents and
occurs in regular, heavy afternoon and evening showers
(Schmieder 1930:6). Sudden, though not extreme,
changes in temperatures occur almost daily during the
rainy season and periodically, for brief spells, during
the dry season as concomitant of <u>nortes</u> (northers)--
cold, damp air masses which move into the area from the
Gulf coast to the north. Annual rainfall patterns
fluctuate considerably and there are periodic draught
(<u>sequia</u>) years (see Kirkby esp. pp. 15-21).

[3]Since June 1978 I have been working as
Principal Investigator in a research project entitled
"Petty Commodity Production, Capitalist Development and
Underdevelopment in the 'Central Valleys' Region of
Oaxaca, Mexico" (in Spanish, "<u>Proyecto de Estudios
Socioeconómicos Sobre Las Pequeñas Industrias de Oaxaca</u>"
or PESPIDEO) which was designed to contribute toward
our understanding of many of the issues discussed in
this chapter. Funding for the initial phase of the
project was provided by a grant from the Social Science
Research Council (June - December 1978), and longer-term
funding (through 1981) has been provided by a grant
from the National Science Foundation (#BNS78-13948).
In Mexico City the Project has been coordinated through
the <u>Dirección General de Culturas Populares</u>, Dr.
Rodolfo Stavenhaven--Director General, and in Oaxaca
through the <u>Dirección General de Desarrollo Económico</u>,
Ing. Fernando Avila Nava--Director General. During
1978-89 the Project conducted survey research and case
studies primarily in the weaving and needlework
industries located in a series of communities in the
districts of Ocotlan and Tlacolula, as well as on
several private and government enterprises specializing
in the purchase and sale of craft products in Oaxaca
City. During 1978-79, the Project was expanded to
include research on several village-based industries
such as cotton-products weaving in Xaagá, palm-weaving
in San Lorenzo Albarradas, and brick-making in Santa
Lucia del Camino. When completed this Project should
provide us with a comprehensive analysis of several
craft and other labor-intensive non-agricultural
industries in the 'Central Valleys' region, and will
specify how these are inserted and function within the
regional, national, and international capitalist
economy.

[4]The idea that small non-agricultural commodity production can function as a pioneer of capitalism or is, in effect, a proto-capitalist form, is present in Lenin's work (1964:335 et passim). He probably should have qualified his argument to indicate that small commodity production may or may not be in a capitalist trajectory. It's overlap with or simulation of early stages of capitalist development, via the commodity nexus, should be considered possible rather than inevitable. It may turn out that commoditization is tied strictly to domestic reproduction and to agricultural operations so that it does not lead to further accumulation in industrial production.

[5]Unfortunately, government data on this matter are contradictory. Two separate volumes of the S.P.P. Informes (1979a and 1979d) contain contradictory figures. According to the first, the 'Central Valleys' region has 103,789.2 hectares (1 hectare = 2.47 acres) of agricultural land of which 91.58% is temporal, 2.94% is de humedad, and 5.48% is de riego (1979a:15); the second report states that the area of arable land within the 'Central Valleys' is 90,000 hectares of which 6,462 (7.18%) are de riego, 4,500 hectares (5%) are de humedad, and 79,038 hectares (87.82%) are de temporal (1979d:122). In any case, regardless of these discrepancies in the official record, it is clear that between 87% and 90% of the region's arable land is cultivated seasonally by rainfall agriculture. The figures on the proportion of land types per district are from S.P.P. 1979a:15-16.

[6]The EAP or Economically Active Population is defined for Mexican census purposes as that part of the population 12 years of age or older that worked sometime during the census year, either for an income or helping some family member in an economic activity, without payment, for an average of 15 hours or more weekly, during the time worked in the year.

[7]For purposes of this study all direct producers who work in a specialized way, either through occupational differentiation or technical specialization, to transform natural resources into raw materials and/or the latter into semi-finished or finished commodities, are to be considered as bearers or 'skilled' labor and, therefore, to qualify as 'artisans' or 'craft workers' (cf. Weber 1961:97). Also, production is classified as 'industrial' when it involves either several direct producers (and usually several domestic clusters) in

23

one locality or production cluster, or several discrete
production clusters, which regularly and systematically
produce commodities for circulation in regional and
extra-regional markets (as opposed to the occasional
or irregular production of commodities for restricted
circulation in a small local market, e.g., other
households in the producer's community).

[8]The controversial problematic of 'articulation
of modes of production' which this statement inevitably
conjures up, has developed over the last decade as a
product of French Marxist scholarship (e.g., P.P. Rey
1976) and those influenced by it (e.g., Assadourian et.
al. 1973; Seddon (ed.) 1978; Clammer (ed.) 1978) but
builds on elements that were present in the writings of
Marx (e.g., part VII of Capital v. 1 on "The So-Called
Primitive Accumulation") and Lenin (e.g., 1964; cf.
Andrianov and Monogarova 1970 for a useful exposition
of Lenin's contribution to the problematic). I
recommend the review articles by O'Laughlin (1975),
Bradby (1975) and, especially, by Foster-Carter (1978)
for a critical evaluation of some of the most relevant
literature on this topic. Regional literature includes
well-known contributions by Laclau (1971) and Cardoso
(1975), and the important debate between Banaji (1972,
1975) and Alavi (1975). Finally, Krader's (1975)
encyclopedic critique of the concept of the Asiatic
Mode of Production in the writings of Marx, Engels and
other 19th century scholars, together with his imagina-
tive exegesis of the theoretical and analytical implications of the AMP concept and the historical trajectory
vis-a-vis capitalism of the social formations it
occupies, is most provocative and merits careful study.

Among the many important issues which have been
raised in this literature, two strike me as being
crucial. First, is the exposure of a methodological
error by many writer who reify the 'mode of production'
concept and, thus, unwittingly transform it into an
historical agent. This tendency has been succinctly
criticized by Foster-Carter who states ironically,
"As modes of production are not the subject of history,
so neither should they be the subject of sentences"
(1978:55) and then observes that real people, not
concepts or thought categories, are the carriers of
historical process. This error is a product of
theoreticism which ignores the operational problem of
formulating agendas for the conduct of empirical
research. This reification can be avoided by rephrasing
the problematic in terms of capitalist/noncapitalist
relations and, for example, replacing the ambiguous

24

notion of 'articulation' with a more specific one like 'relational process' while further specifying the elements involved. This measure may also serve to counteract the economistic tendency to reduce the problematic to one which minimizes or ignores the role of political and ideological elements (cf. Foster-Carter 1978:76-77). A second crucial issue is a rejection of the Kautsky-Luxemburg thesis that the capitalist mode of production necessarily eliminates small-scale, non-capitalist forms as it expands (e.g., Kautsky 1974: esp. Chs. 6 & 7; Banaji 1976:21-28; Luxemburg 1968, Chs. XXCII-XXIX but summed upon on p. 416); and proposing alternatively that capitalist accumulation may, in fact, be partially sustained by subsuming these forms to permanently exploit them as sources of labor-power and profits, a condition which Bartra (1978:64) calls "permanent primitive accumulation." Meillasoux (1972:102-103) and Wolpe (1972) were among the first writers to argue this thesis, although Rey's acknowledgement of the merits of Servolin's critique of his position has probably received the most attention. In Rey's words (1976:253): "Servolin demonstrates, in effect, that the domination of capitalism is not assured by the large agricultural enterprise eliminating the small but by the conservation of the small or medium agricultural-artisan enterprise under the dominion of banking or industrial capital" (my translation of the Spanish version of the original French).

[9]One notable exception in this regard is the unpublished doctoral thesis by C.M. Young (1976) on the 'Sierra Zapoteca.' She characterizes the historical relationship between commodity production and 'monetarization' in this region as follows (1976:296-297): ". . . the Sierra has produced commodities (cash crops) for the international market since the 16th century, but until recently the local economy remain unmonetarized. In the colonial period cochineal was an important export commodity; it was produced as a tribute within a barter economy and the means of coercion used were political. Initially, coffee was produced under a similar system with the local jefe político replacing the colonial administrator as the coercive agent. By the 1930s, however, the area had been freed from this type of direct political control but the peasants continued to produce coffee to meet their economic needs, which commercial capital was already beginning to restructure. In other words, whether a 'cash' crop realized its potential as an agent of the monetarization of a local economy depends upon the nature of the economic development fostered and the relative strengths of the

various segments of the population who encourage such development." What remains unexplained in Young's analysis is the role of merchant or commercial capital in coffee production and circulation, especially from 1930 to the present. Also, one remains skeptical of her assertion that the region had been freed by 1930 from what, in effect, was 'caciquismo' or, at least, one feels deprived of a more detailed explanation of the political economy of regional coffee production in the 20th century.

Additional exceptions to this generalization are to be found in the pioneering regional study of the 'Mixteca Baja' by Alcalá and Reyes (1977), in several licenciatura theses written by students from the Centro de Sociología of the Universidad Autónoma 'Benito Júarez' de Oaxaca (UABJO), and a recently published study of the development of capitalism in the Tuxtepec region by Boege (1980).

A nuclear <u>metatero</u> household in San Sebastian Teitipac

A virilocal-extended <u>metatero</u> household in San Juan
Teitipac.

CHAPTER 2. THE VILLAGE PRODUCTION MATRIX:

LAND, WORK, AND SOCIAL DIFFERENTIATION

A View of the 'Economic' Field

Before embarking on this substantive inquiry into selected aspects of the economic life of Oaxaca villagers, it is necessary to present my delimitation of the field of inquiry or, more specifically, the 'economic' field. In several previous writings I have expressed my views on this issue in detail (Cook, S. 1973a and 1974) and my intent here is simply to highlight and clarify elements of my previously formulated position which, I should also emphasize, was elaborated in constant counterpoint with my Oaxaca research. I depart from a conceptualization of the economic field of human activity as a purposeful, socially organized process of producing and supplying material needs and wants with products, commodities and services. Reduced to its basic elements this process may be conceived as a series of relations between material objects in nature (natural resources), others partially or completely transformed from natural resources (i.e., raw materials and instruments of labor), and human labor power. It is important to emphasize that in this process the initiative and control lies with the human element or labor power, the latter being a concept which denotes the capacity to produce in a double sense: (1) the force, strength or energy to overcome the resistance to transformation inherent in natural resources, and (2) the knowledge, skills or technical know-how and motivations required to humanize labor-power or to insert it in human history. In essence, then, the production and supply of products and services is a 'labor process' (Marx 1967:177-185; cf. Harnecker 1971:19-32). Among the advantages of the 'labor process' concept is that it enables us to avoid the biological reductionist and evolutionist tendencies in the cultural ecological approach, which reduces Homo sapiens to simply another species adapting in the ecosystem (Cook 1973:846-851), through its emphasis on the crucial transformative role performed by human labor upon natural resources, a creative process which is both an original and regenerative source of 'humanity' (cf. Kosik 1967:esp. pp. 224-230; Lukacs 1972). Human populations, according to this conception, do not simply occupy and adapt to habitats or perform natural functions in ecosystems; rather they transform them and are concomitantly transformed themselves.

Having delimited the fundamental nature of the labor process and departing from its postulated pivotal theoretical importance, we can proceed to formulate deductively a more complete and operational concept of the 'economic' field. In a given population (e.g., one of the villages we will examine shortly) individuals perform roles as occupants of statuses in a social structure and, as bearers and wielders of labor-power, they maneuver to appropriate materials from the natural environment, to transform these appropriated materials into utilizable products (combining labor power and tools), and to transfer and use (or otherwise dispose of) these products. These activities, which are empirically observable, together with their explicit and implicit social and cultural content, comprise an economic field of study. This field, in turn, can be defined to encompass three separate yet interdependent event sectors: production (i.e., the labor process), transfer, and utilization (see LeClair 1962; Cook 1974). Taken together, these event sectors circumscribe a process that is materialized through movement, exertion and interaction and is empirically reducible to flows of materials, labor, products, and information; in this process people think and act to create, acquire or dispose of material wealth. The investigator cannot observe this field of study as a concrete totality like, for example, the biologist observes an organism; nor can he or she assume that the specified activities will always and everywhere occur in sequence or at set times and places. Nevertheless, the investigator's job is to observe as many of these activities as is compatible with a research agenda, count or measure their concrete results, question the actors about their activities, and so on.

That an economy is more than a heuristically sectoralized field of maneuver and activity follows from the condition that human life runs its course in real societies with real histories. Even for heuristic purposes it is pointless to formulate a hyper-abstract concept of 'economy-in-general' simply because it will be superfluous to social analysis; all 'economic' activity is internal to specific types of social formations in which specific relations of production prevail. In order to make this argument more

30

intelligible we must briefly digress to clarify the meaning of the concept 'relations of production' and the role posited for these in determining forms of economy and society.

I find it instructive to define relations of production backwards, that is, to depart from their conceptual _alter_, namely, relations of distribution. In my conceptualization of the economic field above I avoided any reference to distribution, a concept which economists define as denoting the process of reward or allocation, operating through a system of explicit and implicit social norms, of the total social product to the so-called 'factors of production' or, in terms of social analysis, those persons or groups directly or indirectly responsible for production. Political economists emphasize the production-to-distribution linkage in two senses: (1) the total social product is distributed to individuals or groups according to their role in the production process (e.g., as laborers and/or controllers or proprietors of the means of production), and (2) that production relations and distribution relations are dialectically coupled as a Hegelian 'unity of opposites' (see Goldelier 1972: xiii-xiv, 269-277). Karl Marx, the premier political economist of the 19th century, succinctly expressed this relationship when he referred to "distribution relations essentially coincident with . . . production relations as their opposite side, so that both share the same historically transitory character" (1967 III: 878), a proposition which he elaborated as follows:

> The so-called distribution relations . . . correspond to and arise from historically determined specific forms of the process of production and mutual relations entered into by men in the reproduction process of human life. The historical character of these distribution relations is the historical character of production relations, of which they express merely one aspect . . . and every form of distribution disappears with the specific form of production from which it is descended and to which it corresponds (1967 III:883; cf. 1904:284).

In other words, when we speak of capitalist relations of production we think immediately of profits, interest, rent, and wages: the principal categories into which

31

income is distributed to the social personifications of the factors of production in any capitalist formation.

On the one hand, these incomes or product shares represent relations of distribution between capitalists who collect profits (and rent and interest) and workers who receive wages; and, on the other, they are linked to underlying legal, political, economic and cultural conditions which create and maintain social divisions between proprietors of the means of production who pay wages and receive profits, and non-proprietors of the means of production who, by necessity, accept wage employment to survive--albeit with employers of their choice. So, in oversimplified terms, we have defined capialist relations of production through their corresponding relations of distribution. We will consider this theme again in this chapter in the final section on 'Social Differentiation and Wealth Distribution.' First, however, and with the above delineation of the economic field as a departure point, let's proceed to examine some of the salient features of the labor process in the metate villages, beginning with the nature of the population, its land and resources.

Land, Population, and Labor Process

The villages, their land and its productive potential. The metate manufacturing villages of San Sebastian Teitipac and Magdalena Ocotlan are located in the eastern and southern arms respectively of the Valley (see Figure 2). San Sebastian lies about 22 kms. from Oaxaca City, approximately 8 kms. south of the Pan American Highway which connects Oaxaca City to the Isthmus, in the district of Tlacolula; Magdalena is 43 kms. from Oaxaca City on the highway connecting Oaxaca City to Ejutla and points south, and is in the district of Ocotlan. Both villages enjoy regular bus service to their district towns and to Oaxaca City.

Each village has municipio status and has a dependent territorial jurisdiction. San Sebastian has a total surface area of approximately 25 km^2 with the habitation area occupying something less than 1 km^2; Magdalena has an area of approximately 14 km^2 (1387 hectares) with the habitation area occupying about one-half km^2. San Sebastian, with a total population of 1677 (339 households) has a density of 67.1 persons/km^2

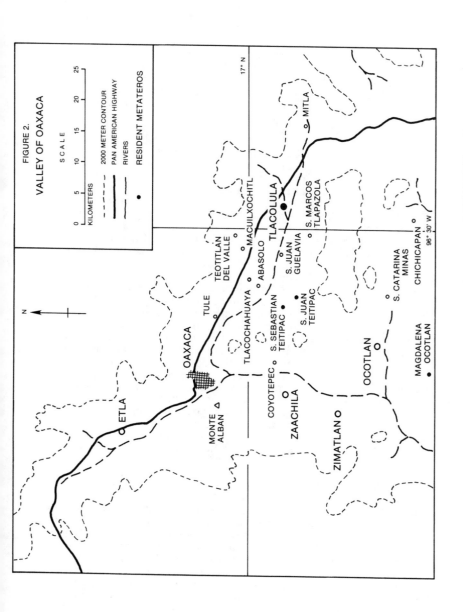

FIGURE 2.
VALLEY OF OAXACA

SCALE

KILOMETERS
0   5   10   15   20   25

- - - - - 2000 METER CONTOUR
━━━━━ PAN AMERICAN HIGHWAY
RIVERS
● RESIDENT METATEROS

33

whereas Magdalena, with a total population of 840 persons (168 households) has a density of 60 persons/km^2.[1]

These figures do not tell us much of ecological importance, e.g., what the population/resource balance is or how the current population compares to the 'carrying capacity' of the available arable land. Given the nature of settlement and land tenure patterns in the Valley of Oaxaca it is reasonable to assume that the land area available to each local population has reached its historical limits (barring a radical transformation of the countryside). Thus, the boundaries of the San Sebastian jurisdiction have remained essentially unchanged since they were surveyed and formally recorded in the 18th century--although recently some additional land was made available to San Sebastianos from a contiguous ex-hacienda (Rancho San Antonio) under the auspices of the ejido program. Magdalena, on the other hand, has had a different historical experience: by 1910 the village had been reduced to the status of a dependent enclave within the boundaries of one of the largest haciendas in the 'Central Valleys' region (the San Jose Progreso-Vergel complex); most of the communal lands of the village had been despoiled by the hacienda during the 18th and 19th centuries so that the village retained title to only 287 hectares (50 of which comprised the habitation area). In 1921, the people of Magdalena petitioned the national revolutionary government headed by President Obregón for a restitution of their communal lands; they were granted 1100 hectares and became an ejido community.[2] The territorial jurisdictions of San Sebastian and Magdalena are bounded on all sides by contiguous jurisdictions of neighboring local populations and, although boundaries are still in dispute at various points, there is little reason to expect future expansion or reduction in land area vis-a-vis contiguous jurisdictions.

The total land area available to these communities is one consideration but its ecological characteristics and economic potentialities are quite another. Looking at the Valley of Oaxaca as a total environment comprising separate ecological zones there is substantial diversity; when one considers micro-environments within these zones the diversity is magnified. Within the boundaries of the territorial jurisdiction of any given local population like San Sebastian or Magdalena there are many different micro-environments--each with unique botanical, physiographic, zoological, and geological characteristics and, consequently, with different economic potentials. This diversity has been documented for the prehistoric period (e.g., Flannery et. al. 1967) and with particular reference to agriculture for later periods as well (Kirkby 1973). However, a comprehensive cultural ecological study of the Valley habitat has yet to be conducted. The following discussion is presented only for the purpose of contextualizing the production and exchange activity which was the focus of my research.

The solution to the problem, faced by every economy regardless of its type or scale, of determining what products are to be produced and in what relative quantities is influenced in various ways by environmental and technological factors. More specifically, the natural environment of any society embodies a set of opportunities and associated limits; through the availability or unavailability of natural resources (e.g., exploitable plants and their seasonal regime; the location, quantity and habits of utilizable animal species; the occurrence of utilizable minerals and potable water; the climate, water supply, soil, and biota as they influence the growth of utilizable plants) the production of certain raw materials or products is made possible or impossible (Wagner 1960:61). In the long run, however, it is the technological factor in any economy that plays a key role, together with human labor-power in transforming environmental potentialities into products. Metates cannot be manufactured if suitable stone is unavailable; but the availability of such stone in sufficient quantities does not assure that it will be quarried, much less that metates will be manufactured from it. Clearly, quarrying and metate manufacturing are not feasible in the absence of a stoneworking technology and a labor force willing and able to employ it. Nor would such a technology be applied to the manufacture of metates in the absence of a need for grinding tools to process certain foodstuffs. Nevertheless, in the complex interplay of natural resources/raw materials, tools and labor power it is clear that the environmental variable, as expressed through available natural resources, is a necessary if not sufficient element in production.

Land types and their productive roles. The following general description of the land-use zones within the territorial jurisdiction of San Sebastian (which is physiographically more diverse than that of Magdalena) gives an approximation of how these villagers make productive use of their habitats.

It should be noted that the productive roles of San Sebastianos and Magdalenans are not restricted by the local ecosystem; they may work for a wage in other villages of the region, in urban centers, or in other regions of the state or nation on a temporary or seasonal basis. In other words, the local ecosystem-- with the territorial jurisdiction of a corporate village as its base--is not coterminous with the 'economy' or economic field in which the village population participates.

Topographically, the terrain of the municipio encompasses three distinct zones which grade into one another at their peripheries: flat, hilly, and mountainous (see Cook 1968:79 for a map of the municipio which designates these zones as well as the named localities or parajes into which they're divided by the villagers). While it is true that nowhere in this area can the present vegetation patterns be attributed to natural influences alone, the degree of human intervention progresses as one moves from the mountainous terrain (which has some secondary forest growth), into the hills, and down to the flatlands. The latter zone, with few exceptions, is under permanent cultivation. Vegetation in the hilly zone has long been exposed to the destructive influences of people and domesticated animals, and certain resources in the mountainous zone have been subjected to several hundred years of human utilization (e.g., stone, trees for lumber, charcoal). This varied terrain, even in the absence of conservation policies, provides San Sebastian with a fairly wide range of utilizable natural resources and serves as a diversified productive base for its economy. Magdalena, by way of comparison, has a substantially different topography (flat to rolling terrain with one large outcrop) and its resource base is less varied; the entire habitat shows evidence of long-term intensive utilization (e.g., there is no secondary forest).

To the residents of these villages all land which lies beyond the habitation area (caserío or pueblo) but which is within the municipal jurisdiction (municipio) is called the campo. The campo in turn is subdivided into (1) terrenos labrados (worked land) or sembradura (planted land); (2) terrenos en bruto or monte (land overgrown with weeds, torn bushes, brush, scrub, etc.) or baldío (wasteland); and (3) cerro or mountainous terrain. The latter, though unsuited for agriculture, is utilized for the collection of firewood (leña) and otate (a bush used by the

36

escoberos or broom makers), to cut wood from several types of trees used for a variety of manufacturing and construction purposes (e.g., charcoal making, house construction), and for its various medicinal and wild food plants. The cerro has additional economic importance as a source of spring water, as pasturage for sheep and goats, for hunting small game animals, and as a source of stone for metate manufacturing and construction purposes.

Monte or baldío, when cleared of brush, thorn thickets, stones, etc., is cultivable but usually low yield. When uncleared it is used as pasture for goats, sheep and cattle, and as a source of firewood as well as certain medicinal and wild food plants collected seasonally.

Terrenos de labranza or sembradura are classified into three broad categories: de humedad propia (naturally damp from high water table), de riego (irrigated) and de temporal (seasonal). These categories are further ranked in a four-class scheme in which humedad propia lands are 'first class' (along with some irrigated lands), and in which various types of temporal lands are categorized as second, third or fourth class. This graded taxonomy of land types is based upon such criteria as topography (i.e., from low and flat to high and steeply sloped terrain), attributes of the soil (e.g., moisture content and retention and depth of water table, soil depth, rock or sand content, color), annual crop yield, and economic use for which suited (e.g., type and value of crop which can be planted, pasturage) (see Cook 1968:81-83, 140).

The terrain in these villages is also divided up into a series of named geographical units or parajes. Each paraje (of which 140 were enumerated in San Sebastian) is identified by environmental signs such as rocks, trees, arroyos, flats, caves, springs, and outcrops or by manmade artifacts such as dams, stone markers, wells, mines, and quarries. These signs (señas) not only provide villagers with a means for identifying a given sector of terrain but enable them to pinpoint a location within it. As one San Sebastiano expressed it: "We, here in the pueblo, find our way around in the campo by means of different signs that exist in a place. . . . The sign is a thing which is seen, a thing that we take as a guide for directing us where we want to go." Large parajes often have sub-parajes. For example, the San Sebastian paraje named detzdañi' (detrás del cerrito or behind the little

mountain) has a sub-paraje named "El huajal" because in
that particular area of the paraje there is a huajal
tree. When referring to this sub-paraje (to distinguish
it from others of the same name) the San Sebastiano
will say "Yalaa niy zub detzdañi" (El huajal que está
detrás del cerrito" or "The huajal that is behind the
little mountain"). (see Cook 1968:84).[3]

Finally, villagers also categorize land in terms
of tenure patterns. For example, in San Sebastian a
basic distinction is between "terrenos de propiedad"
(privately owned land) and "terrenos communales"
(communal land), whereas in Magdalena the basic distinction is between "terrenos de pequeña propiedad"
(privately owned land) and "terrenos ejidales" (ejido
lands). In both villages communal agriculture land
identified with the name of the patron saint are known
as "terrenos del santo" (lands of the saint). Land
under cultivation is also referred to in terms of the
particular type of crop sown, e.g., land planted in
corn is maizal, land with bamboo is carrizal, land with
castor bean is grillal, land with sugar cane is
cañaveral, and so on.

Production in the San Sebastian and Magdalena
economies is rhythmic to the extent that it is dependent
upon seasonal transitions or is adapted to the special
requirements of tillage. Of all production activity
engaged in by these villagers, agriculture is most
intimately bound up with the seasonal cycle and, due
to the necessity of waiting for crops to mature, is the
most complex. Not all seasonal production is directly
related to agriculture. For example, adobe-making,
house construction and repair, cutting and storing of
firewood, and cutting of otate for broom manufacture
(San Sebastian only) are conducted almost exclusively
during the post-harvest months of the dry season. Nor
is all production seasonal in the sense of being performed only during specific periods of the year; animal
husbandry, metate production and some types of
agriculture are among the production activities which
are trans-seasonal. Nevertheless, in generalizing
about economic life in these villages, it is accurate
to state that during a typical calendar year non-
agricultural activity waxes as agricultural activity
wanes, and that during the rainy season production
diminishes in many non-agricultural branches of
production.

The Oaxaca peasant-artisan divides the calendar
year into three discrete seasons (temporadas): the

38

'cold-dry' season which begins in November and lasts through January or February; the 'dry-windy-hot' season which begins in February or March and lasts until April; and the 'rainy' season which usually begins in April or May and lasts to October. The Lenten period (cuaresma) is more or less coterminous with the 'dry-windy-hot' season. The period from July 20 through August, falling in the middle of the rainy season, is called the 'canícula' (canicular or 'dog days'). If the rain continues during this period (or if it ceases but begins again on or before September 8), this is interpreted as an indication that the rainy season will continue into October. If, on the other hand, there is little or no rain during the canícula local wisdom has it that a drought is in the making. It is within this seasonal framework that the villager plans and executes his productive efforts; when the seasons fail to correspond to his expectations, then production plans and efforts are necessarily modified. This relationship emerges most clearly with regard to the agricultural cycle.

Crop tillage in the region involves four sets of opeations: preparation of the field, planting, caring for the crop while it matures, and harvesting and storage. Restricting our discussion to corn cultivation on temporal lands these general operations entail the following specific tasks: clearing or preparing (limpiar or desmontar) the field prior to the onset of the rainy season in April or May; plowing (arar, rayar, or pintar surcos) and planting (sembrar) as soon as the rains begin (early planting is referred to as 'tempranero') and until mid-July; weeding (deshierbo) of the planted fields about three weeks after planting; plowing of secondary furrows (echar orejera) between the original furrows to promote better watering about five weeks after weeding; harvesting (piscar or agarrar cosecha) and storing (guardar cosecha) some four months after planting. The corn tillage cycle on temporal lands, then, lasts approximately six months.

Both San Sebastian and Magdalena have channel (zanja) irrigation systems (and also practice some well irrigation) which make it possible to water fields during drought periods in the rainy season and during the dry season proper. Irrigation facilitates the permanent cultivation of favored plots--especially in Magdalena where the capacity and range of the channel system is greater (reservoir capacity of 330,000 m^3 and a potential range of 270 hectares). During severe drought years, however, these channel irrigation systems may be inoperative due to low water levels

39

(especially in San Sebastian where the 'seasonal' reservoir has a relatively small capacity so that its water supply is depleted well before the next rainy season arrives) [see Lees 1973 and Kirkby 1973:Ch. 4 for further discussion of irrigation agriculture in the region]. Unfortunately, I do not have complete and accurate comparative cost and output data for the cultivation of irrigated and other types of arable land in these villages (see Kirkby 1973:Chs. 5-7). The received local widsom is that irrigated lands regularly produce higher yields--but at a higher cost in labor-- than non-irrigated lands; and, of course, crops on irrigated land are less apt to fail due to lack of water than are those planted on non-irrigated land-- although various sociopolitical difficulties may in- hibit water use in villages with irrigation (cf. Lees 1973:Chs. 2-4).[4]

On the production and use of animals. Animal husbandry is also an important productive activity in these village economies and is one in which all members of the household participate (e.g., tending animals taken to pasture or water, procuring fodder or fetching water, feeding, cleaning stalls). The multiple uses of animals (for example, as instruments of production, objects of consumption, stores of value, sources of cash) are well-known and, in the thinking of most villagers, justify their upkeep (see Chapter 3 'Utilization' for further discussion of this topic). Nevertheless, only a minority of San Sebastianos or Magdalenans raise animals on a relatively large scale; most households keep animals (other than oxen or burros) only as supplementary sources of food or cash.

A 1979 inventory of animals kept by thirty-six randomly selected households in Magdalena show that only two (5.5%) had no animals (three others had only oxen). Of the thirty-four Magdalena households surveyed with animals, the following types were kept in order of descending frequency: oxen--23 households; poultry (chickens and turkeys)--23 households; pigs--16 house- holds; cows--14 households; goats--10 households; burros--5 households; and sheep--3 households. The average market value of these animals per household was 10,020 pesos ($445.33 dollars), ranging from a low of only 200 pesos ($8 dollars) to a high of 31,200 pesos ($1386.66 dollars). These data are consistent with those tabulated from a late-1960's census of 135 ejidatarios in Magdalena; most significant is the fact that the proportion of households without oxen remained constant (33%) (incidentally, this same percentage also holds for a 1966 survey of households in San Sebastian). Also of interest is the relatively low ownership of burros in Magdalena; only 15% of the 1979 sample households and only 11½% of those included in the late-1960's survey. By comparison, 82% of the households surveyed in San Sebastian in 1966 had at least one burro. Whereas the differential ownership of oxen clearly reflects the structure of social differentiation in these villages (see the final section of this chapter), the explanation for the differential frequency of burro-keeping lies, perhaps, in the terrain; Magdalena is relatively flat with most parajes being accessible by ox cart in contrast to San Sebastian which has more hilly terrain with many parajes where ox carts cannot enter.

The 1979 Magdalena survey data on animal inventories may underrepresent the importance of goat- and sheep-herding in the village economy. In the late 1960's the total goat population was 594 mature animals; and there were 206 sheep and 272 kids and lambs distributed among twenty-seven owners. The largest goat herd had 85 animals, the largest sheep herd had about 60, and the largest combined herd had 50 goats, 30 sheep and 20 kids and lambs. Then as now, many of these herds are managed on a share basis: the owner turns over all or a portion of his herd to another villager who assumes complete responsibility for pasturing and managing the herd in return for a claim to one-half of the kids or lambs born during his period of management. Costs of herd management are minimal; the animals feed themselves through grazing so that the principal cost is for the labor required to tend the herds (often provided by young sons of the herd manager). In addition to receiving one-half of the newborn animals, which can form the nucleus for an independent herd, the mediero has rights to all the milk produced by the goats and to one-half of the wool yielded by the sheep. As will be shown in a later section of this chapter ('Division of Labor and Work Organization') and in Chapter 5, share arrangements of this type are quite common in agricultural and non-agricultural production in these village economies.

Land tenure and use. There may be no more important relation between land, population and production in these villages than that mediated through tenure (or tenancy) by which I mean the formal and customary body of norms and rules that establishes the conditions under which land may be owned and used. As is the case throughout rural Mexico, there are three

41

basic forms of land tenure in San Sebastian and
Magdalena: private, communal, and ejido (Reyes Osorio,
et.al. 1974:Ch. 1). It should be emphasized that
these tenure regimes in the Mexican countryside imply
much more than determining how the land is possessed.
They also have profound implications for economic
organization and performance, politics, and social life.
And, when operating side by side within the same rural
community, these tenure regimes are often associated
with social differentiation and conflict and, most
likely, with political factionalism and violence as
well (e.g., Lewis 1949; Stavenhagen 1970; Dennis 1976).
Unfortunately, it is beyond the scope of the present
monograph to discuss many of the broader implications
of these tenure regimes for village life, although in
Chapters 4 and 5 such implications will be discussed
for the metate industry and, in the final section of
the present chapter, some consequences of tenure for
social differentiation and wealth distribution in
San Sebastian and Magdalena will be identified.

While San Sebastian is officially a communal
village (Reyes Osorio et.al. 1974:536-542; Ley Federal
de Reforma Agraria 1974:31-35, 103-104) with private
tenure predominating on agricultural land and residence
lots (ejido tenure was introduced on a restricted scale
in 1969 on lands belonging to the ex-hacienda of San
Antonio Buenavista which is under the jurisdiction of
the municipio of San Sebastian Teitipac), Magdalena
is basically an ejido village with limited private and
communal tenure of agricultural land (and some monte
including a quarry zone) and substantial private
ownership of residence lots. In both villages, however,
there is only very limited private tenure of non-
agricultural lands outside of the habitation areas; in
San Sebastian there is private usufruct of quarries
which, de facto, are communal property (bienes communales) and in Magdalena individual metateros and
ejidatarios are assigned usufruct rights to quarries
(most of which are on ejido property) in accordance
with officially codified Agrarian Reform procedures
(Reyes Osorio et.al. 1974:Ch. VI; Ley Federal 1974:18-
30 et.passim).

In San Sebastian the use of communal land is
under the jurisdiction of a local official known as
the 'Representative of Communal Property" (Representante de los Bienes Communales). All adult male
natives of San Sebastian qualify as ciudadanos
('citizens') and contribuyentes (taxpayers), if their
taxes are paid, and are considered as 'comuneros'

42

(members of the commune); as such they are entitled
to use communal land resources (e.g., cut firewood, cut
otate for brooms, quarry stone, clear monte for cultivation) but are obliged to provide unpaid labor for
tequios (communal labor drafts), pay cuotas and meet
other communal obligations. No comunero, however, can
obtain ownership rights to any portion of the communal
lands. He can solicit a permit from the Representative
for usufruct rights over specified plots or areas
within the communal domain to quarry stone, cultivate
crops or to engage in some other extractive or productive activity. Depending upon the nature and extent of
the use of communal land, the usufructuary may be required to sign a contract and make stipulated payments
to the local government (e.g., as is the case with the
broom-makers and quarrymen). Usufruct rights to parcels
of communal land which is used to cultivate crops or to
quarry stone can be assumed by a usufructuary's heirs
only if they have been in regular use but such rights
are always conditional and subject to dispute with
village authorities or other potential usufructuaries.

Private ownership rights to non-communal
agricultural land or to residence lots are acquired
through inheritance or purchase. The individual owner
holds written documents for each plot which describes
the type of land, number of furrows (surcos), metric
measurements, names of owners of contiguous plots, and
indicates the paraje in which the plot is located.
Inter-plot boundaries are jealously guarded and a
furrow which is plowed a few centimeters off line and
into another owner's field may be the cause of a
dispute.

Plot dispersion or intercalation is a salient
feature of private tenure in San Sebastian and of
private and ejidal tenure in Magdalena; the typical
villager has several non-contiguous plots of land
scattered in various terrain sectors and parajes.
Land inventories of 25 San Sebastianos and 14
Magdalenans support this. The typical San Sebastiano
has a total of 10 separate plots dispersed among seven
parajes, and the typical Magdalenan (in terms of my
sample) has four plots in four different parajes.
Ejido plots in Magdalena tend to be larger than
privately owned plots in San Sebastian. Even though
several small plots in one paraje may be consolidated
by one owner to form a relatively large parcel, the
latter tend to be dispersed even among the largest
landowners in San Sebastian. Thus, the 124 plots of
the pre-revolutionary cacique in San Sebastian, Don

Mateo, were dispersed among ten separate parajes; he did own entire parajes but not two or more contiguous ones.

In Magdalena only 287 out of a total of 1387 hectares of land comprising the village jurisdiction are not ejido property; they are apportioned as follows: 50 hectares are occupied by the caserío or residential area, 60 hectares are set aside as communal fields, and 177 hectares are divided into privately owned agricultural plots. Ejido lands are assigned in usufruct to individual heads of household in accordance with the procedures set forth in the Federal Agrarian Code (Código Agrario) and are administered locally by the Comisariado Ejidal, a group of villagers elected to serve their fellow ejidatarios for three-year periods. The ejidatario's usufruct status is conditional: he or she may not allow an assigned plot to lie fallow for a period longer than one growing season, nor lease or sell rights to cultivate an ejido plot, nor divide up an ejido plot for inheritance purposes (partitioning of a plot may be done by the Comisariado, however). An ejidatario's violation of any one of these regulations is punishable by a nullification and reassignment of his or her usufruct rights. The paradoxical nature of ejido tenure, which grants possession without ownership in a capitalist society that respects only the latter, is compounded when it confronts the value system of rural direct producers in which work is determinant. This becomes clear as we consider the following state-ment on the problem by an astute Magdalena informant:

> I don't have any land. Well, I have
> ejido land but not private property.
> Ejido land is apart. There only the
> nation is supreme ("Manda sola la
> nación"). We have ejido lands so we
> are almost like owners ("Pues casi
> somos como propios"); but we aren't
> owners because we don't buy the land.
> Yet, we have the land. But for what?
> To work. And once the Comisariado
> assigns a parcel of land to us we have
> to work it. If it's uncleared (monte)
> we have to clear it; and then, like
> now in this season (October), we plow
> the land with an ox team. Once it's
> well prepared with the soil loose we
> plant it. Then we are 'owners." Why
> do we consider ourselves to be owners

or to say that the land is ours?
Because we have our work in the land
("Porque tenemos nuestro trabajo al
terreno"). Let's suppose, for example,
that we are clearing a parcel of ejido
land and that we're persons who know
how to read and write and to compute.
Then we will compute the work we do in
pesos--say 20 pesos a day; we add up
the account to see how much the parcel
cost us in pesos. If the sum computed
is 100 or 200 pesos, well, that's what
the land cost us. We are now the owners
and no one can take it away from us.
Again, why do we say that we are owners
of that land? Because we have our work
in the land. A person from the
government might come and ask, "Whose
parcel is this?" The reply is, "It's
Fulano's." Fulano is the owner of that
land because he has his work in it.
And the harvest from the land is his,
too. There's no one to tell him that
he has to hand over such and such an
amount. None of that. The ejido land
is the nation's but the government gave
it to us to be worked.

We have here an incisive peasant discourse on the old
dilemma of proprietorship vs. possession (see Marx
1965:69-71 et.passim; Wittfogel 1957:esp. pp. 270-300)
which lies at the heart of the State's legalized
expropriation, via the route of eminent domain, of the
land from those who possess it and make it productive.

For all intents and purposes, given the
qualifications noted in the preceding discussion and
the labor-centered conception of possession held by the
direct producers, the ejido system in Magdalena--
operating as it does in juxtaposition with a limited
but significant private property sector, serves
essentially as a functional equivalent to the latter.
Thus, usufruct rights to specific ejido plots are
passed on to the legitimate heirs of a deceased
usufructary (which is sanctioned by the Federal
Agrarian Code), or are sometimes alienated through
illegal sale, leasing or sharecropping agreements.

In the concluding section of this chapter I
will examine the distribution of agricultural land in

San Sebastian and Magdalena with particular emphasis on
its relationship to social differentiation and, in
addition, will present and discuss the available
evidence from these villages regarding the possible
relationship between land distribution and the occurence
of non-agricultural occupations among village households.

The Domestic Unit: Its Residential and Kinship Bases and Economic Role

I have asserted in the introduction that the
necessary point of departure in characterizing simple
commodity production as a distinctive economic form
is the household or domestic unit which is the
principal institutional vehicle for bringing together
labor power and means of production, as well as for
pooling cash income or other forms of acquired wealth
for productive ends (including the reproduction of
labor-power itself), among rural laboring populations
of the Oaxaca type. Given the limited, if gradually
expanding presence in the Oaxaca countryside of
capialist enterprise and either the demise or declining
presence of communal or other pre-capitalist supra-
household forms, people's material needs and wants are
circumscribed and their economic destinies are played
out essentially within a structure in which the
domestic unit or household predominates. And this
remains the case even for persons who temporarily
migrate from their home villages. Given the prominent
role I assign to the domestic unit, and to guard
against a tendency to reify it as an idealized
invariant or monolithic form, it is necessary to ascertain its bases and to identify its multiple forms in
the metate villages. First, it will be useful to say
a few words about the spatial or locational dimension
of settlement and residence.

Both San Sebastian and Magdalena, like most
villages in the Valley of Oaxaca, are nucleated settlements in which families are located on separate
residence lots (solares) that may have one or more
households (i.e., a group of persons usually related
consanguineally or affinally and residing in a discrete
dwelling unit). Residence lots cluster to form blocks
(manzanas) which are bounded by streets (calles)
according to a grid layout. San Sebastian is segmented
into two separate residential sections (secciones) of
17 blocks each (146 households vs. 192 households) in
contrast to Magdalena which has no sectional divisions
with the entire village comprising a total of 15 blocks.

The San Sebastian sections are not, strictly speaking, 'barrios'; they function essentially as units of political and administrative expediency rather than as corporate entities of social or cultural identity. Both villages have informal neighborhoods which are sometimes named.

The representative solar in these villages is usually square or rectangular in shape, varies in size from 250 or over 500 square meters, and is enclosed by fences (cercas) of organ cactus, bamboo, or by adobe walls (bardas). From one-quarter to one-third of the surface area of the solar is occupied by one or more buildings of bamboo and thatch, wattle and daub, or adobe construction which are utilized for a combination of habitation, storage, and work purposes. Another portion of the total area is set aside for the maintenance and care of domesticated animals; goats and sheep are kept in pens (corrales) but other animals are tied to trees or posts in shaded areas or are allowed to roam freely. Many lots have wells (pozos) and a small fenced garden (huerta) in which a variety of plants and herbs are cultivated for medicinal and food purposes. Some solares have sweat baths (temascales) constructed of adobe and used principally for post parturition therapy. Given the contours of the spatial organization of these village populations, we can now turn to the social and cultural content of residence and kinship.

Surveys of fifty residence lots (solares) in San Sebastian in 1966 and thirty in Magdalena in 1967, together with the 1979 survey of 37 households in Magdalena, show that the typical lot (solar) has a single dwelling unit in which a nuclear family resides. There is, however, a significant incidence of lots with multiple dwelling units whose residents, considered collectively, constitute an extended family household. The data presented in Table 1 document these generalizations in the case of Magdalena. The modal household in Magdalena (see Tables 1 and 2) is male-headed and has five members, with a tendency for the head's spouse to be several years younger, and with the sex ratio of children 9 years old or younger to be weighted toward males.

TABLE 1. Distribution of Family Types Among 37 Households in Magdalena Ocotlan in 1979.

Type of Family*	(f) of Households
1.	16
2.	8
3.	1
4.	2
5.	0
6.	6
7.	1
8.	3

*The household types corresponding to the numbers are as follows: (1) nuclear--husband and wife with unmarried children; (2) extended virilocal--husband and wife with one or more married sons and daughters-in-law, and may also include other unmarried children and grandchildren as well as parents of the head; (3) extended uxorilocal--husband and wife with one or more married daughters and sons-in-law, and may include other unmarried children and grandchildren as well as parents of the head's wife; (4) widow or widower with children; (5) combination of 2 and 3; (6) childless couple; (7) single person; (8) other. This typology was formulated by Rosa Maria Salgado and Alice Littlefield, with some input from me, for my Oaxaca Project (NSF #BNS-78-13948).

A comparison of data collected from the 1967 and 1979 surveys in Magdalena shows that whereas only 6% of the households surveyed in 1967 were female-headed, some 13.5% fell into this category in 1979, an apparent trend possibly laden with implications but for which I presently have no solid explanation. One striking feature of the data presented in Table 2 is the relative youth of the general population. Indeed, the fact that 30% of the population is 9 years of age or younger and that only 14 (30%) of the households surveyed were without members in this age category suggests, among other things, the significance of children in village economic life. Likewise, the fact that only 8% of the survey population is 60 years of age or older and that 25 (68%) of the sample households were without members in this age category, places the economic significance of the latter in meaningful comparative perspective.[5]

TABLE 2. Age and Sex Distribution of the Members of 37 Households Surveyed in Magdalena Ocotlan in 1979.

Age	Males (f)	Females (f)
0 - 9	33	24
10 - 19	18	24
20 - 29	9	10
30 - 39	9	15
40 - 49	12	5
50 - 59	5	8
60 - 69	5	5
70+	4	3
no data	1	1
TOTALS	96	95

It is a mistake to assume that in these villages all persons who reside on the same lot are, in fact, integrated within a single economic unit. Residents in separate dwelling units on the same lot, even though they sleep apart, may or may not prepare food and eat together, store their crop harvest or fodder together, or operate from a common budget. In such cases, however, there is a strong likelihood of significant production and exchange relationships between them. Still, these are matters which depend upon factors inherent in each particular residence situation and are not always predictable from data indicating the kinship or other relationship between the heads of each discrete houshold. Another feature of domestic organization in these villages which has implications for economic activity is the tendency for heads of household in contiguous lots to be related consanguineally, more often as "primary" but sometimes as "secondary" relatives (Murdock 1949:94-95). The usual pattern is for a father and one of his sons to reside

49

with their respective families on one lot, and for a second son or a brother of the head of the first lot household to reside with his family of procreation on a contiguous lot. The resultant kin-based residence cluster is a compound virilocal form combining family types 1 and 2 in Table 1.[6]

There is no rigid set of rules in these villages to regulate the choice of post-marital residence by a newly married couple. Ideally, each couple aspires to establish their own household independent of the parents of either spouse but, in many instances, they lack the economic means to do so. Consequently, the initial phase of the developmental cycle of the modal household finds a newly married couple living with or near the parents of either spouse, usually in the same residence lot and in a household headed by the groom's father (see Table 1 and Cook 1968:155). This factor accounts for the presence in these villages, at any given point in time, of a significant number of complex or compound family types.

The San Sebastiano or Magdalenan classifies his or her consanguineal and affinal relatives in terms of residence and the propinquity of the relationship which links him or her to them. No specific descent principle dominates the villager's classification of his or her consanguines; kinship is organized exclusively on the basis of a circle of relatives traced outwards from an individual. The resultant organization lacks formalization and uniformity; in the case of one Ego it may be bounded by first cousins and in another by second cousins. Since only full siblings share the same kindred, the latter is not a descent group; its members as a whole do not have a common ancestor. For example, Ego's paternal cousin, as a general rule, does not have common ancestry with Ego's maternal cousin. Though lacking in formalization, the kindred in these villages does have a measure of symmetry deriving from the practice of reckoning kinship by degrees of distance and ignoring the sex of the kinsperson through whom a particular relationship is traced. Given the same sex, then, a relative on Ego's mother's side is structurally equivalent to one occupying a comparable position on his father's side. This symmetry has little generative depth since the villager's knowledge of his or her genealogy rarely exceeds two generations (i.e., does not go beyond the grandparental generation). Even in cases where grandparents are known, informants are often hard pressed to give the names of their grandparents' siblings.

Fictive kinship in the form of ritual god-parenthood (<u>padrinazgo</u>) and co-parenthood (<u>compadrazgo</u>) also operates in these villages along the same lines described for other regions of Middle America (Ravicz 1967). The <u>compadrazgo</u> relationship operates most significantly in production and exchange processes--<u>compadres</u> often cooperate in performing various kinds of work and exchange gifts as <u>guelaguetza</u> partners. For example, one Magdalenan indicated that every year he exchanges labor during the harvest season with eight different <u>compadres</u> (five <u>compadres de pila</u> of baptism and three <u>compadres</u> of confirmation); he either helps them personally or hires a <u>mozo</u> (peón or hired hand). My impression is that the role of ritual kinship arrangements in these village economies is subordinate to that of the kinship system proper--and that both are gradually being displaced by wage labor.

Now that we have identified and described several types of domestic units and related kinship practices in the metate villages, we can proceed to delineate and clarify, in a preliminary way, some of the economic functions which correspond to them. Perhaps the most fertile approach here is to focus on the multi-pronged insertion of domestic units into the division of labor (i.e., the distribution of functions that divides people in a society according to the different economically productive tasks or work that they perform, cf. Bartra 1973:60 and Harnecker 1971: 26-29) and into the division of social production (i.e., the division of production into different branches, spheres or sectors like industrial, agricultural, etc., cf. Harnecker 1971:27).[7] The first connection is 'domestic unit/division of social production' which inserts the members of that unit into an intra-household division of tasks or, if you will, into a series of work roles which do not form part of the occupational structure proper and entail the production of products or services exclusively for use within the unit, the only exception being the reproduction of labor-power and the occasional sale of eggs or some other product usually produced domestically for own-use. In this sphere of domestic work tasks are allocated primarily along lines of age and sex, a process which begins to crystallize around pre-school age children and is firmly structured around older children and adults of all ages, although females carry the major burden. For example, young children fetch water, tend animals, and run errands; women prepare food and wash clothes, men chop wood, crush maguey leaves (<u>pencas</u>) to make strips of fiber for

binding purposes, tend oxen, repair equipment and
buildings, and sweep the residence lot. This division
of tasks is not ironclad and sex-age criteria may on
occasion be inoperative, most typically with women
performing tasks which are reserved for men (e.g.,
tethering oxen) or children (running errands) rather
than vice-versa. Nevertheless, in a majority of
households where a standard sex-age mix is present,
men, for example, don't prepare food or wash clothes
and women don't dig latrines or repair leaky roofs.
The importance of domestic tasks should not be
underestimated simply because they are peripheral (with
the exceptions noted above) to the sphere of commodity
production. Although my research in the metate
villages excluded the systematic study of domestic
work, it is clear to me in retrospect that metate
production is as dependent on domestic work as on anything else because of the indispensable role of the
latter in reproducing the labor-power of metate
industry personnel.

The second and third connections of the domestic
unit, namely, to the inter-household and to the inter-
community divisions of labor, respectively, will be
addressed in detail in the next section. Suffice it
to say here that through these two connections the
domestic units are directly inserted into the sphere
of commodity production and, more specifically, into
money-commodity circuits as sellers of labor-power or
commodities (a sphere with which they are already
familiar at the level of circulation as buyers of
commodities or services).

There are several other functions of the
domestic unit in the economic life of the metate villages
apart from those already mentioned (and the most obvious
one of serving as a vehicle for the biological reproduction of the human population), many of which will be
examined in subsequent chapters. It is through membership in a domestic unit that an individual in these
villages acquires access to and control over means of
production (e.g., land or other natural resources,
instruments of labor) or inherits or otherwise acquires
property rights. Moreover, it is only as a participating member of a domestic unit that an individual's
share of the product of specific labor processes and
of social production as a whole enables him or her to
survive, simply because of the need for pooling labor
and income or wealth in partially proletarianized
societies where the value of labor power is driven
below the minimum of social reproduction (see my

discussion of the "inferior wage" in Chapters 6 and 8).
Finally, it is the domestic unit that serves as a
conduit for transmitting knowledge and ideology which
inject cultural content into the division of labor.
Membership in a domestic unit makes it possible for an
individual to become a bearer of the labor-power
(i.e., the capacity to work which implies the requisite
knowledge and skills) which qualifies one as a metatero
or another as an embroiderer. In essence, the domestic
unit among simple commodity producers assumes a broader
range of necessary functions in the economy than it
does under advanced capitalism. An important aim of
subsequent chapters will be to discuss at length the
nature and implications of the insertion of the domestic
units of rural direct producers in the 'Central Valleys'
into capitalist circuits and will focus specifically
on the contradictory impact of the 'commoditization'
process, that is, the expansion of commodity relations
within the cycle of simple reproduction (i.e., the
replacement and renewal of means of production and of
subsistence) (cf. Wolf 1966:1-17; Cook 1978:293-297,
302-310; Bernstein 1979:424-430; Friedman 1980:164-165).

Division of Labor and Work Organization

Some Concepts Clarified. I prefer to view the
social structure of the metate villages to be fundamentally shaped by the relations of production in which
their populations are involved. These relations, in
articulated combination with the 'forces of production'
(resources/raw materials + instruments of labor +
labor power), constitute a necessary and structurally
dominant element in the Marxist conceptualization of
the 'mode of production' (see Hindess and Hirst 1975:
Ch. 1; Cook 1977:366-367). Relations of production in
a given social formation (and by implication in regional
and local segments of it) are expressed through functions
performed in the process of social production. These
functions relate people to each other and insert them
in the labor process itself, not as individuals, but as
representatives or personifications of social groups or
classes. Recalling for a moment our earlier digression
on the reciprocal relationship between distribution and
production relations, it should not surprise us to
learn that one of the four principal functions of the
relations of production is to determine the distribution
of the total product from specific labor processes and
of social production as a whole (i.e., to determine who
gets what, when, and how). This distribution process

includes remuneration for labor expended in the production of the 'socially necessary' product (that which is required to meet the reproduction needs of labor) and claims for shares of the 'social surplus product' (that portion of the total social product which exceeds the requirements of replacement/renewal of the means of subsistence and production). The three additional functions of the relations of production are as follows: (1) to determine access to and control of rights over the disposition of the means of production or property rights; (2) to assign roles in the labor process or to determine how individuals and groups are inserted in or related to a specific labor process (e.g., as direct producer, worker-owner, supervisor, absentee owner); and (3) to transmit knowledge and ideology which infuses the division of labor with cultural content.

Perhaps the best way to appreciate the significance of relations of production is to consider their actual impact on the material welfare of direct producers. These relations are directly expressed in the direct producers' rights over their own labor, to the means of production with which they work, and to what they produce (Kay 1975:21). The rights of direct producers vary through the course of history within particular social formations (e.g., Mexico) and between social formations (e.g., Mexico and England) which may represent different levels or trajectories of socioeconomic development. For example, in Oaxaca it has been the misfortune of direct producers for centuries to suffer restrictions on their rights over their own labor power, means of production, and labor product which were forcefully and arbitrarily imposed by indigenous or conquering elites. During the late prehispanic and early colonial periods, the rural direct producers in the Teitipac villagers were subjected to exploitation through obligatory payments or tribute in labor or kind (Cook 1968:Ch. 3). Since the latter half of the 19th century, as capitalism has differentially expanded its presence in the regional and local economies of Oaxaca through the spreading commoditization of land, labor and domestic production, the material situation of direct producers has been complicated by the impact of fluctuating and contradictory movements of capital and by the varying persistence of non-capitalist forms of production and exchange. These conditions, which are considered more systematically in the concluding chapter, are very much in evidence in the division of labor and work organization in the metate villages.

Given the broad range of functions attributed to 'relations of production' in the preceding discussion it is clear that these encompass, without necessarily being identical with, work organization. Moreover, it was implicit that work organization (i.e., material or concrete social relationships through which a specific labor process is realized) is a concept both subordinate to and implicit in the more general and abstract concept of relations of production. Let me attempt to clarify the status of these concepts and their relationship in the context of the metate villages where relations of production and work organization may or may not overlap but must necessarily intersect with ideological elements (e.g., property relations, tenure patterns, kinship relations). In any particular line of material production we can observe the workers, measure and record their activities and, also, directly study various physical and technical factors (e.g., location, size, and characteristics of the work place, the resources or raw materials; the instruments of labor) in the specific production situation. As we do this, and focus especially on the social interaction among workers, we are dealing with work organization which is specific to a particular concrete or real labor process. But the relations of production of any labor process have their locus outside of the concrete work situation and depend on ideological or cultural factors. For example, we can observe the activities of three villagers as they extract dirt from a plot of uncultivated land along the edge of a small stream, mix it with burro dung and shredded corn stalks, stir in buckets of water from the stream to make a mud-like mixture and, finally, pour the latter into square wooden molds to shape into adobe bricks which are then laid out in rows on the ground to dry in the sun. In either Magdalena or San Sebastian this adobe-making situation may intersect with 'capitalist' relations of production (if, for example, one of the workers either owns or rents the plot where adobes are being made and employs the other two for a wage and will sell the adobes to make a profit); with semi-capitalist relations of production (if, for example, one of the workers is usufructuary of the plot which is communal or ejido property, another is the usufructuary's son working as a family obligation, and a third is a hired-hand, with the adobe bricks destined for own-use by the usufructuary-boss); or with non-capitalist relations of production (as when the first worker is usufructuary of the plot and has recruited one friend and another compadre on the basis of reciprocity to produce adobes for his own-use). These relations of production are ideologically mediated and, in essence, determine the organization of the labor process (i.e., the status and relationships between the brick-makers) as well as how the adobe bricks or the money into which they may be transformed are 'shared-out' among the direct producers and others (e.g., the absentee owner of the rented plot). In other words, there is a clear reciprocal relationship between ideological relations of production and material relations of a labor process like brick-making; material relations are constituted on the basis of the ideological relations just as the latter are realized through the former (cf. Hindess and Hirst 1975:44-45; Cook 1977:374).

On the Division of Labor. Where does the division of labor enter the picture and what is its relationship to the relations of production and work organization? Recalling the above enumeration of the functions of the relations of production, it can be asserted that the division of labor is the structure resulting from the second function attributed to these, namely, the assignment of roles in the labor process or the determination of how individuals and groups are located in the production sector of the economy, Thus, the division of labor in the metate villages is constituted by the relations of production, within limits set down by ecological and other factors, but is different from these; it is delimited by the specialized work roles performed by individuals with discrete occupational statuses or oficios. In San Sebastian and Magdalena the division of labor has several levels of possible participation for the discrete domestic unit which, for our purposes, can be referred to as the intra-household level, the inter-household level, and the extra-village level; the latter level has many spheres, the most extensive of which inserts village domestic units into the international division of labor. Since we have already discussed the first level our attention here will focus on the second and third levels or with the occupational structure proper.

At the inter-household level, occupations (oficios) integrate village households into a locally circumscribed network of commodity production and exchange. Most households in San Sebastian and Magdalena have at least one member who occupies a status in the inter-household division of labor and who produces a product or supplies a service destined for use by other village households. This level of the village division of labor may be characterized as being fluid and flexible with regard to the participation of its personnel and informal with regard to the social interaction it entails. Recruitment into oficios at this level (e.g., barber, blacksmith, adobe-maker, baker, well-digger, butcher, candlemaker) is usually by achievement rather than ascription, although several criteria may operate in the recruitment and enculturation process. As a general rule, the commodities produced or the services offered by these oficios are exchanged for payment in cash or kind. To reiterate, occupations at the intra-village level directly serve the needs of the local population and reflect an ancient pattern, internal specialization geared to self-sufficiency, which is changing but is by no means dissolving under the impact of capitalist development.

One reason for the persistence of minor occupations in San Sebastian and Magdalena is that they are keyed to other major ones. For example, basket-making, plow-making, cart-making, and harness-making are tied to agriculture whereas blacksmithing is tied to both agriculture and to the metate industry. Also, many dry season occupations like dwelling construction and adobe-making are complementary to wet season agricultural work and year-round occupations like blacksmithing are completely compatible with most other occupations since their activities may be performed during off hours (e.g., early in the morning). One of the two blacksmith-metateros in Magdalena told me that he liked smithing because he could adjust the hours he worked at it to his agricultural and to his metate industry work schedule. Moreover, it had the added advantage of enabling him to temper his own tools which, of course, reduced his cash outlay as a metate producer. Finally, this same Magdalenan pointed out that metate-making was also adaptable to his agricultural work schedule as well as to the necessities of animal husbandry since he could pasture his animals while working in the quarry; and that it met his periodic expenditures for charcoal used to fuel his forge.

The extra-village level of the division of labor which, as the previous discussion indicates is closely integrated with the intra-village level, is comprised of oficios whose products are sold almost exclusively in extra-village markets (including but not restricted to transactions in the marketplace or plaza system). Occupations like metate manufacture, broom manufacture, embroidery, and trading involve work in the village but the commodities produced (or handled) flow into circulatory routes involving at least one and sometimes several money-mediated transactions, and end up, sooner or later, in consumer households located outside of the producers' village (in the case of embroidered articles these consumer households are often located in a foreign country).[8] It is through these oficios, together with certain other productive activities which are either buried under the general occupational rubric of 'campesino' (e.g., alfalfa or other minor cash crop production) or within the category of 'domestic production' (e.g., cheese-making), that villages like San Sebastian and Magdalena produce commodities whose exchange value can be partially appropriated by members of the village or external bourgeoisie. However, the commodities produced or services rendered also provide the corresponding villagers with a supplementary income which helps them to provision their domestic units and, in some instances, yields modest profits for reinvestment purposes.

A salient feature of the division of labor in the metate villages is that many individuals perform in several occupational statuses, simultaneously or sequentially, in their lifelong struggle to make and earn a living. There is, accordingly, no necessary one-to-one relationship between an occupational status and its occupant in these villages; the same individual may occupy several such statuses during his or her work career. It follows from this, of course, that there are relatively few one occupation households. For example, only 9% of the 37 households surveyed in Magdalena in 1979 have only one occupation (see Table 4 below). Some of the implications of 'multi-occupationality' will be discussed in more detail for selected metatero households in subsequent chapters.

There are several ways to classify village occupations and the particular approach one selects is best determined on an ad hoc basis. For expository purposes I have selected an eclectic approach which separates agricultural from non-agricultural occupations and then further classifies each into one of three mutually exclusive categories of production as follows: (1) primary occupations which transform locally-produced or appropriated raw materials into finished products; (2) secondary or intermediate occupations which combine, alter or finish local or imported materials; and (3) service or tertiary occupations which provide labor of a specialized type but do not create material products. Table 3 below presents a tabulation of the approximate distribution of occupational statuses among 356 heads of household in San Sebastian and 135 heads of household in Magdalena

TABLE 3. Occupational Statuses and Their Distribution Among
356 Heads of Household in San Sebastian Teitipac and
135 Heads of Household in Magdalena Ocotlan in 1966-67.

P R I M A R Y

AGRICULTURAL

	Mag. (f)	S. Seb. (f)
1. Campesino (peasant cultivator)	103	240
2. Borregero (sheep raiser)	4	2
3. Vaquero (cattle raiser)	6	1
4. Chivero (goat raiser)	14	8
5. Enjambrero (beekeeper)	0	2
TOTAL	127	253

NON-AGRICULTURAL

	Mag. (f)	S. Seb. (f)
1. Metatero (metate maker)	18	42
2. Leñero (wood cutter)	0	13
3. Escobero (broom maker)	0	13
4. Canastero (basket maker)	5	9
5. Carbonero (charcoal maker)	0	8
6. Jacalero (hut builder)	0	8
7. Adobero (adobe maker)	0	7
8. Cantero (quarryman)	0	8
9. Pozero (well digger)	0	5
10. Labrador de piedra de molino (maker of grindstones for nixtamal mills)	0	4
11. Ladrillero (brick maker)	0	1
TOTAL	23	117

S E C O N D A R Y

AGRICULTURAL

	Mag. (f)	S. Seb. (f)
1. Carnicero (butcher of cattle and goats)	0	3
2. Tocinero (hog butcher)	0	7
3. Trasquilador (wool shearer)	1	1
TOTAL	1	11

NON-AGRICULTURAL

	Mag. (f)	S. Seb. (f)
1. Labrador de mano y metate (finisher)	0	13
2. Tortillera (tortilla maker)	0	12
3. Molinero (miller)	2	3
4. Herrero (blacksmith)	2	2
5. Sastre (tailor)	1	3
6. Costurera (seamstress)	6	2
7. Panadero (baker)	2	3
8. Cohetero (fireworks maker)	0	1
9. Albañil (house builder)	0	6
10. Carpintero (carpenter)	0	8
11. Aradero (plow maker)	9	3
12. Carrocero (wagon maker)	0	
13. Aparejero (harness maker)	1	2
14. Velero (candle maker)	0	4
TOTAL	24	63

T E R T I A R Y

AGRICULTURAL

	Mag. (f)	S. Seb. (f)
1. Pastor (shepherd)	?	7
2. Capador (castrator)	?	
a. bulls		3
b. hogs		2
c. goats		3
3. Jornalero (day laborer)	29	87
TOTAL	29	102

NON-AGRICULTURAL

	Mag. (f)	S. Seb. (f)
1. Regatón de metates (trader)	1	10
2. Peluquero (barber)	1	4
3. Escribano (scribe)	1	2
4. Tiendero (storekeeper)	3	8
5. Músico (musician)	5	24
6. Tamborillero (drummer)	0	
7. Chirimitero (flutist)	0	2
8. Huehuete (marriage broker)	1	3
9. Supulturero (gravedigger)	0	3
10. Partera (midwife)	1	4
11. Curandero (curer)	0	2
12. Huesero (bonesetter)	0	2
13. Sobador (-a) (masseur/masseuse)	0	8
TOTAL	10	73

during 1966-67.[9]

This Table demonstrates the predominance of agriculture in the economies of both villages but, also, shows the importance and diversity of non-agricultural production--especially in the larger village, San Sebastian. In both villages a majority of the male heads of household are campesinos (peasant cultivators) who consider cultivating the soil to be their principal occupation. A substantial number are jornaleros (or mozos) or day laborers who may or may not also be campesinos, and who hire themselves out to local agricultural employers for a wage. In San Sebastian, and to a lesser extent in Magdalena, many individuals who identify themselves as campesinos have little or no land and, in many cases, don't own other necessary means of agricultural production. For example, census data from 1966-67 indicate that only 112 of 356 heads of household in San Sebastian and only 61 of 135 ejidatarios in Magdalena owned ox teams. It could be argued with some justification that the combined proprietorship of land and ox team is the minimum qualification of a true campesino (as opposed, for example, to a jornalero or to a mediero or sharecropper) and, when they are probed on this matter, I have found that many villagers tend to support this approach. Nevertheless, in this monograph I use the term peasant in the less rigorous sense of campesino as this term is understood by any villager in Oaxaca, namely, a self-employed cultivator of the land who may or may not own all of the necessary means of production. My experience has been that most villagers will not use the term campesino (with reference to selves or others) to describe a person who works only as a hired hand in agriculture but rather will label such a person as a jornalero or mozo. The term campesino is regularly used, however, with reference to a person who is known to be a sharecropper (mediero) [i.e., one who cultivates land owned by another with his own or another's ox team and equipment]. These ambiguities surrounding the use of the term 'campesino' need not be of further concern so long as the reader takes into account the fact that they exist among the Oaxacans themselves as well as among those who study them, maintains an awareness of the real complexities of the agricultural labor process and relations of productions in these villages and, finally, interprets the data tabulated in Table 3 (and 4) loosely and with the previous two considerations in mind.

Table 4 provides the basis for extending our discussion of the 1967 data from Magdalena and, most notably, presents evidence of an important new development in the division of labor in that village. Differences in the way in which the two surveys were conducted (e.g., the 1967 survey pertains only to heads of household but covers the entire population, whereas the 1979 survey pertains to all members of the 37 households randomly sampled) make across-the-board comparisons impossible. But limited comparisons focused on the occupational mix and distribution among heads of household can be made. Primary agricultural occupations remain the most widely distributed among Magdalena household heads between 1967 and 1979. Of possible significance, however, is the 10% decline in this predominance in the 1979 survey; this may be attributable to the apparent rise in the proportion of female-headed households (from 6% of 135 in 1967 to 13.5% of 37 in 1979) and to the tendency of females to hold occupations in the secondary non-agricultural sector. The $8\frac{1}{2}$% decline in the frequency of occupations in the primary non-agricultural sector probably reflects a sampling bias in the 1979 survey which resulted in an under-representation of metatero households but might be partially attributable to the proportionate increase in female-headed households.

The most striking comparison between the two Tables is the high frequency of embroidery (bordado) as a female occupation in 1979 and its absence in 1967. Indeed, Table 4 shows embroidery to be far and away the most widely distributed occupation in its category among the survey households (19 of 37 or 51%) and second only to that of campesino in the entire occupational inventory. The emergence of embroidery as an important new occupation in Magdalena merits further discussion at this point, not only because it is illustrative of how and why changes occur in the division of labor, but also because it is merely one local manifestation of the mushroomlike development of a regional capitalist 'putting-out' system disguised as small commodity production (see Chapter 8 for further discussion of this phenomenon).

Several findings from a preliminary analysis of the survey data on embroidery in Magdalena serve to explain why it has spread and suggest how and why it continues to be practiced. Unlike the patterns associated with craft industries which have operated for many generations in a particular village, the young in Magdalena instruct their elders or both young

61

TABLE 4.   Occupations and Their Distribution
           Among 37 Households in Magdalena
           Ocotlan in 1979.

	PRIMARY	(f)	SECONDARY	(f)	TERTIARY	(f)
AGRICULTURAL	1. Campesino (peasant) cultivator)	35	NONE REPORTED		1. Jornalero (day laborer)	7
	2. Borreguero (sheep raiser)	2			2. Pastor (shepherd)	3
	3. Vaquero (cattle raiser)	0			3. Tractorista (tractor driver)	1
	4. Chivero (goat raiser)	8				
	TOTAL	45		0		11
NON-AGRICULTURAL	1. Metatero	2	1. Bordadora (embroid-erer)	19	1. Peón de albañil (construction worker)	4
			2. Labrador de manos (finisher)	1	2. Comisionista de bordado (embroidery commission agent)	1
			3. Panadero (baker)	1		
			4. Molinero (miller)	1		
			5. Tortillera (tortilla maker)	1		
			6. Albañil (house builder)	1		
	TOTAL	2	24			5

and old alike receive instruction together in the village school. Thus, four of nineteen respondents were taught to embroider by their daughters or daughters-in-law (vs. only one who was taught by her mother) and seven were instructed through an extra-curricular program at the school; also, five reported that they were self-taught. Again, in contrast with many 'traditional' craft industries, the population of embroiderers in Magdalena (who, incidentally, are all female) is skewed heavily toward the 39 and younger age categories (80% of 32 persons), with the largest proportion (31%) falling into the 10-19 years category. No embroiderer was nine years or younger and only one was sixty years or older. Accordingly, a significant amount of embroidery work is done by young, dependent, unmarried, and childless females (38% of the sample population), although a majority (51.6%) of the embroidery workers are married and have dependent children. Cross-cutting these differences, however, is one unequivocal finding: regardless of who performs it, embroidery work is relatively time-consuming and is poorly remunerated. An average of about 21 hours weekly is spend on embroidery work per household (which averages out to some 12½ hours weekly per embroiderer). The average weekly income per household from embroidery work is 40 pesos ($1.77 dollars) with the average weekly income per embroiderer hovering around 24 pesos ($1.07 dollars) and the average hourly wage is calculated to be a paltry 2 pesos (ca. $.09 dollars). Out of fifteen households for which detailed data is available, the highest hourly return was 5.83 pesos ($.26 dollars) and the lowest only .60 pesos ($.03 dollars)! When one considers that each embroidery household has an average of 17 pesos ($.75 dollars) invested in tools (i.e., hoops, needles, scissors) which must be periodically replaced, and that more than half of them regularly supply their own thread at an average monthly cost of at least 30 pesos ($1.33 dollars), one wonders how, in fact, embroiderers survive. The answer, of course, is that they don't--at least from their income as embroidery workers which merely provides them with a periodic cash supplement to the household income.

Given these conditions, then, why have the women of Magdalena taken up, and why do they continue to practice, embroidery? One reason lies in the severe inflation that has characterized the Mexican and Oaxaca economies during the past decade (see Chapter 7 under "Levels of Income" for an analysis of the impact of inflation on household budgets in Magdalena) combined with very limited cash-earning opportunities for women

in the village. Embroidery offers them a reasonably
sure and convenient way to convert their labor-power
into much needed cash. It requires a relatively minor
investment in tools, is easy to learn for those who
have the patience (and eyesight), and it requires no
significant rescheduling of domestic work since it can
be done at the convenience and pace of the individual
worker. Last, but not least, the necessary materials,
cloth (in the form of pre-patterned sets which will
later be assembled by the supplier into blouses or
dresses) and thread, are supplied by merchants, most
of whom are residents of larger communities in the
district of Ocotlan with more established embroidery
industries (e.g., San Antonino, San Martin Tilcajete)
and who operate through the Ocotlan plaza on Fridays,
or by their commission agents, two of whom are native
Magdalenans. These merchants or their agents receive
the embroidered materials and pay the embroiderers from
60 to 100 pesos per set, the price depending on the
type or size of the set, the quality of the embroidery,
and on who supplied the thread; sometimes payments are
advanced as a lure and as a means for maintaining
relationships with workers. All of the Magdalena
embroiderers in our survey are outworkers who receive
cloth as described above but many of them buy their
own thread. In short, embroidery has become a significant new source of supplementary cash income for many
Magdalena households. From the perspective of the women
of the household who embroider, the critical issue is
not so much low remuneration as it is no remuneration.
It's not that they're unaware that the return on their
work is meager and that others profit from it, it's
simply that they feel there is very little they can do
to change the situation. As they are apt to express
it, "la necesidad obliga" ("Necessity obliges");
"Que se puede hacer?" ("What can one do?"). As we'll see
in Chapter 8, the greater significance of embroidery
is that it serves as an important point of entry (not
to mention source of profit) for merchant capital into
the productive sector of the regional economy.

On work organization. In considering the
organization of work in these villages, it is essential
to understand that many productive tasks ential cooperation between two or more workers simply because they
cannot be successfully carried out by a single worker.
Some tasks, on the other hand, can be done by single
workers but, often, they lack the instruments of labor
required to do them. Differential access to the means
of production engenders a series of sharing or pooling
arrangements through which those villagers who do not

64

own or have free access to needed tools or resources acquire temporary rights over them by agreeing to share output with their owners. Below I will outline the organizing principles which arise from such conditions, describe the social forms through which they operate, and discuss the range of productive activities which they embrace.

There are five modes of recruiting and organizing labor in the San Sebastian and Magdalena economies: reciprocity (dar mano or 'lend a hand' form of guelaguetza); contract (performance of labor or the manufacture of a product for stipulated wage or salary payment); product sharing or trabajo a medias in which work is rewarded by a share in the output of any productive activity; command of the elected village authorities who mobilize labor for the performance of public work (tequio); and debt repayment by means of which a debtor works for a creditor to repay a cash loan. The first three modes operate according to the mutual consent of the involved parties, and each party's contribution to production is remunerated in kind (e.g., by a reciprocal contribution of labor), by cash payment, or by a share of the product. The last mode and to a lesser extent the next to last involve the performance of work by a subordinate status occupant in an assymetrical relationship (e.g., as a debtor to a creditor), and such work is either unremunerated (as in the tequio) or serves as credit against the worker's debt with his employer.

Guelaguetza is a normative principle and social relationship among these villagers. While operative in both the production and transfer sectors of the economy, its principle is the same: 'If you help me now I'll help you later when you call upon me.' When operational, guelaguetza assumes the form of a dyadic relationship between social equals, and in the production sector may involve the transfer of means of production. The 'dar mano' form of guelaguetza was described to me by one San Sebastiano as follows:

> I say to some member of my family or to anyone for that matter: 'If you are not busy tomorrow and can help me with my work, I will do the same for you when your work requires it.' If he accepts my offer then I owe him a favor and I will repay him--but not in cash. I am

65

obligated to repay that person
with my own labor.

Another San Sebastiano described the arrangement in
terms of the circumstances which make it indispensable:

If a person wants to do some work
which requires the help of a mozo
but has no money to hire one he asks
a friend, relative or compadre:
'Will you be able to do a guelaguetza
with me? Tomorrow we'll go to bring
firewood from the cerro.' And this
person will probably say yes because
he knows that a guelaguetza is
involved. When he needs help in his
work he will ask the other who he
helped earlier: 'Can you work with
me tomorrow?' And he also replies
yes because he knows that it's a
guelaguetza. If one is short of cash
this is how he goes about getting
help.

A Magdalenan gives yet another example of how the
guelaguetza principle operates: "I work according to
guelaguetza in order to acquire rights to use an ox
team. I work two days for the owner of an ox team so
that he will allow me to use it in working my fields.
I don't have to pay for the ox team and he doesn't
have to pay me for my labor." It is difficult to
estimate precisely how many man-days of labor the
typical villager spends annually on guelaguetza work
but my data suggest that the figure is in the neighborhood of five man-days. Only one out of ten informants
interviewed indicated that he had not performed work
on a guelaguetza basis during the preceding year.

Except during the harvest period when
guelaguetza operates extensively between kinsmen and
compadres, the villager who has cash on hand usually will
hire a mozo rather than mobilize labor through
guelaguetza. "With a mozo," one informant confided,
"a wage is paid and that's that; but if the work is
done by guelaguetza then one is obligated to go to work
for the other person, and one must do that work oneself."
Conversely, the villager who is offered a job as a mozo
for a wage may reject the offer and press instead for a

guelaguetza arrangement with the potential employer. This reflects an attitude among many villagers that serving as a hired hand is demeaning of one's status as a 'campesino.' It also reflects an appreciation of the principle of 'deferral of gratification' in the work context: to forgo the short-run benefit of a wage income for a claim upon the future labor services of another villager. The donor of labor services in a guelaguetza arrangement may be planning for the future when he accepts another party's solicitation. He knows that there are seasons during the year when labor is in short supply and hard to obtain by any means; but he is aware that the social sanctions accompanying the guelaguetza principle can attract labor when the market principle cannot.

Product sharing work arrangements (trabajo a medias) involve cooperation between the owners of material means (e.g., land, tools, oxen) and laborers. The most common arrangement of this kind is share-cropping according to which the sharecropper (mediero) agrees to work someone else's land in return for one-half of the total harvest. Often the land worked on this basis belongs to the sharecropper's aged parent or parent-in-law who have indicated that the land will be his upon their death; however, there are many purely contractual arrangements between non-kinsmen as well.

Sharing arrangements are also made in livestock and poultry production. For example, to 'cross turkeys' (cruzar guajolotes) involves the owner of a hen borrowing the services of a gobbler for breeding purposes--usually with an understanding that a reciprocal loan will be made in the future. According to another arrangement known as 'al partido' the owner of an animal (usually a sow) lends it to another villager for breeding purposes. The second party must feed and care for the animal and the lender is given first choice in selecting his share (half) of the resulting litter. Animal fattening is also done on a share basis. The owner of a cow or pig who is short of fodder will seek a mediero (sharer) to fatten the animal. When the animal has been fattened the owner and the mediero agree on a sale price, locate a buyer and split the sale revenue into two equal shares. Finally, in an arrangement known as 'juntar toros' two oxen are united by their respective ownerrs to make a team for plowing and other work purposes. The owners then alternate on a weekly basis in using the team.

During the dry season period from January through
March a great deal of labor is mobilized and organized
into groups to do three kinds fo work: planting of
first class fields (terrenos de humedad) by hoe;
dwelling and other building construction; and adobe-
making. These groups are organized by the person
interested in having the work done (i.e., the patrón),
and are composed of a nucleus of his consanguineal or
affinal relatives and a periphery of his friends,
compadres or neighbors. In most cases the patrón works
along with the group, giving instructions as these are
necessary. A majority of the mozos, who number anywhere
from 2 to 15, provide their labor on a reciprocal basis
with the patrón, whereas the rest are hired on a wage
basis. The patrón is obligated to provide food and
drink for all of his workers. In adobe-making and
house-construction, the patrón customarily hires the
production specialist (i.e., adobero, jacalero or
albañil) on a wage or job contract basis. The laborers
are either recruited by the patrón as described above
or are hired directly by the production specialists.

     In Magdalena in December 1968 I witnessed a
rather unusual 'house moving' project. This required
two days work by ten men--in addition to the elderly
man who owned the house (jacál). Eight of the ten men
recruited were related consanguineally or affinally to
the old man as follows: WiFaBr (2), Br (1), Son-in-law
(2), GrSo (2), and one consuegro (his son married Ego's
daughter). One of the other workers was the old man's
compadre and another was his adopted son. This work
was performed essentially as 'kinship duty' since none
of the workers expected to be repaid by their respected
elder kinsman.

     Work as a means of debt repayment has a relative-
ly low incidence in San Sebastian and Magdalena but does
occur. As an inevitable outgrowth of the inequality
of distribution of wealth in these villages and the
limited availability of credit, this type of work is
initiated by a patrón-creditor who recruits mozos to
perform given productive tasks from a group of villagers
who either owe him cash or depend upon him as a creditor.
If a particular mozo is in debt to the patrón the work
he performs is credited against his account; if he
refuses to work when the patrón requests him to do so,
he will be requested to repay his debt immediately or
told that credit will no longer be available to him.
Often these arrangements are couched in other terms
but the parties involved recognize implicitly what the
reciprocal expectations are. A formalized variant of

68

this arrangement involved one of my key informants in Magdalena who as a young boy in 1944 was indentured by his father to another villager for a period of one year for the sum of 24 pesos. A document was drawn up stipulating the conditions of this agreement. While this is the only case of indentured labor I encountered during my field work, I have no reason to believe that it was restricted to one case.

The tequio is, in essence, a village-wide labor draft through which workers are mobilized by mandate of the elected village political authorities on an ad hoc basis. Each adult male head of household, as a user of communal village resources, is obliged to provide his labor, without remuneration, for tequio purposes. Failure to comply with a tequio assignment results in suspension of the offender's use rights to communal lands (e.g., for cultivation, gathering, woodcutting, quarrying), a jail sentence or levying of a cash fine (in extreme cases all three punishment are suffered). Tequios are called annually to perform seasonal agricultural tasks on communal fields. Specific dates are set aside for these purposes by the village authorities--the work itself being supervised by an appointed work committee.

In agricultural tequios ox team owners (yunteros) are expected to work a pre-assigned number of furrows along with a crew (cuadrilla) of mozos (villagers who are not yunteros) who perform tasks like planting seed or picking the crop. Non-agricultural tequios are organized as the need arises and usually involve the maintenance or construction of a communal facility. During my stay in these villages tequios were organized for the following purposes: to clear weeds and debris from the cemetery in preparation for All Saint's Day festivities; to clear weeds and debris from the channels of the irrigation system; to construct a new school (including quarrying of stone for construction purposes); to construct an addition to the ejido office; to construct a new dwelling for a villager whose dwelling and residence lot were wrecked to provide space for a new village school; to dig a well, construct a storage tank, and perform other tasks required for the installation of potable water facilities. On projects of this sort the labor force is organized into small crews of about 15 workers, one of whom is named as boss.

San Sebastianos and Magdalenans accept tequio obligations in the same spirit as they (and we) accept taxes: as an unavoidable price for residence in their

communities and for the right to use communal resources.
Some villagers openly express their resentment of the
institution or the seeming capriciousness with which it
is sometimes administered; this is especially true of
the metateros who complain that they sometimes pay more
than their fair share of tequio dues (e.g., providing
stone for construction projects and labor on the project
as well). Most villagers, however, control their
hostility and comply. In any case, only when special
projects are undertaken (e.g., construction of a new
school) does the annual tequio obligation exceed one or
two man-days of labor. Most would agree with one villager who ironically summed up his view of the tequio
obligation as follows: "The work is 'voluntary' yet
compulsory; one must comply . . . we villagers are
obligated to have this agreement" ("El trabajo es
voluntario pero forzoso; uno tiene que ir por fuerza
. . . los del pueblo estamos obligados de tener ese
acuerdo").

           Social Differentiation and Wealth
           Distribution

           In this section I will attempt to pull together
various loose ends in preceding sections by focusing on
the social and economic implications of the distribution
of material wealth in Magdalena and San Sebastian. It
should by now be clear that the forms of wealth which
make the most difference in these communities are means
of production in agriculture, especially land, draft
animals, and carts. This is so because agriculture is
their principle mode of livelihood and these are the
most essential and valuable means of agricultural
production. Accordingly, one important task before us
is to assemble the available data (which are by no
means as consistent, relevant or complete as I would
like) and bring them to bear on the relationships, if
any, between household composition and occupational
mix, household status regarding the above-cited means
of production, and their status with respect to the
supply of corn. It is not my intention here to describe
and analyze the 'class' structure of these communities,
not only because of data and space limitations but also
because of the many unresolved theoretical and analytical difficulties surrounding the concept of 'social
class' and its operationalization (see Galeski 1972:
106-118 and my discussion in Chapter 8). What I do
hope to achieve is the construction of a preliminary
framework toward the systematic understanding of the

fundamental socioeconomic divisions or strata in these villages. From my point of view such divisions or strata as exist must be identified by their relation to the means of production, by their role in the division of labor and, consequently, "by the dimensions of the share of social wealth of which they dispose and the mode of acquiring it" (Lenin 1967:213-214). Also, I think that it is both necessary and desirable to deal with subjective and cultural dimensions of this social differentiation so as to conduct as realistic and accurate an analysis as possible. Furthermore, as I discuss more extensively in the concluding chapter, it is misleading and incorrect to circumscribe a treatment of social differentiation within village boundaries and I do so in this chapter only for expository purposes. As was apparent from my brief discussion of the embroidery industry, relations of production in Oaxaca villages extend well beyond their boundaries. Indeed, my treatment of the division of labor has been designed to show that it is structured upon such an extension. Finally, whereas the proposition that the process of capital accumulation in the countryside of a nation undergoing uneven capitalist development creates a stratified rural population split between a 'bourgeoisie' and a 'proletariat' (Lenin 1964; cf. Galeski 1972:109-112) has stimulated much important analytical work (e.g., Shanin 1972; Pozas and Pozas 1973), another consequence of this process which has many ramifications, is often overlooked, namely, that ". . . within the structure of society as a whole the entire peasant stratum is reduced to the position of a 'proletarian with land'" and "in certain countries even becomes the 'lowest social class'" (Galeski 1972:116). This theme will be picked up again in Chapter 8 but the reader should keep it in mind as we proceed through the final section of this chapter.

What is the relationship between division of labor, wealth distribution, and social status in the metate villages? It is worth noting from the beginning that while the data will point to substantial differences in the objective economic circumstances of households, especially in San Sebastian which is the larger and more prosperous village, these are not formally institutionalized or overtly reflected in the daily conduct of interpersonal relations. That is to say, these relations are essentially egalitarian in nature and differences in occupation or wealth are not associated with visible differences in speech, dress or etiquette. In both San Sebastian and Magdalena, for example, I spent many hours squatting on streetcorners

71

in night-time bull sessions with men representing
households which were poles apart in terms of wealth
and status, yet this had absolutely no predictable
impact on their situational behavior; thus handfuls of
dirt or the grossest of obscenities could be casually
launched from any direction and by any hand or mouth
as a contribution to the evening's recreation. Likewise, there are no meaningful distinctions at this
juncture in history between 'ladinos,' 'mestizos,' or
'gente de razon' and 'indios' or 'gentiles'; somatic
differences do not correspond with social or cultural
differences among the villagers and the allocation of
wealth, power and status does not follow ethnic lines
in either of these villages (nor, for that matter, are
these categories applicable to regional society--see
Chapter 8 under "'Class or Ethnicity'?").

It would be a mistake to infer from this that
'egalitarianism' pervades the social consciousness of
these villages; quite the contrary, borrowing an apt
if ponderous phrase from Ossowski (1963:Ch. 2),
"dichotomic conceptions" of social structure are present
in people's thoughts and often expressed in their
converstaions, though with contrasting emphasis between
the two populations. San Sebastianos conceptually
polarize their own village into two strata, the pobres
or pelados and the ricos or gente de categoría, whereas
the Magdalenans are more likely to play down any internal differences that exist and view themselves as
a uniformly poor and exploited collectivity in
opposition to 'capitalistas,' 'terratenientes' or
'canijos ricos' ('feeble rich') in neighboring
settlements--particularly with reference to San Pedro
Apostol where in 1967 there were still several trapiches
which processed sugar cane grown in Magdalena into
panela (caked brown sugar) and, also, several large
stores. However, it is probable that this behavior
by Magdalenans has deeper historical roots and that,
indeed, the contrast between the two villages in this
dimension reflects their divergent histories since
1900, if not before.

Magdalena, as mentioned earlier, entered this
century as a despoiled settlement of essentially landless peones enclaved within the boundaries of one of
the largest haciendas (El Vergel-La Garzona owned by
the Mimiaga family) in the 'Central Valleys' region,
a condition it had suffered since at least late colonial
times. As a consequence of their agrarian struggle,
which was in full swing by 1915 and in which the
Magdalenans employed violent as well as non-violent

means against the <u>hacienda</u>, the establishment of an
<u>ejido</u> from land expropriated from the <u>hacienda</u> was
authorized in a presidential decree dated February 3,
1921 (<u>Archivo</u>, <u>Sec. de al Reforma Agraria</u>: <u>Expediente</u>
14, <u>documentos</u> 15, 28 and 62). Since that date the
trajectory of Magdalena's history has been dominated
by its status as an <u>ejido</u> or federal agrarian reform
community which means that the source of many of its
political and economic problems remains external to it,
albeit with a change in institutional forms (i.e., from
<u>hacienda</u> to State bureaucracy).[10]

San Sebastian, on the other hand, came out of
the colonial period and into the 20th century with its
'original' land base and corporate identity intact.
Its population and economic life had been affected over
the years by the operations of two contiguous <u>haciendas</u>
but it never became as dependent on them as was the case
with Magdalena and, most importantly, never lost any
of its lands through despoilation. However, from about
1880 San Sebastian was dominated by a home-grown
<u>cacique</u>, don Mateo, whose career is a 'rags-to-riches'
tale which left him, at his death in 1915, as proprietor
not only of a large proportion of the best agricultural
lands of his own village but also as owner of significant land holdings within the jurisdictions of several
neighboring settlements. During this thirty-five year
period he was municipal president on five separate
occasions, with his sons serving on others and, in the
style of the Porfiriate, he was the principal link
between the village and the <u>jefe político</u> in Tlacolula.
Don Mateo's career is still a lively topic of debate
among San Sebastianos today. Many of them told me that
their fathers or grandfathers had been pauperized by
signing over land titles to the <u>cacique</u> during drinking
and gambling bouts in his store-<u>cantina</u> (operated by
his daughter and in which everything from <u>pulque</u>,
<u>tepache</u>, and <u>mezcal</u> to machetes, baskets, and cloth was
sold on a cash, credit or barter basis). The Revolution
left don Mateo's land holdings essentially intact
(consisting as they did in a multitude of dispersed
small parcels rather than large unbroken tracts--some
of which he also owned) so that many of his lineal
descendants are among the '<u>ricos</u>' of the village primarily due to lands which they inherited from the <u>cacique</u>
or his wife. Consequently, some of the political
antagonisms in San Sebastian today, not to speak of the
tendency toward a polarized conception of the social
structure, have their roots in this historical
situation (Cook 1968:63-65).

When poor San Sebastianos refer to the 'ricos' in their midst they have in mind individuals like 7, 22, and 23 listed in Table 5, namely, those who are full-time campesinos by occupation, who own substantial amounts of first class agricultural land, as well as the means to make it productive, and who without exception realize an abundant annual harvest.[11] As it turns out, and in support of the previous historical argument, two of these individuals (7 and 23) are grandchildren of don Mateo; the bulk of their respective 5.9 and 7.6 hectares of agricultural land came to them, through their mother (don Mateo's daughter), as their share of the 124 plots (dispersed among ten different parajes) which comprised their grandfather's patrimony (Cook 1968:87-95 and chart on page 96). Yet the third individual cited (22) is not an heir of the cacique and his case is illustrative of another dynamic at work in the village economy, namely, the inter-generational and inter-familial redistribution of wealth. This individual who is a bitter political opponent of the cacique's heirs ironically enjoyed, in the post World War II period, a 'rags-to-riches' career not unlike that of don Mateo himself more than a half century earlier. He was born into a poor peasant family and inherited an insignificant patrimony but with money saved from his earnings as a bracero in the U.S. he began to invest in land and animals. By 1950, and taking into account his wife's assets, he had become one of San Sebastian's acknowledged ricos as well as one of its most influential political leaders (he served as municipal president and has occupied several other important cargos in the civil-religious hierarchy--see subsequent discussion in this section). This case reminds us that we must not look at statistical tabulations like those in Table 5 as portraying a static structure but, rather, as indicating one moment in an ongoing process through which inherited and acquired wealth change hands in a dialectic of fluctuating household fortunes. Land ownership and usufruct status is especially susceptible to change. First there is the tendency, by no means unrestrained, for land parcels to be further parcelized through inheritance. Moreover, given the predominance of the private property regime in San Sebastian, land is bought and sold, leased or rented, and mortgaged and, consequently, changes hands as economic fortunes shift. Nevertheless, to the extent that land holdings are maintained or increased under the ownership or control of various families, who also have the means to diversify their own occupational pursuits while becoming regular employers in agriculture of other villagers, we

74

TABLE 5. Occupations of Heads and
Wealth Distribution in 35
Households in San Sebastian
Teitipac in 1966.

No. of House-hold	Occupations Principal, Others	Land under cultivation (hectares)			Amount of Corn Harvested (kgs.)	Work Animals	
		1st Class	Other	Total		Oxen	Burros
1.	campesino, leñero, escobero	.5	2.7	3.2	2770	2	4
2.	panadero, campesino	1.3	7.2	8.5	2240	3	1
3.	tortillera	.2	1.3	1.5	---	2	3
4.	campesino, castrator	1.0	1.7	2.7	1460	3	3
5.	campesino	.2	2.5	2.7	2268	6	2
6.	campesino, cart maker	.9	1.2	2.1	1900	2	2
7.	campesino, scribe	2.4	3.5	5.9	1764	2	2
8.	metatero, jornalero	.01	.6	.6	900	0	1
9.	mano maker, campesino	0	.4	.4	44	0	1
10.	metatero, jornalero	0	.7	.7	200	0	0
11.	metatero, jornalero	0	.25	.25	750	1	1
12.	campesino, quarryman, mano maker	.2	2.4	2.6	2884	2	0
13.	campesino	.8	.1	.9	1350	2	3
14.	metatero, campesino	.4	1.3	1.7	1550	0	0
15.	campesino, panadero, canastero, leñero	.15	1.1	1.25	1642	0	2
16.	canastero, campesino	0	.5	.5	180	2	2
17.	campesino, metatero	.3	.6	.9	1616	2	0
18.	metatero, campesino	0	2.9	2.9	2786	2	2
19.	metatero, jornalero	0	.6	.6	64	0	1
20.	campesino, mano maker	.5	.6	1.1	2500	2	1
21.	regatona de metates	.03	.5	.53	500	1	0
22.	campesino	7.9	6.0	13.9	14950	2	3
23.	campesino	4.9	2.7	7.6	9750	2	1
24.	metate trader, mano maker	.5	2.7	3.2	2000	0	1
25.	metatero, jornalero	0	.1	.1	---	0	0
26.	metatero, musician, jornalero	0	.1	.1	---	0	2
27.	campesino, metatero	.1	.2	.3	---	2	0
28.	metatero, herrero, campesino	0	.2	.2	---	2	1
29.	metatero, jornalero	0	.2	.2	1000	0	0
30.	metatero, jornalero	0	.7	.7	---	0	1
31.	metatero, jornalero, broom maker	0	.3	.3	---	0	1
32.	metatero, barber, baker, campesino	.03	.1	.13	---	2	0
33.	campesino, metatero, musician	.06	.09	.15	---	2	1
34.	metatero, jornalero	0	0	0	500 (share)	0	1
35.	metatero, jornalero	.05	0	.05	---	0	0
	TOTAL	22.43	46.04	68.46	57568		

clearly have a structural change which is more significant in the long run than any capricious or temporary circulation of households between relative positions of land wealth and land poverty. Unfortunately, the available data do not permit me to further explore this thesis in the San Sebastian case and it remains an important one for future consideration.

Just as an examination of Table 5 enables us to isolate the 'haves' among the San Sebastian households surveyed we can also easily identify the 'have nots.' The salient diagnostic characteristics of this category are relative land poverty (i.e., little or no 1st class land and less than one hectare of other land) combined with the non-possession of an ox team. Of the 35 heads of household listed, twelve (8, 9, 10, 11 ,19, 25, 26, 29, 30, 31, 34, and 35) fall into this category. In comparison with the twenty-three remaining individuals, the statistical record of their poverty is striking: an average of .3 hectares of land per household (with only two having even negligible parcels of 1st class land), vs. a 2.8 hectare per household average (or 2.3 hectare excluding case 22) which includes one hectare per household of 1st class land; and an average of 455 kilograms of corn harvested per household vs. an average of 2568 kilograms (including households 22 and 23) or an average of 1538 kilograms (excluding 22 and 23 which skew the distribution). The reader will note that there are other households whose objective situations in terms of land worked are also unfavorable (e.g., 13, 16, 17 and 27), however, as possessors of ox teams, they are better equipped to overcome this deficiency through sharecropping or rental of their teams which augments their otherwise meager harvest; thus the average harvest for three of these households (excluding 27) is 1049 kilograms which is well above the 455 kilogram average of the twelve 'have nots.'[12]

A survey of the occupations of the heads of the 'have nots' households indicates that in all cases the principal occupation is either metatero or mano maker (1 case only), with the most frequent secondary occupation being that of jornalero or agricultural day laborer. While these data are by no means conclusive (there are exceptions), they do make a strong case for a significant association in San Sebastian households between poverty in the agricultural means of production and the presence of metate making as principal occupation. Likewise, the association between the secondary occupational status of jornalero and poverty in agricultural means is at least as strong. Agricultural

wage labor or agricultural labor for payment in kind
(e.g., in corn or beans) becomes the most viable alternative for survival when employment opportunities are
limited elsewhere (e.g., when metates are not selling);
and it is the most direct means for a household without
an adequate supply of basic food crops to acquire a
claim to some (i.e., in exchange for their labor power).
I will explore this relationship and the situation of
the metatero-jornalero at more length in Chapter 4.

What emerges convincingly, though not with the
extremes displayed in the San Sebastian case, from the
data presented in Table 6 is that there is an uneven
distribution of ejido lands in Magdalena as shown by
the varying amount of hectares worked per household.
The mean size of the ejido holding cultivated per
household for all 35 respondents was 2.7 hectares; 20
households reported cultivating 2.5 hectares or less,
ten as cultivating between 3 and 4.5 hectares each and
two as cultivating 6 and 7 hectares respectively.
Only two of the 35 respondents reported having no land
under cultivation in 1978 and both of these were female
heads of household (an elderly widow and a middle-aged
divorcee). That the uneven distribution of ejido land
is neither a problem of data reliability nor is a
recent phenomenon of temporary duration is suggested
by the results of an official 1966 census of 176
Magdalena ejidatarios in which the recorded number of
hectares cultivated ranged from a low of .5 hectares
to a high of 6.5 hectares, with a mean of 2.9 hectares
per ejidatario household. The same census showed that
53 ejidatarios cultivated 4 or more hectares and that
37 others cultivated only 1.5 or fewer. There is
additional evidence which suggests that this unevenness
reflects the nature of the ejido regime rather than
factors internal to the households themselves. The
1979 data yield no significant correlation between
household consumer/worker ratios and number of hectares
worked per household: ten households have c/w ratios
of 4 or less and cultivated between 1.1 and 3.0
hectares, whereas eight households with c/w ratios of
4.1 - 9 also cultivated the same range of hectares;
and they yield a possible negative correlation between
c/w ratios and number of hectares cultivated per
campesino: 14 households had c/w ratios of 4 or less
and averages of 3.0 or less hectares cultivated per
campesino as opposed to 9 households with c/w ratios
of 4.1 or larger which also had averages of 3.0 or
less hectares cultivated per campesino. With both sets
of statistics, then, the correlations which would have
supported the case for the role of factors endogenous

TABLE 6. Occupations, Agricultural Means of Production, and Annual Corn Harvest for 37 Households in Magdalena Ocotlán in 1979.

House-hold No.	No. of Persons	Occupation-Person Household Mix	Total	Agricultural Land Worked (in hectares) Private	Ejido	Total	Corn Harvest (kgs.) 1978	Regular	Agricultural Means of Production Total Value Pesos	No. Oxen	Annual Rental Pesos	Wage Labor Hired	(man-days) Worked
1.	5	campesino(1), bordado(1)	2	2.0	2.0	4.0	500	1250	10500	2	800	6 @ 300 ps	15
2.	7	campesino-jornalero(2)	2	0	3.0	3.0	0	1000	5500	2	---	---	98
3.	6	campesino(1), bordado(2)	3		2.0	2.0	0	500	8700	2	850	---	0
4.	6	campesino(2), bordado(2)	4	1.0	2.0	3.0	1000	1500	---	2	900	0	0
5.	6	campesino(2), bordado(1)	3	0	2.0	2.0	500	500	---	2	600	0	0
6.	5	campesino(1)	1	1.1	4.0	5.1	1000	2000	7500	2	1200	72@ 360ps	72
7.	2	mano maker-campesino(1)	1	0	4.5	4.5	0	1400	0	0	---	3 @ 150 ps	0
8.	3	campesino-construction peon (1), commission agent bordado(1), jornalero(1)	3							0			0
9.	10	campesino-construction peon (1), bordado(3), campesino (1), shepherd(2)	7	1.0	2.0	3.0	80	1000	500	0	1820	14@ 560 ps	24
10.	7	campesino(1), bordado(2)	3	0	2.5	2.5	500	500	15500	2	1000	0	24
11.	2	campesino(1)	1	0	1.25	1.25	250	300	10500	2	60	0	0
12.	9	campesino-jornalero(1)	1	0	4.5	4.5	0	500	500	0	---	0	0
13.	1	none (elderly widow)	0	0	2.0	2.0	500	1000	5500	2	420	0	0
14.	5	campesino-construction peon (1), bordado(1)	2	0	0	0	500	500	0	0	0	0	0
15.	3	campesino(2)	2	1.5	3.0	4.5	1000	1750	6000	2	400	0	0
16.	2	campesino(1)	1	0	6.0	6.0	500	800	13000	0	200	0	0
17.	6	campesino-jornalero(1)	1	---	---	---	0	---	---	0	0	0	0
18.	11	campesino(2), tractor driver	3	0	2.0	2.0	800	2500	---	0	230	6	---
19.	6	bordado-campesina(2), campesino(1)	3	1.6	3.4	5.0	500	900	---	2	1000	0	0
20.	2	campesino(1)	1	0	2.0	2.0	500	900	9500	2	740	0	0
21.	2	campesino(1)	1	0	1.0	1.0	380	750	---	2	0	0	0
22.	5	bordado (2), campesino-jornalero (1)	3	0	3.0	3.0	0	250	0	0	1650	0	---

TABLE 6. Occupations, Agricultural Means of Production, and Annual Corn Harvest for 37 Households in Magdalena Ocotlan in 1979 (Continued).

| House-hold No. | No. of Persons | Occupation-Person Household Mix | To-tal | Agricultural Land Worked (in hectares) | | | Corn Harvest (kgs.) | | Agricultural Means of Production | | | | |
				Private	Ejido	Total	1978	Regular	Total Value Pesos	No. Oxen	Annual Rental Pesos	Wage Labor Hired	Production (man-days) Worked
23.	6	campesino(3), bordado(2)	5	0	1.8	1.8	0	1500	0	0	---	0	98
24.	10	metatero-campesino-jornalero(1), baker(1), bordado(1)	3	0	1.8	1.8	150	1250	5000	0	1900	0	98
25.	5	campesino(1), bordado(1)	2	3.0	.5	3.5	550	3000	4450	2	---	---	---
26.	3	campesino-construction peon(1), bordado(1)	2	5.5	0	5.5	500	1000	9500	2	1850	8 @ 320 ps	0
27.	2	campesino(1)	1	0	2.0	2.0	500	1000	7500	2	1290	3 @ 140 ps	0
28.	3	campesino(2)	2	0	4.5	4.5	250	2500	---	2	530	0	0
29.	3	campesino-molinero(1)	1	3.0	2.0	5.0	700	1500	0	0	1750	15 @ 600 ps	0
30.	2	campesino(1)	1	1.5	1.5	3.0	300	1250	55000	2	30	3 @ 90 ps	0
31.	6	campesino-jornalero(1), bordado(2)	3	---	---	---	0	---	0	0	---	0	---
32.	6	campesino(1), shepherd(1), bordado(1)	3	1.0	4.5	5.5	0	2500	13500	2	---	11 @ 550 ps	0
33.	2	bordado-tortilla maker(1)	1	0	0	0	0	0	0	0	0	0	0
34.	9	campesino-construction peon(1), bordado(4)	5	1.0	7.0	8.0	---	1250	---	2	---	0	0
35.	3	campesino-jornalero(1)	1	0	2.0	2.0	600	1000	0	0	1400	0	6
36.	9	campesino-construction peon(1), bordado(1), campesino(1)	3	4.0	2.0	6.0	1000	1000	21500	2	---	0	0
37.	8	campesino-metatero(1), bordado(1), shepherd(1)	3	0	2.4	2.4	0	500	8500	2	740	0	0
		TOTALS	83	27.2	87.15	110.91	3360	39050	214000				

to the households were not forthcoming, and it appears
that we must look to the _ejido_ regime itself for the
causes of uneven land distribution. Admittedly, however,
this regime has operated in Magdalena to essentially
eliminate landlessness which, of course, cannot be said
of the private property regime in San Sebastian.

It is significant that 13 (37%) of 35 Magdalena
respondents reported that they owned private agricultural
plots to supplement their _ejido_ holdings (except no. 26
who has no _ejido_ land); the mean private holding per
household was 2.4 hectares with eight households owning
2 hectares or less and five owning 3 or more hectares.
Combining both types of land, these households have an
average of 4.6 hectares each, compared with an average
of only 2.7 hectares each for the 20 _ejidatarios_ without
private parcels. That the ownership of private
agricultural land to supplement _ejido_ holdings appears
to be the key to socioeconomic stratification in Magdalena
is supported by other calculations based on data from
Table 6. For example, the per household average for
respondent estimates (N = 36) of the 1978 corn harvest
(poor due to drought conditions) was 679 kilograms
for the _propietario-ejidatario_ households and only
268 kilograms for the _ejido-only_ households. Furthermore, the total value of agricultural means of production
owned averaged 12,845 pesos ($571 dollars) each for the
propietarios and 4,737 pesos ($211 dollars) for the
pure _ejidatarios_, and the rental of agricultural means
of production averaged 1083 pesos ($48 dollars) per
household annually for the former households and 683
($30 dollars) for the latter (who rent tractors, ox
teams and carts in contrast with most of the _propietarios_
who rent tractors only). Finally, regarding the annual
employment of agricultural wage laborers, eight (67%)
of the _propietarios_ reported spending an average of
790 pesos ($35 dollars) each, whereas only 3 (15%)
ejidatarios reported expenses for hired hands and spent
the negligible amount of 193 pesos ($8.50 dollars) each.
In essence, it appears that the combination of private
and _ejido_ lands (or the possession only of a substantial
parcel of private land as is the case with household
no. 26) is diagnostic of the most successful and
entrepreneurial households in Magdalena and that their
economic situation, as reflected by several quantitative
indices, is substantially better than that of a large
majority of the pure _ejidatarios_. One qualification
to this argument is linked to the fact that three (23%)
of the _propietarios_ reported working an average of 37
days annually as wage-laborers which indicates that they
have by no means been transformed into a true rural

bourgeoisie (though this may possibly have occurred with a few of their co-villagers).[13]

How does the data on household occupational mixes fit into this picture? A tabulation of occupational roles per household (column 4, Table 6) demonstrates a negligible difference between the propietarios and the pure ejidatarios as to the average number of occupational role performers per household (2.5 vs. 2.3). But there are some significant differences between them regarding the frequency of occurrence of occupations and types of occupations in which their members participate. Seven of the 13 (54%) propietarios, for example, are full-time campesinos and report no secondary occupations, whereas this is true of only 45% of the non-private property owners for whom agriculture is less rewarding. The situation concerning bordado (embroidery) is more problematic, especially if one anticipates that it will have a higher frequency of occurrence among the poorer households. The data can be interpreted to show that the reverse is true, namely, that bordado occurs in 62% of the propietario households and in only 42% of the less affluent ejido-only households. Upon closer examination of the data, however, we find that most (75%) of the propietario embroidery households have only one embroiderer but that 66% of the ejido-only embroidery households have two or three embroiderers each. Consequently, it appears that embroidery may, after all, be more intensively practiced in these latter households.

One additional point of interest which should be noted here is that, without exception, occupations with an 'entrepreneurial' dimension and requiring 'modern' skills or operating capital occur exclusively among the propietario households. This is the case with the following occupations listed in Table 6: embroidery commission agent (no. 8; our survey data also indicate that no. 14 probably has a comisionista del bordado), tractor driver (no. 18) and molinero or miller (no. 29). That occupations with these requisites appear in households of this type is, of course, in accordance with a central thesis in the literature of rural social differentiation and class formation under conditions of capitalist development (see discussion under "On the Dynamics of Class Formation" in Chapter 8).

Before concluding this section, which up to now has focused primarily upon occupational and other objective indices of socioeconomic stratification in

81

these villages, something more should be said about the cultural dimension of 'status'--the superstructure based on a series of subjective criteria by which villagers rank themselves and others in a hierarchy of prestige or esteem. We can assume that this status dimension intersects with and provides ideological supports for the socioeconomic structure. But how does this happen? (cf. Stavenhagen 1969:38-42).

My field work experience in San Sebastian and Magdalena has convinced me that material wealth is not the only index of categoría or prestigeful status. Such non-material factors like age, experience, education, knowledge, special skills, and community service can also enhance an individual's status in the estimation of his or her co-villagers. There are old people with few material possessions in both villagers (especially men) who occupy positions of honor and respect and who are treated accordingly by others-- if only kinsmen and fictive kinsmen. Of course, categoría is still most easily achievable with material wealth but not so much through its possession as through its 'generous' distribution (or calculated manipulation?)--especially as an occupant of an office or cargo in the civil-religious hierarchy or as mayordomo or sponsor of a mayordomía (saint's celebration).

Variant forms of the classic Mesoamerican civil-religious hierarchy or ladder system (Carrasco 1961; Cancian 1967) continue to operate in both villages to convert accumulated material wealth into social esteem through displays of generosity in the performance of a series of elected, appointed or voluntary roles. Many posts or offices in the civil-religious apparatus of these villages do not require personal expenditures of wealth or displays of generosity and are viewed simply as 'paying one's dues' as a citizen of the community; but several of the middle and higher level offices do either entail such obligations or evoke such expectations (as do events like birthdays, weddings, and funerals). Since it is beyond the scope of the present study to describe and analyze the civil-religious hierarchy or the mayordomía system (much less other ceremonial occasions which have 'status' implications), suffice it to say that it is through their participation in cargos and as mayordomía sponsors that household heads in the Teitipac villages and Magdalena are informally ranked from the standpoint of prestige and graded on an age basis by their co-villagers. Service in the hierarchy, involving positions of varying responsibility, is obligatory for all adult males and carries no direct monetary remuneration (and, as I've already stated, may require personal expenditures); sponsorship of mayordomías is now strictly 'voluntary.' Nevertheless, informal social pressures toward sponsorship operate as indicated in the following statement by a metatero-campesino from San Juan Teitipac who explained to me how he mobilized the money to fund the sponsorship of a large mayordomía that cost him about 12,000 pesos ($960 dollars) in 1960:

> I put aside money from the oficio (i.e., metate making). And we had an ox team that we fattened which I sold for 5800 pesos; also we have other savings. We began to fatten those animals before I had the cargo. We began to prepare to comply with the promesa (promise to Saint to sponsor the festival) five years earlier. I voluntarily sponsored the mayordomía to comply with my obligations as a citizen of the village. If one doesn't comply with the customs one is not recognized as a citizen. And any of one's neighbors--well you understand about gossip, right? They say, 'Look at that guy, he doesn't undertake a work to help the village comply with its customs.'

Recruitment into cargos, which include posts ranging from acolyte and messenger to judge and mayor) is by public vote or by appointment by incumbent authorities with the usual period of office being three years. Recruitment is increasingly selective as to the experience and qualifications of candidates as the office to be filled becomes more important. This means that the cargo careers of most villagers terminate prior to their occupancy of higher-level executive posts (e.g., Presidente Municipal, Síndico, Alcalde, Fiscal de la Iglesia). At the risk of over-simplifying, and acknowledging the absence of supporting data, it seems to me that the cumulative results of individual cargo careers is to reinforce the prevailing stratification structure by, in effect, restricting the highest-level positions to those villagers who have the means to withstand the strain on their work schedule and budgets, as well as the

capacity to do the job (which in the case of the
executive civil posts is becoming increasingly complex
as the State bureaucracy increases its influence at
the village level). I will deal with some of the social
and economic aspects of mayordomía sponsorship in the
section on "Ceremonial Exchange" in the next chapter.[14]

FOOTNOTES

[1]The population figures for San Sebastian are from the 1970 General Population Census, whereas those for Magdalena are for 1979 and were provided by municipal authorities.

[2]Before the agrarian reform program was initiated during the second decade of this century as an outgrowth of the Revolution, the term 'ejido' referred to communal lands subject to collective usufruct. Following the consolidation of agrarian reform in article 27 of the 1917 Constitution, the term 'ejido' has referred to a system of land tenure based on clause X of article 27 that says: "Los nucleos de población que carezcan de ejidos o que no puedan lograr su restitución por falta de titulos, por imposibilidad de identificarlos, o porque legalmente hubieran sido enajenados, serán dotados con tierras y aguas suficientes para consstituirlos, conforme a las necesidades de su población, sin que en ningún caso deje de concederseles . . ." (1974). It was through the procedure of dotación and not through restitución that Magdalena Ocotlan was established as an ejido (cf. Reyes, Stavenhaven, et.al. 1974:434-466).

[3]One paraje known as Rio Guela has four subparajes called 'Nueve Surcos' (Nine Furrows), Esquina del Rio Guela (Corner of the Guela River), Espinal Rio Guela (Thorn Thicket on the Guela River) and Máquina Rio Guela (literally 'Machine' on the Guela River, so named for an old stone pumping station belonging to a defunct hacienda).

[4]Kirkby 1973 is the most comprehensive study yet published on land use and agricultural systems in the Valley of Oaxaca. It is especially useful for its painstaking analysis of production costs and yields from various types of land and agricultural techniques.

[5]This section outlines the kinship/residence matrix in which metatero households are inserted and, except for the absence of female-headed households among the metatero population, there is nothing which distinguishes its kinship and residence organization

from that of the rest of the population in these villages. See Cook 1968:150-161 for a more detailed description and analysis of residence, domestic group composition, and kinship in San Sebastian Teitipac.

[6]In such cases fences positioned between contiguous lots serve to control livestock and to maintain a certain degree of privacy. In these patrilocal extended household clusters, each household has separate sleeping, food storage, and animal care facilities; but eating, work, recreation and ceremonial activities often involve inter-household cooperation and sharing.

[7]I employ the 'division of labor' concept in an economistic sense which is more narrowly focused on the 'economic field' than is the standard Marxist concept of the social division of labor. My usage encompasses, without being identical with, the Marxist concept of 'technical division of labor' i.e., the division of labor within a given labor process (Harnecker 1971:27).

[8]See Figure 5 which schematizes the circulatory routes for metates and the related discussion in Chapter 6.

[9]There are several reasons why this Table must be interpreted rather loosely. First, I collected first-hand census data from only a limited sample (non-random) of households in these villages (50 in San Sebastian; 30 in Magdalena). Data were also collected indirectly through key informants and from various government censuses. Second, there is the vexing problem of determining what an 'oficio' (occupation) is in these villages; some villagers do not think of secondary or subsidiary occupations as 'oficios' and will mention only their principal occupation for census purposes (which, in fact, is usually the only one solicited). This problem is compounded by the fact that many villagers work irregularly in the secondary occupations or have become inactive in them. Third, there is inevitably an under-representation of female occupations which are directly commodity-producing (excluding domestic work which is exclusively 'use-value' producing and/or reproductive of labor-power) or commodity-handling (e.g., petty trading). This reflects a 'male bias' in my original research which was heavily weighted toward the metateros themselves, as well as the fact that 'official' censuses don't cover the occupational statuses of women who are not 'heads of household." In San Sebastian, for example, there were some 40 female heads of household; roughly

one-half of these women did not regularly cohabit with a male; the rest lived in consensual union but retained their separate 'head of household' status. To the extent that these women gave their principal occupation as something other than housewife (i.e., 'doméstica' or 'ama de casa')--as, for example, tortillera (tortilla maker and seller) or regatona (trader)--they are included in the tabulated census data. Otherwise they are excluded. Incidentally, there is a real need for a systematic study of the nature and role of female labor in the 'Central Valleys' region.

[10]I rarely overheard discussions by San Sebastianos concerning wealth differences which were couched in class struggle terms. In Magdalena, however, the rhetoric tends to be somewhat more militant, perhaps reflecting the influence of Popular Socialist Party literature which was sometimes distributed prior to ejido meetings. That this political current has possibly become stronger since the period of my initial fieldwork is indicated by the fact that the incumbent Comisario Ejidal in 1980--together with a significant number of ejidatarios--is an active member of the Central Campesina Independiente, a peasant organization affiliated with the Communist Party. During 1967/68 it was common in the neighboring village of San Pedro Apostol to hear male villagers refer to the local trapicheros as 'capitalistas.' Since several Magdalenans have been employed as wage laborers in the trapiches side by side with workers from San Pedro, their class consciousness may have been enhanced.

[11]The data presented in this Table derive from interviews which I conducted with a non-random sample of San Sebastianos; the sample over-represented metate industry personnel and under-represented full-time peasant cultivators in terms of their respective proportions of the total village population. Also, the figures on land under cultivation include land which is owned, leased, rented (and in some cases) sharecropped. Finally, the figures on corn yield are informant estimates and are not based on my own measurements.

[12]Crop yield or per plot productivity is one of the principal criteria employed by the villagers to classify and evaluate their cultivated land. The most widely used unit of measure in San Sebastian and throughout the region is the Spanish almud which is equivalent to 4 liters; one almud of shelled corn usually weighs about 4 kilos. Maize yields are

usually given in terms of almudes or fanegas (Spanish bushels equivalent to 25 almudes or 100 kilos) of shelled corn or in carretas (cartloads) of unhusked corn. One carreta of unhusked corn is roughly equivalent to 5 fanegas, 125 almudes or 500 kilos of shelled corn (maíz en grano). See Beals 1975:78-79 for a useful discussion of weights and measures in Oaxaca.

One important aspect of corn production which is not indicated by the data in Table 5 is the annual fluctuation in output or yield due to varying precipitation patterns. For example, according to my own spot estimate, the total harvest on the communal fields in 1966 was approximately 22 cartfuls, with rainfall during the growing season being rated as average to better than average. In 1965, however, not more than five cartfuls were harvested on these same fields due to insufficient rainfall. Likewise, the 1965 harvest for most San Sebstianos was from 1/4 to 1/3 that of their 1966 harvest. This variability in crop yields on temporal lands, itself a creature of capricious rainfall patterns, is a characteristic of 'dry farming' throughout the 'Central Valleys' region (cf. Kirkby 1973:75, 157-160).

[13]A 1968 government census of 135 ejidatarios in Magdalena records substantial differences among them regarding the owernship of ox teams and private land. It shows that only 61 ejidatarios owned ox teams, with 16 of these owning two or more teams, and that 39 (29%) owned private parcels (again with 16 owning two or more parcels). Also, this census records that 32 ejidatarios rented ox teams in that year.

[14]See Cook 1968:165-172 for a more detailed discussion of the civil-religious hierarchy in San Sebastian. B. DeWalt (1974) has compared the cargo system in San Sebastian (using my work as a basis) with others described in the Mesoamerican literature and classified it in terms of a series of indices of sociocultural change. It must be emphasized that my interpretation of this system in San Sebastian is tentative and should not be construed by the reader as applicable to all cargo systems in the region, the state of Oaxaca or elsewhere in Mesoamerica.

Customers examining metates and manos in the Tlacolula marketplace.

Newlyweds with several metates in a wedding gift
display in a Oaxaca Valley Community.

CHAPTER 3.   EXCHANGE AND UTILIZATION

IN THE VILLAGE ECONOMIES:

THE CIRCULATION AND USES OF WEALTH

The Problem

In the preceding chapter we delineated the
nature and characteristics of the production matrix
within which the residents of the metate villages
maneuver to secure their material well-being. We
demonstrated, by focusing on the social differentiation
of the village populations, how and why the production
and distribution of material wealth serves as the
foundation of village economic and social life. What
remains to be done, before concentrating our attention
on the metate industry, is to substantiate the crucial
role of exchange, which we have already posited as
comprising an integral sector of the economic field,
in these village economies and, finally, to consider
some of the uses to which products produced or
acquired by the villagers are put. Let's begin by
elaborating the general principles which underlie
distribution and exchange activities and, then, examine
the relationship between them, both theoretically and
in concrete examples from the villages.

Exchange and Distribution

General principles. It will be recalled from
the preceding chapter that the process of distribution
determines the proportion of total output that is
allocated to laborers and others who contribute to the
production process, whereas exchange determines the
specific products into which the share allocated by
distribution is converted. In other words, distribution
implies a reward system in which products are allocated
among individuals or groups in a society by reason of
their control over the factors of production or for the
labor power they expend in production. Exchange, on
the other hand, refers to the various processes by
which products (and services) move between individuals

or groups as, for example, between producer and consumer, buyer and seller, or donor and recipient.

The producer-product relation, once the product is produced, is not necessarily or immediately one of possession; the rights of a direct producer over the product or his labor are determined by the prevailing relations of production. Consequently, all social formations have explicit or implicit norms governing the way total output is to be shared out among their members which, in turn, necessarily correspond to the prevailing relations of production. It is analytically important to remember that the distribution of product is guided only partly by norms, and that it must not be viewed mechanically merely as a series of acts in response to norms.

It may turn out that the producer of a given product has a primary claim on it; but the "primary claimant" (LeClair 1959:20), the one upon whom other claimants depend for a satisfaction of their claims, might also be a non-producer of some type. For example, in the process of quarrying for metate stone the owner/boss of a quarry claims all stone extracted from his quarry, regardless of whether or not he is present when it is extracted. Stone is not to be distributed among the workers in the absence of the 'owner/boss' or his agent. In rural Oaxaca most claims to output are, as a general rule, established either by producers or by a claimant's role in the production process (as in the above example), and there are relatively few situations in which claims are established on the basis of some non-production relation between producer and claimant (e.g., kinship, compadrazgo) or on the basis of some special relationship of the claimant to the whole community (e.g., office holder in the civil-religious hierarchy). Kinship and compadrazgo are significant in the determination of work group composition and in exchange relationships--but operate only incidentally in the distribution process.[1]

The distribution process in any non-capitalist economy must incorporate means for dividing a joint product among the members of cooperative groups, as well as for compensating the factors of production, especially labor, from a source other than their immediate product. In any analysis of the first problem, it is necessary to ascertain the principles that guide the sharing-out process, whereas the second problem requires a determination of the source of compensation (i.e., money or goods in kind) and of the basis for equating labor and other factor services with goods of a kind other than those immediately produced (cf. Firth 1965:279; Udy 1959:Ch. 6).

Given the almost complete monetization of the Oaxaca economy one would assume that the prevailing distribution principle would approximate the one Firth identified among the Malay fishermen, namely, that "proportionate returns to capital and labor . . . tend to correspond to the degree to which each contributes to the total yield" (1966:256). While my data are by no means complete in this regard, and granting the considerable difficulty in calculating or estimating the value of factor contributions to total product in Oaxaca, there is no doubt that shares in total product are definitely skewed in favor of those who own or control the means of production as against those who provide only labor power. For example, in Magdalena there are three possible ways for a villager who does not own an ox team to acquire one for purposes of working his own private plot or his ejido plot: (1) labor exchange (i.e., his labor power in return for the use of the oxen); (2) rental for a cash payment (50 pesos per half day in 1978); and (3) rental in return for a deferred payment in kind according to the 'a maiz' arrangement through which the owner of an ox team leases it on a yearly basis in return for a stipulated quantity of maize (usually four fanegas or 384 liters) at harvest time. In addition the renter must assume all responsibility for feeding and caring for the oxen and for returning them to the owner in sound condition.

Simon A., one of several Magdalenans who holds oxen 'a medias' from a single owner in the ex-hacienda community of San Jose Progreso, has been a party to this arrangement (to be distinguished from 'a maiz') for eight years. He feeds and cares for the oxen and must replace an ox which dies; he also must pay the owner four fanegas of maize each year and, in addition, must work for the owner four half-days during the year (one half-day plowing, one half-day planting, one half-day weeding, one half-day secondary furrowing). In a bad harvest year the payment of corn can be reduced but must be compensated with a comparable increase in the following year's payment. Even in good harvest years this rent payment represents a substantial production (perhaps as much as one-half) of the campesino's total harvest.

In the metate industry the distribution process generally appears to be more favorable to labor than

in the agricultural sector--although this varies with
the prevailing type of quarry tenure. The least favorable situation is in San Juan Teitipac where the most
productive quarries are owned by non-<u>metatero</u> villagers
and are worked by hired bosses who assemble a group of
<u>mozos-metateros</u> under their direction. The output in
this case is distributed according to the following
formula (assuming a total one-day yield of 12 metate-
sized stone blocks to be shared among 1 owner, 1 quarry
boss who provides tools, powder and fuse, and three
<u>mozos</u>): 6:3:1:1:1. In other words, one half of the
total output goes to the owner (who contributed no work
at all) and the remaining half is shared among the boss
(3 shares) and his crew (1 share each). This contrasts
markedly with the situation in San Sebastian and
Magdalena where quarry tenure is communal or <u>ejidal</u> with
individual usufruct; here the formula guiding distribution (assume 12 metate stones produced by the joint
labor of one quarry boss and 4 <u>mozos</u>) is 4:2:2:2:2.
So, the boss gets two shares of two stones each and
the other workers get one share of two stones each. It
is also common in these villages--especially when a
work-group is comprised exclusively of kinsmen or when
each worker contributes equally of labor and tools--
for each member to receive an equal share of total
output.

Just as we look for the principles which guide
distribution processes in a given economy, so we look
for those which operate in the exchange process. The
Valley Zapotec villager has been portrayed by two generations of anthropologists as possessing a quasi-
instinctive propensity to monetize, to perceive and
evaluate things and events from the pecuniary perspective of a trader (e.g., Parsons 1936:12-13; 445;
Malinowski and De La Fuente 1957:23; Leslie 1960:67-71).
They have been so characterized apparently because of
their alleged ubiquitous and inordinate conversational
concern with 'price' in the presence of the visiting
anthropologists. My experience among the San Sebastianos, Magdalenans and others confirms their periodic conversational inquisitiveness as to the cost of objects
real or imagined, immediate or remote. But I hesitate
on this basis to attribute to them some sort of mystical
'pecuniary impulse.' Rather, it is more plausible to
speculate that this behavior simply reflects the contemporary rural Oaxacans' participation in the inter-
generational transmission of a folklore rooted in many
centuries of being a marketplace-oriented people. Their
repetitive conversational interest in price may also be
nothing more than a situational response to the presence

of interlopers from the affluent, gadget-ridden urban-industrial world.

Perhaps more important to an understanding of the superstructure of exchange among the Valley Zapotecs than price inquisitiveness in their conversational behavior are a series of recurring clichés. These lexical labels contain descriptions and evaluations of the individual; they are not particularized to apply to a specific actor in a certain economic role, but are generalized to apply to the stylized demeanor of the individual actor in all economic roles. By employing these labels the villagers can describe any other villager as a general type of economic actor; they can portray themselves and can evaluate and respond to others in terms of norms implicit in these clichés.

Many of these clichés cluster around two economic personality types: the 'persona legal' (honest or law-abiding person) and the 'persona tramposa' (deceitful person or cheat). The first is a person who meets all of his commitments ("una persona que cumple con todo lo que se compromete"), while the second is a person who makes commitments and fails to meet them ("compromete y no cumple"). The persona legal may be confided in ("es de confianza") because he has a sense of shame ("tiene vergüenza") which he draws upon to protect his honor (honra). The persona tramposa, on the other hand, cannot be confided in ("no se le puede tener confianza"), has no sense of shame ("no tiene vergüenza") and is without honor ("es deshonrado"). As an economic actor, the persona tramposa either does not pay for what he (or she) buys or does not return what he/she borrows ("agarra una cosa y después dice que no lo agarró") or pays a debt only after pressure is exerted by the lender. Usually he does not repay debts and renegs on his work obligations. As a consequence of his conduct, a villager stigmatized by his co-villagers as being 'tramposo' is economically ostracized; he encounters difficulty in obtaining loans or credit (including guelaguetzas) or work as a hired hand. This is a dimension of economic life which, it seems to me, merits more extensive and systematic inquiry.

Intra-village trade. Where, when, how and what do these villagers trade among themselves? Trade occurs daily at the work site (e.g., quarry, blacksmith's forge) or at a business site (e.g., store, grinding mill), at designated marketplaces, on the street, or within the confines of residence lots. Goods and

services are traded by purchase-sale (<u>compra-venta</u>)
with accompanying cash (<u>dinero en efectivo</u>) or credit
(<u>fiado</u>) transactions, payment in kind, or by barter
(<u>cambio</u>). All purchase-sale transactions involve money
pricing, even in the case of payments in kind. For
example, when a commodity like corn or eggs is employed
to pay for goods or services (as in a store or grinding
mill) the exchange value of the commodity accepted by
the seller (store owner or mill operator) is calculated
at a rate below its going market price. Likewise, in
barter transactions rates of exchange are usually negotiated by reference to the market prices of the goods
involved (i.e., with money as a standard of value).
In formally established businesses (stores, mills,
bakeries) prices tend to be fixed; otherwise, product
and specialized service prices are negotiable (the
daily wage for unskilled labor is standard and usually
non-negotiable).

An interesting example of how barter is used in
intra-village trade is provided in a diary kept (at my
request) by one of my Magdalena informants:

>"Thursday, I got up at 6 A.M. and went to
>"La Noria" <u>paraje</u> to check my plot of castor
>beans. There I met Lorenzo G.--a cow-tender.
>He asked me if I would sell him some leaves
>from my castor bean plants and I replied,
>'O.K.' He offered 35 pesos. 'Well,' I
>replied, 'give me 45.' Then he said, 'Will
>you take 40?' Then, I thought to myself,
>what are the leaves going to serve me for
>anyway? and I told him, 'Well, Lencho,
>they're yours.' Then he said: 'I don't
>have the money right now--I pay
>you on Sunday since tomorrow is Friday
>(market day in Ocotlan) and I'm going to
>sell two cheeses.' Then I said to him:
>'If you've got cheeses you can give them
>to me in place of the money.' He responded:
>'Well, then, if you wish I'll give them to
>you--but they are worth 10 pesos each.'
>'No,' I replied, 'I'll pay you 8 pesos
>each.' In the end he gave me the cheese
>for 9 pesos each (18 pesos for two). He
>delivered them that afternoon.

This account also illustrates how haggling is by means
restricted to the <u>plaza</u> where buyers and sellers are

usually strangers. Here in a remote patch of castor bean plants two villagers haggle over the price of cheese as if they were strangers in the plaza. This is what a market economy is all about.

Considered from the standpoint of total volume and value of daily commodity transactions, the tiendas and the molinos de nixtamal are the most important loci of intra-village trade. Most households patronize the grinding mills daily and have at least one member who purchases something in a store (e.g., beverage, candy, cigarettes, matches, chile peppers) each day. Both tiendas and molinos are centers of social intercourse as well as places of business. An important difference between them, however, is that a store can be opened and operated with a much smaller initial investment than a mill which requires expensive machinery and entails substantial operating costs.

Since the village tiendas are patronized only for small purchases of food items, notions and sundries, what profit the storekeeper makes from the sale of these items is derived from his practice of buying in relatively large lots at sub-retail prices and selling in small lots at a markup. The following case study of a tienda in Magdalena illustrates several facets of these village provisioning 'enterprises.'

Filomeno's store was opened in one section of his small adobe house in July 1967 as a consequence of an investment of 600 pesos to prepare the site and 700 additional pesos for the purchase of an inventory (43 different items including soft drinks, mezcal, cigarettes, canned sardines, soap, chewing gum, candy, candles, matches, notebooks, thread, cold tablets, aspirin, alka seltzer, spices, chile peppers, pencils, rubbing alcohol, salt, sugar, lard, rice, bicarbonate of soda, coffee, kerosene). This money was raised through the sale of a small herd of sheep and a calf (F. is a peasant-cultivator with a surplus output of six fanegas of maize from the 67/67 harvest). His basic business strategy is "comprar por el kilo y vender en cantidades de diez, veinte centavos" ("to buy by the kilo and sell in quantities of 10, 20 cents").

In October 1967 F's highest volume
item was mescal; he sold 51 pesos worth of
mescal during that month (he buys at 17
pesos/5 liters and sells 1/2 and one liter
quantities at prices of 2.50 pesos and
5.00 pesos respectively). Beer was the
second best selling item followed by soft
drinks, cigarettes, lard, and sugar. Since
opening, F. estimates that he has incurred
weekly expenditures of between 300-350
pesos--but is uncertain about his earnings.
He kept no systematic financial records
(cash receipts were kept in a jar) but he
estimates that he made about a 100 pesos
profit since the July 22 opening.

From his point of view the major
problem he encountered derived from his
customers' expectations of credit privileges. He did not want to sell on credit
but told me, "La gente aquí piden una cosa
y cuando la tienen en la mano dicen 'anótame
allí en la lista porque no tengo dinero
para pagarte.' (People here ask for something and when they have it in their hand
they tell me to put their name on my list
because they don't have cash to pay for
it)." Since opening day he kept a record
of credit transactions; by October 14 he
had extended credit to 115 separate persons
for a total sum of 485.60 pesos (I made
this calculation from F's records since
he had not bothered to do so). According
to him only a minority of customers fail
to pay their accounts weekly. The typical
pattern is for a customer to repay weekly
what he or she owes but to renew his or
her debt immediately with a new credit
purchase. One transaction I observed in
the store illustrates this: Horacio S.
entered the store at 7:30 P.M. carrying
a sack containing 2 almudes of maíz.
Without weighing it, F. told H. that he
would pay 3.80 pesos for each almud. H.
replied that the current 'plaza price'
(precio de plaza) was 4.00 pesos per
almud and F. agreed to pay this price.
H. had a debt of 6.05 pesos when he
entered the store; after giving the corn
to F. he immediately asked for 5 bottles
of beer and .35 pesos worth of kerosene

but did not give F. any cash. Consequently, he left the store with a debt of 6.40 pesos. According to F. this transaction with H. represents a common pattern. Customers typically renew their debts in this fashion and F. accepts it as part of doing business. His major concern is with several accounts which have steadily built up debts with no payments. His account book showed six persons with outstanding balances of 20 pesos or more and seven with outstanding balances in the 10-20 peso range.

Although he is unschooled in formal cost accounting and bookkeeping procedures, F. and other village storekeepers like him attempt to earn a profit (ganancia) in the process of provisioning their 'household/enterprise' funds (subsistence, rent, ceremonial, replacement). In other words, it is misleading to evaluate F's store operation as an enterprise separate and distinct from his domestic provisioning activities. In fact, the store is simply one circuit in a diversified system which originated in a sum of money accumulated from the sale of animals and corn; it continues to function only so long as it reinforces this corn-cash-animal circulation. F. regularly accepts corn in payment for goods--about one fanega per month. He valorizes corn in these transactions more or less at its current plaza price but resells it several months later to his co-villagers at a higher price (as 'maíz apreciado').

Along with all village storekeepers, F's major problem is controlling the credit flow which he attempts to do by extending credit only to those villagers who established a regular pattern of repayment. As Ralph Beals has observed regarding this sector of the Valley of Oaxaca economy: "A new storekeeper must give credit to attract customers; he is very vulnerable . . . because at first he has little basis for rating his customers and to succeed must be prepared for an initial high loss rate" (1970:240). More than one storekeeper in San Sebastian and Magdalena has been forced out of business due to a failure to withstand this initial overextension of credit; indeed such a fate befell Filomeno in 1970.[2]

Outside of the context of village stores there is a substantial direct trade in goods and services be-

tween villagers involving foodstuffs (especially corn),
fodder, and a variety of products/services produced by
artisans. Most San Sebastianos and Magdalenans who work
in specialized occupations charge set fees for their
products/services and prefer cash payment to payment in
kind. Clients of many of these specialists (e.g., adobe-
makers, jacal-makers, carpenters, tailors and seam-
stresses, candlemakers) are expected to provide the
specialist with all the materials necessary for the
manufacture of the product in question. For example,
the adobe-makers in San Sebastian require their clients
to provide a mud bank along a local stream, a supply of
manure and corn stalks; the tailors require cloth; and
the candlemaker requires paraffin, string for wicks,
decorative materials, beeswax, and other accessories.
It should be noted that much of the business conducted
by these artisans is seasonal--geared either to the
agricultural or fiesta cycles. Thus, a basketmaker in
San Sebastian makes an average of 10-15 baskets monthly
except in October when, with the help of one or two
hired hands, he produces more than 100 baskets needed
by other villagers for harvesting and storing crops.
Candlemakers, bakers and fireworks makers are busiest
during the weeks preceding major mayordomías; metate
makers are patronized by other villagers during the
wedding season from February to May since it is customary
for the godparents of a bride-to-be to present her with
a gift metate.

How much time does one of these artisans devote
to his secondary occupation and what income does he receive from it? These questions will be answered in detail for the metateros in subsequent chapters but it
might be instructive now to briefly examine the case of
one of the two Magdalena blacksmiths, Roberto M.

In February 1967 Roberto purchased a manual
wheel-type bellows (called ventilador and distinguished
from the less sophisticated and less expensive accordion-
type bellows which is known as a fogón or fuelle) for
350 pesos in Oaxaca City to start his smithing business
(cash was raised by selling a cow). Previously he had
tempered his own tools by building a fire with bamboo
roots, fanning it by hand, and using a rock as an anvil
(or took his tools to a blacksmith in another village).
He decided to learn the blacksmith trade and did so by
taking advantage of an opportunity to work as an
apprentice in a blacksmith shop in the nearby village
of San Pedro Apostol. At my request, Roberto kept a
daily record of income, expenditures and work activities
from October 1, 1967 until June 30, 1968 (in late

September 1967 he had decided on his own initiative to keep a record of receipts from his smithing work to determine how much he earned from one 40-peso sack of charcoal).

These records show that during this 7-month period Roberto worked a total of 141.5 hours at his forge (20.2 hours per month; 5 hours per week) and had cumulative gross earnings of 381 pesos (42.33 pesos per month; 2.69 pesos per hour). The only direct operating cost which regularly required a cash outlay was the purchase of charcoal. On October 3, 1967, Roberto bought 40 pesos worth of charcoal (in the Ocotlan plaza but delivered in Magdalena by carboneros from La Garzona) which lasted him until December 21. During that period his gross earnings were 109.75 pesos--yielding him a net return of 70 pesos (about 6 dollars). At this rate of return, his forge would be paid for during the first year of operation.

As in the case of Filomeno the storekeeper, it's misleading to evaluate Roberto's smithing operation as an 'enterprise' separate and distinct from his total economic situation as a peasant-artisan; one of his reasons for pursuing this occupation was to enable him to avoid having to pay someone else to temper his tools (only minor tempering could be done with the fire and rock technique). Moreover, he works at his forge essentially during 'off hours'--between 6-8 a.m. or late in the evening when there are no major competing demands on his time. Blacksmithing, in short, is an occupation which contributes to the provisioning of his household (e.g., by reducing replacement fund expenditures and by increasing cash receipts) and which conveniently supplements his other occupations as peasant-cultivator and metatero (he also makes harnesses).

Inter-village and extra-village trade. When, where, how and what do San Sebastianos and Magdalenans trade with others? While my data are of insufficient scope to support an accurate empirical determination, it is fair to estimate that more than half of the external trade of these villagers is channeled through the plaza system. Nevertheless, by placing the regional marketing system in the Valley of Oaxaca under the analytic microscope, we can discern an 'extra-plaza' network of mutually inter-dependent villages whose economic relationships, at this level, exclude both town and city and bypass the plaza system. Moreover, there is substantial trade between villagers and various

101

outside traders who trade in products which are produced in the national or international industrial economy. The relationships between the levels and dimensions of village external trade in the Valley of Oaxaca economy are schematized in Figure 3.

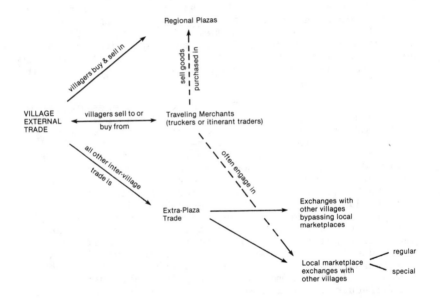

FIGURE 3. Schematization of the Levels of External Trade in San Sebastian Teitipac and in Magdalena Ocotlan.

        Cross-cutting and integrating these various levels and channels of village external trade and linking the latter with intra-village trade is the market pricing process. From this perspective the regional economy is a price-integrated system comprised of a multitude of commodity and factor markets. What do I mean by a "price-integrated market system"? According to the received wisdom of Neoclassical economics the market system is not an entity encompassing a group of interrelated and mutually adjusting commodity and service prices. These are, rather, consequences of the operations or activities of buyers and sellers within a market system. Fraser (1947:131) has said that 'market' refers to a state of affairs; there is a market in a commodity (or factor) when there are a number of buyers and sellers and when the unit price offered and paid by cash is affected by the decisions of all the others. This is another way of saying that a market consists of a group of interacting buyers and sellers or, more specifically, that particular groups of buyers and sellers are connected by a systematic relationship over time between pricing and production decisions. Prices, in other words, are the consequences of interaction among sellers and buyers.[3]

The meaning of the term 'market system' in Neoclassical analysis, then, is that it consists of a series of more or less interconnected markets in different commodities (or factors) and/or in different regions. Economists have long recognized that in a market economy prices of different commodities are interrelated with each other rather than being independent of each other. This reflects the fact that so long as the individuals who appear either as buyers or sellers in one market also appear as buyers or sellers in another market, all commodities are to some degree substitutes for each other. At the very least, if the supply of one commodity changes, it is likely to have some influence on the supply of other commodities; and if the demand for one commodity changes, it is likely to have an influence on the demand for other commodities, at any given time. Of course, these are propositions which remain implicit and essentially untested in application to the Valley of Oaxaca economy.

To summarize our discussion up to this point: trade in San Sebastian and Magdalena is channeled through two spheres, one of which is internal to the village and the other of which is external to the village. The latter sphere encompasses trade conducted through the plaza system, non-plaza trade between villagers and outsiders who are non-villagers, and extra-plaza trade between traders from villages in symbiotic sub-regions which excludes town- and city-based traders. By focusing on the pricing process which is generated through multiple buyer-seller interactions, all of this trading activity can presumably be viewed as one system.

It must be emphasized that this trade involves the circulation of many different commodities--ranging from 'factory-made' clothing and beverages to 'home-made' rope, pottery, or mescal; these commodities are, in turn, associated with a variety of different forms of production (e.g., factory, manufactory, workshop, household) and exchange (barter, fixed pricing, haggling, credit). Indeed, the agents who trade these commodities even utilize different modes of transportation: a majority of the village-based agents travel on burro, horseback or on foot, whereas the city- and town-based agents travel by bus or truck. Also, the intercommunity dimension of this trade is significant as evidenced by the fact that products from the following specialty villages, among others, are regularly sold in San Sebastian: Santo Domingo Tomaltepec (bread); San Pablo Guilá (rope); Rojas (cheese); Atzompa, San Bartolo Coyotepec, and San Marcos Tlapazola (pottery); Matatlan, Chichicapan, and Magdalena Teitipac (mescal); Santa Cecilia Jalieza (wooden spoons); and San Antonio de la Cal (lime) (see Cook 1968:336-338 for a complete list of products). In short, this trade involves many traditional commodities and is by no means monopolized by capitalist agents or interests.[4]

In all the above-cited cases San Sebastianos acquire products from itinerant sellers who come to San Sebastian from the producing villages. There are also a few San Sebastianos who visit other villages as buyers or sellers. For example, some go to Papalutla and to Abasolo to buy tule (a tough plant fiber used in jacal construction) and to San Juan Teitipac to buy maguey leaves which are used as a lashing material. At least one San Sebastiano buys goats and sheep in neighboring villages; others periodically buy oxen. Another individual buys metates in San Sebastian and resells them exclusively in Papalutla (his natal village) but on a small scale and irregularly (about a dozen metates per annum). As a rule, however, the San Sebastianos (and the Magdalenens) conduct their extra-plaza trade within the bounds of their villages; when they leave the village for trading purposes they usually head for the plazas in Oaxaca City or to their respective cabecera plazas (i.e., Tlacolula de Matamoros and Ocotlan).

While both Magdalena and San Sebastian produce various commodities which enter into extra-plaza trade (e.g., castor beans, animal fodder, goats, pigs), there is one staple export in each (excluding metates most of which are traded in the plazas): otate brooms

in San Sebastian and sugar cane in Magdalena. Labor
power is also a significant export of both villages.
A large number of families in each village have teenage
daughters employed as live-in servants or maids in
Oaxaca City and Mexico City, and there is a significant
annual seasonal migration of young adult males from
both communities to temporary jobs in construction,
agriculture, etc. in surrounding towns and villages,
Oaxaca City or in outlying regions (e.g., the Gulf or
Pacific coastal plantation areas). In these and other
villages of the Oaxaca we lack a comprehensive study
of the types and incidence of labor migration (see
Chapter 4 for pertinent data on the metateros).[5]

The otate producers of San Sebastian sell their
brooms through a contractual marketing arrangement between them and the municipal government of Oaxaca City.
Since 1962 the latter has been purchasing tht total
otate output of San Sebastian (apparently one of the
few villages in the Valley of Oaxaca where this wild
plant is found in abundance and is systematically collected) which, according to government figures, amounts
to an average of 1156 dozen otates monthly. Brooms,
made by attaching a handle to a tied bundle of 12
otate branches, are used by Oaxaca City maintenance
crews for sweeping streets, marketplaces, parks, ceme-
teries, etc. At the contracted price of 1.10 pesos
per bundle of one dozen otate branches, the San Sebastianos earn approximately 1270 pesos (just over $100)
monthly from otate sales. Around ten villagers work
regularly in the collection of otates, each gathering
from a minimum of eight to a maximum of 20 dozen
branches daily (the plant grows wild on the hillsides
of the communal land and is similar to bamboo in that
it rejuvenates each spring with the rains). A truck
for the Oaxaca City municipal government picks up
consignments of otate once a month during the rainy
season and twice a month during the dry season from a
storage area in the village.

Sugar cane production in Magdalena is geared
directly to the needs of the panela industry encompassing 20 separate trapiches in the nearby village of San
Pedro Apostol (and one trapiche in San Matias Chilazoa
which used to be ejido affiliated). Cane cultivation
was introduced to Magdalena following the completion
in 1962 of a federally-financed dam/reservoir project
(presa "El Guayabo) which has the capacity to irrigate
270 hectares of ejido land. According to my calculations, the 1967-68 cane harvest in Magdalena yielded a
total of 95.5 meters (wagon loads measured by height of

cane stacked in wagon) involving 11 separate growers.
The average market price was 75 pesos per meter yielding
aggregate gross returns of 7012 pesos or an average
gross return of 369 pesos (about 30 dollars per grower). In
addition to cane, however, each harvest also yields
cogollo (top leafy part of cane stalk which is cut
separately and used as fodder) and zacate (leaves
stripped from the stalk which are dried and used as
roofing material in jacal construction). Therefore, in
the case of Antonio P. who harvested a total of seven
meters of cane, the harvest also yielded 175 manojos
(bundles) of zacate valued at 50 centavos each and 50
manojos of cogollo (valued at 25 centavos each). The
total gross value of his harvest can be calculated as
follows (assuming the price of cane to be 75 pesos per
meter):   75 x 7 = 525 pesos + 87.50 (zacate) + 12.50
(cogollo) = 625 pesos (52 dollars). Antonio estimated his
production costs for this harvest (1/4 hectare plot) as
follows: rental of an ox team for a half day to prepare the soil; labor employed to weed and harvest plus
the rental of a cart to haul the cane from the field
to the trapiche--total 315 pesos. Thus his net earnings
for this harvest were 310 pesos (about 26 dollars)

According to Antonio, he had planted corn on
this plot prior to planting cane for the first time in
1965; in a good year he used to harvest three fanegas
of corn (and 30 tercios or bundles of zacate) with a
total market value of 330 pesos. His total costs for
corn cultivation on this plot were, according to his
estimates, about 120 pesos--giving him net earnings of
about 210 pesos (or 100 pesos less than he earned in
1968 from the cane harvest). In his opinion, given
these profit differentials, other villagers are foolish
to continue to cultivate corn on land where cane can
be cultivated. Moreover, he claims that a high cane
yield is more assured than a high corn yield since the
latter crop is more susceptible to variations in rainfall. Other Magdalenans, however, dislike the unpredictability and capriciousness of pricing in the cane
market, and they especially dislike the arbitrary
control over prices which is exercised by the trapicheros (who they refer to derogatorily as "los canijos
ricos" ("the feeble rich") or "los capitalistas" ("the
capitalists"). Indeed, Antonio himself points out
that he has sold his cane at a different price each
year (1965 @ 40 pesos per meter; 1966 @ 60 pesos per
meter; 1967 @ 59 pesos; 1968 @ 75 pesos). All Magdalenans, including Antonio, are disgusted with what they
allege to be unscrupulous practices on the part of the
cane buyers (e.g., the fact that cane is bought by

volume or measure rather then by weight; also, collusion to set prices among the trapicheros).

In conclusion, the data presented in this section suggest that we can no longer restrict our consideration of peasant marketing in Mesoamerica (i.e., those areas where regional periodic marketing systems operate) to trade conducted through the marketplace system and ignore extra-marketplace trade. It is no longer true, as it was when F. W. McBryde wrote his pioneering study, that the economic role of markets is ignored or under-emphasized or that rural communities in Mesoamerica are portrayed as being completely self-sufficient. On the contrary, there may now be an overemphasis on that role to the extent that the economic interdependence of peasant villages is assumed to operate only through the channels of the marketplaces; it often is implied in the literature that outside of their involvement in regional marketplaces, peasant villages in Mesoamerica exist as autarchies (e.g., Wolf 1966:40-41; Nash 1966: 58-72; Diskin 1969; Beals 1967). The time has come to recognize and analyze the commodity flows in regional economies that bypass the formal marketplace structure.

Ceremonial exchange. If one adopts the insiders' perspective in describing and analyzing physical trans-fers of goods (and services) in Oaxaca villages which do not involve purchase-sale, one is inevitably led to a bifurcation between 'gifting' and 'reciprocal ex-change.' This is so because, in fact, such a distinc-tion is present in the villagers' categorizations of reality. For example, in San Sebastian and Magdalena 'guelaguetza' (galguéz in Zapotec) is the term for re-ciprocal exchange which operates on the principle that the recipient of goods or services is obligated to reciprocate in kind when the donor requests him (or her) to do so (i.e., within a stipulated number of days, weeks, months or years). On the other hand, a physical transfer of goods which occurs strictly within the framework of the fictive kinship system is referred to generically by a Zapotec term which varies with the dialect spoken (see below). Whereas a guelaguetza may be openly solicited by the would-be recipient, the 'gift' (or 'regalo' which is the Spanish cover term for all such transfers, ritual and non-ritual) is presented either as a voluntary prestation by the donor or in accordance with the circumstantially prescribed conduct of ritual kinsmen.

The daily journal (kept at my request) of one of my Magdalena informants has the following entry which illustrates the ritually prescribed type of 'gifting':

> Today, Antonio P. enjoyed a gift that he
> received Saturday afternoon. His compadre
> presented him with the gift as a recom-
> pense for a favor that Antonio had done
> for him. That's our custom here in the
> village; after a baptism of a child, its
> parents take a gift, one or two weeks
> later, to the child's godparents (padrinos,
> who by virtue of their relationship to the
> child, are compadres or co-parents of the
> child's parents--author's note).

I later clarified that Antonio P. was compadre to Pedro
V. because he had accepted the latter's request to be
padrino (godfather) to one of Pedro's children; the
relationship was ritually sanctioned through the baptism
of the infant. In bringing a gift to Antonio, Pedro
was fulfilling a customary obligation as his compadre,
and was reciprocating the 'gift' presented previously
by Antonio, as padrino of Pedro's infant, on the occasion of its baptism. Incidentally, the 'gift' consisted
of 1/2 kilo of chocolate, 2 kilos of sugar, and 15 pesos
worth of bread. Significantly, in Zapotec this transfer is not classified as a 'guelaguetza' but as a
'gandow' (Magdalena) or 'divzaak' (San Sebastian) and
was defined by one informant as "something which they
give for every fiesta, gifts of food for some custom
between co-parents." The 'gandow' customarily involves
all or some of the following items: bread, chocolate,
sugar, cigarettes, and mescal. There are two specific
occasions for such transfers between compadres: baptisms
and weddings. The wedding (fandango) gandow usually
includes a larger array of goods than its baptismal
counterpart, but the direction of the transfer is always from the ritual godparent (padrino and/or madrina)
to the parents of the child being baptized or wed (who
are compadres to the donors).

Still another category of gifts is recognized by
these villagers, namely, those which are not linked to
any ritually sanctioned fictive kinship relationships
and which are neither obligatory nor culturally prescribed. Magdalenans refer to these gifts as 'erzey-
lawdgley' and San Sebastianos as 'ayuda' (assistance).
One San Sebastiano explained this category of gifts
as those "one gives if he attends something to which
he wasn't formally invited, like a wedding or a

funeral" but, in Magdalena, it apparently refers to any gift that's not a gandow.

In short, Beal's distinction between non-ritual and ritual gifting among the Oaxaca Valley Zapotec corresponds to categories familiar to the San Sebastianos and Magdalenans, as does his distinction between "gifting" and "reciprocal exchange." Among the San Sebastianos and Magdalenans, guelaguetza transfers are not considered as gifts; this is because they carry with them an expectation and obligation of repayment: "Son cosas que se paga; tal como se dió así se paga" ("These are things that one repays; one repays them just as they were given"). Guelaguetza transfers are considered to be a type of loan and include ceremonial (mayordomía or fandango related) and non-ceremonial (eggs loaned to a neighbor) transfers.

The fact that these villagers conceive of a series of material transfers as 'gifts' presented in a spirit of generosity does not necessarily mean that they have discounted the desire or obligation for reciprocation in the long run (cf. Firth 1967:9). Mauss' (1954) rule that every gift demands a counter gift and Sahlins' notion of "generalized reciprocity" (1972:193-4) which is based on the principle that material transactions are episodes in continuous social relations should make us skeptical of accepting native categories as definitive approximations of social reality. While it is difficult to prove empirically that 'gifting' among the Valley Zapotec villagers is "generalized reciprocity"--because of the long delay and since the reciprocation hinges upon the discretion of the recipient--it is theoretically more plausible and analytically more fruitful to so interpret it. Ritual kinship-embedded transfers (Beals' "ritual gifting") are certainly illustrative of "generalized reciprocity" and the only reason to suppose that non-ritual gifts aren't is the fact that empirically the anthropologist observes only one-way transfers.

The guelaguetza principle is relied upon by San Sebastianos and Magdalenans to mobilize goods and cash and to help defray costs of mayordomía or fandango sponsorship (or other celebrations). Transactions conducted according to this principle of "balanced reciprocity" (Sahlins 1972:194-5) are certainly larger in volume and more frequent than 'gift' transactions. Below is an excerpt from my field notes describing a guelaguetza transaction which I observed:

Passing Antonio T.'s _solar_ I saw him in
the turkey pen trying to catch a turkey.
I entered and found him with a woman he
identified to me as the mother of his
friend, Juan S. Antonio had the turkey
in his hands and was weighing it on a
scale. Antonio announced that its weight
was 5-1/2 kilos and then gave it to the
woman. After a few words of thanks in
Zapotec the woman left the _solar_ carrying
the turkey. No money changed hands.

Afterwards, I asked Antonio how
much the turkey was worth and he said
50 pesos. I asked him if the señora had
already paid him or would pay him later
and he replied: "_Soy persona legal_." I
asked him to elaborate. He replied that
he would receive a turkey from the Sanchez
family (his friend Juan and the señora)
in return for the one he had just given;
the transaction was a _guelaguetza_. Sra.
Sanchez, he continued, had come to his
solar yesterday afternoon and had spoken
with his wife about a turkey; Antonio's
wife discussed the matter with him later
that evening when he returned from the
fields. They agreed to enter into a
guelaguetza relationship (_trato_) with
the Sanchez household. Sra. Sanchez
had come this morning to find out what
they had decided and to get the turkey
if they agreed. Since Antonio and his
wife did not owe a _guelaguetza_ donation
to the Sanchez family, this was a new
agreement between the two households.
The turkey in question will be used
to prepare a _mole_ for a baptism celebration on Sunday at the Sanchez house.

Most village households keep a _guelaguetza_
account book (_libro de guelaguetza_) containing an
itemized list of donations received and given in transactions with other households. An analysis of these
books shows a predictable uniformity in goods received
and given: tortillas, eggs, turkeys, chickens, beer,
soft drinks, and mescal are the most common items.
Also, the identity of the parties listed (i.e., their
formal social relationship to a given household head)
is similar. In one Magdalena account book the twenty-

110

eight donors were related to Ego as follows: 3
brothers, 1 maternal uncle, 3 brothers-in-law, 7 compadres, 1 godfather, and 13 friends. Such a mix of
consanguines and affines, together with fictive kinsmen and friends, is typical.

Guelaguetza account books vary in terms of format (e.g., some list entries according to type of goods
received, others by the relationship of donor to them,
others simply by household in the order that donations
are received) and, of course, vary in number of entries
and the mix between paid and unpaid donations. For
example, referring to the same Magdalena account book
(showing donations made to help with the sponsorship
of a relatively minor mayordomía), all but one of the
twenty-eight entries were new donations and, consequently, represented future payment obligations of the recipient household. In this case the goods received and
their quantities were: 19 almudes tortillas, 6 cases
of soft drinks, 2 bottles of mescal, 3 cases of beer,
9 packs of cigarettes, 2 turkeys, and 2 dozen eggs.
The Magdalenan who received these donations explained
them to me as follows:

> Those are the guelaguetzas that I owe.
> Now when those who have given me guela-
> guetzas have a festive expenditure then
> we will repay them. My wife asked for
> these guelaguetzas and when the donors
> have a need they will advise us and we
> will repay them. When we are helped
> with guelaguetzas, well, the donors can
> comply without spending any money.
> And when the time comes to repay, well,
> one repays from time to time, one
> doesn't have to pay all at once (in one
> total amount).

It is instructive to compare this Magdalena case
with the following narrative (based on my field notes)
of how one San Sebastian household employed guelaguetza
donations to help defray the costs of a major mayordomía
(Virgen de Juquila) celebration:

> Jorge, the mayordomo or sponsor of the
> celebration, raised a total of 8,540
> pesos ($683.20 dollars) in cash to meet
> the anticipated costs; he sold his ox

111

team for 5,600 pesos, a fattened steer for 1,900 pesos and a cow for 950 pesos. Approximately six months prior to the celebration his wife, Teresa, began lining up donors among relatives, compadres and friends to provide specific donations on preassigned days during the fiesta period. She succeeded in lining up 93 new donors (40 additional households had received donations from Jorge and Teresa previously and were now requested to reciprocate).

As these donations (and return payments) began to flow in during the fiesta period, separate entries were made for each in Jorge's and Teresa's account book; each entry listed the name of the donor and the nature and quantity of his/her donation. When totaled up these donations included: 351 pesos in cash, 85-1/2 dozen eggs, 17 turkeys, 66-1/2 almudes of tortillas, 150 pesos worth of fireworks, 7 almudes of beans and lesser quantities of sugar, cocoa, candles, mescal and cigarettes.

Regarding the social relationships of the donors to Jorge and Teresa, 54 (of the total of 93 new donors) were described simply as 'friends' and 10 others as 'compadres'--which illustrates the extent to which such a celebration is dependent upon extra-familial support. Of the remaining 29 donors, 8 were first or second degree consanguineal kinsmen of either Jorge or Teresa, 13 were most distant consanguines, and 8 were affines.

A comparison of these two cases highlights some differences and similarities in the guelaguetza system in these two communities. For example, in the San Sebastian case not only is the absolute number of donors larger but a larger proportion of them are in the 'friends' category than in the Magdalena case. This reflects the fact that the ceremonial needs of the San Sebastian household were much greater (i.e., it was sponsoring a major mayordomía whereas the Magdalena household was sponsoring a minor mayordomía); and the more goods required the less likely it is that real and fictive kinsmen will suffice as suppliers. Also,

in the San Sebastian case the household in question had
accumulated a substantial fund of guelaguetza claims on
other households (40) as compared with the Magdalena
household (1). Again, this is usually the situation
when major mayordomía sponsorship is involved because
other villagers have advance knowledge of a given household's mayordomía sponsorship status (e.g., 'waiting
lists' are kept) and will tend to solicit donations
from a household which is known to be committed to
future sponsorship (it will be in the interest of such
a household to donate now for future recall). There
is also the practice of "planting" guelaguetzas by
households in anticipation of future ceremonial sponsorship; they build up guelaguetza claims for future
recall by volunteering donations to other households
known to be soliciting (Beals 1970:235).

It's clear from this discussion that a given
household's guelaguetza accounts are an inherent part
of its overall budget (an important dimension of the
"ceremonial fund") (Wolf 1966:7-9). While few households in San Sebastian or Magdalena maintain regular,
systematic accounting of income and expenditures,
most do not appear to regard guelaguetza obligations
as 'current' (i.e., as liabilities which have to be
paid relatively quickly). Of course, implicit in the
guelaguetza loan system is the right of the donor/
creditor to recall his donation at any time. But, as
a matter of fact, any villager by consulting his
guelaguetza records is able to make a probability calculation that one item is likely to be called in the
next month or two, another one somewhat later, and
another later still (maybe several years later). Theoretically, there could be a 'run on the bank' but, again,
the system would collapse if this occurred. Indeed,
guelaguetza relations between households often endure
beyond the generation in which they are initiated; a
father's debt can be inherited by his heirs.

Referring again to the San Sebastian case, a
substantial proportion of the 93 donations received
will be repaid in full and, perhaps, with an increment
during the lifetime of the original recipients. In
other words, through a selective process, relations will
be continued with some of the donors by reciprocating
the initial donation in kind and offering, in addition,
an increment (e.g., two dozen eggs as a counter-donation
plus two additional dozen as an increment). The ultimate pattern of repayment will depend, among other
things, upon the cargo career aspirations (and performance) of a given head of household.

By no means all households in San Sebastian or Magdalena are involved in guelaguetza networks, either because the occasion has not arisen to necessitate it or by conscious avoidance (though this is difficult for most). One Magdalena informant, a <u>metatero</u> born in a neighboring village and married to a Magdalena woman, expressed his sentiments candidly as follows:

> I'm not accustomed to ask for nor to give <u>guelaguetzas</u>. I neither request nor give because those customs are variable. For example: if you come and make a request of me--and I am able to comply, I can give--but you must know that you must repay when I want you to do so, and you say 'O.K.'. Later, the time comes when I am in need and I come to ask you for 'repayment' and you say to me: 'No, because such and such happened to me, I'll repay you later.' Well, 'fuck you!' In order not to have difficulties with people, it's better neither to ask, nor give <u>guelaguetzas</u>. I don't give them and I don't ask for them! When I need something it's better to get it some other way--I get hold of the money and I buy what I need!

This negative view of the <u>guelaguetza</u> probably reflects this particular informant's status as an 'outsider' (i.e., he married into the village and is a native of another region) in Magdalena and, consequently, his lack of a network of <u>personas de confianza</u>--real and fictive kinsmen, friends and neighbors--upon whom he could rely. Yet the fact remains that many villagers are wary of the potential implications of the 'two-sidedness' of the custom (i.e., their concern that reciprocity can be assured only from <u>personas de confianza</u>). A San Sebastiano stressed the importance of this factor in the following statement: "If one believes that a particular person is not honest in his dealings, then, one shouldn't confide in him because with time perhaps that person won't repay a <u>guelaguetza</u>. It would be better to give him nothing in the first place because in the future he'll be of no help."

There are those social scientists who perceive a basic irreconcilability between the dynamics of the mobilization of goods for ceremonial purposes, a process guided throughout by careful planning and calculation, and the disposal of these goods in one celebration--a potlatch-like process which, _prima facie_, appears to be contrary to orthodox principles of economic reasoning. This, of course, is a grossly ethnocentric position which fails to understand the objective situation confronting Oaxaca villagers. Given the structure and dynamics of these village social systems--and the social relations of production prevailing in them--the highest form of rationality is for separate households to mobilize goods as efficiently as possible for 'give away' or redistributive purposes. In fact, the _mayordomía_ and _fandango_ celebrations, like the Northwest Coast potlatch, are not 'give-aways' but multiple exchanges; the sponsor does receive definite social advantages (e.g., enhanced prestige or status), and possibly even short-term material advantages, from the ceremonial redistribution of material goods. And in the long run, of course, this redistributive process operates ideologically to perpetuate and reinforce the dominant position of the wealthier families. Finally, the idea that potential capital accumulation is inhibited by ceremonial uses of wealth and that an important element in the 'development' of the Oaxaca peasantry would be the recircuiting of flows of wealth from 'unproductive' to 'productive' channels serves only to mystify the economic realities of social differentiation in the countryside.

Conclusions. The economic situation of the Valley of Oaxaca peasantry has been characterized by some scholars as one in which the domestic unit participates in two mutually exclusive exchange systems. In the words of Charles Leslie, one of the principal exponents of this view, these are ". . . the _guelaguetza_ system from which the profit motive was excluded and the goal was to cooperate in financing festivals which honored the community-owned saints; and the market system, in which the profit motive combined with fluctuating prices to encourage an impersonal, bitterly competitive scramble for advantage" (1960:60).

The Neoclassical critique of this romanticized dualistic interpretation would be to argue that there is only one exchange sector in the Valley of Oaxaca economy which is governed by the same fundamental economic principles. Rural Oaxacans, like people everywhere (the Neoclassical critique would contend), allocate their scarce resources among alternative ends. The ends among which resources are allocated are culturally defined. These resources are allocated among all of the ends contemplated in such a way as to maximize the return or to minimize loss, be these measured in monetary, prestige, social-ceremonial or other terms.

While this critique provides a rationale for a systematic 'social exchange' type analysis of the Valley of Oaxaca economy that contributes to our knowledge about individual decision-making processes (cf. Belshaw 1969; Schneider 1974), it either precludes or mystifies the analysis of the fundamental processes which determine the production and circulation of commodities and structure social relations within this region. It is true that the peasant-artisan household is enmeshed in a complex network of transactions which differ as to the specific rules of exchange followed by the transactors (e.g., purchase-sale, barter, reciprocity, gifting). Yet, regardless of the rules governing specific transactions, the peasant-artisan's motivations, perceptions, and calculations differ only in degree. They reflect the total economic situation of the domestic unit he represents which, in turn, is determined by his role in the production and circulation process.

One common element in all exchange transactions in which villagers participate is the occurrence of transfer (i.e., the relinquishing or acquiring of rights over products by the respective parties). The empirical fact of transfer is not altered by the social identity of the transactors or by the rules governing the transaction. As seller, barterer or donor, the villager relinquishes rights over products to a second party who, ipso facto, acquires them. Aside from the socioeconomic position of the transactor, what is crucial about this for an understanding of economic process is the circulatory destination of commodities--the type and number of circuits they move through and the degree to which the potential exchange value embodied in them is realized. Our knowledge of the structure of economic process in the region informs us that, inevitably, the destination of many village-produced products is commodity circulation, the realization of exchange value, and, ultimately, the fueling of the process of capitalist development. And it is toward the goal of understanding the dynamics and consequences of these processes that our future research efforts must be directed.

Utilization

The utilization process encompasses two general
types of activities: those leading to further production and those involving direct, immediate consumption;
or, more specifically, those employing material products
to produce additional utilizable products, and those
utilizing material products for the direct satisfaction
of current wants (cf. Herskovits 1952:298-309; LeClair
1962:1192). In the latter sense, utilization is synonymous with consumption, that is, the destruction or
decomposition of a commodity in the process of its use
for provisioning purposes. In the first sense, however,
utilization merges with production and its precise
meaning is ambiguous. Economists attempt to handle
this ambiguity by introducing the distinction between
'capital or producer goods' and 'consumer goods,' that
is, between products which are employed in further production and those which aren't. Unfortunately, the
problems raised here are not contrived or academic;
they arise from the fact that in all economies many
material products have multiple uses, and that 'things'
mask social relations.

Accordingly, one problem in classifying and analyzing material products in the Mesoamerican rural
economy is the relative ease of convertibility of many
of them from one use to another. A simple example is
the metate which is obviously a durable consumer good,
the basic kitchen grinding implement in the peasant
household, which is used principally, though not exclusively, to grind softened maize (nixtamal) into a
dough (masa) for the preparation of tortillas (corn
griddle cakes). However, in a specially decorated form
it is also a prestige good which is ritually presented
by godparents to a goddaughter-bride as a wedding
gift. And when it is used by a professional tortilla
maker (tortillera or molendera) who prepares tortillas
for sale, it clearly becomes a means of commodity production.[6]

A somewhat more complex example is provided by
domesticated (non-pet) animals and poultry. The most
important types of livestock and poultry raised in San
Sebastian and Magdalena are oxen, cattle, cows, goats,
sheep, burros, pigs, chickens and turkeys. These animals, though variously utilized, can best be regarded
as means of production and reproduction. In some cases,
they are directly reproductive and their products, such
as eggs, milk or meat, can be consumed for human nour-
ishment. In a second situation, oxen and burros are

117

used for productive purposes and their status is exactly the same as that of a tractor or plow. In a third situation, animals may be considered to be 'products,' as when a chicken, turkey or pig is fattened over time by special feeding (the process of 'producing' a useable pig, considered as a meat animal, takes a considerable period of time). On the basis of this discussion, the three broad categories of uses into which animals may fall are: (1) as yielding directly consumable products such as milk, eggs, meat, or wool; (2) as means of production which are employed in the production process; and (3) as products whose use may have elements of saving and capital accumulation associated with it.

The uses of animals in the Valley of Oaxaca economy as sources of directly consumable products and as means of production are relatively straightforward, and require no further discussion. Less evident, and somewhat more complicated, is the use of animals as products for exchange or capital accumulation purposes.

As exchangeable products animals or their derivative products are used as objects for sale, as objects of barter, or as objects of transfer to other villagers as 'gifts' or as guelaguetza donations. Calves, goats (and milk, cheese), pigs, sheep (and wool), chickens and turkeys (and eggs) are sometimes sold to other village residents but, more often, are sold in the plaza or outside the plaza to outsiders as the need for cash arises. On the other hand, fattened oxen, cattle and hogs are sold principally in the village to outside buyers who visit regularly in their trucks to bid for these animals. There is hardly a week during the year in which some San Sebastiano or Magdalenan does not sell one or more of these animals for cash. Barter involving animals is occasional; there is at least one itinerant trader who comes to San Sebastian weekly to barter cows and pigs for goats and sheep, offering cash only as a last resort. But barter involving eggs is common in the village stores and molinos de nixtamal. Cash is usually scarce among the villagers and eggs are willingly accepted by storekeepers in exchange for items in their stock and by mill operators in exchange for their grinding services.

Reciprocal exchanges or guelaguetzas involving animals (and eggs) are mostly occasioned by mayordomías and fandangos. Mayordomía donations include a large volume of turkeys and eggs, whereas fandango donations involve these as well as goats, pigs, chickens and occasionally a cow or calf presented as bridewealth gifts. The volume of turkeys and eggs involved in such transfers each year in these villages is considerable. For example, referring back to the account book of Jorge and Teresa in San Sebastian we recall that 45 villagers contributed a total of 185-1/2 dozen eggs and 17 others contributed a total of 18 turkeys to help in the preparation of special foods for this celebration. All told some 57 villagers contributed eggs and/or turkeys on this occasion. When it is considered that there are 14 separate mayordomías celebrated in San Sebastian each year (only one of which, however, entails expenditures comparable to that sponsored by Jorge and Teresa), the total annual volume of such transfers is, by extrapolation, quite impressive. It's even more impressive when we consider that several fandangos are celebrated annually in San Sebastian which may involve expenditures comparable to those of a major mayordomía.

A typical response by a villager (excepting those who specialize in raising animals for sale) to a question about his saving habits is to point in the direction of his animals and say, "There are my savings." What precisely does he mean by this? He does not usually consider animal raising on a small scale to be a 'profit-making' activity but rather as a way to 'deliquify' cash (i.e., to convert a temporary cash 'surplus' into a less liquid asset. This 'deliquification' has two concrete results: (1) it avoids any temptation that might exist to spend cash for something one really doesn't need, and (2) it provides a compromise adaptation to the dilemma of having cash available for emergencies as opposed to investing it in relatively nonliquid assets. With only minimum risk, it's a way of, so to speak, "having your cake and eating it too." The strategy is to buy a young pig, goat, chicken, or turkey, feed it for a time, then resell it as the need arises for substantially more than the original purchase price. This is a practice which Beals (1970:238) refers to (in the specific context of pig-raising) when he observes that the pig is really a "live piggy-bank" among the Valley of Oaxaca peasants.

When I asked one Magdalenan why he raised animals he made the following response which, I think, typifies the thinking of his co-villagers:

Well, in order to have a source of cash
when one needs it urgently. One sells
animals that one has to get a sum of
cash together. For that reason one raises

119

animals: pigs, chickens, turkeys, cows.

Another Magdalenan, when I asked him if it made sense
to raise animals, replied: "Yes, it makes sense, because it gives us a lump sum of cash" ("nos da centavitos
en junto"). For example, when I propose to sell six or
eight chickens I'll get a lump sum of cash." And still
another replied to my question as to why he bought
turkey chicks as follows: "To save money; when I want
to sell them, I have money." Similar responses to such
questions could be quoted many times over among these
villagers.

Most villagers who keep animals as a form of
surrogate banking do not keep track of the costs involved in feeding them. I did find an occasional villager who kept track of costs involved in raising animals (especially pigs or cattle) but this was the exception rather than the rule. Basically, the animal
is considered as a tangible, readily convertible asset
with what seems to be a built-in value increment
factor--where the natural thing to do is to provide the
means for its growth.

When we turn to the utilization of commodities
in direct consumption, the focus shifts to goods and
services as they become objects of use and enjoyment
or appropriation by individual villagers, acting singly
or in groups. Looking at the regional economy as a
circular flow system, consumption may be conceived of
as the process by which the finished product "drops out
of the social movement, becoming the direct object of
the individual want which it serves and satisfies in
use" (Marx 1904:275). In consumption, commodities as
things are embodied in persons; it provides direction
to and represents the culmination of the economic
process.

In all noncapitalist communities ranging from
Bushman bands (Lee 1969) to Malay fishing villages
(Rosemary Firth 1966), we can isolate a kin-based income
pooling unit, typically incorporating males and females
of varying ages, which is the fundamental reproductive,
resource-managing, and provisioning unit. Given the
relative cultural homogeneity of village populations in
the Valley of Oaxaca, variation in needs and wants within domestic units occurs primarily on the basis of age
and sex differences, whereas variation between them reflects socioeconomic and demographic differences
(though we lack empirical studies which document this

120

in crucial areas like nutrition). A crucial determinant of the 'standard of living' of any peasant-artisan provisioning unit in the regional economy is the amount of maize that unit produces relative to its subsistence requirements. Maize is still the principal foodstuff and an important fodder; it also continues to function, if in a reduced and subordinate way, as a commodity money (medium of exchange and short-term store of value) and, in short, occupies a strategic place in the social and economic life of the regional peasant population.

During the principal harvest period (September-November) maize (maíz en grano) is accumulated in the village households' storage places for subsequent use in the preparation of tortillas, gruel (atole) and other foods and drinks, as well as feed for poultry and other domestic animals (especially pigs). Moreover, dried maize husks (totomozle) and dried leaves (zacate) stripped from the stalk, and even the dried stalks themselves (cañuela), are bundled and stored for subsequent use--primarily as animal fodder. In addition to its use as food and fodder, maize is also used as a medium of exchange for a wide range of complementary goods and services required by peasant households but not produced by them or to supplement their own production (cf. Foster 1942:40).

I have already mentioned the fact that maize is commonly accepted in payment for goods at village stores and molinos de nixtamal; it is also widely accepted in payment for agricultural labor (usually through a medias or sharecropping arrangements) and for the rental of ox teams (in accordance with an agreement known as 'yuntas a maíz'). There is also a corn lending institution which is quite similar to money lending, although more seasonal. This is known as 'apreciar maíz' (the corn lent is 'maíz apreciado'). According to this arrangement, a villager whose corn supply is exhausted obtains corn from another villager who has a supply with the understanding that repayment (usually in kind) will be made with an increment when the next crop is harvested. The demand for 'maiz apreciado' invariably begins midway through the dry season in January or February, becomes intense during the middle of the rainy season (as more household supplies are exhausted) and continues until harvest time in September. Specifically, the 'buyer' in such an arrangement acquires a quantity of corn (one or more fanegas) in return for an obligation to pay the seller a stipulated amount of cash (or corn) at the end of the next harvest. In essence, then, three options are available to a villager in a corn short-supply situation: he can (1) buy it as he needs it for cash at the going market price, (2) buy it 'apreciado' (on credit with interest), or (3) borrow it (return an equivalent amount in kind). Most villagers obviously prefer to avoid option 2 if possible but there are many who also dislike option 3 because of pride and a desire to avoid obligations to reciprocate (or possible conflict if the loan isn't repaid when the donor expects it).

The fact that many villagers (especially in Magdalena but also in San Sebastian) buy corn in the plaza indicates that the local village surpluses are not necessarily available to meet the needs of under-producing households (i.e., those that don't produce enough corn to meet their susistence needs). While certain redistributive functions are served by cere-monial and ritual exchanges, inter-household production disparities are not eliminated or adequately compensated for through the internal distribution/marketing systems of the villages. In short, in these villages surplus producers do not necessarily provision underproducers.

How much corn does the typical household require to meet its annual consumption needs? It was beyond the scope of this study to make a detailed investigation of consumption patterns in village provisioning units but a rough idea of these can be extrapolated from interview and household budget data. Estimates by fifteen Magdalena heads of household of how much corn they require annually, of their 1967 harvest, and of the date in 1968 by which their own corn supply was exhausted, suggest that Magdalenans differ widely in their estimates of annual household corn consumption-- the range going from a low of 1.97 kilos per day to a high of 5.32 kilos per day. That these estimates are generally too conservative is suggested by the fact that in only one case was a 'surplus' reported; in all other cases the 1967 harvest ran out before the 1968 harvest began--which means that all of these households were forced to find alternative sources of supply.

Household budget data which I collected for several Magdalena households over varying lengths of time (1 month to two years) suggest a daily corn con-sumption per household of about 4-1/2 kilos. For ex-ample, one family with two adults and three children consumed 4.086 kilos of corn daily between October 1, 1967 and September 30, 1968 (or 817 grams per person daily; this figure includes corn processed for tor-

tillas and excludes corn fed to chickens or pigs).
These figures are supported by daily consumption estimates provided by other Magdalenans.

The 1979 survey data on the corn supply situation
of 34 Magdalena households demonstrates unequivocally
that the crucial determinant of a household's relative
corn supply situation is its status vis-a-vis private
land ownership. Thus, 85% of the private landowning
households reported that they did not have to buy corn
every year to offset a short supply, whereas 71% of
the ejido-only households reported that they did have
to make corn purchases every year. Also, during 1978
(which, along with 1977, was a low harvest year for
most households) the propietario households that purchased corn (23% didn't) did so for an average of 5
months, whereas the ejido-only corn buying households
(86%) bought it for an average of 8 months. However,
this difference is magnified by the fact that 46% of
the propietario households bought corn for four months
or less (vs. 24% of the ejido-only households), and that
52% of the ejido-only households bought corn for 9 or
more months (vs. only 15% of the propietarios). These
findings simply underscore the validity of our thesis
regarding the fundamental division in Magdalena
society.[8]

FOOTNOTES

[1]This is not intended to play down the role of
the 'redistribution' of commodities along kinship and
compadrazgo lines which occurs in the ceremonial context in these villages.

[2]A thought-provoking study of a small village
tienda in the Sierra de Puebla has been made by Barry
Isaacs (1965). He examines various dimensions of the
'function' of storekeeping and stores in a small village, makes a detailed analysis of the way in which the
store is operated on a daily basis, and suggests that,
perhaps, they are best understood from a 'social'
rather than an 'economic' perspective.

[3]It is appropriate here to remind ourselves of
the crucial distinction between the relative exchange
value or price of a commodity and its actual or absolute
value. Marx agreed that at the superficial level of
empirical analysis of market activity prices are indeed
determined by supply and demand and buyer/seller interaction; but he insisted that at a deeper level of
analysis the 'value' of any commodity is determined
through the production process and, especially, is a
function of the amount and quality of "labor power"
embodied in it (cf. Marx 1935, esp. pp. 24-45). The
Marxist approach to value, price and the market carries
different analytical implications than the orthodox
Neoclassical approach (see Chapter 7).

[4]Barter (cambio) is widely practiced as a mode
of exchange in this local trade. For example, about
half of the pottery transactions that I observed during
the 1966 Juquila fiesta plaza in San Sebastian involved
barter; pottery was bartered for fruits (esp. locally
grown guava), vegetables, and seeds in season or for
certain prepared foods like tamales, tortillas, candied
squash or rice pudding. The barter rates differed
slightly from transaction to transaction; money prices
of the objects to be bartered served as a basis for
negotiating the rate of exchange. This money-mediated
barter was reported by Malinowski and De La Fuente
(1957:69) as the most prevalent type of barter found
in the Valley of Oaxaca economy.

In the non-plaza sector of local trade, itinerant peddlers--especially those who sell clothes and sundries--extend credit to their village customers through a system of time or deferred payments (abonos).

[5]During the harvest period from September to November many San Sebastianos work as agricultural laborers in the neighboring villages of Santa Maria Coyotepec, San Sebastian Tutla, Santo Domingo Tomaltepec, Santa Maria Tule, and San Felipe del Agua. Annually, about fifty San Sebastianos are involved in this seasonal labor migration (rough estimate) for periods of two to four weeks. Several of the metateros also work occasionally in the stone quarries of Iscotel on the eastern outskirts of Oaxaca City where wages are paid on a piece work basis. Other San Sebastianos find occasional employment in Oaxaca City on construction projects.

Several Magdalenans leave their village seasonally to seek various wage labor jobs. Some work in the trapiches or as agricultural laborers in San Pedro Apostol; others in construction work in Oaxaca City; and a few go to the coffee haciendas in Soconusco (Pacific coastal area of Chiapas) or to the cane and pineapple fields in Veracruz.

[6]It is logical to assume that the metate, basically a corn-grinding instrument, is doomed to extinction by the molino de nixtamal or mechanical corn-grinding mill (not to be confused with a small metal table grinder which is hand powered) which has been introduced throughout rural Mexico. This may prove to be true in the long run but in San Sebastian and Magdalena, where most women regularly take their nixtamal to the local molinos, they promptly bring the masa home, put it on the metate and grind it some more. According to them this gives the masa a better consistency and, also, 'improves' the taste of the tortillas which are made from it. Metates are still used, wear out and are replaced in these villages.

[7]The estimates given by these informants were in fanegas (24 almudes each); each almud is equivalent to 4 liters or 4 kilograms. The highest estimate made by a Magdalenan of annual corn requirements (547.5 almudes) is equivalent to about 2 metric tons. Only one harvest estimate exceeded this; most were substantially below it. Kirkby (1973:89-94) distinguishes between "levels of satisfaction" and actual "production levels" for corn in Valley villages; she maintains that "an average family of five persons eats about one metric

ton of corn a year at an absolute minimum" (1973:89).
She also contends that there is evidence among Valley
peasants of a "desire not to work more than necessary
to produce a fixed, 'satisfactory' amount of corn"
(1973:94). My own viewpoint is that production levels
for corn or any other commodity in this economy are
not functions of the direct producers' mentalities but
rather are functions of the forces and social relations
of production. We must take into account the crucial
variable of social differentiation (class relations),
together with the nature and consequences of capitalist
development in the regional economy (e.g., what it
means for land tenure and land use), in order to approximate an understanding of differential production levels.

Incidentally, referring back to Tables II-5 and
II-6 we can calculate the corn harvest for 25 San
Sebastian households in 1966 as 2302 kilos (or just
over 2 metric tons per household), and for 36 Magdalena
households in 1979 (bad harvest year) as 371 kilos
(about 1/3 metric ton). However, these Magdalenans,
in regular years, harvest an average of 1085 kilograms
per household according to their estimates. This compares favorably with the average of 982 kilograms per
household for the 1967 harvest.

[8]See Chapter 7 under "Levels of Income" for a
discussion of the metatero household budget; and Beals
1975:Chapter 5 and pp. 318-352 for a comprehensive
treatment of consumption and expenditures in the regional household which includes data on Magdalena collected by me for Beals' Oaxaca Markets Study Project.

Magdalena <u>metatero</u> manufacturing a metate with a <u>barreta</u> in his quarry <u>patio</u> during the rainy season.

<u>Metateros</u> finishing metates with hand picks in their
residence lots.

CHAPTER 4. THE METATEROS

IN VILLAGE ECONOMY AND SOCIETY

The Metateros and Agriculture

Objective indices of the situation. The metate
industry is located within an inter-community division
of labor and is found in only four of the 142 municipalities that comprise the 'Central Valleys' region;
only a minority of households in each metate-producing
community are directly involved in metate production.
In 1966-67, for example, out of a total of 313 households in San Sebastian Teitipac approximately 75 (24%
of the total) were directly involved in the metate industry (42 metateros who extract stone from the quarries
and manufacture metates, and the remainder either
finishers and/or traders); in San Juan Teitipac out of
a total of 870 households there were about 85 producers
of metate industry products and 13 traders (11% of the
total); and in Magdalena Ocotlan out of a total of 135
heads of household there were 18 metateros and 8 finishers or traders (19% of the total).[1]

As pointed out in the discussion of the division
of labor in Chapter 2, the typical village household
is, first and foremost, an agricultural production unit
which may also devote some portion of its available
labor-time to the production of non-agricultural products for sale or to wage labor within and outside of
the village. Consequently, metate production is
typically neither the principal nor the only occupation
practiced by a given household to make a living; rather,
it is the most viable alternative available to many
households which enables them to earn income outside of
agriculture and, often, it is their preferred and most
reliable source of cash income.

Poverty in the agricultural means of production,
the reader will recall, is a prominent feature of the
metatero households in San Sebastian (see Table 5).
Table 7 below tabulates these same data from San Sebastian as well as additional data from 14 metatero households in San Juan. The latter data reinforce my previous interpretation of relative metatero poverty in

129

TABLE 7. Distribution of Agricultural Means of Production and Shelled Corn Yields Among 36 Metate Industry Households in the Teitipac Villages in 1966.

No. of Households	Land Under Cultivation (hectares)					Corn Yield (kilograms)						Oxen			Burros		
	0	.1-1	1.1-2	2.1-3	3.1+	no data	0	1-500	501-1000	1001-1500	1500+	0	1	2	0	1	2
San Sebastian (N = 22)	2	15	2	2	1	9	0	4	3	0	6	15	1	6	9	11	2
San Juan (N = 14)	2	8	3	1	0	0	1	9	3	1	0	9	2	3	10	3	1
Totals	4	23	5	3	1	9	1	13	6	1	6	24	3	9	19	14	3

the agricultural means of production. These combined
data show that 75% of the Teitipac metateros had one
hectare or less of land under cultivation and that 74%
had shelled corn yields of 1 metric ton or less [52%
had yields of 1/2 metric ton or less].   This means that
at least half of these households produced less than
the 730-950 kilograms of shelled corn required to satisfy the minimum annual consumption needs of a family of
four in this region (Beals 1975:93).   Moreover, 66% of
these households owned no oxen and 53% owned no burros.
How do the Teitipac metateros themselves view this situation?   "The rich are rich," one of them asserted,
"because they have land; the poor are poor because they
have no land." And he continued:

> We the metateros, dedicate ourselves to
> making metates because we don't have land
> to cultivate; if we do have land we don't
> get much harvest from it.   Therefore, we
> find ourselves obliged to make metates
> in order to maintain our families.

More than one third of my metatero informants, responding to a question as to why they had taken up this
occupation, attributed their involvement to their lack
of the agricultural means of production.   As one of them
expressed it:

> Since we're poor we don't have means for
> getting money; this is how it has been
> since we were children.   For example,
> my father didn't have much land to culti-
> vate and we are, as the old saying goes,
> "with our hands crossed."   We didn't own
> a team of oxen so even if we would have
> had land to cultivate we wouldn't have
> been able to cultivate it.   For that
> reason, and to avoid leaving the village
> to find work, we have worked as metateros.
> From this work we earn a little bit of
> money to keep ourselves alive; it's the
> only thing we have.[2]

Concerning the possession of land, however,
there is a significant difference between the Teitipac
villages and Magdalena which is illustrated by the mean
size of landholding cultivated per household: San

131

Sebastian--.8 hectares and San Juan--.6 hectares vs 2.3
hectares in Magdalena. As the data presented in Table 8
show, this already substantial difference between the
villages is augmented when we consider that most of the
Magdalena households also possess uncultivated ejido
allotments which, when combined with land under cultivation, increases the per household average to 3.3
hectares. This comparative advantage of the Magdalenans
is reflected in the 1966 shelled corn yields which gave
them an average of 1297 kilograms per household compared with a 1040 kilogram average for San Sebastian
and a very low 412 kilogram average for San Juan. Yet,
considering the situation with regard to oxen, Table 8
shows that only one Magdalena metatero owned any oxen
(just one side of a team) and that most of them are
renters of ox teams and carts. This places the Magdalenans at a disadvantage vis-a-vis one third of their
Teitipac counterparts who own 1 or 2 oxen (and a handful of these have carts as well, though this is not
indicated in Table 7).

The following case study penetrates beneath the
aggregate statistics and exemplifies the difficulties
a Magdalena metatero-campesino without an ox team has
in making ends meet:

> Anastasio harvested 2750 kilograms of
> shelled corn in 1966, an above-average
> yield for his 3.8 hectares of second and
> third class land. His strategy of com-
> partmentalizing his agricultural and
> metate earnings is shown in his response
> to my question as to where he got money
> to meet the costs of cultivating his
> lands. "I meet these expenses," he told
> me, "from what I earn when I sell corn or
> other crops. Last year the harvest was
> good so when the time has come to prepare
> the soil for the next sowing I sell a
> fanega of corn to pay for the rental of
> an ox team. The corn that I harvest is
> to eat and for ox team rentals; metate
> earnings are for kitchen expenses, to
> buy food that we need ("los metates son
> para los recaudos")." Anastasio spent
> 680 pesos on the cultivation of his land
> in 1967, an expenditure which he met by
> selling corn from his 1966 harvest as
> follows: April 1967--sold 5 fanegas
> (500 kgs.) for 62.50 pesos each (312.50

TABLE 8. Distribution of Agricultural Means of Production and Shelled Corn Yields for 13 Metatero Households in Magdalena Ocotlan in 1966-67.

Household No.	Land Holdings in Hectares					Corn Yield (kgs.)		Oxen		Carts
	Ejido			Private	Sharecropped	1966	1967	own	rent	
	planted	idle	total							
1.	3.0	3.0	6.0	0	0	1400	750	0	x	0
2.	2.9	---	2.9	0	.25	---	1400	1	x	0
3.	1.2	.3	1.5	.3	0	1900	---	0	x	0
4.	3.5	.5	4.0	0	1.5	528	1200	0	x	0
5.	1.1	---	1.1	0	0	900	---	0	x	0
6.	2.0	4.3	6.3	0	0	1400	700	0	x	0
7.	1.0	---	1.0	0	0	1400	---	0	x	0
8.	3.8	---	3.8	0	0	2750	625	0	x	0
9.	3.0	.5	3.5	0	1.5	1450	1200	0	x	0
10.	3.0	3.0	6.0	0	0	1138	1614	0	x	0
11.	1.5	.5	2.0	.02	0	1100	450	0	x	0
12.	2.0	1.0	3.0	0	1.0	400	1000	0	x	0
13.	1.5	.5	2.0	0	1.25	1200	620	0	x	0
Total	29.4	18.1	43.1	.32	5.5	15566	9539	1		0
Average	2.3	2.0	3.3			1297	954	--		--

133

pesos); July 1967--sold 2 _fanegas_ for 190
pesos; August 1967--sold 200 kilograms
for 204 pesos. With the August sale
Anastasio's 1966 harvest was exhausted.
Not until late October or early November
would the 1967 harvest come in.

The 'budget compartmentalization' strategy employed by
Anastasio is found in other households but, in his case
and in most others, there is also situational juggling
of incomes from different sources (e.g., metate sales,
animal sales, egg sales, wage labor, loans) to meet
daily, emergency, and seasonal expenses (see Beals
1975:Ch. 5).

There are various ox team rental options open to
Magdalena _metateros_ (cash payment as in Anastasio's
case, payment in labor, payment in corn) but, in the
long run, there is little to choose between them concerning their impact on the household budget. One informant lodged the following complaint about the 'rent
in kind' option known as '_yunta a maiz_':

It's no advantage having a '_yunta a maiz_'
because of the 4 _fanega_ (400 kgs.) payment
in corn you must make at harvest time.
And in a bad harvest year which are the
fanegas I keep and which do I use to pay
for the ox team? If I harvest 8 _fanegas_,
4 go for the _yunta_--and what's left for
me? A lousy 4 _fanegas_! On the other
hand, if a year comes with abundant rainfall one can harvest as many as 5 cartloads
or 25 _fanegas_; you can pay for the _yunta_
and still have 21 left over. In that case
you have a surplus of corn which you can
sell when you need to buy clothes, to
buy an animal, and so on. But when there's
a small harvest? I don't like to rent
yunta a maiz and I'm struggling to see if
I can buy my own. If I'm lucky and have
a good harvest one of these years, I'll
sell half of the corn, sell other animals
we may have around the house like pigs or
chickens, put that money together and
buy, at least, 1 ox.

This informant's proposed solution for the rental problem, namely, buying his own oxen echoes a desire shared by all of his companions.

When we recall from the discussion in Chapter 2 the concrete material benefits deriving from private land ownership in Magdalena, and further considering that these lands are fertile and close to the settlement area [they belonged to the colonial "fundo legal" and were not confiscated by the hacienda], we can sympathize with the following expression of frustration, again by Anastasio, over the obstacles that an 'ejido-only' household must overcome if it hopes to acquire a parcel of private land:

> One thinks about buying but there's no money.
> There are many who have private parcels
> but they inherited them. Their fathers
> bought the land and left it to them as an
> inheritance. Nowadays a parcel of private
> land costs a minimum of 1000 pesos. Some
> people find a way to buy--selling an extra
> residence lot, an ox team, or animals to
> raise the cash. But a complete pauper
> like me lacks the means. When will I
> ever be able to buy a piece of land? I've
> just recently been able to buy a residence
> lot. I can't buy a parcel of land. How
> could I do so? At times I hear that so-
> and-so is selling a parcel and I say to
> myself, 'If only I had the money.'

That this statement could just as easily have been made by any of the Magdalena metateros is indicative that, apart from relative poverty in the agricultural means of production, their socioeconomic situation, like that of their Teitipac counterparts, is characterized by low cash income and chronic indebtedness.

As we will examine more closely in Chapter 7, the level of metatero income from metate sales is, among other factors, a function of fluctuating conditions in the metate market which lead to price instability, and to varying productivity. The metateros generally talk about their annual income from metate sales in terms of a split year (i.e., a 'low price-low income' period lasting roughly from May through October and a 'high price-high income' period from November through April). Estimates of yearly cash earnings

135

between 1966-68 for the San Sebastian and Magdalena metateros ranged from 400 pesos ($32 dollars) to 3000 pesos ($240 dollars), with the average annual cash income for all informants being about 1100 pesos ($88 dollars). For all of these metateros the estimate of income earned during the 'high' period of the year was approximately double that of income earned during the 'low' period. The average weekly cash income for a representative sample of metateros in these two villages during 1966-68 was about 45 pesos ($3.60 U.S.). Only a handful of the most productive metateros earned a regular weekly income in excess of this average.[3]

More than half of nearly 50 metateros I systematically interviewed in San Juan, San Sebastian, and Magdalena during 1966-68 reported that they had debts at the time of the interview; and all of them reported that they had had previous debts. Nine of 14 San Juaneros reported debts ranging from 20 pesos ($1.60 dollars) to 1000 pesos ($40 dollars). Five San Sebastianos reported owing a total of 4500 pesos ($360 dollars) to the same village moneylender (who happens to be the wife of a well-off peasant, No. 22 in Table 5), whereas five Magdalenans reported owing a total of 1900 pesos ($152 dollars) to a combination of storekeepers, moneylenders, and to the Ejido Bank. "There are weeks that I earn money and weeks that I don't," one informant confessed. And he elaborated:

> Those weeks when I work on my own plots I earn nothing but when I work in the quarries or as a jornalero I may earn as much as 80 or 100 pesos. Look, the truth is that in my situation one lives from day to day. The money I earn today I turn over to my wife; tomorrow it will have been spent. That's how our life is. It's impossible for us to save even a few cents. If I were able to save then I wouldn't always be in debt as I am. I've been able to reduce my debts only when I leave the village to work elsewhere. Not long ago I owed a total of 2100 pesos ($180 dollars) to various persons here in the village. So I left, found work elsewhere, and with effort earned as much as 100, 200 pesos a week. So as things now stand I'm in debt for only 800 pesos ($64 dollars).

<u>Metateros</u> habitually seek and readily obtain modest
(but indispensable from the standpoint of household
provisioning) cash loans from <u>regatones</u> (traders) by
agreeing to supply a stipulated type and quantity of
product at some designated future date. These transactions are known as "<u>adelantos</u>" or advances and are
conducted informally on a person-to-person basis. Cash
advances and other aspects of direct producer-trader
relationships will be discussed at more length in
Chapter 6.

<u>The ideological dimension: peasants or artisans?</u>
While I share a growing scholarly skepticism about the
heuristic utility of the 'peasant' concept (e.g.,
Ennew, Hirst and Tribe 1977), I will make a concession
to anthropological tradition by proposing that the <u>meta-
teros</u> are peasants to the degree that they cultivate
the soil on land which they own, rent or otherwise
possess and/or are carriers of an ideology which emphasizes the practice of agriculture as a strategy for
making a living. They are artisans because they are
manual workers who directly manufacture products which,
though collectively stylized, display different degrees
of individual craftsmanship or occupational skill.
Any attempt to measure the 'peasantness' of a <u>metatero</u>
quantitatively (e.g., measuring the proportion of man-
hours or man-days over an annual cycle spent working at
agricultural tasks) would be tedious, just as its results would be misleading--given the multitude of variables which intervene as major or minor determinants
in the work scheduling of only one individual, let
alone of many--because it departs from a behavioristic
misconception. To the extent that a concept of 'peasantness' is heuristically fertile, it implies at least
a two-dimensional process--ideological along one axis
and behavioral along the other. Let me illustrate what
I mean by an anticipatory reference to the case of
Anastasio, a Magdalena <u>metatero</u>, which will be presented
later in this chapter. In Chapter 5, under the section
"Aspects of the Planning and Allocation of Labor-time,"
I summarize the results of a study of Anastasio (who
in that context remains anonymous) which shows that between October 1, 1967 and October 31, 1968 (which en-
compassed 328 work days), he worked 62% of those days
(7.8 hours daily) in some phase of metate production
and on 24% of them in agriculture (6.5 hours daily).
Now in purely behavioristic, quantitative terms, Anastasio would be pigeonholed as an artisan who is a
marginal peasant. Yet if you examine his economic decision-making, his aspirations [two examples of which
the reader has been overtly exposed to in the previous

137

five pages and has encountered covertly in the 'discourse on ejido possession vs. ownership' excerpted earlier] and life history (below in the section on "Work Histories")--that is, his ideological make-up--you will probably agree with me that Anastasio's labor-time mix (metates vs. agriculture) is wholly dependent upon a series of variables subject to change (e.g., status vis-a-vis ox team and private land, size of harvest, metate market conditions). The reader may or may not agree with me that Anastasio is actually a constrained 'peasant' who is trying to realize his peasant aspirations by working as a metatero. You might wish to catalog this for future thought as we proceed.

Regardless of the proportion of their annual labor time that is allocated to agricultural production, most metateros reminisce, think about the present, and plan for the future within an ideological framework dominated by agrarian values. Their occupational and material aspirations are predominantly agrarian: they aspire to be full-time peasant-cultivators and to own sufficient land and other necessary means of production to assure their permanency in that status. They consider this to be a desirable goal, not only because of the relative security it provides for household provisioning, but also because of its perceived potential for capital accumulation. This agrarian ideology emerged clearly in metatero responses to my question as to which village occupation they considered to be the best one. The following is a representative response:

> Cultivating the soil, if one could have sufficient land. That way one can have corn, chickpeas, beans--all the necessary grains. The harvest gives results because one maintains oneself from it; and during the 'dead season' (tiempo muerto) when work's hard to get, those with a good harvest can keep themselves going. Having corn and chickpeas one can buy a pig or a sheep and fatten it; and if he really has a good harvest he can buy a young steer. It's not necessary for a person with sufficient land to have other occupations; he can fatten animals with his own corn and from his heanings will have money available to invest at another time, for example, when the planting season arrives. If I had sufficient land, I would not make metates.

This suggests that the metateros are artisans with a petty bourgeois peasant ideology--which articulates a quest for the possession of land as a means of production with greater security in provisioning the domestic unit and an increased potential for small-scale capital accumulation. Most metateros do not consider the metate industry to offer them the possibility of long-term provisioning success or petty capital accumulation potential; rather they consider metate production simply as a viable means to convert their labor-power, first, into exchange-value and, then, into use-values to provision their domestic units on a periodic, short-term basis. It is only in conjunction with a seasonal involvement in subsistence agriculture that metate production generates long-term commitments, and through senility, death, migration or success in realizing agrarian goals that metate production is abandoned.

Metatero Work Histories: A Dialectic Between the 'Oficio,' Agriculture, and Migratory Labor

Given the preceding discussion, it should not surprise us to learn that metateros who are not successful in achieving a stable relationship between their agricultural and metate production will join the migratory flow and that, on the other hand, those who succeed in acquiring the means necessary to expand the agricultural production capacity of their households may permanently join the ranks of the full-time peasant cultivators. The following work histories of one ex-metatero and two metateros give us a foundation in individual experience from which we can subsequently evaluate the impersonal statistical record for the metatero population as a whole. These capsulized, partial histories vividly document the trials and tribulations of village life, the perserverance and hard work of these men, and some of the strategies they employ to survive.

The Case of Severiano

[At the time of the interview, he was 44 years old, married, and had four children, only 1 of whom was still a dependent. He had a 4 hectare ejido allotment under cultivation and owned an ox team.] What is most interesting about his case is that he had given up metate making for

horticulture which he learned as a jornalero
in the nearby village of San Antonino. I
have very little autobiographical data
from this informant and will present selected statements by him or summarize other data
which pertain to the above-mentioned theme.

S. first left the village to look
for work in 1944 when he was 21. He found
work as a highway construction peon near
Candelaria on the low Pacific coastal
slopes. He worked for 3 months there and
earned 8 pesos daily. "At that time," he
explained, "I had nothing, absolutely
nothing, not even a place to live. I
earned just enough for my wife and me to
subsist." 1955 was a significant year for
S. because he became a metatero and made
his first trip to the U.S. as a bracero
and spent 2 months picking cotton in
Arizona. His net earnings from that trip
were 2500 pesos ($200 dollars) which en-
abled him to buy a residence lot, some corn,
and most importantly, his first ox team
(which cost him 1300 pesos [$104 dollars]).
Regarding his stint as a metatero he stated
the following: "I went with the metateros
to earn some money and I observed them to
see how they made metates. I asked one of
them to sell me a trozo (metate-sized
block of stone) so that I could make a
small metate. Afterwards, I bought pieces
of stone to make metates; I learned that
there are trozos that could be worked
and others that couldn't. That's the way
I learned. But now that work is very hard
for me and I have stopped going it."

In 1957 S. returned to the U.S. where
he picked cotton in Arkansas for 35 days;
he brought home 1300 pesos [$104 dollars]
which he invested in clearing land to plant
sugar cane. In 1964, following a bad cane
harvest and other difficulties related to
his service as head of the comisariado
ejidal, he left the village and took up
residence for 14 months in San Antonino,
an Ocotlan community famous for its garden
cropping (flowers, vegetables) (Waterbury
1976). There he was provided with a
modest place to live by his employer and

140

earned 8 pesos daily. Most importantly, he learned the arts of horticulture and, after returning to Magdalena, he decided to cease being a campesino who plants only corn, beans and cane and became a hortelano specializing in the cultivation of flowers. "From now on," he told me, "I'm going to be a hortelano so that I can be sure about my work." And he made the following comparison between being a campesino planting only subsistence crops and a metatero. "The metatero spends a lot of time getting stone and cutting it but when he sells his metates at low prices, or not at all, he throws away his time and loses a lot of work--just like the corn farmer with a bad harvest. There may be a return but a very small one. The hortelano, on the other hand, simply waters his plants from a well when it doesn't rain." And S. then presents his definitive critique of the oficio of metatero and the subsistence corn farmer: "The way the metateros live in this village, the fact that they don't have a good life is because the prices of metates are unstable; or if they sell at good prices it's almost the same because the metateros have many expenses. They don't have ox teams or good harvests; so even though they might earn good money they don't save any. I'll bet you that not one metatero in the village has even 1000 pesos saved because as soon as they earn money they spend it. And the situation is the same for the campesino who plants only corn."

The Case of Pedro

[At the time this life history sketch was recorded, Pedro was 36 years old, married, and had nine children ranging in age from 17 to 2 months. He had recently become a goat-raiser but also worked occasionally as a metatero. He is the head of household No. 6 in Table 8.]

My father was a soldier during the Revolution and, afterwards, settled here. My grandparents had all the necessary

means of life but my father didn't know how
to take care of them; he was addicted to
mezcal. He had inherited some private land
but he finished everything with mezcal.
That's the background in which I grew up.

The first time that I left the village
was to go south [towards Miahuatlan and
Pochutla] to work on highway construction;
I started in 1953 and worked for about 6
months. Afterwards, I returned to the village and worked as a jornalero--with different people for one day, two days, like
that. But then I started to work for Sr.
Elio at his molino de nixtamal; I worked
for 3 years with him, between 1954 and
1958 more or less. During that time I
also worked clearing brush and scrub from
the land. Then, when he didn't want to
employ me any longer, I left and went to
work again on road construction in the
Sierra Juarez; I lived in a construction
camp for about a month in 1959. Then I
returned to the village to pick up my wife
and everything and went to Oaxaca City to
work as a peón de albañil (construction
peon) for 6 months; we rented a room there.
Afterwards, for another 6 months I com-
muted between Oaxaca City and the village
every Saturday. But I realized that I was
getting nowhere--I was paid only 5 pesos
a day and working at the heaviest jobs.

So in 1960 I came back to the village
and my father-in-law [a metatero] took me
with him to the quarry. I hadn't made
metates until then. My father-in-law bought
semi-finished metates in the quarry and
finished them here at home. I worked in
the quarries during 1960 but toward the
end of that year almost lost an eye when
a piece of stone hit it. I stayed at
home for a month without being able to
work. Once my eye healed I returned to
work in the quarries and worked there
during all of 1961.

In 1962 I went 'north' and worked
for 3 months in Buenavista, California,
in the strawberry harvest. We were paid
every two weeks. The first two weeks I

worked there I earned $45 dollars; the
second two-week period I earned $94 dollars;
the third $105 dollars; and the fourth
$96 dollars. I returned to the village
with 2500 pesos ($200 dollars) in savings.
I bought an ox team, in fact, I bought 3
oxen. I had also bought a radio and
other things in California which I brought
back with me. The ox team cost me 1400
pesos ($112 dollars); with the 1100 pesos
that remained I bought another ox that
cost me 625 pesos. With the rest of the
money I bought corn, fodder for the oxen,
and all the necessary equipment for the
ox team. I spent every cent.

But once I had bought the ox team--
since we have our customs here in the
village--it wasn't long before they
[the village authorities] gave me a _cargo_;
I wasn't able to do business here ("No
pude hacerme negocio aqui"). Well, I
had to sell one ox. Afterwards, when the
corn I had bought ran out, since I didn't
have the time to plant anything, I went
to work as a _jornalero_. Yes, I had land to
cultivate but lacked the resources to
cultivate it. They gave me the _cargo_ of
'Mayordomo de la Pólvora' [i.e., to sponsor fireworks displays on certain festive
occasions]. I wanted to get ahead
("quería aventajarme") but they didn't
let me do so. And that's how it was; I
had to spend another year as a _cargo_
holder. And I had other problems with
my kids so I had to sell the ox team.
Recently I've had to rent an ox team
"a maíz."

Last year's harvest (1966) of 14
fanegas (1400 kgs.) lasted us through
the middle of April of this year (1967).
First I had to pay for the _yunta_, 4
fanegas--that left 10. Those went for
household expenses--one sells 1/2 _almud_,
one _almud_, 2 _almudes_, another _almud_--
and since I've got a lot of family--we
consume 1-1/2 _almudes_ (6 kgs.) of shelled
corn daily. And for necessities like
clothing, food, well, the corn is sold.
So by the middle of April when it was

143

exhausted I had to struggle to find a way to sustain the household and to continue working the fields. Since I had the goats, I sold 4 of them to buy corn.

I started in the goat business on December 5, 1966. I was looking for a way to meet our expenses. And I had been thinking about getting some goats for some time. I spoke with the teacher here in the school and she gave me the goats. [This teacher is a native of the adjacent community of San Pedro Apostol where her husband is a store owner.] She gave me 21 goats on a share basis (a medias). The idea is to get them to breed. She keeps 10 and I took 11. The next time there are newborn kids, she keeps 11 and I get 10 so that things even up. I made another deal with a person here in the village to add his goats to the flock--I now have 63 goats of his a medias. In September, 32 kids were born out of the combined flock; 16 of those are now mine.

My interest is to see if I can succeed with my own animals; to see if I can build up a flock of my own animals like the others have done. I'm still struggling in my life to try to progress. I don't want to continue suffering as we have suffered.

The Case of Anastasio

[At the time of the interview, A. was 34 years old, married and had four children. He divided his work between farming, metate-making, and blacksmithing. His household is No. 8 in Table 8.]

My life as a child was very miserable. I grew up under miserable conditions. When I was 11 I was considered to be school age so I started to attend school--but only for 2 or 3 months each year. School started in February and I attended until April when the planting season approached. The land was ready and I had to help the family earn some centavos by working for others--planting

144

or doing some other job in the fields. That's
where I spent my time, in the fields, and not
in school. [At this point A. interrupted
his narrative to look for a document which,
he said, would be relevant here. What he
came back with was a handwritten document
which he referred to as a "Pagaré" (I will
pay). As you can see from its contents which
I quote below this was an indenture contract;
it reads as follows: "In Magdalena Ocotlan
on the 15 of January 1944 Sr. Agapito H.
(A.'s father) and Sr. Isidro P., both born
and raised in this village, met together in
representation of their own rights and with
legal capacity to make binding commitments
and established a contract with the following
clauses: First, Sr. A. H. receives from
Sr. I. P. the sum of 24 pesos under the
following conditions: a) that Sr. A. H.
voluntarily agrees to give his son Anastasio
as a shepherd's helper ("comprometió
voluntariamente dar a su hijo . . . como
ayudante de pastor . . .") so that he can
tend livestock, and who will earn the sum
of 2 pesos monthly; b) that Sr. Perez (A.'s
employer) agrees to go every day with the
Hernandez youngster, until the year is
completed; c) that Sr. Perez agrees to buy
huaraches and a sombrero or a capisayo (rain
cape) for the youngster. Second, that Sr.
Hernandez deliver the boy on the above date
and continuously until the year ends, only
in the event of illness will he be free of
obligation until he is well and the unworked
days will be compensated." This contract
was in effect from January 15, 1944, to
January 15, 1945, and was signed by Anastasio's
father and by Sr. Perez. A.'s narrative continued as follows:] When the school year was
about to end I would begin to attend classes
again but then they would end. When I was
12, the same story: I attended school until
agricultural work season arrived and then I
would cultivate and tend the milpa. I could
do all the necessary tasks. The same when I
was 13. When I was 14, my father died and
I was orphaned--my mother had died when I was
only 2 years old.

My father owned only a residence lot
and a jacal (hut) when he died. I had to

sell it to pay for his burial. And since
we have the custom here of the <u>novenario</u> (9
days of mourning)--with what money? Well,
I had to find someone who was willing to give
me a job. I went to see Sr. Elio who had a
corn grinding mill (<u>molino de nixtamal</u>) to
ask him for work because I needed a few
<u>centavos</u>. He said he was familiar with what
I could do--plant and tend <u>milpa</u> and to take
care of oxen, and that he would pay me 10
pesos a month to do this work for him.   I
told him o.k. but that I needed a 50 peso
advance. He gave it to me and I paid for
my father's <u>novenario</u>. That was March 23,
1947. And I had to sell a few other things
to raise additional money because the
<u>novenario</u> cost me 100 pesos.

On April 2 I started to work for Sr.
Elio and remained with him until August 1947.
Then he told me: "I can't force you to work
for me; it's a voluntary thing; if you are
willing to continue working for me then
we'll continue." Well, I stayed on with him
since I had no other place to go. I came
to feel at home and to learn about all of
his problems. He knew that I took good care
of his oxen. I worked with him for 10 pesos
a month until 1950 when I got married.

After getting married I stayed with
Sr. Elio for another month but the arrangement no longer worked so we went to live
with my father-in-law. I worked as a
<u>jornalero</u> for 5 months--until my father-in-
law taught me how to work stone. I didn't
know how to quarry stone or make metates
until he taught me. He taught me everything. I worked in the '<u>oficio</u>' [i.e., as
<u>metatero</u>] in 1952, 1953, 1954 and, finally,
in 1955 I bought a <u>yunta</u> (ox team). Since
we had fewer children then [2 had been born
by that date], I was able to save money from
metate sales. With that money I bought
pigs which I fattened and sold for 700 pesos;
the ox team cost me 900 pesos ($72 dollars).

In 1959 I had to sell the ox team to
buy a place to live. I sold it for 1700
pesos and paid 1200 pesos for the lot with
a <u>jacal</u> (hut). I sold a pig for 700 pesos,

put that money together with the 500 pesos left over from the ox team sale, and bought another ox team in 1960 for 1200 pesos.

In 1961 the 'accusation' came and I lost almost everything. [A. was accused of abusing another villager who was drunk. A. was then serving as a village policeman and had been ordered by the Presidente Municipal to pick up the drunk and put him in jail. But, according to A., as he was hauling the drunk off to jail he struggled free and fell to the ground, striking his head on a rock. A. was charged with assault and was jailed in Ocotlan. He was not supported by the Presidente Municipal.] I had to sell the ox team to pay for legal expenses and I have not been able to buy another one since.

[In 1963 A.'s wife was badly scalded with boiling water in a kitchen accident and was bedridden for two months. She was finally cured but A. spent more than 1000 pesos on medical expenses. Shortly thereafter he went to Salinas, California, as a bracero with 1000 pesos borrowed from his father-in-law to pay for the trip. He picked strawberries for a 2-month contract period in the hope of earning enough to pay back his debt and buy another ox team. But as he told me, "I didn't figure out how to pick strawberries" ("No encontré la forma de pizcar las fresas"). As it turned out he earned only enough to repay the 1000 peso loan from his father-in-law. The last time I visited with A. in Magdalena (October 1980) he still had been unable to acquire a yunta.]

What these three case studies illustrate in microcosm, the data in Tables 9 and 10 demonstrate for the metatero population as a whole, namely, that their careers span many types of work and take them well beyond the confines of their villages. From the raw data which is tabulated in Table 9 I have computed the average number of major extra-village work experiences per metatero as 3.8 (San Sebastian 4.4, Magdalena 3.3, and San Juan 2.6) and that the average duration of each experience is 3.6 months (Magdalena 5.7, San Juan 4.5, and San Sebastian 2.0). As can be inferred from this

TABLE 9. Frequency and Duration in Months of Major Extra-Village Work Experiences Among 45 Oaxaca Metateros.

Number of Experiences	Duration of Experiences (months)										Total
	no data	0	less than 1	1-4	5-9	10-14	15-19	20-24	25-29	30 or more	
no data											
0		6									6
1			2	1	1					3	7
2	1				3	1			1	1	7
3	1			4	2	1				1	9
4					2	2	1				5
5	1				1			1		1	4
6					1	1		1	1	1	5
7											0
8											0
9							1				1
10								1			1
Total	3	6	2	5	10	5	2	3	2	7	45

148

table only six (13%) of 45 metateros in the 3 villages
reported having no major extra-village work experiences.
The seven cases (16%) with work experiences of 30 months
or longer include two long army enlistments and cases
where the entire household moved to the vicinity of the
head's employment (e.g., tropical crops area of Tuxtepec-
Veracruz). The typical work experience of 3 to 4 months
duration, however, is usually a solo venture with the
worker's family remaining behind in the village. One
of my informants expressed concisely why he had periodically had extra-village work experience of long duration:

> By necessity, the lack of money. I left
> the village to earn centavos in order to
> have the necessities ("para tener lo
> necesario"). For that reason I had to
> leave to get work. Here in the village
> the pay is low, 15 pesos a week (1967)
> and there [cane fields in Tuxtepec] the
> pay is 15 pesos a day. That's why I left
> the village, because the pay is better
> elsewhere.

What kinds of jobs do these individuals get and
where do they get them? An examination of Table 10
provides some answers. As might be anticipated, 72% of
the jobs are in the agricultural sector and, of these,
45% were in the United States as contract laborers or
braceros; most of these involved cotton picking in
Texas or Arkansas or garden crop/citrus harvesting in
California. During my first weeks in San Sebastian in
1965, being a somewhat naive student of liberal persua-
sion, I expected daily to be assaulted by irate ex-
braceros who would use me as a whipping boy to somehow
redress past grievances against unfair and unscrupulous gringo employers. Much to my surprise quite
the opposite occurred, and I was asked time and again
by ex-braceros and would-be mojados to "fix papers"
("arreglar los papeles") or otherwise make connections,
contacts or arrangements to facilitate either re-entry
or first entry into the U.S. for work purposes. Indeed,
and without exaggeration, if I would have followed
through on all such requests during my periods of work
in these villages, I am convinced that their male populations would have been temporarily depleted in the
15-50 age range--and that the metate industry would
have experienced a marked decline in activity. In retrospect, I have a hunch that some of my informants

149

TABLE 10. Sectoral Classification and Location of 135 Major Extra-Village Work Experiences Among 37 Metateros

Sectoral Classification	Location of Extra-Village Work									Total
	Elsewhere in District	Outside District but in Region	Outside District Region Unspecified	Oaxaca City	Tuxtepec-Veracruz	Pacific Slopes	Chiapas	Mexico City/Borderland	U.S.A.	
AGRICULTURE										
Local Subsistence Farming	7	19	1	0	0	0	0	0	0	27
Coffee	0	0	0	0	1	6	3	0	0	10
Sugar Cane	0	0	0	0	8	0		0	0	8
Pineapple	0	0	0	0	5	0	0	0	0	5
Cotton	0	0	1	0	0	0	2	1	20	24
Garden Crops/Citrus	0	0	0	0	0	0	0	0	23	23
CONSTRUCTION										
Buildings	0	0	0	6	0	0	0	1	0	7
Highway	0	1	8	0	0	0	0	0	0	9
Quarrying	2	2	0	0	0	0	0	0	0	4
FACTORY	0	0	0	0	2	0	0	2	0	4
SERVICES	3	1	0	2	0	2	0	4	0	12
MILITARY	0	0	0	0	0		0	2	0	2
TOTAL	12	23	10	8	16	8	5	10	43	135

150

cooperated with my repeated and bothersome requests for data with the veiled hope of a guelaguetza from me which might have conveyed them across the frontera. These statements should not be misinterpreted; I did talk to villagers who had experienced "fracasos" ("failures") as braceros and who had little desire to risk another trip to the frontera (border). Moreover, I did encounter metateros and other villagers who displayed anti-gringo behavior (especially when under the influence of that unexcelled relaxant of the subconscious, mezcal), and others who told me of abuses suffered on their way to or from the frontera or inside the U.S., which sometimes involved gringos but more often involved other Mexicans or Chicanos. The point that should be made, however, is that the metateros or other rural direct producers in Oaxaca don't move into the migratory labor stream because they like unfamiliar people and places or out of a perverse wanderlust. They do so to seek a possible way out of the vicious cycle of non-accumulation and persistent poverty in which they find themselves mired (as I think my analysis up to this point has demonstrated). The blunt truth is that hard manual labor is much more poorly remunerated in Oaxaca (or anywhere in Mexico for that matter) than it is (and was) in Texas, Arizona, California or elsewhere in the U.S. (see Gamio 1971:171; Fernandez 1977:Chs. 5 & 6; Van Ginneken 1980:61 et passim; Reichert 1981). And, as eminently rational calculators in matters affecting their material livelihood, rural Oaxacan direct producers will take any reasonable opportunity to substantially augment the returns on the labor-power they sell. They also know from their own daily experience that they don't have to cross the U.S. border to suffer exploitation by capitalist employers so that prospect hardly serves as a deterrent to migration.

The comparative data on net earnings for agricultural employment in Mexico and in the U.S. by the metateros (pertaining to 1966-68 and earlier) vividly, if not conclusively, reinforce the above argument. According to my calculations (derived from net earnings reported by informants for 19 separate work experiences in Mexico and 34 in the U.S., all of which were included in Table 10 tabulations), the average monthly net earnings per work experience in Mexican agriculture by these migratory metateros was the incredibly trifling sum of 51 pesos ($4.07 dollars) in contrast with a still meager but comparatively enormous sum of 1004 pesos ($80.33 dollars) per U.S. work experience! [The reader is referred back to the case studies to find some examples of the purchasing power of pesos in the good old 1960s.] These computations may be unsophisticated and the sample limited but their meaning is clear.

If I would have included minor (i.e., short-term) extra-village work experiences in Table 10 it would have become unmanageable--especially regarding agricultural jobs in places within easy commuting range (by walking, burro, bus or truck) of the home villages [this includes places within the same district and sometimes those within adjacent districts], since these are sources of a great deal of seasonal wage-labor. As it stands, however, 27% of the major experiences were in other communities in the same district or region which have agricultural regimes differing little from those in the metate villages themselves [except in some cases with more irrigation and garden cropping,] followed by 14% in the Tuxtepec-Veracruz region of intensive tropical agriculture where metateros work in the sugar-cane and pineapple harvests and, lastly, by 11% in the Pacific coastal slopes of Oaxaca and Chiapas where they work in the coffee harvest (and the coastal plain of Chiapas where they pick cotton).

With regard to work experiences in the non-agricultural sectors, they were most frequent in the construction industry with 40% of the total; these were about evenly divided between building construction in Oaxaca City and road or highway construction in the 'Central Valleys' and other regions. Also, there were a few long-term experiences by metateros in quarrying activity--mostly in the Ixcotel quarries on the outskirts of Oaxaca City; however, the significance of these is overshadowed by the fact that several metateros periodically work in these quarries on a short-term (i.e., 'minor') basis, sometimes commuting daily between Ixcotel and their villages (i.e., San Sebastian and San Juan). Given the burgeoning growth of Oaxaca City since 1970, combined with the absence of any major highway construction program in the 'Central Valleys' region during the same period, my impression is that there has been a corresponding diminution in the proportion of metatero work experiences in this activity and an increase in their participation in construction work in the city. The relatively small proportion of extra-village work experiences in the urban services sector (16% in Oaxaca City or Mexico City) reflects a tendency for labor demand here to be met primarily through either permanent or very long-term rural-to-urban migration or, in the particular case of Oaxaca City, through daily commuting from heavily populated band of rural communities surrounding the city in the

152

<u>Centro</u> district.

How can the impact of these work experiences on the ideology of the <u>metateros</u> be summarized? One must guard against a tendency to respond to this question by exaggerating the effect of such experiences and arguing that those individuals with more extra-village work experiences in either urban or extra-regional contexts [especially as <u>braceros</u>] were, for example, less suspicious of my intentions, were generally more cooperative and articulate in expressing themselves, and had broadened [more 'modern'?] aspirations for themselves and their children--particularly for their sons. In my case these would be impressions which don't find much support in the systematic data I have collected. What does strike me as meriting emphasis is the extent to which most of their major extra-village work experiences has contributed to the development of more systematic, sophisticated thinking about their own labor-power as a commodity. Without exception, their work as <u>braceros</u> in the U.S. and in the sugar cane, pineapple, and coffee harvests in Mexico--and even in the quarries of Ixcotel--exposed them to payment on a piece work basis, according to the weight or volume of the crop harvested (or the stone quarried). Under such a payment system, the premium is on individual rather than cooperative effort--a factor which, as I discuss in Chapter 5, seems to have had an effect on quarry work organization in the metate industry. In most of the rest of their extra-village work, the <u>metateros</u> were paid wages on a time basis (per hour, per day or per week) which would also reinforce and formalize their thinking about 'time as money' which had already (and inevitably) been fostered by their independent involvement in the production of commodities for sale in the regional marketing system. I will return to this topic and elaborate on aspects of it in Chapter 7.

In concluding this section, and to summarize the discussion, I think it is fair to say that the withdrawal of <u>metateros</u> from the metate industry due to their inability to develop or sustain a viable involvement in agricultural production in their villages pushes them into unskilled extra-village labor markets, thereby inserting them in a process of proletarianization which operates in the economic and ideological spheres. In the last analysis it's not simply 'land' or 'land with metates' but 'land and/or metates and/or work (wage labor' which represent the economic alternatives for these rural direct producers (see Martinez-Alier 1977: 130-146 for a suggestive analysis of the Cuban peasantry

153

where a parallel argument is made which has influenced
my thinking here). A metatero can become a 'peasant'
or a 'proletarian' but as a metatero he is neither.
Rather, he is simply a rural direct producer who may
be peasantized, proletarianized or remain an artisan
with partial peasant and proletarian status.

The "Oficio"

Introduction. The principal source of pride in
their craft or, as they call it, "el oficio")"the
trade"), lies in their recognition that not every man
in their villages who has similar objective material
conditions of life has the aptitude, physical endurance,
or the inclination to work as a metatero. Moreover,
the metateros seem to share an underlying belief in
predestination which binds them to and excludes others
from the oficio, combined with an historic sense of
its ancestral prehispanic origins. One of my informants,
who, incidentally, has never left his village of San
Juan Teitipac to earn a living, articulates several of
these themes as follows:

> Well, all things considered some men are
> destined for this oficio. In the first
> place, not all human beings can serve in
> it ("no todos los seres humanos pueden
> servir en esto"). Some dedicate them-
> selves to agriculture, others to making
> charcoal in the hills. Some also work
> as jornaleros and leave the village for
> other places and still others have the
> oficio of selling goods as traders. But
> we understand that men are assigned to
> oficios and in those oficios they have to
> remain. For example, some people say to
> me. 'What's wrong with you? Your work
> is very hard, damn! With all those heavy
> sledge-hammer blows! 'Listen brother,'
> I tell them, 'let's agree that I was
> destined to be a metatero.' I say this
> because we know that in ancient times
> those men were also metateros. We know
> this to be so because I have a quarry
> here where I've found tools from the olden
> days, from the times before the white
> people arrived with the Conquest (Porque
> en la antiquedad vamos viendo que también

aquellos hombres fueron metateros desde
mas tiempo . . . mas o menos antes que la
raza blanca viniera a la Conquista). [The
reader can read more about his ancient tool
find in Chapter 5 under the section on
"Historical Aspects . . ."]

This philosophic view of the oficio is accompanied by a more pragmatic one of its concrete economic
importance. "From metate work," said a Magdalenan, "I
sustain myself, I maintain my family. From there," he
continues,

> I make money for corn and other foodstuffs.
> From there I make money for clothes. With
> this oficio I make money.

A San Juan informant in a similar vein explained:

> This work leaves something to sustain us.
> In the first place, work in other oficios
> like that of jornalero doesn't give re-
> sults. One earns a minimum. And with
> the metate I can work a lot at home and
> according to my own schedule--I have time
> to gather fodder for the animals. One
> works calmly without being bothered by
> someone telling him to hurry up with the
> work. We work according to our own hours;
> at 8 or 10 in the morning we can begin--
> at whatever hour we please. As everyone
> knows, a jornalero must begin work punc-
> tually at 6 a.m. and work until 6 p.m. for
> a miserable wage of 5 pesos. What good
> are 5 pesos for sustaining a family?

In short, then, participation in the "oficio" which is
sanctioned ideologically as the historic vocation of a
select few must constantly survive the test of economic
performance. That it still manages to do so as we
enter the penultimate decade of the 20th century is
diagnostic of the paradoxical Mexican variant (given
that nation's vast, nationalized petroleum wealth) of
a worldwide malady called by various names like "underdevelopment," "uneven development" and so on, but having
one underlying common denominator--national development
priorities are dictated by the needs and objectives of

industrial capital whose regional interests and activities are selectively focused (or enclaved) economically and are tentative (or contested) politically. In Chapter 6 we will examine how, why and when the oficio scores well or poorly in the economic performance test which constantly is imposed upon it by its practitioners.

Internal organization. The metateros are informally organized into functionally differentiated status groups which are ranked on the basis of worker skill and knowledge of the strategy and tactics of the craft. Unlike many craft and skilled occupational groups known to students of economic history and comparative economic organization, the metateros have no established leadership, no formal corporate organization, and no institutionalized mechanisms to promote solidarity or esprit de corps and to control dissension or conflict.

The informal organizational structure of the metateros (i.e., characterizing each local industry), consists of three functionally differentiated and ranked sets of statuses. The maestros (masters of teachers) are capable of organizing and directing quarry operations, of instructing others about the strategy and tactics of quarrying and stonecutting, and are the most skilled and knowledgeable quarrymen and stonecutters. Only a handful of metateros in each metate-producing community are recognized as maestros.[5] The mozos metateros comprise the majority of the active working population in the industry; they lack the knowledge and experience of the maestros in the quarrying phase of production but are competent stonecutters who can make any stone product (i.e., metate, mano, molcajete). Apprentices, who are for the most part young men between the ages of 14 and 21, are in the process of learning (through trial and error, imitation, and instruction) how to make metates and manos. They typically go through a period of on-the-job training during which they provide unskilled labor (e.g., clearing and hauling tasks) in return for stone and instruction or guidance. The informal status hierarchy (maestro--mozo metatero--aprendís), considered sequentially, represents developmental stages in a metatero's career. This is not to imply that all apprentices become full-fledged metateros nor that all metateros become maestros but does mean that those who do attain higher ranks necessarily passed through the lower ones.

In Magdalena Ocotlan somewhat less attention is paid to distinctions between maestro, mozo, and aprendís than is the case in the Teitipac villages. This is explicable, to some extent, because of the smaller scale of the Magdalena metate industry and also because of a lesser tendency for quarrying activity in Magdalena to be conducted by large work companies. Most of the quarrying in Magdalena is done by small groups (2-3 men) of affinal or consanguineal kinsmen; larger work groups are strictly ad hoc in nature (i.e., several men working in adjacent quarries will cooperate on certain tasks) and don't involve relationships explicitly organized on a maestro-mozo-aprendís basis.

One significant difference between the metate industry in the Teitipac villages and in Magdalena is the presence in the latter of an individual recognized as 'encargado' or 'jefe' of the metateros. This position was held for several years by a retired, elder metatero who was widely respected by a large majority of the younger, active colleagues. His position, however, was primarily of a ritual nature and was linked to the annual celebration of the mayordomía of Nuestro Señor de las Peñas--a saint's cult celebration held exclusively by the metateros in Magdalena--presumably for the combined purpose of promoting solidarity among them and for displaying their civic spirit. Some informants preferred to refer to this elder's position not as 'encargado de los metateros' (as he was referred to by some metateros and by many non-metateros in the village) but rather as 'Presidente de la Comisión de la Fiesta del Señor de las Peñas'; they denied the relevance of this status for matters related to quarry tenure or other occupation-related problems. On the other hand, some informants insisted that the 'encargado' served as a spokesman for all metateros in village matters--representing their interests as a group before the local authorities-- and, also, gave examples of how his knowledge of quarry affairs helped him to provide counsel or good offices in mediating disputes or conflicts in the quarries. Nevertheless, given the absence of a clear consensus among the Magdalena metateros regarding both the position of 'encargado' and the 'Mayordomía de las Peñas' itself--combined with the fact that I observed resistance among them regarding the payment of cuotas for financing the latter--it is clear that the Magdalenans have not achieved a corporate organization of their craft.

Recruitment. The typical metatero career begins between the ages of 10 and 20 years, with the mean starting age of a sample of 35 Teitipac informants being 17-1/2 years. Recruitment into the occupation

157

tends to be through ascription. Of 30 active Teitipac
metateros interviewed in 1967 only four reported having
no consanguineal relatives in ascending generations who
were metateros. Of the remaining 26, 16 reported a
three-generational patrilineal continuity in the occupation (i.e., from FaFa or FaFaBr to Fa or FaBr to
EGO). Direct three-generational partilineal succession (FaFa to Fa to EGO) occurred in 14 of these cases,
with direct two-generational patrilineal succession
(Fa to Son) occurring in the other two. A total of 13
of these informants have metateros in both their matri-
and patri-lines in at least one ascending generation;
however, occupational succession has a definite partilineal bias. Similar patterns characterize the metatero population in Magdalena Ocotlan.

Only four of 30 Teitipac informants reported
having no consanguineal relatives of the first or
second degree who are active metateros. All of the
others reported having either first or second degree
consanguines (in most cases both) who were at that time
active metateros. Moreover, all of the informants reported having affines who were practicing metateros.
Some idea of the extent of the consanguineal and affinal
networks among the metateros can be provided by tracing
these relationships for one metatero as is done in
Table 11.

TABLE 11. Consanguineal and Affinal
Relatives of a Teitipac Metatero
Who Are Also Metateros

Generation	Patrikin	Matrikin	Affinal
2nd Ascending	FaFa (1)	MaFa (1)	
1st Ascending	Fa (1)	MaBros (3)	FaSisHu (1) MoSisHu (1) WiFaBr (2)
Ego's	Brs (3)	MoBrSo (3)	SisHu (1) MoSisSo (1) WiFaBrSo (1)

Certain families in the Teitipac villages and in
Magdalena are known as metatero families. For example,
it is often said of such families by others in the

community: "Son del oficio desde sus abuelos y bisa-
buelos" (They have been in the occupation since their
grandfathers and great-grandfathers). Such reputations
are, more often than not, supported by the genealogical
facts. For example, the Cruz family in San Sebastian
is identified as a metatero family. The genealogy of
the direct male descendants of Jose Cruz, the progenitor,
is represented in Figure 4:

FIGURE 4. Genealogy of the Male Metatero Descendants of Jose Cruz

*represents deceased person

As it turns out, all 14 of the direct male descendants
of Jose were or are metateros. Since Jose was himself
a metatero his occupation has been transmitted through
a total of 3 descending generations. Between the Cruz
and three other patrilines in San Sebastian society,
the metatero population there has a deep and extensive
kinship base.[6]

Enculturation. In San Sebastian and Magdalena
the finishing tasks in metate and mano production are
taught in the residence lot; all preliminary and intermediate production tasks are taught and learned on location in the quarries. In San Juan, on the other hand,
where the quarries are close to the village and are
more accessible, metate-size blocks of stone (trozos)
are carted from the quarry to the metatero's residence
lot; in many instances, then, the latter becomes the
San Juan metatero's workshop--a situation which also
prevails among the San Juan metateros residing in
Tlacolula.

159

In the Teitipac villages as well as in Magdalena apprentices are taught by instruction from more skilled metateros; the instruction takes the form of tips and pointers periodically volunteered or solicited rather than systematically programmed training. Much of what any apprentice learns is acquired on his own initiative through trial and error or imitation. The San Juaneros, unlike the San Sebastianos or the Magdalenans, often congregate on street corners in groups of five or six persons to labrar (finish) their products. In this informal street corner setting a spirit of friendly competition prevails which is conducive to the development or perfection of production techniques. In the words of one San Juanero:

> . . . After I was able to make metates, we would meet on the corner to finish them. Well, there they taught me how to do a better job of finishing them--Guillermo Cruz, who's now dead, was my maestro. There we competed with each other--with our other companions--to see who could finish the best product. Well, of course, with patience we turned out well made products.

Only one of 24 metatero informants in San Sebastian claimed to have had no teacher; eleven stated that their father was the key person in their occupational enculturation; three learned from affines and one from an elder brother. The remainder were taught by non-relatives, two maestros being responsible for training four of them. Of 15 San Juan informants, 7 were taught by their fathers, two by mother's brothers, one by his elder brothers, and another by his FaSisHu. Four of these informants were taught by non-relatives as apprentices in quarries owned by their bosses. Of ten Magdalena informants from whom this information was solicited, five learned the oficio by working with their fathers, one with an elder brother, one from a MoBr, one from a FaSisHu, and two from other metateros. In short, patrilineal kinship ties between teacher and apprentice are crucial to the process of metatero enculturation.

During his period of apprenticeship the apprentice is economically dependent on his maestro-patrón; he helps the latter in those quarry tasks which require a minimum of skill but considerable effort (e.g.,

hauling waste stone out of the quarry) and is rewarded
with an occasional piece of stone, access to the maestro's tools, and with advice or instruction. The apprentice is also entitled to the revenue from the sale
of his products---which are few in number and poor in
quality. Usually for a period of several months the
pecuniary reward for the apprentice's work is minimal
and he must rely on patience and perseverance to get
him through his apprenticeship.

The essential features of the maestro-aprendís
relationship emerge from the following conversation
which I had with a San Sebastian maestro:

Q: How is it that one gets to be a
metatero here in the village?

R: According to his family. Or, if not
that way, some say, 'No one wants to
give me work; I'm going to see if they
will teach me something in the quarry.'
He comes to the quarry. He lends a hand
to the metateros who are working there;
he helps them push dirt or toss away
waste stone. After a time they say to
him: 'Grab that crowbar and make yourself a mano; this is how you do it.'
Now this is how he becomes a metatero;
he begins in that manner.

Of course, there are persons who
are there in the quarry with the metateros
and never learn to make metates. I have
a neighbor who never could learn. Every
time he picks up a crowbar he screws up
the trozo; he breaks it and he gets disgusted. He can do the finishing tasks
but even those he doesn't do well. He
will never have the name of metatero.
It's just like school, some study but
never learn anything.

Q: How does the maestro go about teaching
a person who wants to learn to be a
metatero?

R: Well, he begins on a block of stone.
He gets a leaf for marking lines on the
stone to guide the cuts. The apprentice
cuts along the lines marked by the
maestro. When he's finished the maestro

161

looks over his work and tells where additional cuts are needed. In any case, the first metates never come out well. But little by little they improve.

Q: And how is it that a maestro knows when an apprentice has learned to make metates?

R: When he no longer asks the maestro for advice or guidance. He simply grabs a block of stone and his crowbar and begins to cut away. When he's finished, he says: 'Maestro, look and see what defect it has.' And the maestro replies: 'Look, here it needs a little more work.' But when it's well done, well, then, he's learned. Right? Some of them. But others never learn to make metates alone; they always need guidance. They always need someone around to tell them where cuts should be made. Some never understand; they just aren't cut out to be metateros. They just can't do it. They will never be metateros.

There are variations in the recruitment and enculturation process as can be inferred from the following account by a San Juanero of how he became a metatero:

From the beginning I was a peasant. But in 1933 one of my compadres, Efren Carranza, introduced me to the occupation. He said to me: 'Compadre, if you want to learn I will teach you; give me a peso to buy you a handpick so that you can begin to make manos.' I gave him the peso and with it he bought me a little hammer—second hand—I remember. And with that second-hand hammer he went to Jose the blacksmith who made two picks from it. Until this day I remember that Jose charged me $1.50 for those two picks. And the day that he finished making those tools, I went to pick them up very contentedly and, then, went to see an old metatero named Manuel Cruz. Manuel sold me some pieces of stone, some unfinished manos, for 5¢ each; and on that first day I finished a mano. I returned to my house very pleased with myself

162

because I had gone to the house of Sr. Cruz
so that he could teach me. However, I was
somewhat pensive as well because, on that
first day, a little piece of stone got into
my eye; that night I saw little lights and
I said to myself: 'What will I do to pto-
tect my sight?' But that week I finished
6 manos and we went to Oaxaca to sell them.
There I bought myself a pair of dark glasses
which I've worn ever since to protect my
eyes.

Little by little I began to make 1
mano daily, then, 3 every 2 days. Afterwards I was making 2 daily. That was enough
because in those days a laborer earned only
25¢ from sunrise to sunset--a hard day's
work; I was able to go to the fields to
bring alfalfa for my animals and then by 6
in the afternoon finish 2 manos; that gave
me an income of 50¢ daily.

I began to make metates without a
maestro; I observed how others did the work
and then I made some wooden models--tracing
the form from an old metate. Then, I began
to cut stones using a ruler and a pencil to
mark the cuts. I started using a little
chisel--about 15 centimenters long--and
slowly but surely I perfected my finishing
techniques. In 1939 I began to make specially decorated metates (carved in bas relief)--those that sell for 200 pesos each
now and then were worth only 8 pesos.

A Magdalena informant explained to me the conditions under which he was invited by a metatero friend
to learn the craft:

. . . He invited me to work so that I could
help to clear away debris and dirt and quarry the stone and, afterwards, we had stone.
We finished one part while he was teaching
me. Once that I learned to work along to
set blasts, to cut--then I looked for my
own quarry.

And, finally, another San Juanero--who, at the

163

time of the interview was 44 years old, a quarry proprietor and a recognized master of the oficio (who also
was elected to be Presidente Municipal in the early
1970s, the first of his oficio in many years to serve
in that post in any of the metate villages)--explained
to me how he had learned the craft from his father:

> I began to acquire knowledge of this work
> from my father when I was 14. I watched
> him working; he was a maestro-metatero.
> Probably, one gains all of his knowledge
> from one's father. I saw how he worked
> the stone, how he broke bedrock in the
> quarry to look at its texture, how he
> worked in the quarry. He told me: "Be
> careful, this stone is no good so let's
> break it up and get rid of it because it
> keeps us from reaching the good stone
> underneath." And once we had blasted
> and cut away the good stone, we started
> cutting it up. Here the teacher has to
> give examples to the apprentice. My
> father taught me by tracing out the form
> of a metate on the stone with a leaf.
> Then he knocked off pieces with a sledge
> hammer and after that I would begin to re-
> fine it with the crowbar. Fathers have
> the right to criticize us when we're
> wrong and he would tell me: "Well, that
> work is not well done, you need to cut
> off a little more here." It took me two
> years of instruction to learn. By the
> time I was 16 I knew how to fracture bed-
> rock by inserting wedges (cuñas), how to
> plant a powder charge for blasting it up.
> That's what my father did for me.

So much then for how the oficio is transmitted from
generation to generation in these villages.

Not all learning about the oficio occurs in a
context of father-son or master-apprentice relations,
however. The peer group is also important here--espec-
ially among the neophytes. For example, in San Juan
where I found more young boys working in the metate
industry than in the other villages, several of them
were accustomed to wander through the quarries picking
up discarded pieces of stone [a practice they referred
to as "pepenar la piedra"] which was unsuited for

making full-size metates or manos but suited for making miniature products for sale as curios or toys. Some of these boys (some as young as 8-10 years of age) made agreements with traders regarding the sale of their products. And, they would work together on the street-corners or in other favorite gathering places to fashion their products in a context of mutual criticism. By the time they reach their teens, many of these San Juan youths are skilled in the use of hammer, chisel and hand pick, and have only to gain instruction in the use of the crowbar to qualify as full-fledged metateros.

As mentioned earlier, several Teitipac metateros have, over the years, periodically hired themselves out as stonecutters in the Ixcotel quarries located on the eastern outskirts of Oaxaca City or to work as mason's helpers in urban construction projects; this work ex-perience has provided them with knowledge of 'modern' techniques of quarrying and stonecutting. Nevertheless, metate making itself retains an artistic element which cannot be reduced to an ensemble of technical proce-dures. A San Sebastian maestro of the oficio told me the following anecdote to illustrate this point:

> Making metates is a question of pure
> sight and thinking. Do you think that we
> have a model or an apparatus to do this
> work? No! The square or the ruler are of
> no use in making metates. I will never
> forget the day when a master stone mason
> visited our quarry; he was a skilled stone
> cutter who could build anything with stone.
> I said to him: 'Let's see if you can make
> a metate.' He came over, took out a pen-
> cil and ruler, marked the stone, and began
> to cut it. At times he used a square to
> measure and mark the stone. But when he
> finished the metate it was formless; it
> had no style (gracia). He looked at the
> metate and then asked me: 'What went
> wrong?' I replied: 'In our occupation
> you can't depend on the tools of your
> trade like squares and rulers. Look at
> that metate; it's very well squared but
> has no form. To give a metate style and
> class it does no good to square and measure
> everything; one must simply have the know-
> ledge of how to do it.'

This anecdote, of course, leads us right back to the ideological underpinnings of the oficio which we discussed above, and is one manifestation of how these are renewed through metatero discourse. Regardless of how this ideology is maintained its central theme is the same: every man cannot be a successful metate maker; the oficio selects for those men who combine physical ability, strength, and endurance with patience and perseverance, and for whom the working of stone involves stylistic shaping as well as precision cutting.

A Comparative Review and Preview of the Metateros and Their Industry

In this concluding section I will present additional background material on the metate industry and survey several aspects of production and exchange internal to it, as well as identify problem-areas which will be examined in more depth in subsequent chapters. Table 12 presents a synoptic comparison of population, tenure, work organization, marketing, and rituals and corporateness in all four metate-producing communities (cf. McBryde 1945:60-61; 72-73 for comparative data on production and marketing of metates in 3 villages in SW Guatemala).

The metate craft is not indigenous to Magdalena Ocotlan; it was first introduced there by the grandfather of a recently deceased metatero who migrated to Magdalena from San Juan Teitipac early in the present century. Since Magdalena lies about equi-distant between the plaza towns of Ocotlan and Ejutla, products originating there could theoretically be marketed with equal facility in either plaza. However, there is reason to believe that the Magdalena metateros were somewhat more involved with the Ejutla plaza until the 1940s.[7] That the Magdalena metate industry was firmly established by the latter period is evident from the following summary description of it published in the 1949 Mendieta y Nuñez volume:

      In Santa Magdalena Ocotlan there are twenty individuals who manufacture metates as a secondary occupation.

      The stone utilized in the manufacture of these metates is obtained gratuitously by these individuals from a hill

TABLE 12. Synoptic Comparison of the Metate Industries in Four Communities in the Valley of Oaxaca

	SAN SEBASTIAN	SAN JUAN	MAGDALENA	TLACOLULA
POPULATION	Total personnel: 75 41 metateros; active population fluctuates with seasonal, ceremonial and agricultural cycle but several are 'full-time;' 11 are mano producers and the remainder are finishers or traders; many are landless	Total personnel: 100 75 are metateros or quarry workers; 12 make only mortars and pestles; 12 are traders; seasonal fluctuation in quarry activity is extreme; many metateros are landless but only a few are full-time	Total personnel: 25 metateros 1 trader; none of the metateros are full-time; seasonal fluctuation in quarry activity is extreme; all metateros have arable ejido land	Total personnel: 6 metateros All are natives of San Juan; 3 are 'full-time;' rest have alternative sources of income but regularly produce metates* *Note: 'full-time' metateros do supplement their income irregularly as day laborers but they make metates throughout the year.
TENURE SITUATION	No ejidos but communal lands Ideal private ownership vs. legal reality communal ownership reconciled via conditional individual usufruct or quasi-ownership; quarries located on communal cerro No land scarcity but unequal land distribution Endemic disputing between metateros over quarry boundaries and use rights	No ejidos Quarries located in privately owned fields; no communal tenure Land scarcity and unequal distribution Disputes between owners and workers over product sharing but no disputes over quarry boundaries or use rights	Ejidos Quarries located on ejido property but individual usufruct rights granted Relatively equal distribution ejido lands but scarcity and unequal distribution of prime arable land Some disputing over boundaries and use rights but situation controlled by ejido authority	Ejido and communal lands Quarries located on both communal and private lands; rights and boundaries are in dispute; neither quarrymen nor metateros are owners Land scarcity and unequal distribution Private vs. communal property rights and boundaries in dispute; metateros indirectly involved in factionalism between the 'cantero-comuneros' and the 'propietarios'
WORK ORGANIZATION	2 basic patterns: 1) 'loners'—individual exploitation with occasional cooperation; 2) 'company'—loosely organized cooperative work group with director who distributes output and laborers; volatile composition leads to 'roaming' and 'claim-junping'	1 dominant work pattern: 'company' with non-metatero owner, a quarry boss (encargado) who is a metatero and directs work and distributes product, and a group of laborers (mozos)	'Companies' are unknown; work is conducted via reciprocity and cooperation between 'owners' of contiguous quarries; some informal cooperative work arrangements but no formal status differentiation into 'maestro,' 'encargado,' 'mozo'	Metateros either lease a quarry to work themselves or with hired labor; but stone from the quarrymen or work with the latter on a product-sharing basis. More highly rationalized forms of work org.

TABLE 12 (Continued)

	SAN SEBASTIAN	SAN JUAN	MAGDALENA	TLACOLULA
MARKETING	Village traders important but not dominant in marketing	Village traders dominate metate product marketing	Village traders unimportant; producers dominate marketing	As local traders; all products marketed by producers in plaza or by encargo
	Most sales are in bulk lots to wholesalers; relatively few sales to private buyers	Some sales to wholesale buyers but retail trade most important	Majority of sales to private buyers	Majority of sales to private buyers
RITUALS & CORPORATENESS	There are no rituals or ceremonies unique to the metateros; there is no corporate spirit or organization among the metateros	On New Year's Eve metateros place offerings and build makeshift altars in their quarries to bring them luck during the New Year; there is no metatero organization	The metateros celebrate annually an exclusive 'mayordomia' (Señor de las Penas); all metateros contribute toward the expenses; the metateros have an 'organization' with a leader and spokesman who organizes the annual fiesta and serves as liason between the metateros and the ejido authority	There are no ritual practices or organization unique to the metateros though some of them participate in the 'comunero' organization along with the quarrymen

situated on the outskirts of the village which has the Zapotec denomination of <u>Yeg Canoa</u>.

The tools utilized in this activity have a total cost of 14.00 pesos and are the following: a <u>barreta</u>, a sledge hammer and six wedges (<u>cuñas</u>).

The first operation which the <u>metateros</u> must perform is extracting the stone from the quarry, by means of explosions provoked by planting powder charges which cost one peso each.

From each blast they extract sufficient stone to manufacture 12 metates.

The time required for making a metate of standard proportions is six days and its manufacture is done in the quarry itself.

Since they work on Sundays, each individual manufactures five metates per month.

The metates are sold in the neighboring town of Ejutla de Crespo at a price that fluctuates between three pesos and 3.50 for each metate, but they have to pay for the right to sell in the <u>plaza</u> the sum of thirty cents per metate.

The transport of the metates is on burros of their own property, so that the cost of production is not increased by that expenditure.

Since they manufacture an average of five metates per month, they obtain a monthly income of 16.25 pesos, or a daily earning of forty-nine centavos.[8]

Thus, through a combination of factors including historical accident, natural resource endowment, available labor supply, and a ready-made market-area, a one-man specialty occupation in Magdalena grew into an established craft industry.

Although native Tlacolulans have, in past gen-

erations, manufactured metates the present metate industry there is organized exclusively around a group
of several migrants from San Juan Teitipac, all of whom
now reside permanently in Tlacolula. These individuals
are considered to be 'afuereños' (outsiders) by the native Tlacolulans and still maintain close economic,
social and sentimental ties with their native village.
The output of these Tlacolula-based San Juan metateros
accounted for roughly 60% of total metate/mano sales in
the Tlacolula plaza between 1966-68, a pattern which
still held true in 1980, with the remaining 40% being
accounted for by San Juaneros selling products manufactured in San Juan (some San Sebastian products are
occasionally sold in Tlacolula).

   With respect to marketing, our data show that
metate price levels in the plazas of Tlacolula and
Ocotlan tend to correspond more with each other than
either does with price levels in the Oaxaca City plaza
over a given calendar period. Time series data on
average monthly metate sales prices for an 8-month
period between September and April indicate that the
only serious divergence in the movements of these two
price curves is in October, a situation which reflects
hyperactive trading associated with the patron saint's
celebration in Tlacolula. This ceremonial plaza draws
an unusually large number of sellers from both Teitipac
villages with the effect of creating a 'buyers' market
with unseasonably low prices. In any case, the metate
price levels in Ocotlan and Tlacolula remain uniformly
higher than the price level in Oaxaca City throughout
the period for which comparative price data is available (i.e., 1967-68, 1977-78).

   This latter pattern undoubtedly reflects the
differing marketing functions performed by these respective markets. The Oaxaca City metate market has
developed a regularized wholesale function which is not
found on a comparable scale in either Tlacolula or
Ocotlan; in Oaxaca City it is customary for metate
sellers to deal regularly with bulk-lot buyers who
purchase in relatively large lots but at low prices.
Moreover, in Oaxaca City when buyer movement is slow
the producer-sellers (who in 1981 are no longer prominent in a market now dominated by traders) prefer not
to store products in the marketplace from one week to
another and 'unload' their products with numerous retail stall owners (puesteros or caseteros) who pay even
lower prices than do the big-lot buyers. In Tlacolula
and Ocotlan, as a general rule, metates are sold singly
to private buyers who are looking for high quality

170

metates which bring premium prices and have a relatively low turnover.

There is no uniform pattern of quarry tenure in the metate producing communities: each local group deals with the problem of quarry ownership and use rights in accordance with the tenure regime prevailing in its particular community. The Teitipac villages provide a basic contrast. San Sebastian presents a case in which the ideal of private proprietorship is continually clashing with the legal reality communal ownership; the metateros seek and are nominally granted 'quasi-ownership' status in the quarries which, however, remain communal property. In effect, what happens in San Sebastian is that conditional usufruct rights are granted to individuals who then proceed to exercise private control over a section of quarries located on communal lands; however, because of the contradictions in the tenure situation, such private control is often contested by others. In San Juan, on the other hand, the quarries are located on privately owned land and, consequently, have a series of owners who, in most cases, are not metateros. This seems to contribute to a stable work and tenure situation but gives rise to an inequitable distribution of product.

Magdalena Ocotlan manages to reconcile the ideal of private appropriation with the legal reality of communal ownership through its ejido organization. All of the Magdalena quarries are located on ejidal lands and the metateros can obtain usufruct rights to a quarry by filing a claim with the local ejido authority (comisariado ejidal). However, ultimate control and ownership of the quarries rests collectively with the village through its ejido authority, and the metateros find themselves caught in a bind between private usufruct and collective tenure which is manifested in constant disputes between them and village authorities regarding a property use tax.

In Tlacolula, the quarry tenure issue is deeply intertwined with the larger issue of a continuing state of indeterminancy regarding the delimitation of permanent boundaries between communal lands (terrenos comunales) and private lands (pequeñas propiedades) within municipal jurisdiction. A protracted and sometimes bitter political and legal struggle has been waged in Tlacolula for several decades between factions seeking to consolidate communal holdings (los comuneros) and those protecting or seeking to expand private property interests (los propietarios). The local canteros

(quarrymen), as comuneros, have been the prime movers
of the first faction since the difficulties first erupted in the mid-1930s; the metateros, as newcomers, have
been caught in the middle of the tenure dispute and
have been forced into a series of shifting alliances
with both factions.

Over the years the comuneros' interests have
been served by a series of local officials (represen-
tantes de bienes comunales)--at least one of whom,
along with several of his constituents, has suffered
incarceration and harassment as a reward for his attempts by legal means to eliminate violations of the
federal Agrarian Code (Código Agrario) in his home town.
The propietarios, on the other hand, have spent large
sums of money on lawyers and bribes of local, state and
federal officials in their partially successful attempts
to acquire ownership of communal lands (see El Imparcial,
Oaxaca de Juárez, February 10, 1973, for one account of
an episode in this conflict).

The Tlacolula quarries, then, are located on
both private and communal property; some metateros have
made profit-sharing or rental agreements with private
proprietors of quarries to obtain usufruct rights;
others have aligned themselves with the cantero-comunero
faction (which suffers periodic suspension of quarrying
privileges as a result of the ups and downs of the
tenure conflict) and obtain stone either by purchase
from the canteros or as a trade-off for labor services
provided in quarry operation. By 1977 two enterprising
metateros had managed to acquire usufruct over a communal quarry by paying a substantial use-tax to the
municipal authorities; this payment (300 pesos monthly)
is made from revenue obtained through the weekly sale
of 2-3 truckloads of stone for construction purposes
in addition to revenue from metate sales. These metateros are engaged in a rationalized operation which
enables them to raise additional income from quarried
stone which is not suitable for metate manufacture;
previously in Tlacolula (and still in the Teitipac
villages and in Magdalena) such stone either is unused
or is 'contributed' to the municipio for construction
projects (via the tequio mechanism and in lieu of
labor service). In short, given their immigrant status
and the muddled tenure situation, the Tlacolula-based
metateros are confronted with greater uncertainty than
other metateros in gaining and maintaining access to
their primary raw material but are also presented with
the opportunity to increase the income-yielding potential of their work.[9]

FOOTNOTES

[1] The fourth municipality with *metateros* is
Tlacolula de Matamoros which in 1966-67 had 6 *metateros*,
all of whom were migrants from San Juan Teitipac. A
1978 inquiry about the situation in San Sebastian suggested a possible decline in the metate industry population since 1966-67 to include only 41 (approximately
10%) of the village's 400 households. A similar inquiry regarding Magdalena indicated that 25 (ca. 15%)
of its 168 households had metate industry personnel
(16 *metateros*, 8 apprentices, 1 *regatón*). In February
1979 a survey questionnaire was administered to a 20%
random sample of 168 households in Magdalena. Since
only 3 of the 37 households included in the survey had
metate industry personnel, it appears that the occupation was underrepresented in the survey. Metate market
records from the Ocotlan marketplace for 1978-79 reinforce the 1978 estimate that approximately 15% of all
Magdalena households participate in the metate industry.

Though San Juan Teitipac has a larger population of individuals qualified to perform work roles in
the metate industry and, at one time had a larger active *metatero* population than San Sebastian, it now
(late 1970s) appears that the latter village has a
large number of active *metateros*. This trend may be a
reflection of the fact that San Juan has a more re-
strictive tenure system in the quarries and fewer
quarries (with little area for opening new ones) than
has San Sebastian. Symptomatic of a decline in the
production of the San Juan metate industry is the increased traffic of San Juan based *regatones* to San
Sebastian to buy metate products and the migration of
San Juan *metateros* to Tlacolula. In 1966 and continuing
throughout 1967, this traffic had become so heavy (and
the competition so intense) that many of the regular
San Sebastian *regatones* have been hard put to find regular suppliers among their fellow villagers.

The term *barretero* refers to any villager who is
skilled in cutting stone with a long pointed crow bar
(*barreta*)--the principal tool of the Oaxaca Valley
quarryman and metatero. Not all *barreteros* in the Teitipac villages are *metateros* but all of the latter are

173

barreteros. The term is not employed to denote an oficio (occupation) but to denote a skill which is often required on tequio work projects or by a patron. It is a label for a particular work role which many male villagers can perform.

Metateros and maneros (mano makers) may also be regatones; but, in most cases, the latter are either labradores (finishers) only or play no role in the production of the products they trade.

[2]That metatero land poverty is not a fiction is suggested by the fact that several of them in San Sebastian engaged in a struggle to secure an ejido grant for the village. In 1966 a formal petition was filed by 24 San Sebastianos with the Federal government (Asuntos Agrarios) requesting an ejido land grant from the remaining lands of the ex-hacienda of San Antonio Buenavista. Eight of these petitioners, including one of the chief organizers of the petition, were active metateros. Since the absentee owners of the defunct hacienda do not cultivate the land remaining in their possession, the San Sebastianos, in accordance with relevant sections of the Mexican Agrarian Code, hoped to succeed in having the land titles transferred to the village for cultivation by themselves as ejidatarios. Their petition was in fact successful and an ejido was established by 1970.

[3]Estimates of weekly expenditures in 1967-68 by Magdalena metateros yield an average of 50 pesos ($4 dollars) per household. Our 1979 survey in Magdalena yielded the following figures on the distribution of cultivated land, income, and expenditures: an average of 3.22 hectares (median 3 hectares) of land was cultivated per household (vs. 2.9 hectares average for the three metatero households); the average weekly income per household was 202 pesos ($9 dollars) (vs. 263 pesos or $11.70 dollars for the metatero households), whereas the average expenditure per household was 196 pesos ($8.70 dollars) (vs. 220 pesos or $9.80 dollars for the metatero households).

[4]In an open-ended questionnaire which I administered to 45 metateros in the Teitipac villages and in Magdalena, two questions designed to measure occupational and economic aspirations elicited, almost unanimously, agrarian oriented responses. The first of these questions was: If you had the opportunity to select any occupation you wanted, here in the village or anywhere else, what occupation would you select?

The response to this question was invariably 'peasant-cultivator' (campesino). The second question was: If you had the luck of finding 5000 pesos how would you spend it? Most informants indicated that they would buy land and oxen.

[5]A survey of 15 metateros in San Sebastian Teitipact indicated that there is a broad consensus as to what constitutes a maestro, the 3 salient traits cited being skill in appraising and cutting stone, skill in the manufacture of metates, and ability to organize and direct group quarrying activities. Below are some representative definitions of a maestro given by my informants:

1. He's a maestro because he knows how to do it. He knows how to make metates and manos. Also he can make 'carved de-sign' (calado y dibujado) metates. He knows the work from the beginning--the cutting of stone in the quarry. Not everyone does that well. That's a maestro.

2. The maestro has the quality of saying how one is going to blast and cut stone in the quarry. He can even say--as if he were divining the stone--how many metates a block of stone will yield. That's a maestro; he is a director. The worker who doesn't know how to cut stone asks advice from the maestro in his quarry. The maestro tells him: 'That stone should be cut like this.'

3. The one who turns out the best work is a maestro. In every sense he knows stone. He can appraise stone in the quarry. Just by looking at stone in the quarry he can estimate how many metates will come out of it.

[6]In San Juan, as in San Sebastian, certain fam-ily surnames predominate among the metatero population. In only one section of the village 15 Cruz's are meta-teros, as are 10 Mateos, 8 Carranzas, and 4 Noriegas. One member of the Carranza family traced his occupation from his great-grandfather through his grandfather to his father; his brother and son are also metateros.

This is one documented case, then, of five-generation patrilineal succession to the occupation.

In both Teitipac villages the metatero population tends to be concentrated in particular residence areas. About 2/3 of the San Sebastian metateros reside in a two-block sector of section 1 in that village; in San Juan just under 2/3 of the metatero population resides in the northern section of the village which is near the quarries--a total of 34 living in an area made up of 6 contiguous blocks. Given the close association between kinship and residence in the social organization of the Teitipac villages, as well as the important role of kinship in occupational recruitment, the above pattern is predictable.

[7]Thus, in a brief section on the Magdalena metate industry in the Mendieta y Nuñez (ed.) volume (1949) the following statement is made: "The metates are sold in the neighboring town of Ejutla de Crespo . . ." (1949:560). My Magdalena informants corroborate the past importance of Ejutla as a marketing outlet; however, a certain portion of the Magdalena metate output has always been marketed in Ocotlan--although stiff competition was once provided in that plaza by the Teitipac sellers. Apparently as a result of the opening of the Oaxaca City-Miahuatlan highway in the late 1940s, Ocotlan gradually displaced Ejutla as the most important plaza town for Magdalenans.

[8]Aside from the comments by Malinowski and De La Fuente (1957:154-155), this is the only published statement on the Oaxaca valley metate industry that I have encountered. The reliability of the data, as well as of some of the inferences drawn from them, is open to question but, nevertheless, they are useful. The metatero population figure is not far out of line with the present one which contradicts the judgments of certain elderly Magdalenan informants who claim that there used to be more active metateros in the village than there are now.

The price data contained in this statement, while having to be corrected for the effects of intervening currency devaluations and generalized inflation in the Mexican economy as a whole, do indicate a rather remarkable appreciation in the metate price level since the 1940s. It is worth the trouble to pin down these price level increases more precisely. Tamayo (1962:605) provides us with estimates of the GNP in the Mexican economy for 1940 and 1960 respectively; to facilitate analysis he converts the value of the 1940 GNP into 1960 pesos by multiplying the former by a factor of 5 (implying that the value of the peso has decreased to 1/5 of its 1940 value). His conversion factor is apparently reliable, being based upon a separate study of the value of the Mexican peso (i.e., Indice de Moneda Nacional, Banco de Mexico). Consequently, it is probably not a great distortion of reality to assume for our purposes that the 1940-41 peso was worth 1.00 whereas the 1966-67 peso is worth .20.

According to Malinowski and De La Fuente (1957: 155), metates were sold (in the Oaxaca City plaza) within the price range of 1.50-6.00 pesos depending upon size, the average price being 5.00 for regular-sized metates. My data show that the average price for a regular-sized metate in 1966-67 was 35 pesos. In other words, in the space of some 25 years the average money price of metates has increased 7 times by 700%).

What does this mean in real economic terms to the metate producer, on the one hand, and to the metate consumer, on the other? Using 1940-41 as our base year for the value of the peso, the average price of a metate in 1966-67 is 7 pesos--or 40% higher than in 1940-41. In other words, the real value of a metate has risen by 40% between 1940-41 and 1966-67: the consumer in 1966-67 pays 40% more for a metate (in terms of constant purchasing power) than did his 1940-41 counterpart and, conversely, the 1966-67 producer earns 40% more on each metate (other things remaining equal) sold than did his 1940-41 counterpart.

[9]Another result of the quarry tenure situation in Tlacolula has been to encourage one metatero-entrepreneur to operate on a highly rationalized workshop basis. To counteract the difficulties in gaining access to quarries, he maintains a large inventory of trozos in a storage area adjacent to his workshop. Periodically, he hires quarrymen to exploit a quarry which he has managed to lease on a temporary basis; stone suitable for the manufacture of metates is hauled by rented trucks to the storage area. On one visit to his workshop I counted some 100 trozos (a several month's supply) in the storage area. Over the years, this individual has hired a series of helpers from his native village of San Juan Teitipac to manufacture metates in his workshop. At the time this study was conducted, two of his WiBrSo worked in this capacity. To facilitate production, he has assembled a wide array of stoneworking tools as well as a bellows for smithing.

He and his workers use hammers and chisels (instead of barretas) in their cutting operations; they specialize in the manufacture of large, high-quality (and high-priced) metates. An important part of his business is conducted on an encargo basis with clients from Tlacolula and surrounding villages.

Work company in the Mesa Grande Quarry in San Sebastian Teitipac

Metateros at work in the quarry in San Sebastian
Teitipac.

180

CHAPTER 5. MEANS OF PRODUCTION

WORK RELATIONS, AND THE LABOR PROCESS

IN THE METATE INDUSTRY

The Means of Production

Historical Aspects of the Technology of Stonecutting and Quarrying in the Valley of Oaxaca. Quarrying and stonecutting have a long history in the Valley
of Oaxaca as is evidenced in the monumental prehispanic
architecture of sites like Monte Albán and Mitla. Fortunately, the archaeological record of quarrying and
stonecutting at one important site, Mitla, has been
studied by Holmes (1895) and by Williams and Heizer
(1965). Blanton (1978:96) has unearthed evidence which
leads him to estimate that during the Classic period
(ca. 500 A.D.) at Monte Albán, the ancient Zapotec
"capital" centrally located on a hilltop site in the
Oaxaca Valley, there were metate and mano "workshops"
(i.e., strictly an empirical term without social content which refers to "concentrations of products produced, used, or discarded in production"--Blanton
1978:17) involving from 52-104 direct producers who
apparently manufactured these products for the use of
the locally resident population (estimated at between
15,000 and 30,000--Blanton 1978:58). We can expect
additional evidence of prehispanic Zapotec metate and
mano production from other areas covered by the Valley
of Oaxaca Settlement Pattern Project (Blanton 1978,
1980; Kowaleski 1980) but, unfortunately, the prospect
for ethnohistorical reconstruction of the socioeconomic
aspects of late prehispanic/early colonial metate and
mano production in the region are not good. This prog-
nosis is based on facts such as the apparent lack of
direct reference to this industry in the primary sources;
the 16th century Spanish chroniclers, for example, do
not mention its existence in the Teitipac villages or,
for that matter, anywhere in the Central Valley's region. Burgoa (1934:416) does make one passing reference
to metate production among the Valley Zapotec (see p. vii

181

above) but makes no mention of it in his discussion of Teitipac.[1]

Oral tradition among the _metateros_ points to San Juan Teitipac as an ancient center (_matriz_) of metate production in the Oaxaca Valley. In the absence of any material more directly relevant, it is worth quoting Chapple and Coon's (1942:165) perceptive synoptic inter-pretation of Holme's description of prehistoric lithic industry in Mitla since it is logical to assume that essentially the same conditions must have prevailed among the _metateros_ of that time:

> The stonecutters of Mitla did their work without metal tools; they used only crude stone hammers and picks, held in the hand; many of these tools remain in the quarry. The actions were simple and la-borious, but required considerable plan-ning and skill; it is apparent that a planned organization, with directors and workmen, was necessary to operate the quarry. Probably stonecutters were part-time or even full-time specialists. In transporting the stones from the mountain slopes to the city, they had no force at their command other than that of human muscle, aided by whatever leverage devices they could employ.

> . . . it is apparent that people who employ simple, nonmetallic tools and hand labor alone, are able to conduct mining and quarrying operations of con-siderable complexity, and on a moderately large scale.

The only direct evidence I found suggesting the presence of prehispanic quarrying and metate manufac-ture in the Teitipac area are a series of crude stone implements discovered by a _metatero_ from San Juan in 1962 (Cook 1973b:1487). While clearing debris from his quarry one day, this individual uncovered a burial which contained the remains of seven human skeletons along with various clay urns and pots, a metate and mano, and four stone implements, three of which are hammerstones (weighing from one to five pounds each, and undoubtedly used for crushing and breaking) and one of which is a hand pick for chipping. All of these implements were grooved for the attachment of hafts, although no trace remained of the latter. The burial site (which I visited in 1966) was constructed from a combination of dirt, mortar, and stone flakes which, according to the metatero discoverer, appeared to have been debitage of metate manufacture. In the absence of systematic archaeological investigation in the Teitipac area and in the quarries, in particular, the significance of the above find remains merely suggestive.

The technology of quarrying and metate manufacture in Teitipac was transformed by the Spanish during the Colonial period: wooden and stone tools were replaced by more efficient and durable steel tools, and blasting powder came to supplement human labor power as a basic energy source in quarrying. However, these changes did not occur immediately, and the process has been both discontinuous and selective in nature. The earliest opportunities for innovation occurred in the sixteenth and seventeenth centuries when the Teitipacanos worked in the gold and silver mines operated by the Spanish in the nearby communities of Magdalena and Santa Catarina. Burgoa, the Spanish chronicler, wrote of their experience in the Santa Catarina mines: "They were lowered down into dark and gloomy pits, by torch-light, with heavy crowbars (barretas), wedges (cuñas), mauls (masos) in their hands" (1934:220). The tool combination of crowbar and maul was, again according to oral tradition, the basis of metatero technology until early in the present century when the steel sledge hammer replaced the wooden maul and, somewhat later, when tempered steel tools replaced heavier and less efficient iron tools.

Although blasting powder, steel wedges, and the steel sledge hammer were available earlier, it was apparently not until early in this century that their use became widespread among the metateros in the Teitipac villages, probably as a direct result of contact between them and masons and stonecutters from Ixcotel, Oaxaca City and elsewhere. It should also be noted that the importance of mining activity to the metate industry is inferable from other evidence as well. Even today the quarries from which the stone for metates is extracted are called minas (mines) and not canteras (quarries); the latter word is present in the metatero vocabulary but is used mostly to designate a quarry where stone is extracted exclusively for construction purposes. Finally, metateros are sometimes referred to as mineros (miners) but almost never as canteros (quarrymen).

183

There was still another colonial experience, aside from mining, which introduced the Teitipacanos to Spanish stoneworking technology, namely, church and monastery construction organized and directed by the Dominican friars beginning in the latter half of the sixteenth century (Del Paso y Troncoso 1905:109; Burgoa 1934:95; Arroyo 1961). The ambitious Dominican construction program in the San Juan Teitipac must have resulted in the opening of new quarries and the expansion of already existing ones with obvious implications for the native labor force and technology.

Some of the changes in tool technology which have occurred in this century and their impact on quarry work organization and productivity are indicated in the following statement by one of the oldest living metateros:

> In the old days we had to work with at least three partners in each quarry; alone one could not handle the work. Now, since we're part of another civilization, the metateros buy long steel pinchbars (pulseta) and they work alone. In the old days, we didn't even have knowledge of such tools. We didn't have the steel sledge hammer but only wooden mauls (masos de madera). Then one day my father told me: "Now they have steel hammers." So we bought one. Before that we used to suffer a lot! That maul weighed several kilos. Sometimes the maul would split apart and pieces would fly off and hit us. But with the steel hammer nothing like that happens. Now things are different; now they are advanced. In a little while they can now cut 4 or 5 blocks of stone for metates--because they use the steel sledge and steel wedges (cuñas). In the old days we didn't have wedges. They must have existed but none of us knew about them. We split stone with brute force, with blows of 5 kilo crowbars (barretas). And now, with the sledge and the wedges, a large block of stone can be split in five or six minutes. In the old days it took us a whole day or, at least, a half-day, to make only one cut. There were times when a whole day was spent working and no stone was cut. Tomorrow they would say! Those were the

terrible days! What did we earn? But, today,
cutting lots of stone--there's money.

The Instruments of Labor in Quarrying and Metate Manufacture.

The complete metatero tool kit
today includes several implements. First a series of
three steel bars varying in length, diameter, weight,
point type, and use. These tools are, in order of
decreasing length and weight, as follows: (1) pulseta
(pinchbar)--5-6 ft. long, 12-15 lbs. in weight, about
2 inches in diameter, with a special half-moon shaped,
wedge-like tip suited for boring deep holes in a rock
bed (to insert powder for blasting purposes); (2)
barreta (crowbar)--usually about 4-4 1/2 ft. long and
1-1 1/2 inches in diameter, weighing between 8-10 lbs.,
and with a sharp, spearlike tip for flaking stone
(basic tool for cutting a metate or mano out of a stone
block); (3) barreno (short pinch bar)--shorter than the
barreta with a pulseta-like tip for boring into stone
and a blunted end (striking platform) to receive hammer
blows (used with sledge hammer to bore holes in bedrock).

Other steel implements used by the metateros
are the pico or hand pick which is 8-10 inches long,
1 1/2-2 inches in diameter, weighs about two pounds
and has a tapered, pointed tip on one end and a wedged
tip on the other, and is designed for stone chipping
(the basic metate and mano finishing tool); cuñas or
wedges, from three to six inches in length, with one
wedge-shaped end for splitting and the other round and
blunt to serve as striking platform (used to split large
stone slabs or blocks of stone when struck with sledge-
hammer); sinceles or chisels which are longer and thin-
ner than wedges (though they may approach the size of
picos) and used, along with a small hammer, to flake
and cut stone in place of the barreta or to cut designs
on a finished metate; the long-handled, 4-5 lb. sledge
hammer and the short-handled, 2 lb. hammer (marro)
the long-handled spade shovel(pala); the cucharilla--
a 3 1/2-4 ft. long steel rod, about 1/2 inch in diameter,
with a spoon-like scoop on one end (used to scoop
stone dust and debris out a hole being bored into a
rock bed for blasting purposes); and the lima or file
used for filing points on the various cutting tools.

A tool inventory for metateros from three villages shows that the two indispensable tools are the
barreta (crowbar) and the pico (hand pick). The

sincél (chisel) is found exclusively in San Juan Teitipac where the hammer and chisel technique is a popular
alternative to the use of the barreta for basic cutting
and flaking operations. In San Sebastian and Magdalena
the latter technique is used exclusively. The limited
distribution of pulsetas among San Sebastianos and Magdalenans and their absence among the San Juaneros reflects the presence of the "loner" (i.e., a metatero
who, by preference, works mostly unassisted) pattern of
work organization in San Sebastian and Magdalena and
its absence in San Juan. The pulseta, a long and heavy
boring tool, enables one individual to bore a deep hole
in bedrock unassisted; this task is usually performed
by a two-man team using a heavy sledge and a barreno.
The relatively high cost of the pulseta combined with
the extra strength, skill, and endurance required of
the worker who uses it are factors limiting its distribution and use.

The estimated costs (according to estimates provided by the metateros in 1967) of the tools inventoried
ranged from a low of 16 pesos ($1.25 U.S.--case no. 4)
to a high of 238 pesos ($19 U.S.--case no. 26); the
average total estimated cost for all cases was 87.50
($7.20 U.S.). Among a sub-sample of eight Magdalena
metateros from whom I elicited information on tools and
technology, I found that seven had specific plans to
acquire additional tools; they knew what the approximate price of these tools was and intended to allocate
earnings from metate sales into the purchase of these
(e.g., "I'm going to get that money here from my metate
work" or "I'm going to pull it [money] out of the
stone"). ("Ese dinero lo voy a consequir aquí del
trabajo del metate" or "Lo voy a sacar de la piedra").
These planned acquisitions would either relieve the
metatero in question from the necessity of borrowing or
renting a particular tool and/or would increase his
productivity (e.g., pulseta or barreno and marro,
chisels for carving special decorations). Only one of
these metateros aspired to own a modern, presumably
innovative tool--in this case a motor-driven stonecutting saw.

In addition to the cost of the tools themselves,
there is a constant outlay for maintenance--mainly for
sharpening and tempering points on the barreta and pico
(which must be done at least twice weekly under conditions of normal use). Metatero estimates for this
expense range from 3-15 pesos weekly with 6 pesos as
the average.

The purchase of blasting powder and fuse is another necessary and regular expenditure in metate production. During 1967-68 powder ranged in price from 4.50 to 7.50 pesos a kilogram, and fuse cost from 1.00 to 1.50 pesos per meter depending upon the place of purchase (lower prices prevail in Oaxaca City). Considering that one kilogram of powder is sufficient for three or four separate blasts, the approximate annual consumption of these materials is roughly five kilograms of powder and five meters of fuse per metatero.

It should be noted that these production costs may not be paid by every active metatero. For example, in San Sebastian where the work company (companía) arrangement is common, the quarry boss (maestro-como dueño) often pays for powder and fuse; or the expense is shared among the various members of the work company. Also, it is not unusual for apprentices to agree to pay for powder and fuse in return for learning quarrying techniques from a more experienced metatero (one such arrangement in Magdalena involves two brothers).

Stones and the Quarries: Resources and Raw Materials. It is axiomatic that the natural environment of any society provides opportunities and establishes limits with regard to the labor process. In other words, through the availability or unavailability of natural resources (e.g., exploitable plants and animals; utilizable minerals and potable water; climate, water supply, soil, biota as they influence the growth of utilizable plants) certain kinds of production are facilitated or precluded (cf. Wagner 1960:61). However, these environmental requirements, limits, and opportunities are not mutually independent, nor are they absolute. It is obvious, for example, that the availability of suitable stone deposits--in the absence of a water supply or cultivable soil--would not suffice to attract and support a population of stoneworkers. While metates clearly could not be manufactured in Oaxaca communities if suitable stone were not available for quarrying, the availability of stone does not assure that it will be quarried, much less that metates will be manufactured from it.

The 'Central Valleys' region encompasses zones with abundant igniumbrites and the stone which is quarried by the metateros appears to be granitic in composition (not basaltic) though some of the quarries appear to yield a metamorphosed granite (i.e., a

granite-gneiss). The metatero's taxonomy of stone,
like that of land in general, is organized by a combination of criteria. At the broadest level, stone is
categorized into two classes: useful stone (piedra que
sirve) and useless stone (piedra que no sirve). The
latter type occurs in the form of loose surface debris
(ranging in size from small rocks to huge boulders)
and outcroppings on flat and hilly terrain throughout
a village's territory. Stone which is useful in metate
production occurs in the form of sub-surface beds and
is found predominantly in hilly or mountainous terrain.

In classifying stone the metateros are most concerned with hardness or workability, texture, and color
(which determine saleability and durability in use of
metates and manos). Color is the trait most often employed by metateros in describing stone, and other
traits tend to be subsumed under it. Blue-green (verde-
azul) and brownish (cafe) types of stone are considered
to be "first class" (primera clase) because the metates
made from them tend to maintain a better grinding surface longer than those made from stone of other colors.
However, first class stone, while preferred by the
consumer, is relatively hard to locate and is difficult
to quarry and cut (because of its hardness and brittle-
ness); therefore, metates made from it sell at premium
prices.[2]

Metates are usually made from "second class"
stone (de segunda clase) which resembles first class
stone in color (it's called verde or green and morado
or purplish) and texture but is more workable--yielding
more readily to the metateros' barreta blows. The
'second classness' of this type of stone derives from
the fact that metates made from it are said by the
metateros to be less durable than those made from the
harder first class stone. But since the metatero is
more directly concerned with workability than with
durability, this class of stone is preferred by him
(and is also more abundant and more easily quarried).
White (blanca) and whitish (blanquisca) stone is considered to be "third class" (tercera clase) because
metates made from it sell poorly; buyers generally
dislike the color and consider metates made from this
stone to be of low durability. The metateros, who
operate on the principle of caveat emptor, manufacture
and sell metates of second class stone under the pre-
tense that they are of first class stone. That they
succeed in this deception reflects, aside from the natural monopolistic aspects of their market position,
the fact that buyers are unaware of the difference and

that the metates sold are reasonably durable. It should also be pointed out that the <u>metateros</u> are aware of the advantages to them of selling metates made from more workable (but less durable) stone; demand is maintained by making and selling metates which will wear out and have to be replaced periodically (this is especially true since metates are used less intensively now than they were prior to the introduction of alternative grinding facilities, namely, the <u>molino de nixtamal</u>).

The terms <u>cinta</u> (ribbon) and <u>ventiada</u> (joint) or <u>realíz</u> (fissure) refer to visible structural or compositional flaws in quarry stone. An important task of every quarry boss is to discover and evaluate the significance of such flaws in exposed bedrock and to adapt quarrying strategy accordingly. More specifically, a <u>cinta</u> is a ribbon or vein of quartz which is visible on the surface of bedrock or a block of stone but usually penetrates deeply; it is of harder composition than the stone into which it is intruded [in much the same way that a knot is harder than the wood into which it is embedded] and, for this reason, makes cutting difficult. The <u>ventiada</u> or <u>realíz</u> (joint or fissure), on the other hand, is a structural flaw which, rather than presenting an obstacle to the quarryman, presents a line of least resistance along which bedrock or stone is most easily split or factured. Whereas the <u>cinta</u> is a vein of hard intrusive material, the <u>ventiada</u> is a deposit of sedimentary material in a fissure which structurally weakens the mass of solid stone surrounding it. Thus, a block of stone (<u>trozo</u>) with a visible <u>ventiada</u> is rejected by the <u>metatero</u> since he knows that it will not withstand the strain of the metate manufacturing process. The type of stone which the <u>metatero</u> seeks as a result of his quarrying efforts is "<u>piedra limpia</u>" (clean stone) or flawless stone (i.e., with no <u>cintas</u> or <u>ventiadas</u>); stone which is rejected is called <u>piedra podrida</u> (rotten stone) or <u>piedra defectuosa</u> (defective stone) which either has visible structural flaws or is crumbly (<u>solo se desvorona</u>).[3]

Another series of terms in the metatero vocabulary refers to the shape and structure of stone in a quarry. A large bed or bank of native stone within a quarry is referred to as a <u>paderón</u> or <u>banco</u>. Separate native slabs of stone within each bed are called <u>vetas</u> or <u>tiras</u>. The basic quarrying strategy is to plant charges of blasting powder in such a manner that entire slabs will be loosened from their beds. The key to a successful blast lies in planting the charge so that the force it generates when exploding will fracture the bedrock along its joints. A large slab of stone which is blasted loose from a bed is called a plancha, and each metate-size block which is cut from a plancha is called a trozo.

The relevance of jointing to quarrying has been emphasized by two geological writers as follows:

> Joints are of considerable importance to mankind. The quarryman both loses and gains by the presence of these natural rock fractures. If the joints are too close together he cannot quarry dimension the stone; if they are too far apart his blasting costs may be excessive (Landes and Hussey 1948:293).

Jointing patterns (ventiado o realíz de la piedra) in a bed of stone must be studied and evaluated by the master stone cutter (maestro de la piedra) before decisions are made about how to prepare a blast. The success of a blasting operation depends upon the accuracy of this preliminary diagnosis of jointing patterns. An incorrect diagnosis means that a given blast will probably yield little more than worthless fragments of stone. Hours and sometimes days of work may be wasted as a result of this. Not even the most experienced and knowledgeable stonecutters are infallible in their judgments and blasting strategies, as is evidenced by the occasional wagers that are made on the outcome of a blast.

The Labor Process

Phases in the Extraction and Transformation of the Raw Material. There are two basic phases in the labor process of metate production: the quarrying phase in which operations revolve around the extraction of stone from the quarry (i.e., the transformation of stone as a resource into a raw material); and the post-quarrying phase of the manufacture of metates (and manos) (i.e., the transformation of the raw material into finished products). In the idiom of the metateros the quarrying phase is referred to as la sacada; the post-quarrying phase is divided into two sub-phases called la echura and la labrada (see below, Table 13).

190

The tasks of the quarrying phase are the most labor-time consuming, as well as the riskiest, of the entire production process. Contingent upon such factors as the condition of the quarry (e.g., position of the beds, amount of debris), the number of workers, and the skill of the quarry master (not to mention luck), this phase may last from one to several days before yielding a sufficient quantity and quality of stone.

The strategy and tactics of quarrying, as well as the organization of work and patterns of worker interaction, depend significantly upon the physical layout of the quarry. A bed of native rock is usually inclined or tilted (if its angle is measured from the horizontal plane of the quarry floor), and in their quarrying operations the metateros must follow a course dictated by the natural position of the rock bed they are exploiting. The physical structure of the quarry is altered accordingly. "When one first begins to work a new quarry area," explained one metatero, "the place is flat. If with time a good bed of stone is uncovered it must be followed wherever it leads. For that reason a quarry becomes deep." In deep quarries (where the distance from the floor to the ground surface ranges anywhere from 25 to 50 feet), the metateros sometimes find it necessary to dangle from ropes suspended from the top of the quarry walls or to support themselves on crude scaffolding in order to work a promising bed of stone.

The first step in the quarrying phase is the "descombro" (descombrar = to disencumber, clear away obstacles). This is hard, tedious, unimaginative work requiring more exertion than skill. It involves the use of shovels to clear away dirt and stone debris, baskets to haul the waste material out of the quarry, and crowbars, sledge hammers, and wedges to break up and move larger pieces of waste stone. Machetes are also used during these operations to cut down bushes or trees which will encumber planned quarrying activity. The actions involved in this process include prying, striking, cutting, picking, chopping, crushing, splitting, shoveling, scooping, lifting, pushing, hauling, and dumping; human labor is the only source of power. Typically, these tasks are performed by two or more workers; their aim is to expose an underlying bed of native stone so that it can be blasted loose. Tasks are assigned to allow the most experienced quarry workers to focus their efforts on locating and exposing the bed; less experienced workers haul away debris.

191

The second step in the quarrying phase consists
of a series of tasks referred to collectively as "co-
hetear" or blasting. This process begins only after
the bedrock has been exposed and is done with the
barreta, the pulseta, or a barreno and long-handled
sledge hammer. The objective of these tasks (cutting,
boring, hammering) is to bore a hole into the exposed
bedrock for planting a powder charge. The most experienced workers perform these tasks, an important preliminary to which is the "sizing up" (tanteo) of the exposed bedrock to decide where the hole should be bored
to assure optimum results from the blast. This "sizing
up" process sometimes evokes lively discussions among
the metateros concerning the structure and composition
of the exposed bed of stone (i.e., where its joints
are, the depth and course of the ventiadas and cintas,
and the angles of its component slabs). When a decision
is reached, a few downward cutting strokes with a
barreta are required to start the hole, then a barreno
is inserted and is rotated slowly by one worker while
his partner hammers it with a sledge. This task is
called "barrenar" and, depending upon the estimated
depth and structure of the bed of stone, the hole will
be sunk to a depth of sixty to seventy centimeters.
At five minute intervals the hammering is halted to
enable one of the workers to scoop debris out of the
hole with a cucharilla; after each sequence the working
partners usually exchange tasks. Two men can complete
this task in two hours or less, depending upon the
hardness of the stone, etc. This task can also be
performed by one worker with a pulseta in approximately
the same time.

After the hole is bored it is packed with a mixture of blasting powder and damp earth. This task is
performed by one worker who inserts the mixture into
the hole with a cucharilla, until about twenty centimeters have been filled. The mixture is packed down
with a wooden ramrod (atacador). Next a layer of paper
wadding is stuffed into the hole and a length of fuse
is inserted. Finally a layer of damp earth is packed
into the hole on top of the wadding and around the fuse
to complete the process. The fuse is ready to be lit
about twenty minutes after the process begins.

If the blast is successful in dislodging usable
slabs (planchas) of stone, the next step in the quarrying process is cutting them into metate-size blocks
(trozar la piedra). If not, then these same tasks must
be performed again in the same sequence. As with the
previous two steps, this one is performed by the most

experienced stonecutters since it involves a crucial "sizing up" (tanteo) of the results of the blast. All of the maestro's knowledge of the composition and structure of stone is required here to assure that as many trozos (metate-size blocks) as possible are extracted from the parent slab. The jointing and flaw structure (patterns and channels of ventiadas and cintas) of the latter must be diagnosed correctly to achieve optimum results. The tools utilized in this process are the barreta, the sledge hammer, and several wedges. The principal actions performed are measuring (hand lengths), flaking, cutting, holing, inserting the wedges into the holes, and hammering the wedges until the stone fractures. A single worker (or two workers in alternation) performs all of these operations.

When asked to explain this "sizing up" and measuring process the metatero will reply, "I'm sizing up the stone to figure out where the cuts can be made," or "I'm looking for the joints to see if it will split so that the wedges can be struck in." Lines are traced on the slab (using a green leaf) to indicate where cuts will be made. Even before a blow is struck to split-off a trozo from its parent slab, the metatero has visualized the trozo-to-be as a metate. Thus, during his appraisal of a freshly extracted stone slab the metatero makes judgments such as, "It has no third leg so it won't be good for a metate" or "It's hard to tell how many metates this trozo will yield since it has several flaws." The estimate of the anticipated trozo yield of a given parent slab of stone also becomes on occasion an object of friendly wager among the involved metateros.

The termination of the "sizing up" of the results of a blast is signaled by a statement like the following: "The lines to tell us where to cut are drawn and measured; now we'll slice it up to measure." The "slicing-up" process involves preliminary boring with the barreta; then wedges are inserted into the holes and are hammered with a sledge until the slab is split-up into several trozos. Normally, not more than an hour elapses between the time the post-blast appraisal begins and the splitting of the parent slab into trozos. The average trozo is rectangular in shape, weighs around 100 pounds, and measures a minimum of 20 x 15 x 20 inches.

After this task has been completed, the trozos are moved out of the quarry proper to a work patio adjacent to the quarry. Barretas are employed as levers

(palancas) to move trozos up steep inclines; on level
ground trozos are pushed end over end out of the quarry
and into the patio area. Before trozos are brought to
the patio the metatero 'shapes' them by knocking off
protrusions with a sledge hammer. The purpose of
"shaping" (arreglar) or "squaring up" (cuadrar) a trozo
is to assure that it is free of hidden structural
flaws, to lighten it for easier manipulation, and to
ready it for the metate manufacturing process proper.
Once the trozo is moved into the work patio, the quarrying phase of the labor process ends and the post-
quarrying phase begins.

The first step in the post-quarrying process of
transforming a trozo into a metate is the destronco
(Sp. destroncar = detruncate). This task is described
by a metatero as follows: "Now I'm going to begin to
detruncate, to make the trozo look more like a metate.
I already know where the tail and legs of the metate
will be and now I'm going to measure the length of its
face." Using green leaves yanked from a nearby bush
or tree, the metatero traces out the shape of a metate
on his trozo and then proceeds to lop off slices of
stone from it. With a series of forceful, continuous
downward strokes of the barreta (from fifty to ninety
strokes per minute)--striking the trozo at approximately
a forty-five degree angle, a metatero can complete this
task in less than thirty minutes. A detruncated trozo
is shaped like a truncated pyramid with a rectangular
base. The 'base' actually becomes the grinding surface ("face") of the metate, and the truncated top
portion of the trozo is transformed by the metatero's
cutting strokes into the three-legged base of the metate. At this stage in the manufacturing process the
metatero has a clear mental image of the metate he is
fashioning but the trozo is not yet called a metate.

The second stage in the transformation of a
trozo into a metate is the "emptying" (vaciar) operation during which the three legs and the sides ("lados"
in Sp.; kweyeh in Zapotec) of the metate are cut out.
This is a crucial task in the manufacturing process
since it requires precise yet forceful cutting strokes;
one misplaced blow of the barreta can ruin the trozo.
As he works the metatero traces out the pattern of his
cuts on the surface of the trozo and, as it slowly but
surely begins to assume the form of a metate, the metatero will say something like, "Now you can see that the
stone is no longer a trozo but a metate," to indicate
that the crucial transformation from trozo to metate
has been made. This typically takes from thirty to

thirty-five minutes. On the completion of this task one _metatero_ described his product as follows: "I have now finished emptying the _trozo_. Now that it's emptied out it can be called a metate. It lacks refining but, at any rate, it's a metate because its legs have been formed out of the stone."

The "refining" (_refinar_) task involves thinning out the body and legs of the _metate vaciado_ (emptied-out metate) through steady, firm flaking action with a _barreta_. The flaking strokes are restrained to avoid shearing off too much stone. When this task is completed, the metate is said to be "_barreteado_" (worked with a _barreta_) and is then hauled from the quarry usually by _burro_) to the village residence lot of its owner where it will undergo the final finishing operation ("_la labrada_"). Anywhere from three to five man-hours of work have been expended from the time the first _barreta_ blow was struck against the _trozo_ and its transformation into a metate _barreteado_. Among other factors, the differences in labor-time expended during this operation reflect differences in _metatero_ strength and skill, work tempo, and hardness and size of the _trozo_ being worked. Those _metateros_ using the _barreta_ technique (all but a few San Juaneros who use the hammer and chisel technique) work from a standing position during all the pre-finishing stages of manu-facture. So the work demands considerable arm and shoulder strength as well as skill and patience.

During the finishing process the worker's only tool is the hand pick (_pico_) which is used to chip away steadily at the surface of the metate until it is smooth (_liso_), the operation requiring from four to six hours for a regular size metate (about two hours per mano). Finishing and decorating (painting) are the only steps in the metate manufacturing process in which women and children sometimes participate.

There are two ways in which a metate can be decorated: by painting or by sculpture in low relief (_calar_ or _bordar_). Painting is the most common form of decoration for a variety of reasons. It requires less time and skill than the sculpture technique; it has wide consumer appeal; and it serves to camouflage re-paired breaks or other defects in a metate. Until twenty or so years ago, prior to the ready availability of low-priced paint, metates were either sold undecora-ted or were decorated by chiseling--a painstaking pro-cess requiring considerable patience and skill. Undec-orated metates are still sold in significant quantites and there is still some demand for chisel-designed metates on a special order (encargo) basis; but most metates sold today are decorated by painting. Decoration by chiseling requires a minimum of two days (16 man-hours) of work, a special set of chisels and hammers, and is done at the village residence lot of the metatero; decoration by painting requires about one hour of work, no special tools, and is often done in the marketplace sales area.

Labor-Time: The Social Average

Table 13 summarizes the stages in the "labor process" (Marx 1967, I:177-185) of metate production, and tabulates the socially average amount of work required to produce a standard metate. The numerical figures shown are derived from actual observations of a cooperative quarry operation in 1967 in San Sebastian Teitipac; they are in substantial agreement with computations in this and other communities. I should emphasize that these figures do not represent actual averages computed on the basis of an extensive scientific sample of separate production occasions; my opinion is, however, that they would not diverge significantly from such computations if these were available.

Given the availability of utilizable stone in a quarry (i.e., in the raw material state as a result of prior quarrying activity), it is quite possible for the most proficient metateros to manufacture two semi-finished metates in an 8-hour period and, in an additional 4-6 hours each, to finish these metates. However, there is variation among metateros in the number of man-hours required to complete the manufacturing process which reflects, among other things, differences among them in age, strength, skill, and work habits, as well as differences in the stone itself. On more than one occasion in the quarries, I observed a metatero complete two semi-finished metates in the same time required for others to complete only one (size, hardness of stone, etc. essentially equal). I have timed the manufacturing of standard-sized metates in 3-1/2 hours which, I believe, is approaching the minimum possible manufacturing time. This is supported by the fact that my observational data indicate that, on the average, 4-1/2 to 5 man-hours of work are required to manufacture a semi-finished metate from raw stone; they also show that, on the average, an addi-

TABLE 13. Labor Process in Metate Production*

| | Quarrying Stage--Production of the Raw Material | | | | Manufacture of the Metate | |
| | "LA SACADA" | | "LA ECHURA" (semi-finishing) | | "LA LABRADA" (finishing) | |
	1. "Descombrar"	2. "Cohetear"	3. "Echar corte"	4. "Barretear"	5. "Labrar"	6. "Pintar"
Nature & Order of Operations	shovelling, cutting, hauling debris; cutting brush, trees; purpose to expose 'bed' of stone	pre-blast survey; boring hold for powder; prepare blast; post-blast survey and stone selection	cut and split selected slab of stone into metate-size blocks (trozo)	cut semi-finished metate from trozo with crowbar	chipping metate surface with pico to smooth it out	decorate sides of metate with painted floral designs
Tools Required	shovel (pala) crowbar (barreta) sledge (marro) wedges (cunas) machete baskets	barreno, powder cucharilla, fuse barreta, atacador pulseta (pinch bar) marro (sledge)	barreta marro cunas	barreta marro	pico (hand pick or chisel)	enamel
Stages in Material Transformation	Native stone in natural beds (bancos)		plancha (slab) to trozo (block)	trozo to metate barreteado (semi-finished)	metate labrado (finished)	metate pintado (painted)
Work Organization	cooperative male (4)	cooperative male (3)	cooperative male (2)	individual male	individual male, female or child	individual male, female
Duration of Operation	1-1/2 hours	4 hours	3/4 hour	4 hours	6 hours	1 hour
Amount of Social Work per Metate in Hours of Individual Labor-Time	4 x 1-1/2 = 6 6 ÷ 4 = 1-1/2	3 x 4 = 12 12 ÷ 3 = 4	2 x 3/4 = 1-1/2 1-1/2 ÷ 2 = 3/4	1 x 4 = 4	1 x 6 = 6	1 x 1 = 1

SOCIALLY AVERAGE AMOUNT OF WORK FOR ONE STANDARD METATE

= 1-1/2 + 4 + 3/4 + 4 + 6 + 1 = 17-1/4 hours

*See Cook 1973 and Chapter V for a more detailed description of metate technology and manufacturing procedures. Table adapted from Godelier 1971:57.

197

tional 4-6 hours are required to finish the standard-sized metate (more for large metates, less for small ones).

Since metates are customarily sold with companion manos (mullers), which require a maximum of 25-30 minutes to semi-finish and an additional 1 1/2 to 2 hours to finish, a minimum of two work-hours must be added to the social necessary labor cost of the standard metate (with mano) to arrive at an approximate labor equivalent of the market price. Finally, given typical quarry conditions it is reasonable to estimate that a minimum of 1/2 man-days of quarrying work (4-6 man-hours) is required for every metate manufactured (e.g., clearing away debitage, preparing for blast, blasting, extracting stone after blast). It is the socially average amount of labor expended during this pre-manufacturing or quarrying phase of production which is subject to the greatest variability in the short-run, and which is the major stumbling block to making an accurate long-run (i.e., one year or longer) estimate.

On a subjective basis the metateros approach consensus in estimating their work time in producing a finished metate (regular size, etc.) as, on the average, three days, proportioned among tasks as follows: one day for quarrying ("la sacada"), one day for manufac-turing the semi-finished metate ("la echura"), and one day for finishing the metate ("la labrada"). They do not specify voluntarily the hour-equivalents for their work but will attempt to estimate these when pressed to do so; this is complicated by the fact that they do not use watches or clocks and, as a general rule, estimate time during the day by the position of the sun. The metateros know that if quarry conditions are favorable or if they are successful with a blast on any given day, they can produce a finished metate in ten or twelve working hours--but this is not a predictable situation.

In short, given a combination of subjective and objective estimates, we can reasonably assume that the 'social average' for labor-time required to produce a standard metate lies between an absolute minimum of ten (10) hours and a maximum of 24 hours (3 work days), and that the 17 1/4 hour estimate arrived at in Table 13 is an acceptable approximation of the actual social average.

Aesthetics vs. Economics in Metate Manufacture.
The decorative phase in metate manufacture raises the
issue of the role of aesthetics and pride of craftsmanship in the manufacturing process. During this
process the metatero is often confronted with the
conflicting demands of economy and artistry, that is,
whether to economize his productive efforts (e.g., by
using softer, less durable and/or off-colored stone)
or to satisfy certain aesthetic criteria or standards
of quality in his product. These demands have practical as well as aesthetic aspects; practical to the
extent that they require efficiency in the allocation
of labor-time and effort, and aesthetic to the extent
that they are concerned with the ultimate form or
style yielded by the metateros' techniques for over-
coming the inherent tendency of stone to resist their
efforts to transform it. These two demands are not
irreconcilable but the metateros tend to view them as
contradictory. As one of them put it: "A metate
made rapidly is not well-made; one which is made
slowly and with care will be well-made. It's better
to work slowly at a metate, to take a whole day to
finish it, so that it will turn out fine."

The metatero works stone by his eye and by the
feel of his tools. His success in cutting stone is,
for him, a matter of pura vista (pure sight); and he
expresses his preference for soft over hard stone in
terms of the pulso (pulse) of his barreta--the feed-
back to his muscles from the impact of the tool upon
the stone. For the metatero workmanship involves more
than the pace of individual work; it involves qualities
of intuition and judgment as well.

This artistic concern with work technique among
the metateros is paralleled by their aesthetic concern with standards of quality in their products.
Stylization and uniformity in the manufacture and form
of Oaxaca Valley metates do not preclude variation.
Just as an outsider can readily learn to distinguish
between Oaxaca Valley metates and those produced
elsewhere (e.g., Sierra de Puebla or Chiapas highlands
in Mexico, or Maya-Quiche area in highland Guatemala),
or between, for example, a Magdalena metate and a San
Sebastian metate, so the insider (the metatero and
the regatón) can distinguish between a metate made
by villager X and one made by villager Y. The distinguishing criteria become more subtle (and less
relevant) as one moves from the inter-regional to the

inter-village to the intra-village level, but they are no less real.

The criteria by which workmanship is judged among the metateros themselves are evident in the following description by one metatero of the attributes of a "well-made" metate:

Its sides and edges must be cut smooth and straight. The metate must stand up properly (bien parado). Some metates are crooked from the face downwards and they need to be reworked to give them form and grace (gracia). The metate is like a woman: those that are best dressed look prettier. Sometimes a metate is well balanced but its arc is crooked. The metatero must have an understanding of what he's doing to turn out a "well-made" metate. If he doesn't have this understanding of what he's doing, he can make metates but make them badly. This occupation is an art because not everyone can work in it.

In essence, certain subtleties in line and shape, which are so crucial in the metateros' judgments of their own products, are idiosyncratic elements which lend metate production its artistic quality.[4]

Aspects of the Planning and Allocation of Labor Time. Over the annual cycle the metateros must plan and allocate labor time (and other resources) between two major brances of production: agriculture and stoneworking. To a significant extent the general logistics of this planning and allocation process are necessary responses to seasonal changes; the wet vs. dry season bifurcation provides a framework within which work schedules are established. While there are elements of risk and uncertainty in both of these branches of production, which may have an impact on productivity, the overall dynamic of work planning and labor-time allocation is a creature of the seasonal program of the regional economy and of the production structure which is keyed to it. The metateros do have some room for maneuver within the framework of this seasonal program and production structure (e.g., temporary wage-labor) but short-term fluctuations and irregularities in work and income patterns conform over the annual cycle (and from one year to another) to the

200

constraints of this program.

How, specifically, is the labor-time of a _metatero_
allocated over the annual cycle? The tentative results
of my analysis of a work diary kept for me by a
Magdalenan between October 1, 1967, and October 31,
1968, present us with the following picture. Of a
total of 397 days during this calendar period, there
were 340 weekdays (i.e., 57 Sundays were excluded
since they are generally defined as "days of rest").
Considering that twelve of these were secular or
religious holidays, we arrive at a total of 328 potential work days during this calendar period. This
informant worked on some aspect of metate production
on 206 days (62% of 382) for an average of 7.8 man-
hours daily--but ranging from a maximum of 15-1/2
hours to a minimum of 1 hour daily over this period.
In addition, he engaged in some type of agricultural
work on 80 days (24% of 328) at an average of 6-1/2
man-hours daily; and he engaged in marketing on 58
days, travel on 17 days, ritual-ceremonial activities
on 11-1/2 days, and in meeting civic obligations on
8 days. Finally, the diary shows that this individual
was incapacitated by illness for a total of 11 of the
328 days.

Of the total of 1358-1/2 work hours this individual devoted to metate production during this
period, 847 man-hours (62%) were spent in quarrying
activity and the remainder in post-quarrying activities.
The least proportion of work time spent in quarrying
during any single month was 57% and the most was 77%;
this supports my earlier statement that quarrying is
the most time-consuming and least predictable aspect
of metate production.

The month when the greatest number of work-hours
was allocated by this individual to metate production
was May 1968, which culminated a trend beginning in
December 1967, and, also, initiates the rainy-season
decline which bottoms out in September. While May
is somewhat below the monthly agricultural work average
for this informant of 42 hours (36.5 hours in May),
it is a month of relatively high expenditures in
agriculture (seed and equipment for planting). Thus
his high labor commitment to metate production during
May reflects this urgent cash need. August and September, on the other hand, are months during which this
(and other) _metatero's_ labor commitment to metate production is relatively low but when his (and others')
commitment to agriculture is greatest (84 and 74 hours

respectively committed in these months because of the harvest). In other words, over the annual cycle the labor commitment to metate production and agriculture tend to be inversely related.

Given the constraints of the seasonal program and its related regional structure of production, uncertainty and risk are important in the strategy and tactics of metate production. As one perceptive _metatero_ expressed it: "When good luck comes you win a little; when bad luck comes you lose a little; this occupation is just like a game." So, to some extent, the _metatero_ is a gambler; he must take risks to minimize the impact of uncertainty upon his production activities. He can't eliminate uncertainty from his production activities. He can't remove the uncertainty factor from his milieu but he can exercise some control over it by calculated risk-taking. A case from the Mesa Grande quarry area in San Sebastian will suffice to illustrate this:

> L. spent all day blasting and clearing debris in his quarry along with his brother-in-law, R., his brother Bartolo, and others. After an afternoon blast, a survey of its results indicated that there would be enough _trozos_ for each member of the 'company'--if the parent slabs were cut properly. The 'boss' of a contiguous quarry was called over for consultations about cutting operations. He and the others agreed with L.'s judgment: "It can't be said exactly how many _trozos_ this stone will yield because it has many flaws." The cuts were made and each member of the company got a _trozo_; everyone left the quarry.

> Upon arriving in the quarry the following morning L. moved his _trozo_ into the patio and, after examining it closely, said: "I don't think it will hold up because it has a flaw (_ventiada_) where the tail of the metate will be." But he proceeded to work on it with his _barreta_. "This _trozo_ is a gamble because of its flaws," he said, "but I'm going to take the gamble to see if it turns out o.k. If it doesn't I'll lose my work. But why should I toss it away? I'll take the

gamble." During his work on the trozo L.
paused periodically and said: "It's a gamble
I'm taking; it's not a sure thing," or "It's
nothing but a gamble because it's defective;
I'm taking a gamble but I can't lose hope."
During the entire "emptying out" process L.
handled the <u>barreta</u> carefully and without
his usual force because, as he explained,
"the flaw holds up in some places but
crumbles in others."

In this case, metate production simulates a game of
chance (<u>una rifa</u>). If L. had chosen not to take a
chance (<u>rifar</u>) on the defective <u>trozo</u> his only other
alternative was to start from scratch by preparing
another blast since no other <u>trozos</u> were available. By
altering his work tactics (e.g., easing up on the force
of his cutting strokes and aiming the <u>barreta</u> with
special care) he was able to minimize the risk of frac-
turing the <u>trozo</u> and losing his work. If the <u>trozo</u>
had failed to yield a metate (which it did not in this
case), L. would have lost only a few hours of work at
most. On the other hand, to have to prepare another
blast would not only have involved a loss of the labor
time expended to obtain the defective <u>trozo</u> but would
have increased the risks separating L. from the manufacture of a metate (i.e., each step in the production
process has its own set of risks which are not operative in subsequent steps).

Aside from the decisions of a specific work
situation, the <u>metateros</u> must plan the allocation of
their labor time for periods as long as 15 days. When
a particular deposit of stone has been exhausted in a
quarry, it is necessary to spend several days in clearing out debris to locate and expose a promising new
deposit. Under these circumstances the <u>metateros</u>, who
invariably seek to extract sufficient stone for manufacturing several metates, will plan a 15-day schedule
(which is a set of expectations rather than a rigid
program) as follows:

4 days--clearing debris from the quarry to
        expose suitable deposits

1 day --blasting (<u>cohetear</u>)

2 days--cutting trozos (<u>trozar</u>)

4 days--manufacturing metates and manos(<u>barretear</u>)

3 days--finishing (<u>labrar</u>)

1 day --marketing

There is considerable variation from this idealized
work schedule especially during the quarrying phase.

When questioned directly about their work plan,
<u>metateros</u> are inclined to respond in terms of a six-
day week (Monday through Saturday). But plans, even
for this relatively short period, are usually qualified
with a series of 'ifs.'

> Monday we will blast; if the blast is un-
> successful then we'll blast again on Tuesday.
> If the Tuesday blast is successful we'll
> make metates on Wednesday and Thursday. If,
> however, we get good stone from the Monday
> blast, we'll make metates on Tuesday and
> Wednesday; then on Thursday and Friday we
> can finish them to take to the Saturday
> <u>plaza</u>. If good stone happens to be avail-
> able on Monday we can make a metate then
> also.

Uncertainty, then, is inherent in metate production
and is a constant to which <u>metateros</u> must adapt.

In Magdalena the quarries drain poorly and,
during the rainy season, many of them are likely to fill
up with water and become unworkable. The way in which
one enterprising <u>metatero</u> copes with this situation
provides an illustration of long-range planning;

> Pedro works in a quarry which was previously
> worked by his father who died in 1961. After
> his father's death, the quarry was divided
> between Pedro and his older brother who
> died in 1966. P.'s brother's share of the
> quarry went to the latter's 15-year-old son
> who is not yet a <u>metatero</u>.
>
> P. worked with his father when the
> latter was alive on a product sharing (<u>a
> medias</u>) basis together with his older
> brother. They quarried the stone (their
> father did not work in the quarrying opera-
> tions) and divided the <u>trozos</u> into three

204

equal shares. <u>Trozos</u> were made into metates immediately; no inventory of <u>trozos</u> was built-up for future manufacture. This caused serious problems during the rainy season when the quarry filled with water. They adapted by seeking work arrangements with <u>metateros</u> in other quarries until the rains passed and their own quarry could be pumped out.

After the death of his older brother P. began planning his production differently. He decided to build up an inventory of trozos during the dry season for use during the rainy season when the quarry became unworkable. He planned his work in accordance with his judgment about precipitation patterns ("<u>segun como va pintando la lluvia</u>"). Each year he attempts to spend one month's work in accumulating a <u>trozo</u> inventory. In 1965, the first year of his new strategy, he accumulated an inventory of 30 <u>trozos</u>; in 1966, 22 <u>trozos</u>, and in 1967, 20 <u>trozos</u>. In the latter year the quarry was flooded from June through December (pumped dry in January). P.'s inventory lasted him until October; after that, and until January 1968, he worked on a share basis with another <u>metatero</u>.

When not under pressure to raise cash for an emergency, P. prefers to hold his <u>trozos</u> until the 'high price' dry season arrives. To avoid manufacturing and selling metates from his <u>trozo</u> reserve during the wet season (when metate prices are generally low), he sells crops and animals. In 1967 sales of castor beans (<u>higuerilla</u>) served this purpose; he also sold a few goats and sheep from a herd of 15.

It was noted above that my analysis of a work diary for a Magdalena <u>metatero</u> yielded an estimate of 7.8 hours spent working on some aspect of metate production on the average work day. However, the typical work day in the life of a <u>metatero</u> involves him in activities other than those directly related to his principal occupation. During his 16 waking hours (6 a.m. to 10 p.m.)--and subtracting about 2-1/2 hours for eating, rest, recreation and personal activities

205

(e.g., praying before the family altar, bathing, shaving)--he performs certain household chores (e.g., sweeping the residence lot, fetching water, feeding animals) and other miscellaneous tasks (e.g., conducting business in the municipal or ejidal office). In Magdalena, it is common for a metatero to keep an eye on his grazing animals while working in the quarry. In short, the daily life of the metateros is short of leisure or inactivity; and requires, in addition to planning and decision-making, considerable physical exertion.

The Social Relations of Metate Production

Bases of Work Relations. Metatero work organization is a function of material and ideological factors. In the absence of certain environmental conditions (e.g., scarcity of arable land, availability of deposits of utilizable stone) there could be no metate production in the region. Of course, the availability of stone in the natural habitat of the metate villages does not imply, ipso facto, that its utility is self-evident nor that its extraction is feasible. That its utility has been recognized and that it has become an object of the labor process are tributes to the ingenuity and physical effort of generations of Zapotec workmen.

From the environmental standpoint, the natural occurrence of igniumbrites in extensive beds near the ground surface facilitates systematic quarrying activity. Different quarry sub-types (variation being measured in terms of size and depth) and their spatial locations correlate with patterns of work organization and worker interaction. For example, in the Mesa Grande quarry area in San Sebastian, three quarries are relatively shallow--containing extensive beds of stone near the surface--and can be quarried by a single worker or by small groups of workers. Also, since these three quarries are located on higher terrain than other quarries in the area, their workers tend to interact more among themselves than with workers on the lower level. This situation reinforces the independent work habits of the upper level workers--all of whom, in fact, are 'loners' with regard to their work ideology and skills. One quarry is larger and deeper than other quarries in the area; its stone beds are tilted and relatively deep below the surface. Consequently, this quarry is worked by crews with 3 to 8 members each. On

the lower level of the area--where this quarry is lo-
cated--there is frequent communication and interaction
between workers in different quarries, a situation
which tends to reinforce cooperative work patterns.

From the technological standpoint, differential
use and ownership of tools is correlated with different
modes of stone extraction and, consequently, with different quarry types and work arrangements. There is a
tendency for metateros with few tools to work with those
who have more tools, and it is technologically impossible for a metatero to work alone without special tools
which make it possible for him to perform a series of
quarrying and stonecutting tasks unaided. The metateros
themselves are quite aware of these relationships as
the following statement by a maestro confirms:

> Now they have all the tools: barrenos and
> long pulsetas; a sledge hammer with 8 or
> 10 wedges (cuñas); fuse and blasting powder.
> All the requisites. Why should they want
> to depend on others? There are times when
> out of need for a tool I ask a person who
> has it to come and work with me--he has
> tools which I don't have. In that situa-
> tion one is obliged to have a work compan-
> ion. There are some who make an effort to
> get a complete set of tools. At times he
> may have to pay a helper 'but, in any case,
> all the stone that falls is for him alone.

From the cultural perspective, traditional
metatero technology and modes of stone extraction have
encouraged cooperation. Cooperative effort, however,
has always been organized on a small scale, never involving groups of more than 8 workers. Instability and
inefficiency have been characteristic of even this
small scale organization; petty feuds over ownership
rights, use of tools, and product sharing cause a
fairly steady turnover in the membership of even the
smallest, kin-based work groups. The traditional metatero dilemma has been that cooperation was a technological necessity but that quarreling, envy and dissension
generated by the contradiction between privatistic vs.
communal property and production ideologies encouraged
an atomistic worker orientation. That this dilemma
has not yet been resolved is implicit in the following
statement by a young Teitipac metatero who, while ap-
preciating the 'economies of scale' which could result

207

from a large, rationalized, cooperative work organization, has himself elected to become an independent operator:

> We could make a set of rules and regulations as a group; in company arrive at the same hour in the quarries and work the stone together as a single job. We could blast and cut the stone together, and, then, each one could work his own piece of stone. But it's not possible to work together on the same schedule because the work is voluntary, not obligatory. There are no bosses to tell everyone what to do and when to do it. Each worker is his own boss. The metateros can't be organized because their work is not done for the government; it's not ordered by decree. It's personal work.

The 'loner ideology' implicit in this informant's statement reinforces the older 'atomistic orientation' which, as we've seen, was an outgrowth of the realities of the traditional metatero work situation. The newer ideology, however, is, at least in part, an outgrowth of exogeneous conditions which have greatly affected the experiences and thinking of many younger generation metateros.

Cooperative Work Arrangements. The basic collective work arrangement among the metateros is the company (compañía), a group of mozo-metateros or compañeros-metateros who work under the direction of a maestro-dueño or a maestro-encabezado depending upon the prevailing quarry tenure situation. In San Sebastian where quarry tenure is allotted on an individual metatero basis, the maestro-dueño (master-owner) who directs operations derives his status from his superior knowledge of quarrying coupled with his 'ownership' of the quarry. On the other hand, in San Juan where quarries are often owned by non-metateros, the patrón-owner hires a maestro-metatero as an encabezado or encargado (boss) to direct quarry operations. The status of the San Juan 'boss' is similar to that of his San Sebastian counterpart except that it does not derive from his ownership of the quarry but from his appointment by its owner.

208

The usual arrangement between a quarry boss and its owner in San Juan is made on a product-sharing basis (a medias with the boss being the mediero)--the owner claiming half of the total product (i.e., blocks of stone) and the other half going to the boss to distribute among his mozos, usually on an equal share basis. Stone produced from quarry operations is set aside by the boss and is distributed only in the presence of the owner. If, for example, 12 trozos are on hand when the owner arrives in the quarry, he will claim six and the boss will claim six. If the company consists of two mozos in addition to the boss, then each will receive two trozos. In those cases in which the boss is also owner (propietario) of the quarry, he allots himself more than equal share of the product. One San Juanero in this position who has two mozos describes his policy as follows:

> If 12 trozos come out, I give 2 to each mozo and keep 6 for myself. But this depends upon the quality of the trozos. If they're good I give only 2; if they're bad I give 3 to each mozo. Everything depends upon the attendance of the mozos. If they show up for work every day during a two-week period and we take out 30 trozos, I will give each mozo 5 or 6 trozos. But if there are days that they fail to show for work and only 8 or 10 trozos are taken out, then each mozo gets only 2. I always give an equal share to each mozo because they are reliable (son de mi confianza). They are workers who can be told how to do something and, even if I'm not around, they will go ahead and do it as I instructed them.

Clearly, then, private proprietorship, not labor power expended, is the critical determinant of product distribution in the San Juan metate industry.

My San Sebastian field assistant, a metatero who accompanied me on excursions to the San Juan quarries, made the following astute comparison between the quarry work situation in the two villages:

> In San Juan the owner of the quarry carries many guarantees. In the first place, the owner of the quarry doesn't work there.

He just waits until the stone is quarried
and then goes and grabs half of it. If
there are 12 _trozos_ the quarry boss grabs
6 and the owner grabs 6. Then the boss
divides up his portion among the _mozos_.
For that reason the owner has more guarantees than his workers. And the owner
doesn't do any work in the quarry.

Here in San Sebastian it's easier
for the workers. The workers in San Juan
suffer more because they quarry stone without having any guarantees. Here in San
Sebastian the owner of the quarry works
together with the rest of the workers who
are helping him. Here, for example, if
there are a total of 8 in the quarry, 7
mozos and the owner, and if 8 _trozos_ are
taken out, each worker grabs one. Here
we make no distinction between owner and
worker because each gets an equal share;
each puts in an equal amount of work and
must get an equal share.

There in San Juan the problem is
this: the _patrón_ or the owner of the
quarry is an exploiter (_aprovechado_). He
gives no guarantees to his workers. That
is to say, he gets more because he already
has (_vale porque tiene_); and the poor workers, since there is no available territory
where they can look for their own quarries,
are forced to work with him even though
they are not compensated on the same basis
that he is. The owner decides things
just because the quarry happens to be on
his land.

Although in San Sebastian the owner-boss does not claim
a disproportionate share of the stone quarried, his
relationship to his _mozos_ is, in other respects, similar
to that of the _maestro-propietario_ to his workers in
San Juan. In both cases, the differential relationship
of _maestro_ and _mozo_ to the means of production is the
basis of quarry work organization.

How does the quarry boss direct the work activity of his helpers? The master quarryman (_maestro de
la piedra_), as boss (_dirigente_), makes basic production
decisions regarding the strategy and tactics of quarry

operations. He decides where and what kind of work will be done; selects the most appropriate spot in the quarry to blast stone loose from its bed; and, if the blast is successful, directs the cutting and apportionment of the stone. A San Juan boss describes the kinds of decisions which are typical for any given day in the quarry:

> The first thing is to look for a place which looks promising. For example, if we arrive in the quarry and we see a bed of stone which looks like it might yield a lot of stone but needs to be cleared off first, and another smaller one where it appears that stone will be yielded more readily, it's better to move to the latter; we can earn some money from it and then knock down the big one. It's more difficult to take on the big one first because it will require more tools and more time.

> When one intends to discover a new quarry, one has to invest more work. But in a quarry which is already opened up, if a lot of debris is not inside, the job is easier. For that reason I always make sure that debris is cleared out of the quarry where I'm working; when one wants to go back there, all that's necessary is to set the blast and knock down stone.

> If I appraise a stone and decide that it will be difficult to cut up, then, I will cut it myself. In that way, if the cut doesn't give good results, I have no one to blame but myself. I make nearly all of the cuts myself; since I'm more expert things usually turn out better that way.

Unless there is a special understanding to the contrary, the mozos in a company will not perform basic quarry operations in the absence of the boss. The latter directs and coordinates these operations until enough stone has been accumulated to enable each member of the company to make at least one metate or several manos. The accumulated stone is sometimes distributed among the workers on the principle 'from each according to his ability to each according to his work' (typically in San Sebastian and Magdalena). Or, as one San Sebastian quarry boss put it, "When trozos accumulate I divide them up; each worker gets his due according to the amount of work he contributed."

Unfortunately, this formula for determining an individual metatero's share in total quarry output is imprecise and difficult to apply. Consequently, a major source of conflict in the quarries, which contributes not only to the circulation of metateros between separate quarries but also between individualistic and cooperative work arrangements, are disagreements about stone distribution. The following account by one San Sebastiano, who circulated from a 'loner' situation to a 'company' and back again, illustrates how this occurs:

> "I came down to L.'s quarry and he sold me a trozo. Afterwards I asked him: 'Will you give me a chance to work with you?' "Why not,' he replied, 'but you must bring your own blasting powder, your crowbar and sledge; we'll cut this stone and I'll give you a share.' 'O.K.,' I told him, and I went to bring my tools. Then we cut a large slab of stone into several trozos. We each grabbed one-half of the trozos; we cut four and each grabbed two. When there were no more trozos I brought powder and we blasted; a lot of stone came out. Well, that's how it went with us for about a month and a half."

> "Well, there we were and at first he treated me very well, but then he began to show his displeasure. It was o.k. for me to work very hard there--but what he didn't go along with was that I made 2 metates daily. He didn't accept that. He wanted me to make only one metate--he makes one and I make one. But by mid-day I finished one and in the afternoon I work on another trozo. And when it's time to quit for the day, I have 2 metates. 'No,' he said to me, 'for that reason I ran off S. (another loner who had temporarily worked with him)--because he made too many metates.' The next day I went to the quarry and he didn't come but sent word that I should clear away debris. But I didn't do this and instead went to cut stone for trozos

to make <u>metates</u>. I found a good slab and
cut two <u>trozos</u> for metates and 6 manos;
then I began working a metate. I finished
one and the next day another along with
8 manos. When he finally came to the quarry
on the 3rd day he asked me who had cut stone
in the quarry. I told him that I had. He
cursed me: '<u>Hijo de la chingada</u>!' 'No,'
I said, 'You're too old for that now.' I
had my crowbar ready and if he had decided
to get tough I would have given him a blow
(<u>chingadazo</u>) on the head. I left the quarry
early that day. I didn't go there again to
work."

To summarize: the Teitipac <u>metateros</u> consider
the work company to be a mode of expedient cooperation,
not necessarily desirable but often imperative ("We
help each other out because one cannot do the work a-
lone"). Those quarry operations which cannot be performed by an individual worker are performed by groups
in which each member agrees to work for only a share
of the total product--the allocation of that product
being done by the quarry boss. In the past few decades,
the increased availability of certain tools has gradually weakened the economic need for cooperation in the
performance of quarry tasks, the company has declined
in importance (especially in San Sebastian). Yet, such
factors as the unequal distribution of tools, quarry
skills and, in the case of San Juan, quarries themselves,
will continue to perpetuate the existence of this type
of work arrangement.

The company is by no means the only arrangement
for cooperation in <u>metatero</u> productive activity. Often
the need arises among the <u>metateros</u> to establish a production relationship on the basis of the reciprocity
principle (<u>dar mano</u> form of <u>guelaguetza</u>). Such a relationship can be entered into by two <u>metateros</u> at any
stage in the production process (i.e., in quarrying or
post-quarrying phases). It may involve an exchange of
labor services or the products of labor (e.g., <u>trozos</u>,
or metates or manos in various stages of completion).
The most important of these reciprocity-based relationships among the <u>metateros</u> are described below in the
words of a <u>San Sebastiano</u>:

1) Labor exchange: quarrying operations
If one of my regular working companions does

213

not show up on a day when we are going to
set a charge, then, I speak to someone else
in another quarry: 'Do you want to make
guelaguetza with me to come help set a
charge? My regular partner didn't come.
When you need help with setting a charge
then I'll help you.'

2) Labor exchange: post-quarrying operations
If I am in need of finishing unfinished
metates which I have on hand but am pressed
for time, then, I ask one of my partners or
some metatero relative: 'Let's make a
guelaguetza deal; finish a metate for me
now and next week I'll finish one of yours.'

3) Product exchange: trozo
I blasted and the stone which I got was not
good; and I had to go to plaza on Saturday
to make some purchases. So I asked another
quarry owner: 'Lend me a trozo so that I
can make a metate to take to the plaza on
Saturday. As soon as I'm able to get some
trozos out of my quarry I'll return one to
you.'

4) Product exchange: finished metate or manos
For example, if one of my partners or any
other metatero in the quarry says to me:
'If you can make me a metate this week, next
week I'll make one for you. Let's go a
guelaguetza.' Or, to take another example:
I want to go to Oaxaca this Saturday but I
have only 1 metate and want to take 3 to
plaza; and I don't have time to make 2 more.
In such a case, I'll speak to other metateros
to find out if they'll help me with two additional metates. I agree to make metates
for them during the next week.

Though not engaged in regularly, all of the above transactions are viewed as continuous social relationships
in a framework of mutual self-interest. "These are not
gratuitous favors," one informant told me, "because
any day one is asked to return it and the return represents one's work." Even such simple transactions as
the borrowing or lending of a tool are informally

214

enmeshed in this network of mutality. "Everything is guelaguetza with us," commented one metatero, "because all help is paid for sooner or later."[5]

The following summary of observations I made in 1968 in the "Piedra de Canoa" quarry area in Magdalena illustrates how the guelaguetza principle operates in a specific quarry situation:

> This morning I accompanied M., A. and J. to the 'Piedra de Canoa' quarry. We arrived in the quarry at 11:00 A.M. and found G. already at work (with a mozo who was being paid 5 pesos daily with meals) clearing stone out of his quarry--and was moving a trozo from the quarry floor up to the work patio. M. works alone in an adjacent quarry; A. works in one section of the same quarry which G. (who is A.'s br-in-law) works. J. (together with his brother V. who arrived later) works a quarry adjacent to those worked by G. and A.

> Shortly after we arrived in the quarry area, M. asked J. and G. for help in prying a large slab of stone loose from its bed (it had been jarred loose by a blast the previous day). Both responded positively to M.'s request and ten minutes later were joined by V. (J.'s brother). After twenty minutes or so of prying (palanquear) with barretas used as levers, the large slab was extracted and fell to the quarry floor where M., now working alone, proceeded to cut it into trozos. J., G. and V. returned to their own sections of the quarry and began work. No compensation for their effort was asked for nor was given.

> I asked M. if all the trozos he was cutting belonged to him and he said yes. I asked him if any of the others were entitled to a share of his stone, as compensation for helping him, and he responded negatively. He explained that their help was provided in the spirit of 'dar mano' guelaguetza, and that the metateros were accustomed to exchange labor among themselves on a reciprocal basis.

215

He indicated that he also has the obligation
to lend a hand to his companion workers
when his help is requested.

    Individualistic Work Arrangements. The 'loner'
is a metatero who has his own quarry (as usufructuary)
which, as a matter of principle, he works with only
occasional help from others. The 'loner' is characterized by his mastery of the technology of quarrying
(i.e., its strategy and tactics) and metate production,
his ownership of an appropriate set of tools, and a
unique attitudinal syndrome or mental set which combines
opposition to cooperation and sharing with support of
individual initiative and self-appropriation of the
products of one's labor. According to the 'loner,' the
competent and efficient quarry worker is penalized by
having to share output with partners who are often less
reliable and efficient workers. The salient traits in
the loner ideology emerge from a sampling of their
statements presented below:

> 1) Not all work equally. Various individ-
> uals work in one quarry, some arrive early,
> some late. The ones who arrive early do
> more work than those who arrive late. The
> conscientious worker does more work but
> earns the same as the others. For that
> reason I don't like to have helpers. That's
> why I work alone. Only me blasting; only
> me cutting the stones; only me finishing
> the products.

> 2) At times a blast yields very little
> stone and there's not enough to go around
> for all the workers. Some don't want to
> put in the same amount of work as their
> companions. Some arrive later than others
> in the quarry. The one who gets there
> first screws himself more and, after-
> wards, to share the trozos equally--it
> doesn't result.

> 3) I prefer to work alone; that way all
> the stone I take out of the quarry is for
> me. Since I learned the occupation I
> haven't liked to work in company. One

is always doing another's work. Some
are lazy and don't do their share of the
work.

4) I work alone because I don't want to
have difficulties with anyone. I have
all my own tools and I work the hours that
I want to work. All the stone I cut is
for me. Otherwise, somebody else is always
grabbing stone which you cut. When you
work alone all the stone you cut is yours.
So my motto is 'each person with his own
work.'

A Magdalena informant provided an example of an incident
which led him to prefer working alone rather than in a
cooperative arrangement with other metateros:

Q: Do you work alone or with other companions?

R: Alone.

Q: Why do you work alone?

R: Because at times things get out of
control--somebody grabs a trozo
larger than the next guy's and he gets
mad.

Q: Have you worked before with others?

R: Yes, that's how I know about the
situation.

Q: When was the last time that you worked
with others?

R: Last year. We started off well and
ended up bad.

Q: What happened?

R: I made two metates in a day--well the
stone yielded very well, and my partner
made one. But I wasn't trying to take
unfair advantage of the stone; it's
that I needed money, I was in a tight

financial situation. I made two and
he made one; for that reason he got
mad and afterwards he didn't want to
work with me.

Then, I said to him: 'There's
still another slab of stone; let's go
and wreck (desbaratar) it.' He replied,
'Tomorrow,' or that he didn't have time.
Well, that's the way it went, and
that's how I learned that he was mad.
I tried to reason with him but he only
got madder.

Q: What was the agreement between you?

R: He was owner of the quarry and we worked
there between the two of us. And what
came out--one metate each or two
metates each. The agreement was that
the following week he made two metates
and me one--because I made two this
week--in that way we would remain even.
Only that he didn't want to continue.

What common variables or experiences characterize
the 'loners' and perhaps, contribute to their ideology?
(The data from the Teitipac villages represented in
Table 14 provide some leads in this matter.) As it
turns out, all eight of the 'loners' are members of the
younger generation of metateros, their average age
being 34 years. All of these individuals have had
several extra-village work experiences as wage-
laborers; the average number of separate experiences
being 4 per person, ranging from periods of 1-1/2 to
6 years for the total length of time spent outside the
village. Six of the eight 'loners' have worked as
braceros, thus, experiencing a work environment rad-
ically different from that in their home villages.
Perhaps, then, the 'loner's' alienation from the traditional forms of quarry work in his village stems, at
least in part, from repeated experiences as a wage
earner where he could acquire an economic orientation
in which the level of his income is perceived as a
direct function of his own decisions and work.[6]

Any prospector who participated in the 19th
century California 'Gold Rush' with its cycle of
prospecting, claim-staking, and claim-jumping would
understand the situation confronting the San Sebastian

TABLE 14. Age, Marital Status, Occupational Recruitment and Work History Data for 8 'Loner' Metateros

Informant No.	Age	Marital Status	Age	Recruitment Mode	No. of extra-village jobs	Work History Length and Nature of Work
1	28	married; 3 children	18	no metatero relatives; self-taught	3	8 months as bracero
2	35	married; 4 children	14	father was metatero but died young; self-taught	4	6 months: 3 as bracero; 3 as laborer in Mexico City
3	32	married; 1 child	14	learned from older br.	8	16 months: 6 as bracero; 6 as laborer in Mexico City
4	35	married; 2 children	15	learned from Fa; several metateros in family	6	20 months: 8 as bracero; 3 in Oaxaca City; 9 in other areas of Mexico
5	37	married; 2 children	12	learned from Fa; several metateros in family	3	6-1/2 months: all as bracero
6	36	married; 2 children	23	learned from friend; Fa was metatero but died young	2	1-1/2 months as highway construction laborer in Mexico
7	30	married; 5 children	15	learned from Fa; patrikin are metateros	2	6 years: 5 years in Veracruz sugar cane; 1 year in highway construction
8	42	married; 2 children	16	learned from FaBr; Fa and other relatives also metateros	4	9-1/2 months: 5-1/2 months as bracero; 4 months in Veracruz in sugar cane

219

metatero. The competitive rush to stake a claim on a
productive quarry motivated by opportunism, which characterized the California situation, parallels, on a
reduced scale and for much smaller stakes, the
present-day situation among the San Sebastian metateros.
According to this pattern, one metatero 'discovers' a
rich bed of stone and other metateros gravitate toward
the area either to contest the 'discoverer's' claim or
to establish new ones of their own in a contiguous area.

There is a rhythm to metate stone quarrying re-
sembling that which characterizes, for example, ore
mining. In metate stone quarrying, as in mining, extractive activity diminishes in proportion as the yield
of the extracted material diminishes. Beds of stone
are exhausted through continuous, intensive quarrying,
just as veins of gold ore, for example, are exhausted
through continuous, intensive mining. Quarrying in
San Sebastian, like gold mining in the 'Wild West,'
has a history of booms and busts, runs and exoduses,
ups and downs, as well as its cycles of discovery, extraction, abandonment, re-discovery, re-extraction and
re-abandonment. By necessity, then, the metatero is a
roamer: in the highly competitive game of quarry
prospecting, claim-staking or claim-jumping, and quarrying, his is a constant roaming quest for stone. It
was this aspect of his occupation which led one metatero
to reflect: "Each one of us searches for a place
where there's good stone because good stone is not to
be found everywhere. One must keep moving from one
place to another until he finds good metate stone."
This is both a statement of the 'roamer' philosophy and
of the situation which underlies it.[7]

The roaming of any given metatero varies, however, as to immediate cause and ultimate result.
Causes include involvement in disputes with working
companions, exhaustion of a bed of stone, difficulty
in working a particular type of stone, decline in demand or buyer interest in metates made of a particular
type of stone, invitations from fellow metateros to
combine production efforts, and opportunistic decisions
to move into another quarry area where others are having
good luck. Roaming may result in staking a claim to a
quarry, becoming a partner with or assistant to an
already established quarry 'owner,' or a failure to
adapt to the new quarry situation (e.g., due to un-
suitable stone, rejection by other workers, disgust,
etc.) and a continuance of the quest.

Though the causes and results of roaming vary,

the phenomenon itself is constant since it involves all metateros. The typical San Sebastian metatero will, most likely, change quarries at least once during any given year and, from one year to another, will probably have experienced a change in quarry areas (e.g., from the Mesa Grande to the Mesa Chiquita). During a career the typical metatero will have worked in most of the quarry areas found within the village jurisdiction. The various aspects of roaming emerge in the following account by a 34-year-old metatero who has been working in the occupation for 16 years:

> I've worked in five different quarry areas: in Cacalote, in Ticulute, in the Mesa Chiquita, in the Mesa Grande, and below the Atzompa hill. I used to like the occupation a lot and I moved about looking for a place to get myself in so as to make a living. I really liked it there in Cacalote where I first started to work. But, then, good stone began to be found on the Mesa Grande and several began to work there with the purplish stone that's still being quarried. After that the buyers in Oaxaca stopped buying the white stone from Cacalote. So it was in 1963 that we moved to the Mesa Grande; in 1962 I was still working in the Cacalote quarry with Lorenzo and his sons Dario and Marcelino. Also with Juarez; it's only a short time ago that Juarez moved up to the Mesa Grande. Salvador, Felipe--all of those who now work on the Mesa Grande--used to work in Cacalote.

> One moves about looking for the best results; where there's stone which is selling good, that's where one tries to get in. The whole point is not to get stuck in a situation where there are no metates. I had a quarry in Ticulute but we kept going down after the stone and the quarry got too deep. I've wanted to find another quarry of my own but I haven't been able to get a helper to work with me in clearing off a place. My father is now tired of it all and my brother is bored with the whole situation--he doesn't want to work in the quarries.

But, for example, if I make a new
quarry some place, as soon as the stone began
to give results, then the others will come
to try to get me out of there. So to avoid
fights I don't make the effort of opening my
own quarry. I go and help other owners.

Older metatero informants recall causes for
shifts in quarry extraction patterns which are no longer
operative. For example, prior to the abandonment of
the haciendas (i.e., Santa Rosa and San Antonio) which
are contiguous to the village jurisdiction on its
north and south boundaries, respectively, the adminis-
trators made periodic attempts to appropriate the
stone quarries nearest to their haciendas. One old
timer recalls an incident he witnessed at the Frente de
Coyote quarry involving the administrator of the San
Antonio hacienda and the metateros who were working the
quarry:

I don't remember the name of that administrator but he came up to the quarry one
day. I happened to be there to take my
father his lunch. My father and his partners were eating lunch when the administrator came and told them to stop working
in the quarry because it belonged to the
hacienda. When my father heard those
words about 'suspension' he became tough
and yelled, 'What did you say?' And the
administrator took out his pistol and the
metateros picked up stones. Well, they
ran that administrator off and the dispute
ended.

Another metatero recalls the conditions which led to
the discovery of the Mesa Chiquita quarry by his grandfather, father and others in 1917--during the revolutionary era:

We opened up that quarry on account of a
rumor. In 1917 the village police went
looking for two wood cutters who were lost;
they went up to the Mesa Grande and brought
down two individuals from San Agustin de
las Juntas and put them in jail. And, after
they had left, some other villagers found

222

the two woodcutters dead. Afterwards, the village of San Agustin persuaded the state police to move into our mountains to look for the two villagers who we had locked up. They began shooting at us and a battle broke out in which 4 soldiers were killed. That was in 1917--in November. Of course, all that month and until March no one worked in the Mesa Grande Quarry; it was remote and bandits came down to get water there. Not until the end of 1918 did they begin to work there again. Five workers, during that period, decided to go down to the Mesa Chiquita to look for stone. They moved down due to the rumor that bandits had occupied the Mesa Grande. They divided up the Mesa Chiquita and opened quarries. My father got a share there.

The causes of metatero roaming, then, have varied over the years but the pattern itself is an old one which is now an inherent aspect of the metatero situation.

Tenure Ideology, Work Relations, and Conflict in the Quarries

Each of the metate-producing communities is characterized by a distinctive mix of quarry tenure principles, or at least, by a distinctive configuration of quarry tenure patterns. Yet, with the exception of San Juan Teitipac where all quarries are within privately owned lands (pequeñas propiedades), the fundamental reality of quarry tenure in the Valley of Oaxaca is the contradiction between private and communal (or ejidal) tenure. In San Sebastian, Magdalena and Tlacolula, quarries are within the boundaries of communal or ejidal lands, and are assigned through private usufruct; or they are within the boundaries of privately owned parcels and are owner-worked or are rented. Regardless of the de jure quarry tenure regime (communal, ejidal, private), the principle which all metateros recognize, and which inevitably shapes the day-to-day use of quarries, is that the worker who discovers and/or clears and works a quarry is its de facto 'owner.'

The Teitipac villages provide a basic contrast between communal and private tenure regimes. In San

Sebastian all quarries lie within communal lands and are, de jure, communal property; however, specific quarries are, de facto, controlled by individual metateros (who are referred to as "dueños" or owners)--but only so long as they actively work them. For the most part, these so-called 'owners' do not have documents to support their de facto status. Moreover, there is no consistent policy by local authorities to regulate use of these quarries (in sharp contrast to the situation in the ejido community of Magdalena). As will be discussed below, this inconsistency is associated with almost perpetual instability and conflict in quarry use and work organization (compared to only occasional problems in Magdalena). In San Juan, on the other hand, the quarries are located within the boundaries of privately-owned parcels and, consequently, have legitimate owners who, for the most part, are not metateros. This is associated with relatively stable use patterns and work organization but, as documented above, generates inequities in the distribution of quarry output.

Ejidal vs. Communal Tenure: Magdalena and San Sebastian Compared. A private property ideology is predominant in both communities--but a much higher proportion of total arable land is privately owned in San Sebastian than in Magdalena. As discussed in Chapter 2, most of the land suitable for agriculture in San Sebastian is privately owned as pequeña propiedad; communal tenure prevails on most of the non-agricultural land and on certain selected agricultural tracts which are held and worked communally in the name of the patron saint or the school (i.e., terrenos del Santo, parcela escolar). With the exception of these cultivated tracts, the communal lands (terrenos comunales) are hilly and wooded or covered with thick growths of scrub or brush, and are used primarily for grazing animals, woodcutting, collecting wild foods or other usable plants, and for quarrying. All of the important quarry areas are within the communal sector and usufruct is regulated by village officials--particularly the Representante de Bienes Comunales and the Síndico. However, on a day-to-day basis problems pertaining to the nature of usufruct (e.g., rights and duties of the usufructuary, jurisdictional boundaries, entry and exit routes to and from the quarries, etc.) are handled informally by the metateros themselves. Village officials directly intervene in metatero affairs only in reaction to crisis situations which they usually resolve through a combination of 'site visits' and hearings, the results

of which in terms of judgments are enforced by threat
of punishment (e.g., jailing, fines, suspension of work).

There is no formal code of conduct imposed upon
the metateros by local officials; but there is an unwritten code of conduct and agreements among the metateros, together with a series of precedents established
through rulings by local officials, which serve to regulate quarry tenure and use. This contrasts with the
situation in Magdalena where, in addition to unwritten
rules of conduct, tenure and use of the quarries--which
are all ejidal property--are closely regulated by the
local ejido authority (Comisariado Ejidal) in accordance
with rules and regulations set forth in the federal
Agrarian Code (Código Agrario).

The right of the individual villager to exploit
communal or ejidal land derives from his membership in
the corporate community (usually by birth) and his
satisfactory compliance with the duties of citizenship
(e.g., paying taxes and other levies, contributing labor services to tequios, serving in elective or appointed positions). One villager expressed his understanding of this situation as follows:

> Do you know what our guarantees are? Or
> what are the payments that we make to the
> village? We give tequio service whenever
> this is required. That's the payment we
> offer. The village government tells us
> what to do. For that reason we have the
> right to use communal property, for ex-
> ample, the quarries.

It became clear to me during the course of my
research that Magdalena metateros were subject to tight-
er corporate constraints and control than were the
metateros in San Sebastian. For example, I learned of
no instance in San Sebastian of the suspension of quarry use rights as punishment for alleged 'misconduct'
but recorded several such instances in Magdalena. This
is somewhat paradoxical in view of the fact that San
Sebastian is more class-differentiated than Magdalena
and that its government is usually controlled by the
wealthier peasants--many of whom either express contempt
for the metateros or automatically pigeonhole them as
belonging to the poorest stratum of village society.
Thus, during a hearing in San Sebastian concerning a
conflict among several metateros over use rights in one

of the quarries, the <u>Representante de Bienes Comunales</u>,
a member of one of the dominant landowning families of
the village, made the following statements which were
directly insulting to the <u>metatero</u> plaintiffs:

> ". . . let's see in what way we can control
> you people there. You can't be fighting
> like this all the time. It's entirely
> like a pig with an ear of corn in its mouth--
> you go here and there following each other
> and fighting. And you move elsewhere in
> the same way--fighting. You already did
> it in another quarry--damn! Pure fighting!
> It's like the comparison I just made;
> because in the same place you come together
> with pure fights."

> "They (the <u>metateros</u> in question)
> remind me of a story: 'When a burro is
> lying dead, the fiercest dog wants to take
> advantage of the best meat.' That's how
> these <u>metateros</u> are; just dogs! Those
> things are bad."

Verbal castigation of this type, combined with threats
by the local authorities to suspend work rights or to
call in outside authorities, seems to work in San
Sebastian to keep conflicts in the quarries from getting
out of hand (although there were some past incidents
that necessitated incarceration).

There are a number of non-<u>metateros</u> in San
Sebastian and Magdalena who argue that the <u>metateros</u>
should be more tightly controlled by local authorities
and should pay fees for quarry use rights (in addition
to <u>tequio</u> and other obligations). The <u>metateros</u> emphasize, in refuting this argument, that the high element
of risk and uncertainty in locating and successfuly extracting stone from a quarry merits special consideration. They point out, by comparison, that the peasant
who clears a plot for cultivation is assured of planting his crop and, even if the harvest is poor, he does
not completely lose the work he invested in land preparation, whereas the <u>metatero</u> may spend many days in
quarry work without obtaining stone suitable for producing metates.

In San Sebastian most villagers recognize that
the use rights of a majority of the <u>metateros</u> derive

from the fact that they are carrying on old family traditions in quarries that were originally discovered and
worked by their ancestors. In the words of the Repre-
sentanté de Bienes Comunales:

> "...once indicating to each (metatero)
> his place (in the quarry area) there will
> be no risk of problems. We, precisely
> because we're not of the occupation (of
> metateros) aren't covetous of the place
> (quarries). Nephews and great-nephews are
> in the quarries today. No one has opened
> a new quarry; they were there when we were
> born. We don't know who the men were who
> were working back in those times. It
> corresponds to an heir who works there
> and then he sends for his friends and three
> or four begin to work there. For that
> reason they all gather together in a quarry,
> like a society. But afterwards within the
> society itself they fight."

Some San Sebastian metateros seek to convert their
possession of use-rights over a quarry into actual proprietorship by obtaining 'documents' from a village
official which confirm their claims to a particular
quarry. Such documents serve to support the inheritance
rights of an heir (if these should be disputed) or as
a basis for purchase-sale of a quarry--although according to the Mexican Agrarian Code communal lands are not
alienable through purchase-sale.

For the most part, however, the San Sebastian
metateros possess quarries as comuneros and their individual usufruct rights are sanctioned by the informal
consensus of their companions. As one San Sebastian
metatero expressed it:

> Among us the basis of ownership is approval
> by our metatero companions. One is recog-
> nized as owner. Almost nobody goes to see
> the Presidente or the Síndico to ask them
> for a place to work; they find a place on
> their own. Then if the authorities arrive
> on the spot and ask who works a particular
> quarry, the owner answers, 'I do, sir.'
> Then the authorities say: 'When stone is
> needed for a village project you, as the

227

boss of this quarry, will have to donate
so many stones of such and such size.'
In other words, they recognize him as
owner. But he is an 'as if' owner. But
if he stops working in that quarry no one
else can go to work there because the one
who left is recognized as boss of that
quarry.

In other words, the San Sebastian metateros generally
accept the relative and conditional nature of quarry
tenure, and do not claim absolute and unconditional
proprietorship rights (though many of them seek and
would prefer these). At the heart of their 'quasi-
ownership' code there is, however, the idea of exclusive
private possession based upon mutual respect for work
expended. Most disputes among the metateros do not
arise from disagreements over tenure rights, per se,
but over the precise boundaries of the quarry area to
which they pertain.

The following statement by one member of the
municipal government in San Sebastian during 1966-67
is representative of the 'official' view of the quarry
tenure situation there.

We recognize the metateros as owners because they work there and are given preference. For example, they go there,
find a place and clear it, and then take
out stone for metates. Over time the
quarry gets larger and anyone who asks,
'Who's working here?' is told: 'It belongs
to so-and-so.' But it belongs to so-and-
so in word only; in reality all the terrain
on which the quarries are located is communal.

This is not to imply that the interests of municipal
officeholders and the metateros always coincide. There
are occasions when these conflict. For example, there
is the thorny issue of how revenue should be distributed from the sale of quarry stone for construction
purposes to outside buyers. In 1962 a neighboring
village needed stone for construction purposes (for
a new municipal building) and sent representatives to
bargain directly with the metateros. When the municipal
authorities of San Sebastian were informed of the

situation they communicated with their counterparts in the neighboring village and told them that all future negotiations should be handled on an official village-to-village basis. They claimed that the metateros were granted sale rights only to that stone which could be utilized in the manufacture of metate products, and that transactions of all other types of stone fell within the jurisdiction of elected village officials. Nevertheless, on other occasions individual metateros did succeed in selling stone directly to outside buyers although a portion of the sales revenue was paid as a surcharge to the municipal treasury.

When inter-metatero quarry disputes arise they are resolved in one of three ways: by withdrawal of one of the disputants, by a voluntary compromise between the disputants, or by forced arbitration by the municipal government. Withdrawal is the outcome of the operation of a peck order principle in metatero social relations according to which the toughest or most intimidating individual prevails. In metatero jargon the victor in such cases is said to have "put himself in by his balls" (se metió por sus güevos) or by his superior ability to intimidate ("por su valentía"). Tools (e.g., barretas, machetes) or firearms are sometimes employed as threats in these conflicts but physical combat is customarily restricted to fist fighting or rough and tumble matches.

An example of voluntary withdrawal is provided in the following account by one San Sebastian metatero of a dispute with a paternal cousin (FaBrSo):

There was envy (envidia) there on the Mesa Chiquita (one of the communal quarry areas). I was working alone there, setting my own blasts. When others saw that some large stones were blasted loose, they came--three of them, including my cousin. They asked me where I had gotten permission to work in that place. I replied to my cousin: 'Look, cousin, our fathers used to work here together and, now, why are you impeding my work?' He responded: 'I have been working here regularly; why is it that you came up here just recently?' I replied: 'It's now that I need money; I came here to earn a few cents.' He then told me: 'No, you must ask me permission before you come to work here.' I replied: 'Yes,

229

cousin, I will ask your permission when I
want a block of stone which you've already
cut; but not when I'm going to put in my
own work to get stone for myself from the
quarry.' And then I told him: 'Look,
cousin, here is the stone I've gotten with
my work; go ahead and cut it, it's yours.'
And I left that quarry and haven't returned
since. Instead of losing my time there
fighting with them and having them look
at me in a bad light, I decided to go into
the mountains and make charcoal.

When quarry disputes in San Sebastian are brought
before municipal officials for settlement, a series of
hearings are held between all of the disputants and,
in serious cases, a group of officials visits the disputed quarry to make a survey (often taking measurements and making notes on boundary markers). The
outcome of official arbitration typically involves the
division of the contested quarry into equal parts for
each of the disputants. The 'compromise' is recorded
in a written document called an 'Act of Conformity.'
By resolving disputes among metateros according to this
formula, municipal officials maintain an 'uneasy peace'
at the expense of rewarding the aggressive disputant
with a share of the contested quarry. But they are
also reinforcing the underlying 'communal' nature of
quarry tenure.

By way of contrast, in Magdalena—where all matters pertaining to quarry use and tenure are handled
by the local ejido organization whose members are all
essentially class-equals of the metateros or are themselves metateros—temporary or permanent suspension of
quarry use rights does occur. Below is a chronological
synopsis of salient events in a 1969 quarry dispute in
Magdalena which was reported to me in a written document by one of the involved metateros.

Jan. 15 - Comisariado Ejidal solicits two
          wagon loads of stone from each
          of 20 metateros for use in the
          construction of a wall around
          the local ejido office. The
          stone was to be provided free of
          charge.

Jan. 15, 18 & 20 - The metateros meet with

the Comisariado Ejidal to request that the donation of two
wagon loads of stone release
them from one day's tequio (many
of them complaining that they
had already met their tequio
quota for the year).

Jan. 25 - A public meeting (junta) of all
ejidatarios to discuss and take
action regarding the request of
the metateros. The majority
consensus was that the quarries
are ejidal property and, therefore, the metateros must contribute stone as requested or have
their quarry use rights suspended. The metateros must contribute the stone and also give one-
day's labor as tequio.

Feb. 8 - Forty mozos (laborers) and 18
wagoneers arrive at the quarries
to collect the stone; the group
is confronted by three of the
metateros who protest that stone
suitable for metate manufacture
should be seperated from stone
suitable for construction. The
leader of the group of ejidatarios
responded: "We have to take the
stones because they belong to
the ejido; the quarries are not
private property." The metateros
armed themselves with several
large rocks and threatened the
ejidatarios. No stone was taken
from this quarry.

Feb. 11 - The 3 metateros involved in the
incident of Feb. 8, together
with another companion who early
in the A.M. of Feb. 8 hauled a
load of stone from the quarry to
his village residence lot, are
warned that their arrest is im-
inent. They leave the village
for Oaxaca City to seek help from
the regional ejidal office (jefe
de zona). After spending a day
in Oaxaca city they succeeded in

231

           obtaining a document from this
           official which prohibited their
           arrest by village authorities.

Feb. 12 - A general meeting of ejidatarios
           is called (attended by more than
           100) and a motion is approved to
           indefinitely suspend or withdraw
           quarry use privileges of three
           of the involved metateros and to
           permanently expel another from
           the village (he was not a native
           of the village but his wife was).

Feb. 14 - The involved metateros ignore
           this ejido directive and continue
           working in their quarries. They
           are arrested by the local police
           and taken to the district jail in
           Ocotlan, held for 24 hours and
           then are released after paying
           fines of 100 pesos each.

Feb. 25 - The Jefe de Zona from Oaxaca
           city comes to Magdalena to hold
           a meeting regarding the quarry
           problems. The result was that
           the three native metateros (the
           fourth was permanently expelled)
           would be permitted to resume work
           in the quarries if they agree to
           pay a fee of 500 pesos each year
           because "they earn a lot of money
           with metates since there are
           metates that are sold from 150
           to 200 pesos each." The metateros
           protest that they can't pay such
           an unreasonable fee. But the
           motion is passed, an act is for-
           mally drawn up, and all ejidatarios
           present are forced to sign on
           penalty of being jailed.

The latest information I received on this matter (contained in a letter from one of the involved metateros)
is that following the election of new ejidal officials
in the village in May 1969, that he resumed working
in the quarries. On June 8 he was arrested and jailed.
The newly elected comisariado told him that he could
not continue to work in the quarries because the other

<u>ejidatarios</u> would be angered. He concludes his letter by saying: "It was best for me to stop going to the quarry; now I just don't work."

A case in San Sebastian, involving an intra-quarry feud between individual <u>metateros</u> over boundaries and exit/entry routes, illustrates, among other things, the dynamics of fission and fusion in the organization of quarrying activity. In San Sebastian quarry work organization is inherently unstable because of the technological exigencies of the quarrying process itself (e.g., as stone is quarried its immediate source, a bed, is destroyed, and the shape of the quarry itself is permanently altered) combined with contradictory tenure arrangements (communal ownership with private usufruct) and work ideology (cooperativism vs. individualism). The following sequence of events which occurred over a two-year period in the Mesa Grande quarry area shows how these contradictory forces operate to transform the organization of the quarrying process.

Pre-1965   - A. worked a quarry with his Mo-in-law's Br. (<u>tio</u>), J., who was recognized as the 'owner-boss' (<u>dueño-maestro</u>). When J. passed away without direct male heirs, A. assumed the status of 'owner-boss' of the quarry because he had worked closely with J. and was allegedly told by J. before he died: "You are going to remain there so that no one else can work there." But A. had to agree with J.'s widow, who had a 'legal' claim to inherit J.'s property, to compensate her regularly with metates (i.e., a form of rent in kind) in return for his assuming direct control of the quarry.

Summer 1965 - A. was respected as 'owner-boss' by other <u>metateros</u>, and assembled a group of them to work with him as '<u>mozos</u>'(two of his brothers and 5 others). A. apparently paid his 'rent' to the widow on an irregular basis for a short period. One <u>metatero</u> who worked with A. described the situation in the quarry as of late 1965: "The widow had an

233

arrangement with A. according to which he had to give her metates. He did this at first. He became the boss of the quarry and would recruit people to help him but stopped giving metates to the widow. One day she asked him: "Where are my metates A.? Either give me metates or buy the quarry from me." A. responded that he was not going to give her more metates and had no intention of buying the quarry because he was already 'owner.'

Early 1966 — On the basis of advice from relatives and certain metateros who were envious of A.'s control of this highly productive quarry, the widow registers a formal complaint with the village authorities to the effect that A. was breaking a contract. A local official (Síndico) drafts a document showing the widow to be 'owner' of the quarry and obliging A. to give her 2 metates every 2 weeks as 'rent.' If A. refused to comply his quarry use rights would be suspended. A. signed the agreement but his brothers refused to help him meet the rent cuota.

April 1966 — A. fails to make the stipulated rent payment and the widow lodges a second formal complaint with the Síndico. A.'s quarry use rights are suspended though he is permited to work in another quarry area. Various metateros (including those who had influenced the widow) assert claims to parts of the disputed quarry--arguing that J.'s widow could legitimately claim only a small section where her husband had actually worked. The Síndico decides to partition the quarry into four separate sections among the following individuals: (1) A.'s brothers; (2) J.'s widow's DaHu and his brothers; (3) the 'owner' of a contiguous quarry (who had worked near but not with A.); and (4) a

'claim jumper' who had worked many
years earlier in the quarry but
who opportunistically asserted his
'rights' through intimidation of the
other metateros and by spurious
claims to supporting documentation
(A. said of him: "Se metió por sus
guevos o sea por su valentía").

March 1966   - Boundary conflicts and conflicts
over entry and exit routes erupt
among these four parties and culmin-
ate in a series of hearings presided
over by the Representante de Bienes
Comunales and the Síndico. It is
in these hearings that the former
official likens the contesting metateros to a "pack of dogs fighting
over a burro carcass" and threatens
to put the entire matter into the
hands of extra-village political/
judicial authorities.

   How does A., in retrospect, evaluate the situation? He resents the decision of the village authorities to partition the quarry, and he is determined
to eventually try to reassert his rights because, in
his words, "Allí tengo mi trabajo y él que trabaja
alli es el dueño" (I have my work there and the one
who works there is 'owner').

   The dilemma of village officials regarding possible solutions of quarry tenure problems is an inevitable derivative of a fundamental contradiction in
Mexican national agrarian ideology and policy between
privatistic and communal concepts of property (Stavenhagen 1970:229). The partitioning strategy which is
regularly invoked by San Sebastian authorities to
attempt to resolve quarry tenure problems reflects their
desire to conform to the widely shared norm of private
proprietorship and individual progress without vio-
lating traditional (and legal) notions of communal
tenure and common welfare. Whereas this strategy seems
to be partially effective in the area of agricultural
tenure, it is doomed to failure in application to quarry
tenure because of the unique dynamic of the labor process in quarrying.

   For example, in the above case the section of
the quarry assigned to party 2 encompasses the only

available exit/entry route for the larger quarry area. And since this route would necessarily be obliterated in the quarrying process, the other parties in the quarry area were understandably disturbed. One of the metateros in party 2 described his quarrying strategy during the hearings in a way which leaves no doubt as as to the ultimate consequences of the unrestrained assertion of individual rights of 'possession' in the quarry:

> . . . as things now stand in the quarry,
> I won't know if I'll have to keep moving
> in that direction (which would destroy
> the exit/entry path) until we see the
> results of another blast. Only then will
> we be able to judge where the rock is
> going to come out. So, for my part,
> this subject is of no concern to the rest
> of you. I will have to come out where I
> can and the rest of you will do likewise.
> What have I to do with you? I must
> follow the stone where it obliges me to go.

As this case suggests, the form and position of rock beds in a given quarry determine quarrying strategies and these, in turn, delimit quarrying tactics as well as the structure of interaction between quarry workers. One conclusion seems inescapable: in the absence of cooperative arrangements between metateros working in contiguous sectors of a quarry, which can be achieved and maintained only if communal ownership is enforced to the exclusion of 'conditional' private usufruct, conflict between them is a predictable by-product of the quarrying process itself.

FOOTNOTES

[1] In an unpublished paper William B. Taylor (1971:1) is not encouraging about the prospects for reconstructing, at the socioeconomic level, craft production in the colonial economy of the Oaxaca Valley: "In principal, the time dimension could shed light on any facet of the market economy of Oaxaca; but in fact, the kinds of questions and hypotheses which an historian can pose and hope to answer hinge directly on the nature of the historical records at his disposal. The documentation for colonial Oaxaca would not, for example, permit the duplication of Scott Cook's work for metateros. . . ."

[2] One metatero described this stone selection and grading process as follows: "In order to determine the quality of stone one first grabs a barreta and knocks off some pieces to see if it's hard or soft. Before proceeding to cut one must also examine the stone for flaws (ventiadas or cintas). Then one tries to cut away the flaws so that the good stone remains. Every type of stone has flaws. For that reason one must choose a piece that's good (un pedazo que sirve). Stone can be compared to a fat steer (Las piedras vienen dando como un toro gordo). It has its loin that is pure meat; and it has its fat and gristle. There's stone that is pure good stone and there's stone with lots of flaws. Well, we toss away the latter. It's just like a steer. Even a fat steer has lean meat-- but, of course, it has fat and gristle. We metateros are also like cattle buyers who know how to price a steer. When a stone is blasted loose we know how much it will yield right away. When we see the stone we know which side has flaws and which side is good."

[3] Jointing is a common feature of granitic formations (Landes and Hussey 1948:292). On the relevance of this geological phenomenon to human exploitative activity Landes and Hussey note: "Joints are of considerable importance to mankind. The quarryman both loses and gains by the presence of these natural rock fractures. If the joints are too close together he cannot quarry dimension stone; if they are too far apart his blasting costs may be excessive" (1948:293).

Jointing patterns in a given bed of stone must be appraised by the metatero before he makes decisions of a strategic and tactical nature. The success of his blasting operation depends upon the accuracy of his estimate of the jointing patterns. An incorrect estimate means that a given blast will yield nothing more than worthless fragments of stone. Hours and sometimes days are often lost from the metatero's work schedule on this account. Not even the most experienced and knowledgeable quarry masters are infallible in their decisions.

The terms "ventiada" and "realíz" are commonly used by the metateros to refer to joints or fissures in bedrock or stone and are here spelled phonetically. My Spanish dictionaries yield a verb 'ventear' which, among other things, means 'to split'; presumably its past participle 'venteada' is the standard Spanish equivalent to the metateros' "ventiada." Unfortunately, the term "realíz" or any reasonable cognate does not appear in my dictionaries.

[4]The interested reader can find a complete photographic record of the various steps in the labor process of stone quarrying and metate manufacture in Cook 1973.

[5]The product exchange type of guelaguetza is not frequently practiced; it is often a last resort for a financially pressed metatero who needs cash but has a poor credit status with village moneylenders and regatones. One variant of this type of guelaguetza is quite common, however. A quarry owner who has several trozos on hand will set aside a certain portion of these to another metatero who is short on stone. The latter will make metates from these trozos with the understanding that half will be returned (in a semifinished state or barretiado) to the owner. The other half remain the property of the metatero in compensation for his labor services. The reader will note that the same 'sharing' principle is operative here as in the 'al partido' arrangement discussed above.

[6]It is interesting to note in this regard that there are few 'loners' among the San Juan metateros where quarrying is performed almost exclusively by companies. Of a sample of 12 San Juan metateros from whom work histories were collected, not one had worked as a bracero and only one informant had prolonged experience in the extra-village wage labor system. Several of these informants have never had work experi-

ences outside their village and others have left periodically only to neighboring villages or to Tlacolula.
Incidentally, most of the 'braceros' were employed on
a 'piece work' basis.

[7]The metateros have no term which literally
translates as 'roamer' but do refer to opportunistic
types as "conveniencero" ("El que busca pura convenien-
cia; quiere beneficiar sin trabajar mucho"--he who looks
for pure convenience, who wants to benefit without
much work) or "pepenador" (from the verb 'pepenar'--
to pick up, seize, grab). The latter is a sort of
quarry scavenger who selects from waste or reject
stones pieces which are suitable for making manos or
molcajetes (mortars) or miniature metates. The
pepenador, who is neither quarryman nor a metatero,
may attach himself to a particular quarry and help with
simple clearing tasks or restrict his activities to
abandoned quarries. The conveniencero, on the other
hand, moves about from quarry to quarry temporarily
attaching himself to a work group when he judges the
situation to be favorable. He is usually a metatero
and a quarryman and helps with quarry tasks just
enough to justify a claim to a share of the output.

'Prospecting' for stone deposits has always been
a principal metatero activity; but the Teitipac land-
scape no longer contains virgin areas which have stone
suitable for quarry exploitation. Consequently,
'prospecting' by the metatero now consists in re-open-
ing abandoned quarry areas. As a San Sebastiano expressed it: "One has more or less of an idea where
stone can be found because our ancestors had quarries
there. One comes to such a place and says to himself:
'Those ancients worked here; now one must look for
stone in a spot nearby.' If not in the abandoned
quarry itself at least to one side of it. There one
has a good idea that he will find stone for metates."

Metate Sellers in the Tlacolula Marketplace.

CHAPTER 6. MARKETING, MARKETS AND MARKETPLACES
IN THE METATE INDUSTRY

The Market Concept and Metate Marketing

Marketing, in abstract terms, is the process of the physical transfer of commodities from producers to consumers or from production sites to exchange sites to use sites. Obviously, marketing depends on production to generate and sustain it just as it, in turn, facilitates and supplies utilization. More specifically, the marketing of metate industry products can begin any time after the final stage in their production is completed; it operates through exchange and ends as the initial stage of their utilization begins. In systemic terms, marketing implies regularized, inter-dependent relationships between people, commodities, and sites in a circulatory process activated and co-ordinated by flows of information, and patterned to reflect the prevailing relations of production.[1]

Before proceeding with the analysis, it will be useful to distinguish between three distinct notions of the 'market' concept to avoid possible confusion in subsequent discussion (cf. Firth 1967:5). First, it refers to a theoretical or ideal state of affairs relating to transactions between abstract categories of suppliers and demanders and focussing on the behavior of prices and quantities, as well as on the allocation of rewards to producers and marketers. Second, it refers to a particular time and place locality where buyers and sellers meet to trade, and emphasizes their behavior and the observable, quantifiable results of that behavior. Finally, it may denote a distributional area for products which is dependent upon particular marketplaces and/or upon the production centers which supply products to marketplaces. We can label these the notions of 'market,' 'marketplace' and 'market-area' respectively.[2]

Given these preliminary distinctions and focussing on the commodity class 'metates,' it is legitimate to posit a metate market as being generated through a series of multiple buyer/seller transactions occurring in marketplaces and resulting in the transfer of metates into various market-areas. The locus of such transactions need not be (nor is it exclusively

so in the case of metates) a particular marketplace
or series of marketplaces. However, in the 'Central
Valleys' economy a large majority of metate sales are
marketplace (plaza) mediated. Or, expressed differently, each market-area is supplied through market transactions occurring in a particular marketplace. Theoretically, of course, a market for a particular commodity
can be posited as independent of either a market-place
or market-area (i.e., simply as a transactional arena
where the forces of supply and demand converge and are
manifested in trading behavior); although empirically
in the Valley, as in other regional peasant economies
of Mesoamerica, it is usually associated with both
(see Foster 1948; Marroquín 1957; Swetnam 1973; Tax
1953; 13-19 et passim).

    The four metate production centers (the Teitipac
villages of San Juan and San Sebastian, the village of
Magdalena Ocotlan, and the town of Tlacolula de Mat-
amoros--refer again to Figure 2) supply at least one of
three specific marketplaces; and each marketplace provides an inter-actional arena for the operation of a
series of potentially competitive markets. These
latter, in turn, are the transactional basis for maintaining a series of partially overlapping metate
market-areas. One such market-area centers on the
Oaxaca City marketplace (Benito Juarez Maza until mid-
1970) and is supplied by the Teitipac villages; another
centers on the Ocotlan marketplace and is supplied by
the Magdalena producers; and the third centers on the
Tlacolula marketplace and is supplied by the Teitipac
producers together with a group of locally resident
producers.

    Throughout my research, observation and analysis
started from the production center and then shifted
to the marketing system, as opposed to starting with
the latter (or with one of its component marketplaces)
and shifting to the production center (or ignoring it
altogether by focussing exclusively on marketing). I
view the market-area as the dependent distributional
hinterland of a discrete production center and not of
a marketplace; I consider the latter to be nothing
more than a way station in the flow of products between producers and consumers (or sellers and buyers).

    Given this perspective, I interpret the mar-
ket data to indicate that metates produced in the two
Teitipac villages follow marketing paths which overlap only partially so that, in effect, the Oaxaca City
marketplace (to a larger degree than the Tlacolula one

where both of these producer-seller groups also compete) is an intermediate marketing site (i.e., bulking
and dispersing station) for two metate market-areas.
This apparently reflects the fact that the Oaxaca City
marketplace in 1966-67 capsulated a structurally (and
spatially) bifurcated metate market: a wholesale
market involving most San Sebastian sellers and a retail market involving most San Juan sellers (although
the bifurcation is complicated by product transfers
between San Sebastianos and San Juaneros and by occasional dual participation by both sets of sellers in
wholesale/retail transactions). I will discuss these
market-areas in more detail later in the chapter; what
I will do now is to delineate the general structure of
the metate market, i.e., the transactional arena in
which metate suppliers meet metate demanders.

On the General Structure of the Metate Market

Single market or multiple markets? My earlier
reference to a series of potentially competitive metate
markets implies that I have rejected the notion of a
single industry-wide competitive market, i.e., one
transactional network which integrates all buyers and
sellers of metates and cross-cuts localities. It is
possible to define such a market a priori as encompassing all buyer-seller transactions in which a metate
changes hands--implying that transactions in the Oaxaca
City, Ocotlan and Tlacolula marketplaces (not to mention those occurring outside the marketplace) occur in
the same market. But this assumes contact (direct or
indirect) between buyers and sellers in the separate
marketplace and the concomitant transmittal of current
market information between them, a situation which does
not obtain in the metate industry.

On the contrary, the metate data suggest that
the inter-marketplace circulation of market information, like the circulation of metates and their marketers, is irregular and discontinuous. There are, to
be sure, both potential and actual buyers and sellers
of metates who move between the Tlacolula and Oaxaca
City marketplaces or between the Ocotlan and Oaxaca
City marketplaces. But, to my knowledge, there is
no buyer or seller who regularly travels between all
three marketplaces--or between any two of them--to
trade in metates. As might be expected, the Oaxaca
City marketplace does serve as a conduit for the flow
of market information between Tlacolula and Ocotlan

(and vice-versa), and the same persons who transmit this information presumably are also informed of conditions in the Oaxaca City marketplace. Theoretically, then, at any given time there could be potential transactors with direct or indirect knowledge of prevailing metate market conditions in all three marketplaces. But, to reiterate, I have no evidence to suggest that such knowledge is employed to support activity in the purchase and sale of metates which could operate to regularly and systematically link together metate price negotiations in the three separate marketplaces (or even in two of them), even though their periodicity would be conducive to this. In short, the data indicate that metate transactions occur in three essentially separate and independent site-confined markets rather than in a single site-free market which crosscuts localities and integrades metate trading in discrete marketplaces.

Perfect or imperfect competition? The issue of a single market vs. multiple markets for the metate industry dovetails with the issue of whether the inter- and intra-marketplace marketing situation is characterized by perfect or imperfect compention. The above discussion of the inter-marketplace situation implies that on an industry-wide basis metate marketing is conditioned by various imperfections which tend to create a series of potential perfectly competitive submarkets, rather than a single industry-wide imperfectly competitive market. It is appropriate here to identify and discuss some of the conditions which contribute to the compartmentalization of the metate market at the inter-marketplace level.

What, for example, are some of the empirical generalizations which derive from an analysis of the metate price data that bear on the competition issue? Data collected over an eight-month period in 1966-67 in the Tlacolula, Ocotlan and Oaxaca City marketplaces show marked differences in the average monthly price levels among these markets. The widest gap was between the price level in the Oaxaca City market and those prevailing in Tlacolula and Ocotlan (i.e., the combined average price curve for the latter two was consistently around 15-20 pesos above the Oaxaca City average price curve). On the other hand, the Tlacolula and Ocotlan markets never displayed an average price curve difference as high as 15 pesos and only for two months did they display a difference greater than 10 pesos. As we will see, these price differentials reflect a variety of factors including imperfect buyer/

seller knowledge, moderate product differentiation creating quasi-brand loyalties, transportation costs, and wholesale vs. retail trade volume.[3]

Transportation costs (i.e., bus and/or truck fare plus whatever is required to compensate the individual who carts metates between locations) represents one important factor in discouraging inter-marketplace trade. Given the price differences between the Oaxaca City and Tlacolula/Ocotlan marketplaces, together with their relative locations vis-a-vis each other and the metate production centers which supply them, arbitrage (i.e., buying metates in the most favorable price location and transporting them for sale in locations of higher prices) would only be feasible from Oaxaca City to Tlacolula or Ocotlan. On the basis of transport costs alone such an arbitrage might appear to be profitable in the short run. But, in reality, other factors intervene to alter the situation. For example, any middleman who acquired metates in Oaxaca City for resale in either Ocotlan or Tlacolula would have to compete against the producers who supply these marketplaces; in the case of the Tlacolula marketplace he would, in many instances, be competing with his own suppliers. While the arbitrager would not be operating under this disadvantage in the Ocotlan marketplace, other factors discourage a Oaxaca City to Ocotlan trade. For one thing, the sales volume is much smaller in Ocotlan (and in Tlacolula) than it is in Oaxaca City, so that even if the trader could successfully conduct business in the market his cash returns would be low. Also, the metate buying public in Ocotlan (and in Tlacolula) have developed strong preferences for particular traits in metates (i.e., special qualities of workmanship, type of stone, size, color) which are usually not present in the lower-priced metates sold in Oaxaca City. In sum, there are many factors which minimize the inter-marketplace trade of metates in the Valley of Oaxaca.

One important difference, alluded to earlier, between the Tlacolula and Ocotlan metate markets, and the Oaxaca City market, is that the former involve mostly retail transactions at a relatively low volume of total sales per given time period, whereas the Oaxaca City market involves a larger proportion of wholesale transactions at a higher volume of total sales. Thus, out of a total of 624 separate transactions (transferring 1320 metates) recorded for a period of 100 trading days between 1966 and 1968 in the San Sebastian sales area of the Oaxaca City marketplace, approximately 62% comprised purchases of two or more metates for resale purposes. A single big-lot buyer who resells in Ejutla and Miahuatlan pur-chased 45% of the metates sold (582); another 24% of total metate sales during this same period was to several big-lot buyers from the Isthmus; 8% was to one middleman from Ocotlan who resells along the Ejutla-Miahuatlan-Pochutla axis, and 7% were purchased by traders from San Juan Teitipac for resale in the Oaxaca City marketplace. In other words, about 84% of total metate sales by San Sebastian sellers in the Oaxaca City marketplace was to resellers who purchased in lots of two or more metates per transaction and who may acquire as many as a dozen or more metates on any giv-en trading day. This is in marked contrast to the situation in the Ocotlan and Tlacolula marketplaces over the same period where more than 95% of all re-corded sales were to individual buyers for private use and involved only one metate per transaction. Obviously, then, the role of big-lot buyers in the Ocotlan and Tlacolula metate markets is minimal.

A reasonable inference from regular and high-volume wholesale buying in the Oaxaca City metate market is that bargaining advantages lies with the buyers. Such an inference would, after all, support the case for imperfect competition in the metate in-dustry. Yet an examination of the supply side of the market with special reference to the problem of free-dom of entry of potential suppliers suggests the pos-sibility of countervailing forces. It is an axiom of economic theory that natural or cultural conditions can produce monopoly--i.e., the position of the seller of a commodity with no near substitutes. Within the total market-area served by the Valley of Oaxaca metate industry (or within each of the three market-areas supplied by a particular production centers), it can be argued that the metateros as a collectivity occupy a semi-monopoly position. This does not mean that they are in a formal collusive posture with respect to the buyers or that they have complete control over price; there is ample data to demonstrate that neither of these conditions exists. What it does mean, however, is that certain natural and cultural factors are present in this regional economy to sig-nificantly restrict entry as supplier into the market for any locally produced commodity.

In the metate industry, for example, a pre-requisite of production is the availability of access-ible deposits of the proper kind of stone. Moreover,

246

for any individual to gain entry into metate production he must first satisfy a whole series of particularistic requirements (e.g., citizenship rights in a corporate village, acquisition of the necessary technical knowledge and skills). It is very difficult for a non-native of a metate village to acquire ownership or use rights to land for purposes of cultivation, quarrying or other use; it is also more difficult for a non-metatero native villager who wishes to learn the craft to do so if he does not have real or fictive kinsmen among the active metateros. In essence, and one of the many examples in the Valley of Oaxaca of production specialization by community, combined with a tendency toward intra-community occupational specialization by family, the metate industry is relatively well insulated against possible competition from new producers.

The lack of cooperative marketing organization within and between metate-producing groups precludes a formalization of natural monopolistic elements into a collective market strategy. Nevertheless, these factors do function indirectly to protect the metate sellers from the price negotiating power of big-lot buyers, and to make the individual producer (and the industries) somewhat less vulnerable to the rigors of competition. Of course, the producer-seller does compete against many other producer-sellers in the market; but the big-lot buyer is also competing against several other big-lot buyers. In the context of price determination it is probably true that the big-lot buyer has a short-run advantage over the small-lot seller. But considered in the broader context of the organization of production in the Oaxaca Valley economy, it is the big-lot buyer who is dependent in the long run upon the small-lot producer-seller as the only viable, direct and regular source of metates. Given the presence of competing buyers and the relative freedom of entry into the trading sector of the economy, it can be argued that the middleman-trader, not the producer-seller, is most vulnerable to the forces of competition.[4]

Differential atomistic competition at the intra-marketplace level. Up to this point I have presented data and arguments in support of the thesis that, at the inter-marketplace or industry-wide level of analysis, the structure of metate marketing is imperfectly or monopolistically competitive. Locational factors, including location of production sites vis-a-vis primary marketing outlets and the relative locations of the latter, together with transportation costs, are certainly of demonstrable importance in determining the compartmentalized structure of metate marketing. When we concentrate our attention on the marketplace-specific market, however, several nonlocational factors are operative which tend to reinforce compartmentalization of the inter-marketplace structure. In this context metate trading tends to approximate the economist's model of "differentiated atomistic competition" (Dorfman 1964:89). This is a situation in which producers (or sellers) of moderately differentiated products like metates sell at different prices because ". . . the customers have come to perceive differences in the qualities of the products . . . and, while some customers avail themselves of the cheaper variant, others are willing to pay a premium for the one they consider superior" (op. cit.).

Such characteristic differences in metates as size, style, fineness of finish, handsomeness of decoration, color and hardness of stone (i.e., indices of the expected durability of a metate) are all factors over which the metatero has varying degrees of control and provide criteria by which buyers perceive, judge, and purchase metates. The Tlacolula metateros, for example, limit their work to prime stone (i.e., as measured in terms of hardness, composition, texture and color) which is relatively difficult to cut but which yields large, durable, high-quality metates. Moreover, these metateros exercise special care and patience in finishing and decorating their products. This combination of factors, which results in a larger input of man-hours per unit of output, has given the Tlacolula metate a deserved reputation for style and quality; it has also been reflected in the relatively high average price level for metates in that market. A comparable situation exists in Ocotlan where several of the Magdalena metateros have created and maintained large clientele on the basis of the durability and quality of their products.[5]

To propose the presence of brand-like configurations in metate-marketing is not to imply the absence of heterogeneity in marketplace inventories. In fact, on any given trading day in each of the market-places the metate inventory is varied--ranging from poorly made, small, utility metates to expertly made, large, luxury or gift metates--and the range of final selling prices is correspondingly wide (again reflecting the Marxian law of value). Yet, the central tendencies of product traits, quantity and quality of embodied labor, prices and buyer/seller behavior

248

incline each marketplace situation toward a distinctive
market configuration. Despite intra-marketplace heterogeneity of inventory, buyer preferences and loyal-
ities to a particular type of metate are reinforced in
the marketplace by seller behavior. In the bargaining
situation buyers are often reminded of the positive
attributes of, say, a Magdalena or a Tlacolula metate
compared to those produced elsewhere; differences between metates of the seller's own group are not emphasized as much as differences between these and
metates produced in other communities. Thus, the occasional appearance of a seller in the Ocotlan marketplace with metates produced in the Teitipac villages
invariably elicits criticism from the local sellers
which emphasizes the putatively inferior quality and
workmanship of their competitors' products. In short,
between marketplaces (and between separate producer-
seller groups) there are a series of real and fictive
differences among metates of the same general type
which function to limit substitutability and to provide a partial basis for differential pricing.[6]

Disregarding for a moment moderate product differentiation within and between marketplaces, and at-
tempting to understand the nature of competition in
metate marketing from a somewhat different perspective,
the following state of afairs can be posited as typ-
ifying each of the three markets: on any given trading
day metates with similar characteristics tend to be
sold at different prices (though the differences may
be slight--and are larger between metates with dis-
similar characteristics). This is true because transactions in these markets occur as a series of semi-
independent events, partially independent of past and
contemporary transactions in the same market. Individual transactions are conducted through bargaining
but are not unique and wholly independent of each other.
Any individual entering into a bargaining sequence is
aware that there are other potential buyers or sellers
of metates in the marketplace and may, in fact, have
already negotiated with one or more of them in previous bargaining sequences on that or another trading
day. This knowledge and/or experience does not imply
that the individual has an understanding of supply
and demand concepts but does imply an awareness of the
possibility of a better deal for a similar metate with
another trader. Consequently, if a potential buyer
perceives a particular seller's minimum selling price
as being too high (even if the quotation is below the
maximum price the buyer is willing to pay) he or she
may withdraw from negotiations and seek a seller

whose minimum selling price is lower. It is, of course, entirely possible that non-price considerations will also have a bearing on a buyer's decision in such a situation.

One of the few notable exceptions to this pattern of price determination is a tendency among some sellers and buyers to establish semi-formalized trading partnerships ('marchante' relationship)--a tentative sort of 'gentlemen's agreement' typically linking a San Sebastian producer-seller (propio) to a regatón and often entailing cash advances by the latter to the former. These arrangements tend to be brittle and are not perceived as long-term relationships which are binding upon either party. Either buyer or seller may do business elsewhere when he or she feels that it will be advantageous to do so. In other words, such loose 'partnerships' are constantly tested against actual market conditions.

Spatial Patterns in Metate Marketing

On the structure of the metate market-areas. I have compared the Tlacolula-, Oaxaca City- and Ocotlan-centered metate markets in several basic dimensions of marketing analysis. But how may the market-areas which they supply be characterized and compared? As is the case with price levels, Ocotlan and Tlacolula resemble each other more than either of them resembles Oaxaca; that is, the market-areas centered in Ocotlan and Tlacolula contrast sharply in structure and size with the Oaxaca City-centered market-area. A large majority of the buyers who purchase metates in Ocotlan and Tlacolula either reside in villages within the judicial-administrative districts of which they are the head towns (cabeceras) or are residents of these head towns. Indeed, out of a total of 380 transactions recorded (390 metates sold) in the Ocotlan marketplace on sixty-two trading days over a two-year period, 64% of the metates sold were bought by persons living within the cabecera jurisdiction of Ocotlan, 20% by persons from the contiguous jurisdiction of Zimatlan and 4% by persons from the contiguous jurisdiction of Ejutla. All told, buyers from 68 different communities purchased metates from Magdalena sellers in the Ocotlan marketplace; 71% of total sales were to buyers representing 17 different communities of origin--the six most important being San Miguel Tilquiapan, Ocotlan de Morelos, Santiago Apostol, Asuncion Ocotlan, San Pablo Huistepec, and San Baltazar Chichicapam (only one of

which is not within the Ocotlan district). Even
though the market-area boundaries are not coterminous
with the jurisdictional boundaries of the cabecera,
the total area supplied is culturally homogeneous and
geographically continuous--if diverse in ecology
and economy. The data from Tlacolula reinforce this
pattern: out of a total of 80 transactions recorded
over a 12-week period only 11% involved buyers from
outside the cabecera jurisdiction.

The Oaxaca City-centered metate market-area contrasts sharply with the Tlacolula/Ocotlan pattern.
Approximately 53% of all metates sold in the Oaxaca
City marketplace by San Sebastian sellers over the
two-year period (total = 1320 metates) were distributed
either in peripheral districts of the 'Central Valleys'
region (e.g., Ejutla, Sola de Vega, Miahuatlán) or
outside of the region in the southern highlands or
Pacific coast (e.g., Salina Cruz, Tehuantepec, Juchitan,
Matias Romero); and the remaining 23% were distributed
in the Sierra de Juarez, the Sierra Mixteca, and in
areas of the 'Central Valleys' not included in the
Tlacolula and Ocotlan market-areas (e.g., Zaachila,
Etla). In short, the Oaxaca City-centered market-area
is spatially discontinuous, culturally heterogeneous,
more extensive in territory, and supplies a much
larger population than the other two market-areas. The
specialized wholesaling function of the Oaxaca City
metate market, combined with the magnitude and diversity
of its market-area, demonstrate the existence of a
centralized and rationalized distributional system
underlying the ostensible chaos and unpredictability of
weekly trading activity.

The circulatory routes of metates. As durable
consumer products, the metate and mano follow routes
of exchange which terminate only as they enter into
the process of utilization in the individual consumer
household. However, there are several alternative
routes of circulation for these products which are
associated with contrasting spatial, social structural,
behavioral and statistical patterns. The accompanying
Figure 5 schematizes the spatial patterns in metate
marketing and serves as a point of departure for a
discussion of related problems.

Before turning to a discussion of the Figure
and in order to cut through some of the semantic
ambiguity characterizing popular usage among Oaxacans
in the labeling of marketing roles, it is useful to
distinguish between roles originating on the producer

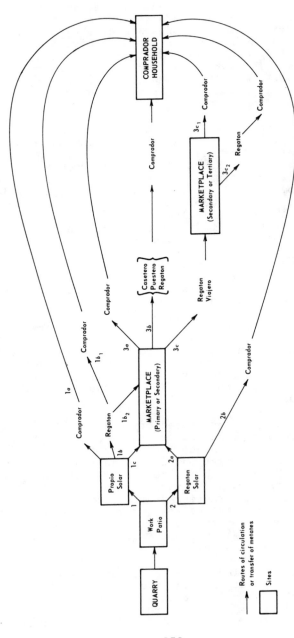

FIGURE 5. Circulatory Routes in Metate Production

or supply side of the marketplace (i.e., those associated with circulatory routes 1 and 2 in Figure 5) and those originating on the demand or consumer side of the marketplace (i.e., those associated with routes 3a, 3b and 3c in Figure 5). In the former context the propio is an individual producer who sells products which he personally has manufactured; the term is also employed (along with comprador or cliente) to refer to the buyer who purchases products for use in his own household-- and to avoid confusion I have used the term 'comprador' to refer to this private buyer-consumer. Regatón is another term with multiple referents among the Oaxacans. In the village context it refers either to an individual who regularly buys metates (or other products) from propios for resale in the marketplace, or to an individual who is not a native of the producing village and who buys metates for resale in his home village or elsewhere. These petty trading regatones may also be finishers (labradores) of metates or manos and often buy semi-finished products.

In the producing villages there are some individuals who combine activities as propios and regatones but this occurs occasionally and involves only a few of the propios. Many regatones are also finishers but this does not make them full-fledged metateros or propios; the latter status implies that its occupant works in the quarrying and pre-finishing stages of manufacture, as well as in the finishing stages. The distinction between propio and regatón is made by the villagers themselves; they do not use a hyphenated term like propio-regatón or metatero-regatón to refer to those individuals who combine two roles. Such an individual will be locally identified by his role in manufacturing (i.e., as propio or metatero). In summation, the following generalization can be made about marketing roles on the production side of the marketplace: whereas only a few propios occasionally enter the market as regatones, a majority of regatones regularly work as finishers (labradores) of the metates (or manos) they buy to resell.

On the demand or consumer side of the marketplace, the word regatón (regatona for female traders) is employed by the metate sellers as a cover term to refer to three basic types of middlemen: (1) those who are regular big-lot buyers of metates for resale on a wholesale/retail basis in distant marketing centers (e.g., Salina Cruz, Tehuantepec, Juchitan, Miahuatlan, Pochutla); (2) those who are regular small-lot buyers of metates for resale on a weekly retail

253

basis in the Oaxaca City marketplace, in smaller hinterland marketplaces (e.g., Zaachila, Zimatlan, Sola
de Vega, Ayoquesco), or periodically in fiesta marketplaces held in the Valley or beyond (e.g., San Pablo
Huistepec, Juquila, Canderlaria); and (3) those who
periodically buy small lots of metates for resale on
a daily retail basis in the marketplace as one line
of their shop-(caseta) or stall-(puesto) based trade.
In contrast to their counterparts on the other side of
the marketplace, these middlemen deal only in finished
products; they perform no manufacturing or finishing
tasks whatsoever (except for an occasional touch-up
job).

With these terminological distinctions in mind
it is appropriate to focus attention once again on
Figure 5. Two principal circulatory routes for
metates, each with alternatives, are illustrated: (1)
the propio-centered route with two extra-marketplace
alternative routes (1a and 1b) and two marketplace-
mediated alternative routes (1b$_2$ and 1c); and (2) the
regatón-centered route with one marketplace-mediated
alternative route (2a) and one extra-marketplace
alternative route (2b). All routes originate in the
work patios adjacent to the quarries, and transfers
from there to residence lot work places in the village
involve semi-finished metates. A majority of metates
transferred from either propio or regatón residence
lots are finished and ready for use. However, finishing tasks are sometimes performed in the marketplace
sales area (especially in Ocotlan).

The route with the highest volume of circulation
is that through which the propios transport their own
semi-finished products from the quarry work patios to
their village residence lots for finishing, and then
transport the finished products to the marketplace.
This route (1c) accounted for approximately 2/3 of
total sales (606 metates) in 1967-68 by San Sebastian
sellers in the Oaxaca City marketplace. Or, alternatively, the propio sometimes transfers (by sales, gift,
or barter) his finished metates directly to consumers
without going to the marketplace. This alternative
(route 1a) typically involves encargos (special orders)
or ceremonial transfers (e.g., propio gives gift
metates to bride who is relative or godchild) but may
also involve direct cash sale (usually to a fellow
villager or to a buyer from a near by village). Still
another alternative route (1b) is for the propio to
sell (finished or unfinished) metates from his residence lot inventory to regatones (from his own or a

254

nearby village) who, in turn, resell them in the marketplace (1b$_2$) or in extra-marketplace transactions (1b$_1$).
That these are important routes quantitatively is shown
by the fact that from August 1967 through June 1968 approximately 27% (255) San Sebastian metates were sold
by propios to regatones from other villages (especially
San Juan Teitipac), and that just under one-third of all
transactions in the Oaxaca City marketplace involved
San Sebastian regatones as sellers. So much, then,
for the propio-centered routes for marketing metates.

The regatón-centered routes (2a and 2b) are
those originating with the acquisition by local regatones of semi-finished products in the quarry work area.
These metates (or manos) are then transported (by burro)
to village residence lots for finishing. Typically, the
regatón, either with members of his or her own family or
with hired help, finishes these metates for subsequent
transport to the marketplace (2a) or directly to the
consumer in extra-marketplace transactions(2b). Those
regatones who take physical possession of semi-finished
products in the quarries have usually acquired a prior
claim to a given metatero's output by having paid him a
cash advance (adelanto). The regatón's trip to the
quarry is made to assure prompt repayment and to enable
him (or her) to choose a metate he wants. Certainly no
more than one-fifth of all metates marketed by local
regatones are directly appropriated in the quarries.

It is interesting to note that by no means all
metates which pass from propio to regatón in the producing village do so through purchase or sale (i.e.,
via cash-mediated transactions)--although this is the
predominant mode of transfer there and is the exclusive
mode of transfer in the marketplace. While I have only
limited and random data on metate transfers in the producing village transacted without money payment, I do
have records of some gift transfers and of twelve instances of barter between propios and other villagers
(usually regatones) in which metates were exchanged for
other products or services. Of these twelve recorded
transactions (occurring in San Sebastian Teitipac in
1967-68), six (6) saw propios exchanging semi-finished
metates in the quarry for prepared food (chicharrón) or
beverages (tejate). One of these metate-for-food exchanges was a multiple transaction which went as follows:
various metateros in a work company (companía) drank
tejate (non-alcoholic beverage made from ground corn)
offered by a vendor, then each contributed labor toward
the semi-finishing of a metate which, when semi-finished,
was given to the tejate vendor (a woman from the village

255

who was a regatona). Of the six remaining instances
of barter, two involved the exchange of semi-finished
metates for the use of an ox team for plowing the
propio's fields; one involved the transfer of a metate
for a quantity of dried beans; another saw a semi-finished metate exchanged for finishing services on three
unfinished metates; and the last entailed the exchange
of one small finished metate for one barreta (crowbar).
In most of these cases, the metates exchanged were
eventually brought into the marketplace for resale by
the village regatones who either originally or subsequently acquired them. [8]

Just as metates follow three routes into the
marketplace there are three routes they take out, regardless of whether they enter as property of propio
or regatón. The first of these (3a) is the most direct
route to the ultimate destination of every metate,
namely, utilization in the food preparation area of a
peasant household: the buyer represents the household
and acquires one metate directly from its seller
(either propio or regatón). This seller-to-comprador
route accounted for roughly 8% of the total sales by
San Sebastian sellers in the Oaxaca City marketplace
in 1967/68, but for 95% of total sales by Magdalena
sellers in the Ocotlan marketplace during the same
period--clearly demonstrating their overwhelming retail
specialization. The second route (3b) is somewhat
less direct, having one intervening link between the
market-place and the comprador, namely, a stall-based
retail vendor (puestero, casetero, regatón) who buys
from the propio or from the village-to-marketplace
regatón and resells to the comprador. This route accounted for about 13% of total sales in the Oaxaca City
marketplace (by San Sebastian sellers) in 1967/68, but
for only 2% in Ocotlan. Finally, the third route (3c)
is the most circuitous and not only finds the metates
passing through another marketplace in the hands of a
regatón (i.e., the big-lot buyer/intermarketplace
trader) but, in many cases, being resold to yet another
regatón (marketplace-to-village type) before coming to
rest in the comprador household ($3c_2$). The wholesale
specialization of the San Sebastian sellers in the
Oaxaca City marketplace is demonstrated by the fact
that 69% of their sales in 1967/68 followed this
regatón-dominated path, as compared to only 3% of the
sales by the Magdalenans in Ocotlan.

Metate Sellers in the Marketplace: Bargaining
Strategies and Tactics

   For propios and regatones alike the plaza is
viewed as a place where a multitude of commodities are
bought and sold at prices that are usually negotiable
(except in tiendas where they are fixed). The plaza
is recognized as an arena of concentrated supply and
demand where one can find buyers for what one brings
to sell and sellers of what one needs to buy. One
informant expressed this dual function of the plaza as
follows:

       Around here one says, 'Let's go to the
       plaza; that's where we go to spend our
       money. I get what I earn during the week,
       I earn it, in the plaza; and I spend it
       there buying what we need to maintain
       ourselves.

As sellers, the metatero and regatón alike are quite
sensitive to buyer preferences. One metatero, for example, gave the following explanation of why he had
worked in several different quarries during his career:

       Well, I've worked in nearly all the quarries
       in the village because the plaza commands.
       At times buyers seem to prefer greenish
       stone; other times they go for the purplish.
       If they ask for the one, I'll find it; if
       they want the other I can get it too.

Over the years, quarries have been abandoned and later
reoccupied by metateros as they attempt to satisfy
fluctuating consumer preferences for stone. The metateros don't necessarily like this and they do behave to
reinforce uniform preferences among their clientele,
preferences which fit the specifications and logistics
of their stone resources and quarry situations.

   One principle which all metate sellers follow in
their transactions with buyers is that of 'caveat emptor'
('Let the buyer beware'). In the metate market this
implies allowing the buyer to examine the product which
interests him or her and to reach a decision to buy it
at his/her own risk. Since the sellers' tactics are
designed to counter those of buyers, this means that

all of the sellers' comments about their products are positive (e.g., "This metate is made of hard stone") in contrast to the buyers' queries or disparaging remarks ("Is the stone hard?" or "It seems to me that the stone's no good"). A typical response among metate sellers to my question, "In the plaza how do you try to get the best price from a client?," was as follows: "Showing him the metate, so that he may see that it's good, clean, well-made--that it has no defects. And one demonstrates the metate [grinding corn] and, thus, the client can be convinced to pay the price."

In accord with the 'caveat emptor' principle, flaws or breaks in metates are carefully and skillfully camouflaged by painted decorations, broken legs are cemented back into place, and the repaired metates are sold as if they were in mint condition. The metate sellers rationalize this by saying that the client is responsible for judging the quality of their products and for deciding whether or not to buy. The metate seller will not mention a repair to a client, and if the latter should discover it, the seller will deny that the product in question has been repaired. The following description of an incident which I witnessed in the Ocotlan marketplace in December 1967 will illustrate this sales strategy:

> The most interesting incident of the day involved Jaime who brought a metate to plaza which had been broken and repaired. Two weeks ago he broke off one of its legs while cutting it. He brought it to his residence lot from the quarry, and proceeded to fasten it back on the metate using a mixture of cement and glue. He then finished the metate and painted it with a special design large enough to camouflage the break. According to J. this is approximately the sixth time that he has repaired a metate since he became a metatero.

> In the plaza J. consistently made a high opening quote for this metate. At 10:00 he opened a negotiation with a quote of 85 pesos which the buyer countered with a 60 pesos bid--more in line with the going market price of a metate of this size and finish (without the flaw). J. made a final counter-quotation of 80 pesos and the

buyer withdrew. I was surprised by J.'s strategy since I had assumed that he would 'dump' the metate on the first buyer who made a reasonable offer. J. maintained his posture all morning and finally sold the metate for 70 pesos. The buyer had spent at least two hours in the sales area examining all the available metates (11) and bargaining actively with several different sellers. His final choice was between two metates, one of which was J.'s flawed one. The buyer sought assurances from J. that the metate was made of good stone--which J. obligingly provided. The buyer closely examined the metate from all sides and never detected a flaw. After buying the metate the buyer asked for J.'s name and then gave his own which, ironically, turned out to be the same as J.'s.

After the buyer had left the sales area with the metate I asked J. if he was concerned about the possibility of a request for a refund if the buyer discovered the flaw. J. admitted that this was a possibility but didn't expect it to occur. His attitude was that, after all, he had not forced the decision to buy the metate upon the buyer; the latter's choice had been his own. J. manifested no overt indication of any remorse over his deceit in selling a defective product. He had done the same on five prior occasions and had never had a buyer protest or seek a refund.

I told J. that I had seen a metate seller taken to the police station in Oaxaca City for selling a broken metate; that the metate had been confiscated by the authorities, the purchase price returned to the buyer, and the seller fined 20 pesos (which was true). This seller was a regatona and could argue (as she did) that she herself had been deceived by the metatero who sold it to her (which wasn't true--she bought it cheap as a flawed product). J.'s reaction was that if such an incident were to arise that he would also claim that he is a regatón and is not responsible for the deceit.

As this latter incident suggests there are times when the informal code of the metate sellers comes into conflict with the formal laws of the marketplace. The regatona incident involved an irate buyer who returned a metate to the seller in the marketplace where he had purchased it the previous week and demanded a refund. The surface of the metate, he claimed, crumbled under the friction of grinding--and he had no intention of eating stone in his tortillas! The regatona described the incident in her own words as follows:

> Eight days ago I sold a pretty metate of good stone to a cllent--and today he returns the metate and tells me he wants a refund. I told him: "'A deal's a deal'--an article that I buy, do you think I would return it to the seller?" And he replied: "Don't give me any trouble or you'll suffer the consequences." "But sir," I told him, "how was I to know if the stone was good or not? Now, I repeat, I'm in business, and a sale is a sale." She said that she also told him, "Don't you think that we have failures too? For example, we buy oxen in the plaza but how do we know if they're any good? We come home and discover they're no good. What can we do about it?"

The regatona's spirited defense of her position was to no avail (she was aware beforehand that the metate in question was made of inferior stone)--as she suffered the penalties described above.

One further example illustrates not only the principle of caveat emptor but also the effectiveness with which the ethical code for marketplace behavior is enforced:

> The most interesting incident of this day involved R. (metate seller--propio) and an ambulatory fruit vendor. R. was on the verge of consummating a negotiation for his metate with a buyer when an apple vendor walked into the metate sales area. As she passed by R.'s metate she accidentally brushed against the mano (which was resting on the metate) causing it to fall to the cobblestone sidewalk and split in half--

much to the consternation of everyone. R. had been patiently assuring and reassuring the buyer that the metate and mano were made of the best quality, most durable stone. The ease with which the mano broke vividly demonstrated the contrary. A heated argument immediately erupted between R. (and his wife) and the fruit vendor. The latter, disclaiming any part in the incident, slowly walked away from the area and R. went hurriedly to find a policeman while his wife kept the fruit vendor under surveillance. When the latter saw R. approaching with a policeman, she promptly paid R.'s wife for the mano. In the meantime R.'s prospective buyer had left the scene without buying the metate.

Another informal rule of the metate market is the essential inviolability of the discrete transaction. Once serious negotiations have been initiated between buyer and seller, the latter will not entertain bids from interloping potential buyers. This is illustrated by the following excerpt from my field notes for January 26, 1968:

At one point in the transaction involving M.--which consummated in a 50 pesos sale to a buyer from San Cristobal--negotiations were deadlocked; and a second buyer who had been observing the proceedings tried to elicit a separate quote from M. But M. refused saying "Estoy tratando con otro señor."

This is not to imply that metate sellers do not consciously play off one buyer against another; indeed they do so regularly--but only after negotiations are deadlocked. For example, I witnessed the following bargaining sequence in the Ocotlan marketplace (October 13, 1967):

Quote	Bid
80	40
75	40
50	45
50	50
65	55
60	55
60	55
60	60

After his first quotation of 60 pesos the seller said
to the prospective buyer, "partimos el queso" ("let's
split the difference")--implying that the 65-55 deadlock
could be resolved by agreeing on a final selling price
of 60 pesos. At this point, a second prospective buyer
began to express interest in the seller's metate; but
in response to the second prospective buyer's inquiry
the seller asked him to wait until the ongoing negotiation was terminated. After making the 60 pesos quotation a second time, the seller said to the first
prospective buyer: "Por cinco pesos está la parada"
("The deadlock is over five pesos"). This was his
euphemism for "put up or shut up." After receiving
another bid of 55 pesos from this buyer, the seller
turned to the second prospective buyer and said,
"Entre muchacho" ("Come in, boy")--which indicated his
readiness to negotiate with him. Before this could
begin, however, the first buyer agreed to the 60 pesos
selling price. The seller's tactic had paid off.

In other words, metate sellers negotiate with
prospective buyers consecutively, not simultaneously--
but in deadlocked negotiations do employ the tactic
of playing one potential buyer off against another.
Incidentally, this same rule also operates between
sellers: no effort is made to interrupt negotiations
between another seller and a potential buyer--but there
is often a quick follow-up of deadlocked or aborted
transactions by competing sellers.

The metate seller arrives in the marketplace
with definite expectations as to what his day's earnings should be; these are based upon his knowledge of
current market conditions gained through conversations
with his companions or through his own marketplace experiences in previous weeks. So prior to his entry
into the marketplace on any given plaza day, he has an

accurate idea of the going market prices for various types of metates and will negotiate accordingly, always trying to keep the buyer's offers as high above his minimum acceptable return (i.e., "supply price") as possible.

As a general rule, the seller makes an opening quotation at the prospective buyer's request to open negotiations. The act of quoting is not a price-setting act. On the contrary, the initial quotation is understood by both parties to be provisional and is invariably altered during the course of subsequent haggling. The prospective buyer's initial bid usually undercuts the seller's opening quotation by an amount proportional to the gap between that quotation and the going market price (about which buyer knowledge is selective); and the final selling price is typically a compromise-- falling midway between the initial quotation and the initial bid. Thus, if a seller makes an opening quotation of 60 pesos for a metate whose going market price is around 45 pesos, the buyer's opening bid will be 30 pesos. If negotiations continue beyond the initial phase to consummation, the haggling process will converge at a price in the neighborhood of 45 pesos. If the bargaining process fails to close the quotation-bid gap to 10 pesos, the transaction will abort. As we will see in the next section, however, there are exceptions to this typical pattern. One metate seller summed up the bargaining situation as follows: "To haggle means not to have a set price but that the buyer buys and the seller sells. The seller asks the amount of money that he estimates the product to be worth. And the buyer that haggles offers a little less than what the seller asks. It goes that way until a deal is made, until they reach an agreement."

The form of bargaining is standardized but its conduct may vary from transaction to transaction. Verbal interaction between traders is customarily intense and often sarcastic but rarely is carried to the extreme of forcing the withdrawal (e.g., via insult) of either party. The _plaza_ is recognized as a unique setting for interaction in which a particular style and intensity of behavior is evoked. Thus, a common remark by a seller after a buyer tells him emphatically that his quotation is ridiculously high is, "I won't get angry with you because we're in the marketplace" ("_Estámos en la plaza, por eso no me enojo_"). Or, to elicit a bid from a buyer who snickers in reaction to a high opening quotation, the seller will remind the buyer of the context and urge him to bid: "We're in the marketplace, merchant; let's have your offer!" ("Es-támos en la plaza, marchante; a ver que ofrece ud!').

The buyer for private use is typically the most fastidious and deliberate bargainer. If a female, she will kneel down near the metate, pick up its mano, and assume the grinding position; often she requests corn from the seller to test the grinding qualities of the metate. Next, she will rub her hand over the grinding surface, pick at any possible flaws she detects there, and will carefully examine the underside of the metate. Finally, she will measure the metate, test its balance, and study its proportions and all aspects of its appearance. Male buyers often lift a metate to get an idea of its weight; both male and female buyers will sometimes test the hardness of the stone by chipping on the metate with a hand pick provided by the seller. In short, the metate is given a rigorous physical examination and visual appraisal in the course of haggling interplay between buyer and seller.

Various verbal tactics are employed by the metate seller to enable him (or her) to get the best of the prospective buyer in bargaining. If, for example, a buyer makes an especially low bid, the seller may comment cynically, "Ud, no tiene ganas de comprar" ("You really don't want to buy anything") or "Lo guardo en la bodega primero" ("I'll leave it in the storage place first"). In the case of a buyer who lingers in the sales area but who is hesitant to negotiate, the seller will offer assurances by saying something like, "You can get metates which are less expensive than mine but the stone is no good" or (if the season is appropriate) "You better buy a metate today because after the fiesta which is coming prices will be soaring." Buyers display an equally wide repertory of haggling tactics which are often employed in an attempt to bid down a seller's quotation. A common one is to belittle the quality of a metate ("It's made of soft stone"; "It has a flaw"; "It's too small"; etc.); another one is to accuse the seller of holding a grudge against him (e.g., "You must be mad at me, you're really teed off"; "You really want to push me"; "You're taking out your frustrations with others on me"). Many buyers will emphasize that they are buying a metate for their own use and not as a gift for a bride or to resell ("No quiero el metate para un fandango o para vender, es para que muela mi mujer"); others will simply argue that their offer is a fair one ("Le pago bién; no le castigo").

A transaction may be consummated in a few minutes

or may drag on for an hour or more--during which time the buyer may break off negotiations with one seller and initiate them with another, only to re-open negotiations subsequently with the first seller. Prolonging negotiations is usually to the buyer's advantage since the metate seller, especially the propio, is anxious to convert his products into cash to facilitate his own purchases in the marketplace. During periods of maximum buyer activity (e.g., January-April when there is a "sellers' market"), however, competition between buyers is keen (especially in Oaxaca City) and they wait for the sellers in the bus terminal and open negotiations with them as they unload their metates. This situation rarely occurs in Ocotlan where buyer activity--even during the peak demand season--never reaches the volume and intensity of Oaxaca City. My records show that most sales in the Ocotlan marketplace occur between 10:00 and 11:00 a.m.--with activity beginning by 9:00 a.m. and ending between 3:00 and 4:00 p.m. This differs from the Oaxaca City situation (for the propio trade) where trading begins earlier (between 6:00 and 7:00 a.m.) and ends sooner (usually by noon).

Miscalculations in negotiating are sometimes made by the metate sellers either through a lack of correct information about going prices or an incorrect judgment of buyer intentions. I observed one transaction in which a private buyer made a bid of 35 pesos to the seller's opening quotation of 60 pesos. As the negotiations progressed, the gap between bid and quotation narrowed to 5 pesos (quotation of 50, bid of 45) at which point the seller held firm and the buyer left the sales area. The seller anticipated the return of the buyer and expected to consummate the sale at 50 pesos. But the buyer did not return and the metate was sold later in the day for 40 pesos. Of course, I have also witnessed negotiations in which the seller's hedging paid off in a higher selling price.

Between 1966 and 1968 I observed several transactions in which a metate seller undersold a metate (in relation to the going market price) because of a failure to observe the negotiations of other sellers. In one instance, a metate seller arrived late in the marketplace and a buyer who had been bargaining for a half hour with another seller (opening quotation 120 pesos, bid 75) immediately approached the newly arrived seller requesting a quotation on a metate which was similar to that for which he had been haggling; these latter negotiations had reached a deadlock (quotation,

100, bid, 75). Unaware of the details of this previous negotiation, the newcomer quoted a price of 70 pesos which the buyer promptly accepted. Afterwards, when informed of the details of the previous negotiations, the newcomer was visibly chagrined and in subsequent negotiations for the remainder of his metates he kept his opening quotations on a par with those of the other sellers.[9]

Competition appears to be more intense between village-to-marketplace *regatones* than between *propios*. The former often criticize each other for engaging in unfair competition (e.g., spying on negotiations, making clandestine counts of product inventories of other sellers, stealing customers), whereas *propios* rarely make such complaints about each other. *Regatones* are also much more prone than are the *propios* to employ current price data in 'cutthroat competition' to undersell their competitors. This pattern carries over into the marketplace from the village where there is keen price competition among the *regatones* in purchasing metates from the *propios*. Space in the marketplace sales area may also be a source of conflict among *regatones*; it is allocated on a first-come, first-serve basis. Even though kinsmen, *compadres* and friends tend to occupy contiguous positions in the sales area week after week, there are occasions when a late-comer has difficulty in finding a space to occupy with his products. This tendency among some sellers to display aggressive competitiveness is referred to derogatorily as "*echando competencia*."[10]

By and large competitive prowess is not considered by the metate sellers to be a cause of any given seller's success as a seller. Both *propios* and *regatones* alike, when asked why some sellers get better prices than others, attribute this to a combination of luck and product differences. "Luck, they have luck," responded one seller to this question. "It's the luck of each person." "And, also, it depends on the metate," he continued. "If they sell dear the metate is well made; if they sell cheap the metate is not well made."

How does seller attendance at the marketplace vary over the annual marketing cycle? As might be expected my records show that variations in seller attendance correlate closely with variations in price and output (see Chapter 7). For example, over a two-year period (96 trading days) from September 1966 through June 1968 an average of 7 sellers per *plaza* day came to the Oaxaca City marketplace (San Sebastian sales area) or approximately 30 sellers per month. The months of highest attendance (October and December-April) are also the months of highest output and price (see Figure 10).[11]

When the metate seller arrives in the marketplace sales area he (or she) places the metates (and manos) together in rows on the pavement (or ground) in front of him. He either stands directly behind the products or stands toward the rear of the sales area and waits for a prospective buyer to show interest in the products. As a buyer comes into the sales area the seller will stay close to the products looking for an opportunity to open negotiations with the buyer. Only after a seller has spent several hours in the sales area will he leave the area to seek out buyers (e.g., the puesteros or stall owners).[12]

Before initiating negotiations with a prospective buyer, the metate seller--on the basis of cues like mode of dress, speech and general appearance--will have made a social character judgment about the buyer which will influence the seller's negotiating strategy and tactics. For example, the seller will have categorized the buyer as a campesino (peasant), turista (tourist), regatón (trader), and so on, and will probably have identified the buyer's place of origin (e.g., a particular village or town in the Valley, or a particular region like the Sierra, the Isthmus). Thus, if the seller identifies a buyer as a "serrano" (i.e., from remote highland areas who often appear 'Indian' in dress and speak broken Spanish), he will be more aggressive in bargaining--open with a higher quotation and display extra perseverance in maintaining this position. While there is some tendency on the part of sellers to deride "serrano" buyers (behind their backs) for peculiar speech patterns (or by referring to them as "atrasados"), discrimination in pricing is not attributable solely to 'ethnic' prejudice--but also reflects the fact that sellers are simply taking advantage of what seems to be relative market strength. This is especially true of the Magdalena sellers in Ocotlan who realize that they hold a monopoly over the supply of metates in their market-area and that a "serrano" who has traveled a long distance to attend plaza is not likely to travel elsewhere to purchase a metate.

The metate sellers tend to classify buyers (with reference to bargaining tactics or conduct) as "good" or "bad"--with one explicit and one implicit sub-type in each class. Table 15 lists these types and gives selected informant statements which are descriptive of each sub-type. The two explicit sub-types are the "necesitado" and the "baratero." These terms are never employed with reference to the same buyer; they are mutually exclusive terms in the metate sellers' usage. A "necesitado" is usually a buyer who displays the characteristics of a "serrano." The "baratero," on the other hand, is typically employed with reference to 'hard-nosed' bargainers from villages within the home district of the sellers or to regatones (either inter-village traders or big-lot buyers).

Price Determination: A Graphical Analysis

Among other things, the previous discussion points clearly to the price-setting nature of the metate market: metate prices are negotiated between sellers and buyers through a haggling process which involves a successive series of quotations and bids in discrete bargaining sequences. In Chapter 7 we will examine the variability of average price, output and sales levels in the metate market--and raise the question of the extent to which price determination on discrete trading days reflects or relates to these movements at the macro-level. In the present section, through the use of price determination graphs derived from data collected during a ten-month period and covering over 100 separate bargaining transactions in the Ocotlan marketplace, I will attempt to link the micro-level of the separate transaction to the macro-level of aggregate price and output for a sector of the metate industry. In other words, I will focus on the hows and whys of specific situational pricing behavior in the context of more generalized market structures and processes.

Figure 6 displays data which show the patterned, seasonally programmed nature of metate market activity. Curve AQ in graph A shows clearly that metate sellers vary their opening quotations monthly and seasonally-- and that buyers, on the average, bid anywhere from 17 pesos (January) to 36 pesos (June) below the sellers' initial quotations (an average of 27 pesos below for the ten-month period). A comparison of curve AQ and AB with AP demonstrates, also, that while the initial quotations of sellers tend, on the average, to vary widely from final selling prices (20-30% above) the

Table 15. Types of 'Customers' According to the Metate Sellers

1. The 'good customer' (El 'cliente bueno')

A. The 'needy buyer' (El 'necesitado')

". . . he/she begs, and begs, and begs and one knows that he/she wants to buy" (". . . ruegue, ruegue y ruegue y ruegue y sabe uno que tiene ganas de comprar")

"He/she comes down [from the mountains] to buy" ("Baja [de la Sierra] a comprar")

B. The 'fair trader'*

"They put higher prices" ("Ponen precios mas altos")

"Right away they put a price on the metate; they don't offer 40 or 50 pesos but right away offer 70, 80 pesos ("Luego, luego ponen precio al metate; ellos no dan 40, 50 pesos pero luego, luego ofrecen 70, 80 pesos)

"They offer a price that the metate is worth" ("Ofrecen un precio que vale el metate")

"They like our stone and pay better prices" ("Les gusta la clase de piedra que tenemos nosotros y pagan mejores precios")

". . . a reasonable person who comprehends that the work that one does is difficult. They tell us to sell our work for what it's worth" (". . . una persona de razon que comprende que el trabajo que uno hace es muy difícil. Luego dicen: que vende su trabajo en lo que vale. Se dan cuenta que no so consique un metate dondequiera")

2. The 'bad customer' (El 'cliente malo')

A. The 'cheapskate' (El 'baratero')

"They make one hesitant to negotiate because they offer bad prices" ("Esa gente da miedo para tratar porque ofrecen malos precios")

"They offer cheap prices" ("Muy baratos los precios que ofrecen")

"They are the stingiest when it comes to buying; they fool around a lot to arrive at a price; they want what's chea;" ("Son mas duros para comprar; dilatan mucho para que lleguen al precio; puro barato quiere")

B. The 'shopper'*

"As a passer-by he asks: 'How much is the metate worth?' He offers a lower price and goes away, and one knows that he stopped simply to ask prices" ("De pasadita dice: ¿cuanto vale el metate? Se ofrece otro precio mas bajo y se va; y uno se da cuenta que aquel nada mas vino a informarse de los precios")

"He comes only to ask . . . to compare prices" ("No mas viene a preguntar . . . a comparar precios")

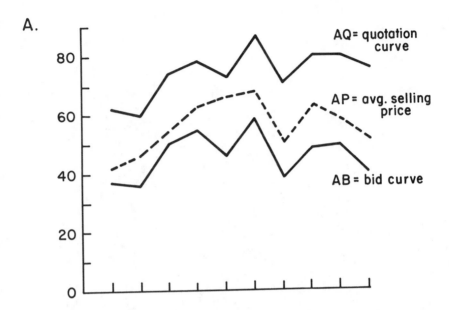

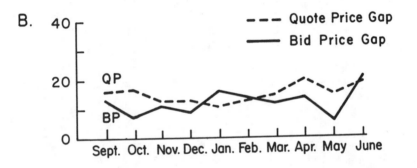

Figure 6.   Graph A: Average initial quotations and bids for 108 negotiations for metates in the Ocotlan marketplace between August 1967 and June 1968.   Curve AQ represents average initial quotations; Curve AB represents average initial bids; Curve AP represents average selling price.

Graph B: Average gap between initial quotation and final selling price and initial bid and final selling price for 76 consummated metate negotiations in the Ocotlan marketplace between August 1967 and June 1968.   Curve QP represents the initial quotation-final price gap; Curve BP represents the initial bid-final price gap.

initial bids of buyers have a fairly constant relation to them (10-15% below).

Starting in November it is obvious that the metate sellers consistently make higher opening quotations across the board--a trend which peaks in February. On the other hand, as the rainy season approaches (April, May) opening quotations become lower (see Curve AQ). Finally, the March decline is clearly reflected in the quotation curve which drops substantially in March from its February peak--indicating that sellers responded to the oversupply situation by decreasing opening quotations.

Graph B illustrates the shifting positions of buyers and sellers in the metate market over the ten-month period. Between September and December and again between March and May, buyers are apparently in the strongest negotiating position; they are able to purchase metates at prices which are closer to their initial bids than they are to the sellers' initial quotes. This position is reversed in January and February, however, and as the rainy season begins in April and May the sellers' position weakens again as the buyers' position becomes stronger (except in June when their respective positions appear to be, more or less, balanced).[13]

At the level of the individual negotiation how can we judge whether bargaining favors the buyer or the seller or determine which party enjoys the strongest position? Fortunately, the basis for such a judgment or determination is quantifiable, and in strict minimax terms either buyer or seller succeeds in minimizing costs or maximizing returns at the expense of his co-negotiator. Yet given the fact that the seller is, by convention, the initiator of negotiations-- coupled with his or her tendency to open with a quote well above the anticipated final selling price (and the minimum expected return)--it is probably not accurate to characterize his negotiating position as subordinate because of buyer success in minimizing expenditure. Rarely does a metate seller offer an initial quotation which corresponds to an estimate of going market price; it's usually closer to the price he or she would like to get, not to the price he or she thinks will be negotiated.

In examining a large corpus of price determination graphs the analyst is confronted with problems of classification before he can turn to those of analysis.

Perhaps the basic distinction, which is manifest in graph profiles, is between the consummated, the aborted, and the interrupted transaction. Each of these has a unique profile as illustrated in Figure 7 below.

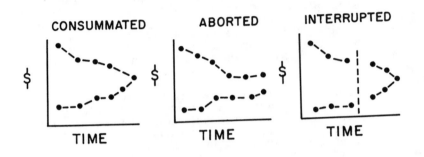

Figure 7.   Graph Profiles of the Consummated, the Aborted, and the Interrupted Transaction

Another basic distinction is between the assymetrical and the symmetrical transaction, the former favoring either buyer or seller and the latter favoring neither, as illustrated in Figure 8. Also, one must consider the factors of duration, the number of quotes and bids, the size of the initial quotation-bid gap, and others. Most of these factors will be dealt with in the analysis of the Ocotlan metate market data.

In our analysis we will focus primarily on consummated, uninterrupted transactions which are either symmetrical or assymetrical. As it turns out, 75 (23%) of the 108 negotiations recorded and graphed were consummated; of these 37 (49%) were assymetrical in favor of the buyer, 21 (28%) were assymetrical in favor of the seller, and 17 (23%) were symmetrical (favoring neither buyer nor seller). It should be emphasized, however, that on any given trading day during the year a particular negotiation may assume almost any pattern; the data do not yield evidence of any particular negotiating pattern which is uniquely characteristic of a given trading day, month or season. The existence of such patterns is perhaps implicit in some of the aggregate time series (see Chapter 7) but they do not emerge

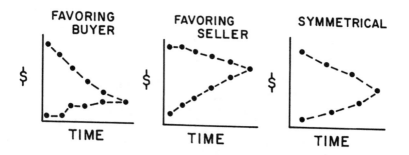

Figure 8.   Graph Profiles of Assymetrical and Symmetrical Transactions

at the level of the trading session. There are enough
sources of variability inherent in the market conditions
of each trading day to preclude patterning in negotiations which is specific to a particular moment in the
marketing cycle.

    This does not mean that the careful observer-
analyst cannot isolate patterns in negotiations which
reflect particular market conditions, nor that these
latter may not, in fact, tend to occur at one period
during the year rather than another. The analysis
in Chapter 7 of aggregate price, output and sales data
will demonstrate conclusively the presence of cyclical
patterning on a seasonal and inter-annual basis. Moreover, the price determination data themselves display
patterns which correspond to market conditions operating
at the aggregate level. Accordingly each graph in
Figure 9 represents a bargaining sequence which I selected to illustrate a market situation shown in the
aggregate data in graphs A and B in Figure 6, and implicit in the price, output and sales time series (Figures 10 through 14 in Chapter 7).

    To reiterate, I have selected those cases from
my trading records that are most representative of my
sample for a particular month. This does not mean that
either my sample or the cases selected from it are
completely representative of all the negotiations which

273

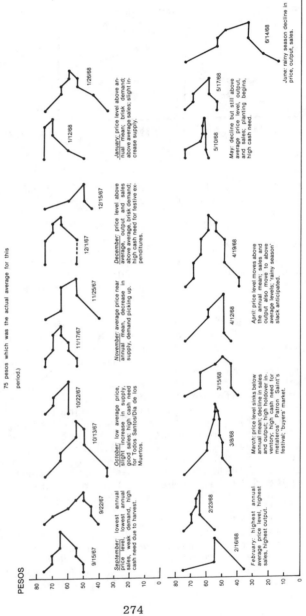

FIGURE 9.

Price Determination in Metate Bargaining in the Octotlan Marketplace between 9/15/67 and 6/14/68.

(All graphs are adjusted to uniform intervals on the time axis, and to a sellers' opening quotation of 75 pesos which was the actual average for this period.)

September: lowest annual price level, lowest annual sales, weak demand, high cash need due to harvest.

October: low average price, slight increase in supply, good sales; high cash need for Todos Santos/Día de los Muertos.

November: average price near annual mean, decrease in supply, demand picking up.

December: price level above average, output and sales above average, brisk demand; high cash need for festive expenditures.

January: price level above annual mean; brisk demand; above average sales; slight increase supply.

February: highest annual average price level, highest sales, highest output.

March: price level sinks below annual mean; decline in sales and output; high holdover inventory; high cash need for metateros' Patron Saint's festival; "buyers' market.

April: price level moves above the annual mean; sales and output also move to above average levels; "rainy season' slack anticipated.

May: decline but still above average price level, output, and sales; planting begins, high cash need.

June: rainy season decline in price, output, sales.

LAPSE OF TIME

274

occurred during that month. I do believe, however, that they are responses to the forces and conditions operative in the wider market at the time they occurred. We are not dealing here with abstractions but with the behavior of real individuals and the movements of real commodities.

To facilitate analysis I have adjusted the prices in each negotiation in proportion to a seller's initial quotation of 75 pesos--which is the actual average for the ten-month period. The vertical axis in each diagram represents prices in pesos scaled at ten peso intervals; the horizontal axis represents the time consumed by the negotiation. All graphs have been adjusted to uniform intervals on the time axis, with actual time required by a negotiation indicated on the graph when available (19 minute average per negotiation for all cases during the ten-month period). In the graphs the upper line represents the seller's quotations, and the lower line the buyer's bids; the final negotiated price is the point of intersection of the two lines. Each point on the graph represents a successive quotation or bid made by one party; it is the total configuration of the graph, not the level of the final price, which is most significant for purposes of this analysis.

A characteristic shared by all negotiations is the wide gap between the seller's opening quotation (which always comes first) and the buyer's opening bid; while there is some variation in the width of this gap it is not as great as the variation in the time required to close the gap. The range between the shortest and the longest continuous bargaining sequence is from two to forty minutes. Only a few of the graphs approximate complete symmetry (23% of the total sample), with both buyer and seller making concessions by regular increments. In all of the other graphs the shape is assymetrical, with either the buyer (49% of total sample) or the seller (28% of total sample) being more successful in resisting price concessions. There was only one negotiation (10/22/67) in which resistance was sustained throughout the negotiation by the seller but, significantly, none in which the buyer's initial bid was accepted.[14]

Most rural Oaxacans seem to enjoy the give and take of haggling and the seller or buyer who refuses to haggle (regatear) is atypical. During the two years that I observed marketplace trading for metates in Oaxaca I never witnessed a sales transaction consummated

without bargaining. The specific shape of the graphs
depicting negotiations is an outcome of the interplay
of two factors: the prevailing supply-demand conditions
and the negotiators' knowledge of them, and the bargaining skills of the negotiators. Among the metate
sellers there was substantial variation in attitudes
toward and skills in bargaining.

It is appropriate at this point to examine in
detail one of the bargaining sequences depicted by a
graph--in this instance 3/8/68.

This bargaining sequence began at 9:00 a.m.
The buyer (accompanied by wife) opened
the sequence by asking the seller, Florencio:
"What's the price?" F. responded with an
opening quotation of 60 pesos. The buyer
then queried: "What's your lowest price?"
F. replied: "Well, what do you say?" The
buyer then gave his opening bid of 30 pesos.
F. responded with a quotation of 55; the
buyer held his bid to 30. F. then lowered
his quotation to 50 and the buyer followed
with a bid of 35. After a brief pause in
negotiations, during which the buyer closely
examined the metate, he asked F., "What's
your best price?" F. replied immediately:
"I'll take off another 5"--making his quotation 45. The buyer, after another short
pause, then asked: "Well, what's the least?"
F. replied: "The least is 45." The buyer
again bid 35 and F. said: "It doesn't come
out, it's all work." But the buyer persisted
and said: "Well, what do you say?" F.
responded: "I already told you; in a little
while a regatón will come along and pay me
40." And he continued: "It's hard stone,
it's not false stone. The stone from San
Juan (Teitipac) is false--that stone is
nothing but mud!" The buyer nodded in
agreement but then repeated: "Well, what
do you say?" F. replied: "It doesn't
come out. The metate is just the right
size for you people that travel a long way."
(Note: When I asked F. where he thought
these buyers were from he answered: "From
there below, those people who bring apples"--
probably referring to mountain people from
Miahuatlan.) F. then said: "I'm going
to take off two pesos--43." The buyer then

276

made a bid of 37 to which F. responded: "It doesn't come out; a mano is worth 12 pesos--it's preferable that I sell only the metate at that price; in a little while the regatón will come along and pay me 12 pesos for the mano."

The time was now 9:20 a.m. The buyer reexamines the metate; he takes F.'s hand pick (pico) and begins picking at the metate. F. then says: "That's the hardest stone." The buyer lays down the pick, looks hard at F. and says: "Well, will you give me a better price?" F. responds, "No."

The buyer and his wife turn away and walk slowly out of the metate sales area (9:25 a.m.). F. whistles the buyer back and quotes a price of 42 pesos. The buyer says no and F. quotes a price of 41. The buyer responds: "Paint it and I'll give you 40." F. replies: "No, painted it's worth 45; I'm giving you a good price-- in a little while the prices will change when the other sellers arrive. Now's the time to buy when I'm here alone; in a little while the prices will be fixed." The buyer, unmoved by F.'s words, says, "Well, what do you say?" F. responds: "I gave you my price."

At this time the buyer's wife sits down behind the metate for the first time during the negotiations, picks up the mano, and goes through the motions of the grinding process; her husband observes with interest. Time: 9:30 a.m. The buyer says to F.: "37 pesos, unpainted." F. replies to the buyer firmly: "Now, I have really set my price." The customer and wife walk slowly out of the sales area. F. sits down and begins to chip away at an unfinished mano. The buyer stops in front of the nearby basket sales area, says a few words to his wife but does not begin bargaining for a basket. At 9:35 a.m. they come back to the metate sales area, and make an offer of 39 pesos. F. quotes 40 without looking up from his work. The buyer sits down near the metate and begins to repair a broken strap on one of his huaraches. He says nothing. At 9:39 another buyer stops, examines F.'s metate and asks: "How much is it worth?" F. quotes a price of 60 pesos and the new client remains. At this point the previous client, with a worried look on his face, stands up, pulls out a new 50 peso bill and gives it to F. who queries: "40?" The client nods his acceptance and the transaction is consummated at 9:40 a.m.

Though longer than most, this was a representative sequence in many ways. As the first transaction of that particular trading day, it set a precedent for subsequent negotiations. This day remained a 'buyer's market' and sellers were repeatedly making price concessions to buyers. Also, it provides a good illustration of one way in which the Magdalena sellers reinforce their natural monopoly position and build up consumer loyalties to their products by downgrading the quality of Teitipac metates. Finally, it incorporates a representative selection of the bargaining tactics and ploys utilized by the metate sellers. For example, Florencio alludes to the regatón who will arrive to buy his metate at the price he is asking; he emphasizes the hardness and durability of the stone, reminds the buyer that the price is low because it's early in the day (if they don't buy now they'll pay more later), and, finally, he successfully plays one buyer off against another to consummate the transaction.

Another issue raised by this case is the extent to which the bargaining skill of individual sellers operates to promote differential returns among the metate sellers. Florencio is among the most astute metate traders in Ocotlan yet he was unable to sell his metate at a price which exceeded a seasonal average (i.e., he could not overcome buyer's market conditions). At most his astuteness earned him a bonus of five pesos which it would have cost him to paint the metate. Yet there are certain sellers who regularly get higher prices for their metates than do other sellers. According to the sellers themselves, some factors at work here in addition to the bargaining skill of individual sellers include the differential quality of metates, the differential need for cash (e.g., emergency vs. regular cash needs) and, finally, just plain luck. All of these factors operate to contribute to sales price differentials. Although, as it turns out, the most astute bargainers (apart from the regatones) are also the most skilled manufacturers whose metates have the best appearance and, consequently, will command higher prices. Another contributing factor which has not been mentioned is metate size; as a general rule larger metates bring higher prices than medium or small metates (see Table 16).

TABLE 16. Final selling price and size of metates sold by Magdalena sellers in 66 separate transactions on 11 plaza days between April 12 and June 28, 1968, in the Ocotlan Marketplace.

Size of Metate (inches)			Selling Price (pesos)		
	length	width	40 or less	41-70	71 and higher
Small	10-11 x	14-15	10	--	--
Medium	11½-12½ x	15½-17	3	28	1
Large	13 x and larger	18	--	7	17

My data clearly indicate that the metateros expect and seek to negotiate prices in the marketplace which exceed value estimated exclusively in terms of work days expended in producing a metate, even though the latter does serve as the major cost component of their Minimum Acceptable Return (MAR).* On several occasions I observed metateros refuse to sell metates to prospective buyers whose final bids fell only a few pesos short of the sellers' final quotations (which are often equivalent to the MAR). In such negotiations (which abort if the buyer fails to increase his or her bid to meet the seller's quotation) the metateros complain that the prices offered by the buyers do not adequately compensate their work. This is expressed in statements like "El trabajo no vale así" ("My work is not worth so little") or "El trabajo no resulta" ("The work doesn't may off"). There is a surprising

*This concept will be discussed more fully in Chapter 7.

279

uniformity among the metateros as to the basic procedure they follow to estimate the money cost of metates. A prevalent tendency is to apply an 'opportunity cost' formula according to which they count the total number of work-days spent in producing a metate and convert this to a money equivalent by referring to the going wage for a day laborer (jornalero). On one occasion during the 'slow period' (May-October) in the metate market, I observed a metatero refuse an offer of 35 pesos for a metate which was part of an inventory held over from previous weeks, an action which surprised me under the circumstances. To my question as to why he had refused the offer, this metatero responded categorically that the metate was worth 40 pesos (his MAR) because it had required four work days to produce which, in money terms, he figured as equivalent to 10 pesos per day.

Many metateros will also explicitly include the cost of transporting metates to the marketplace, as well as marketplace surcharges and storage charges, in their rockbottom quotation especially in those circumstances where the potential buyer's bid is approaching the MAR (which tends to be computed strictly on a labor cost basis). Often, in a deadlocked negotiation with only a few pesos separating seller's quotation and buyer's bid, the metatero held out in an effort to cover his incidental non-labor costs. I witnessed one negotiation in which the price of a metate was agreed upon but the sale was not consummated at the last minute because the buyer refused to pay the metatero a small fee (1 or 2 pesos) to haul the metate from the sales area to the local bus terminal. Typically, the extra-labor overhead costs of metate production (e.g., tool maintenance and replacement, powder, fuse, pumping water from quarry, hired labor for quarry work) are not incorporated in the metateros' explicit MAR estimates--if only because of their lack of formal accounting skills which would facilitate the per unit computation of these. In any case, since the bargaining strategy is to sell metates at a price which exceeds the MAR and, since supply and demand conditions over the annual cycle fluctuate so as to make this strategy successul, the margin between MAR and average selling price will, over the long-run, compensate the metateros for their overhead costs of production.[15]

The metateros adopt a bargaining posture which anticipates the possibility of profit realization but they often sacrifice this possibility to the exigencies of household provisioning and the necessity to convert their embodied labor-power to cash at a rate which, in the last analysis, is a creature of the market. To facilitate their purchase of complementary goods and services, the <u>metateros</u> prefer to sell their metates as early in a <u>plaza</u> day as possible; on slow days some <u>metateros</u> will 'dump' their metates with local retailers at rockbottom prices so that they can attend to their provisioning activities. The extent of their involvement in the <u>plaza</u> as producers/provisioners/consumers is illustrated by the case of one San Sebastian <u>metatero</u> who, after several years of selling his metates in the Oaxaca City <u>plaza</u>, was persuaded to sell his entire weekly output to a <u>regatón</u> in the village. He held to this agreement for several months but, then, abruptly cancelled it, giving me the following explanation for his action:

> I felt strange when I no longer took metates to the <u>plaza</u>. I had become accustomed to going to Oaxaca with my metates. It seemed very strange to me that I was going to <u>plaza</u> only with cash (from metates sold in the village). I didn't sell anything there; I only walked around. I felt badly because I got no money in the <u>plaza</u>. I would run into my former customers (middlemen) and they wouldn't pay me. What are they going to give me if I have nothing for them? I had become accustomed to them asking me when I arrived in the <u>plaza</u>: "How many metates did you bring today?" And I would tell them and then they would ask me, "How much do you want for them?" I felt very strange going to the <u>plaza</u> to spend money without having sold anything there to get it. One must take something and bring something back. Right? It's like a business. A businessman sells something in one place and buys something in another. As a <u>metatero</u> I bring something from the village to the <u>plaza</u> and there I buy something to bring home.

This <u>metatero</u> was selling every metate he could produce (semi-finished) to a village middleman who paid him 25 pesos per metate and extended him cash advances of up to 200 pesos in return for claims on his future metate output. Since the <u>metatero</u> did not have to spend time on finishing operations, he was able to

devote all of his labor-time to quarrying and manufacturing semi-finished metates--thus increasing his
weekly output of semi-finished metates and eliminating
the risk (and expense) of marketplace trading. While
he was apparently satisfied with this arrangement in
financial terms, he seems to have terminated it uni-
laterally simply because of his commitment to the plaza
routine. As a producer for the plaza, he felt that it
was in the nature of things for him to sell his own
products there so that he, in turn, could purchase
someone else's. On the other hand, his decision might
have reflected his unexpressed belief that over the
long run weekly metate price fluctuations in the plaza
operate to the material advantage of the producer-
seller.

Yet, from the perspective of the structure of
regional economic process, this metatero, by removing
himself from direct involvement in marketing activity,
was operating against the logic of the system. The
latter operates on the principle that 'value represents
labor,' that exchange in the marketplace is the necessary culmination of the inter-community division of
labor. Marketplace exchange is the main route in this
regional economy for the realization of the value of
commodities by linking up social production with social
demand which, ultimately, assures the reproduction of
the system. Any break in the direct link between social production and social demand, which the activity
of middlemen represents, poses a threat to the reproduction of the regional economy. For when producer-
sellers cease to deal directly with producer-buyers,
as the predominant relationship in the social exchange
process, then the simple commodity sector of the regional economy will dissolve into its capitalist matrix.

Petty Trading and the Circulatory Process: Metateros and Regatones

It is the mythical figure of Juan Garabato (origin in the Riuz cartoon series?), of whom it is said
in a popular Oaxaca saying, "He buys dear and sells
cheap" ("Compra caro y vende barato"), that reminds
metatero and petty regatón alike of their vulnerability
as consumers who must produce and/or sell in order to
consume. In some situations the metatero sees himself
as Juan Garabato: he is often forced to accept a low
price for his products in a buyers' market and, then,
turn around and pay high prices for certain complemen-

tary goods and services he buys. This is especially
true from May-September, the rainy season, when metate
prices decline and prices of corn, beans and other basic foodstuffs increase. During such a slump (few
buyers, low prices for metates) I asked one metatero
why he continued to quote high prices for his metates;
he responded: "Why are we going to buy dear and sell
cheap? That's no joke. One must sell dear too" (see
Marroquín 1957:210-214 for a discussion of the 'price
scissors' in the Mixteca Alta).

Nevertheless, the metatero considers the petty
regatón to be more likely to fall into the predicament
of Juan Garabato because of his (or her) obligation to
recoup a cash outlay when selling metates. They consider that the risk factor is greater for the petty
regatón than it is for themselves; given the capriciousness of market fluctuations regatones can never
be assured of a profit margin, something which is not
of ultimate concern to the metatero.

Although the Juan Garabato theme (which crops
up spontaneously in casual conversation) reminds the
metatero of the risk element in middleman activities,
it does not discourage some of them from periodically
entering the market in that capacity. The metatero-
regatones, in addition to manufacturing finished metates, buy semi-finished metates from their co-workers
which they will finish and resell in the plaza. The
following excerpts from an interview with a metatero-
regatón from Magdalena Ocotlan illustrate the salient
features of the marketing strategy of this group:

Q: During the past year have you traded
metates that you did not manufacture
yourself?

R: Yes, I bought about 30 semi-finished
metates and I finished them.

Q: Why did you do that?

R: Because they brought me a profit. For
example, I buy a semi-finished metate
for 40 pesos. I finish it and sell
it for 80, 90 pesos. Let's discount
10 pesos for the mano. That's 30-40
pesos that I earn in one day. That's
money!

283

Q: Why did you buy metates from others instead of going to the quarry and making them yourself?

R: Because sometimes I'm working at home and other _metateros_ come by and ask me if I want to buy metates from them. From the month of August I begin to buy; I take out about 500 pesos to buy in September and October. Then, in November and December I begin to sell. I buy only the better quality metates. I store them and afterwards, when I have time, I take them out of storage, finish them and paint them. And they give me a profit of more than half of my original investment. Rather than having my money on my hands, I invest it in metates.

Q: Where do you get the money to buy metates?

R: I take it out of my own work or I sell something, a hog, a calf or any animal. And after selling the metates I bought, I get some more animals and keep the money that I earned. Last year I put aside 500 pesos. And I made 950 pesos from selling metates. I earned 450 pesos.

Q: Why do you buy metates to resell instead of buying more animals?

R: Because of the weather. Because of the sickness that comes; it's risky to buy pigs. Instead of investing money in pigs, it's safer to invest in metates. I invest my money in metates. I buy in August, September, October. This is preferable to lending money for interest. Because money lent pays no more than 10%--100 pesos loaned for two months yields 20 pesos. If you buy two metates at 50 pesos each, you invest 100 pesos-- in two months you can sell them for 100 pesos each. Do you come out better or worse? But many who have gotten into this business have failed. I don't understand why. One must know how much it's worth when he buys it, and how much it's worth when he sells it--that's all there is to it. If I buy a metate in August or

September, I pay 40 or 50 pesos; in
December I'll sell these same metates
for not less than 80 or 90 pesos. Many
have done it and they fall flat on their
faces. When I buy I'm sure that I'll
earn half again what I paid for it when
the time comes to sell. There are some
who are buying now (May) in order to
resell in one or two months from now.
But by that time the price will have
dropped (it's still high), and they'll
be selling when the price is lower.
How the fuck? (Como chingao?) It
doesn't come out. One must wait until
the price is low to buy, and sell when
the price is high.

Several key elements in the metatero-regatón
marketing strategy are illustrated here. First, it's
clear that an objective of the trader is to make a
profit on a sum of money invested; this is a petty mercantile capitalist activity. Second, there is an explicit commitment to arbitrage which is geared to the
seasonal variation in the metate trade cycle. Metates
(and manos) are acquired and stored in the village when
the price level is low (June-October) and brought to
the marketplace for resale when the price level is
higher (December-May), a strategy which some of the
propios also follow. Third, the metatero-regatón has a
preference for the manipulation of highly liquid non-
cash assets (especially animals) and does not usually
invest money to earn interest (through making loans
or saving in a bank). This reflects, aside from the
relative absence of formal banking facilities (in
1966-68 these were located only in Oaxaca City), the
peculiar problems and needs of village life. Cash on
hand, hidden away for a time of need, is notably unproductive from the perspective of a petty entrepreneur, whereas animals, though susceptible to premature
death by disease, or metates are a liquid alternative
which also serves an 'investment' function. Finally,
the metatero-regatón is a relatively sophisticated
calculator of alternative courses of action: he moves
back and forth between metates and animals, according
to market and seasonal fluctuations, and usually
avoids options like money lending which can have unde-
sirable social and economic consequences. While he
is aware of the risk and unpredictability of metate
market fluctuations in the short run, his experience
has taught him that these tend to balance out over the

annual cycle. If he can withstand the impact of short-run crises (of family or market origin), he is confident of the probability of long-run success. Of course, there is a relatively high rate of turnover among petty traders; many are not as successful as this informant says that he is.

Petty metate traders (including women and men who are not also _metateros_) view their trading activity as a self-sustaining business. After accumulating a sum of money to begin trading operations, the trader finances subsequent purchases of metates from revenues derived from the sale of metates purchased with the original cash outlay (which varies from 25 to 500 pesos). In other words, a portion of cash earnings are kept in circulation to maintain inventory, often being disbursed by the trader to _metatero_ suppliers as cash 'advances' (_adelantos_).

When hard pressed, petty traders will sell a metate for a net return of 5 pesos (and occasionally will absorb a loss on a metate). On the other hand, profits as high as 30-35 pesos per metate are not uncommon. Usually, the 'profit' earned on any particular metate is spent on consumer purchases in the _plaza_. For example, if a trader purchased a finished metate in the village for 25 pesos and spent 1.00 peso on transporting it to the _plaza_ and .50 for the marketplace surcharge, and sells it for 40 pesos, he or she will have made a profit of 13.50 pesos. The latter sum will most likely be spent in the _plaza_ on consumption articles and the balance of 25 pesos will be 'reinvested' in the purchase of another metate in the village.

In short, while the _plaza_ is a place where the petty trader does business at a profit, it is important to note that he or she remains enmeshed in a process of simple commodity circulation along with the _propios_. The trader operates to provision his or her household, to meet the costs of maintaining the household and the 'business,' and not to expand the latter through increasing profits and investment.

Recapitulation and Conclusions

In this chapter I have outlined the salient features of the objective and subjective economic framework in which metate marketing is conducted. To this end I have identified various market conditions to which buyers and sellers adapt (and perhaps alter as well), I have indicated certain aggregate statistical results of their behavior during a finite time period, and I have described how the metate sellers evaluate market performance. The aggregate results were measured as the flow of products between locations, and it was assumed that these products circulate through a process integrated by the multiple forces of supply and demand. The metate market was found to be compartmentalized into three site-confined segments through the operation of various imperfections (e.g., location and transport factors, moderate product differentiation); or, at the inter-marketplace level of analysis, the metate marketing process was found to be monopolistically competitive.

At the intra-marketplace level of analysis, however, the data indicate that a more perfectly competitive situation tends to prevail--at least in terms of trading behavior (i.e., as measured by the degree of control over prices exercised by sellers or buyers, which depends on the number of traders, the uniformity of products, and the freedom of entry for potential traders). Only in the wholesale section of the Oaxaca City metate market do conditions exist which incline the trading situation toward a monopolistically competitive pole. The other essentially retail markets appear to approximate the perfect competition model since activity in them ". . . rests on the free interplay of buyers and sellers, with price established through the interaction of buyers who do not buy enough to set price with sellers who do not control enough of the supply to set price" (Nash 1966:70).

As a means for ascertaining the hows and whys of economic behavior, the practitioner of the Neoclassical approach often finds himself obliged to infer human behavior from price and quantity behavior. One of the implicit aims of this chapter has been to foster the illusion that the understanding of marketing processes lies at the level of marketing itself, and that commodity flows and price determination through haggling can be reduced to patterns, quantitatively or qualitatively derived, which suffice to explain these market processes as consequences of the inter-action of the invisible forces of supply and demand.

In the next chapter, by contrast, we will analyze the circulation of products in the metate industry from the Marxist perspective which assumes that this process can only be superficially approximated at

287

the level of commodity flows and pricing behavior; and that it is ultimately understandable only in relation to the labor process and the structure of production relations which determine the movements of commodities and prices. To compartmentalize the economic process for heuristic or expository purposes is a matter of expediency but to formulate explanations which mirror this compartmentalization is to mystify the approximation of reality. So, to isolate marketing from the economic process and then to analyze it in terms of transfer or pricing behavior internal to it is to be victimized by "commodity fetishism," that is, approaching the 'commodity' as a thing which is related to other commodity-things exclusively through exchange and, thereby, masking the social relations of commodity production (see Marx 1967, 71-83). Moreover, to recognize that transfer and pricing processes imply social relations but to include these in analysis only at the level of marketing (ignoring production) is to combine "commodity fetishism" with "circulationism." We will examine these tendencies in the next chapter as we demonstrate that commodities like metates are exchanged only because human labor power has been organized, expended and transformed to meet a social demand. In other words, metates circulate between sites, and are aggregated and dispersed during the circulatory process, only because they are creatures of the labor process and are products with use-values to satisfy a social demand. The meaning of circulation, then, must be found in the labor process and the relations of production.

[1]Obviously this definition restricts 'marketing' to commodity economies. In economies where use-
value (non-commodity) production predominates, the
circulation of products beyond the producing unit may
be described as 'exchange' or 'trade' but not as marketing. Of course, to the extent that such circulation
flows through a 'marketplace' then the latter term might
be appropriate. Since the following discussion focus-
ses on the metate, a commodity which has a rather
unique status as the only durable consumer product displayed in the contemporary Mesoamerican peasant marketplace which has its origins in the prehispanic economy
of the region, the extent to which aspects of its
marketing situation are applicable to other commodities
is problematic. My feeling is that what is characteristic of metates may also be characteristic of other
artisan products which are produced and circulate
wholly within the peasant sector, but that when we turn
our attention to agricultural products the relevance
of metate-related patterns diminishes.

[2]To approximate social reality through any of
these concepts it would have to be assumed that marketing is merely a process lying between the labor process
and the social relations of production, on the one
hand, and distribution and its social relations, on
the other. The commodities marketed may serve as sources of the realization of exchange value at any point
prior to their passage into the realm of use. In
other words, we must avoid the 'fetishization' of the
market concept under the cover of the phrase "for
heuristic purposes only."

[3]That the Oaxaca City marketplace (San Sebastian
sellers) has much higher total metate sales as well
as a higher proportion of wholesale transactions vis-
a-vis the Ocotlan marketplace (Magdalena sellers) is
clear from the following figures: between September
1967 and June 1968 a total of 307 metates were sold by
Magdalena sellers in 297 transactions in Ocotlan,
whereas a total of 865 metates were sold by San Sebastian sellers in 301 transactions in Oaxaca City.

[4]The question of the degree of exploitation of
the metateros by the big-lot buyers arises here. Obviously, these buyers enter the market to make a profit

by re-selling peasant-artisan commodities; the fact that they do so regularly, week after week, month after month, and from year to year, demonstrates that they find metate trading profitable. And the metatero, always hard pressed for cash, is vulnerable to the 'cash advance' (adelanto) arrangement according to which the big-lot buyers loan a sum of money in return for claims to future output at prices which are below the average negotiated market price. To some extent, of course, trader profit appropriated from the purchase and resale of metates (or other peasant-artisan products) can be justified as a return for marketing services rendered. Yet the class relations implicit here cannot be ignored and must ultimately lead to an analysis of the exploitative nature of the 'market' in a developing capitalist economy. In any case the degree of exploitation of labor is minor in the metatero-/big-lot buyer situation compared to that which exists when merchants establish more direct controls over the labor process, as has occurred in the weaving industry in the Valley (see Beals 1975:266-269).

[5]The Marxian law of value is obviously at work here since the Tlacolula metateros obtain higher prices to compensate for the relatively higher quantity and quality of the labor embodied in their products. They regularly ask and receive higher average prices for their metates than do any other group of producer-sellers--but their metates are generally larger, more finely worked, and of better quality stone. Comparatively speaking, the workmanship of metates manufactured in Magdalena for the Ocotlan marketplace is inferior to that of Tlacolula metates--however, the stone is of comparable quality. While many metates produced in the Teitipac villages are comparable in workmanship to those produced in Tlacolula, and superior in this respect to Magdalena products, the stone from which they are manufactured is usually of inferior quality. 'Value' in the Marxist sense is, of course, ultimately a function of 'socially (vs. individually) necessary labor'; and there is a limit beyond which labor inefficiency will be penalized.

[6]In other words, a certain percentage of actual price differences reflects these 'competitive' elements as well as differing quantity and quality of socially necessary labor.

[7]See Chapter 7 for a more detailed analysis of the dynamics of pricing with emphasis on the labor-cost element.

[8]As far as I could ascertain, it was in 1944-45 that the first Teitipac widow (not all regatonas are widows or divorcees but a majority are) entered the metate business which she learned while she was the concubine of one of the most successful regatones. He described this affair and its ironic results as follows:

> Then came Esperanza. She was widowed and I was then in my heyday as an 'exploiter' of women. And since I saw that she was good-looking I said to her one day; 'Why don't you get into the metate business?' 'Well, all right,' she replied, 'if you agree to teach me.' Well, I taught her and not long afterwards she was buying more metates than I was. Since she was a woman no metatero would refuse her offer to buy metates.

Following the precedent set by Esperanza, a series of female villagers were to appropriate a sizeable chunk of the Teitipac metate market through a unique blend of sexual charm and business acumen--a position they have not relinquished since.

Beginning with Esperanza, the unattached regatonas have apparently found their sexual charms to be advantageous in their dealings with the metateros. It is apparently quite common (at least according to 'hearsay') for an amorous relationship between regatona and metatero to have also been a trading partnership. Two such arrangements occur: (1) the regatona operates as a 'metatero prostitute'--accepting metates and manos in exchange for her sexual favors; and (2) the regatona establishes a quasi-concubinage relationship with one particular metatero from whom she gets metates and manos in exchange for sexual services on a regular basis. In either case, the couple does not live together but meets for brief encounters, usually in the 'hotel' areas of the marketplaces.

[9]This is not collusion with monopoly implications. Rather it is simply a way of reducing competition between sellers so as to force buyers to select metates mainly on the basis of non-price criteria (i.e., metates of similar size and workmanship will be quoted at similar opening prices). In the incident described above, the 'newcomer' opened his negotiations with a quotation approximating his MAR. Some metate sellers

(propios) who have no flare for haggling use this direct approach. A majority, however, are keen hagglers
and, as a matter of principle, open negotiations with
quotations that are well above their MARs and are in
line with the seasonal trend in price levels. Moreover, since most metate transactions occur in the close
quarters of the marketplace sales area it is difficult
for buyer and seller to maintain secrecy regarding the
details of their negotiations. Payments are usually
made in full view of other buyers and sellers. A
seller's outward indifference to the negotiations of
other sellers conceals a keen interest in price formation. The typical seller will tactfully 'eavesdrop'
to acquire such information which he will employ in his
own subsequent negotiations.

[10]It is important to recall here that in 1967
the metate sales area in the principal Oaxaca City
marketplace (Benito Juarez Maza) was bifurcated into
two groups of sellers who occupied opposite sides of
the street on market day (dia de plaza). The San
Juan sellers occupied the south side of the street,
while the San Sebastian sellers occupied the north
side--directly facing each other. There was no open
antagonism between the two groups altough they tended
to depreciate each others' products when talking to
buyers; the San Juaneros (who are predominantly regatones or regatonas since the propios tend not to sell
their own products in the plaza) regularly buy metates
and manos from the San Sebastianos (who are predominantly propios) in the plaza. The San Sebastianos
tend to sell on a wholesale basis with a relatively
small portion of their sales going to private buyers.
The San Juaneros, on the other hand, conduct most of
their business with buyers for private use; they buy
two or three metates at a time from propios and sell
one metate at a time to private buyers. These conditions, among others, tend to diminish the competition
between the two seller groups. The competitive syndrome, as describe above, is most characteristic of
the behavior of sellers on the San Juan side. Since
the mid-1970s when the main Oaxaca City market was
moved to a new location the San Sebastian sellers
attend less frequently and metate sales are dominated
by the San Juan traders.

[11]In Ocotlan, between September 1967 and June
1968 (43 plaza days) an average of 10 metate sellers
per plaza day came to the marketplace to trade (ranging from a low of 6 on September 1 and November 10
to a high of 15 on May 3). There is little difference

in attendance patterns between *propios* and *regatones* (in Ocotlan and among the San Sebastianos in Oaxaca City); they tend to follow similar patterns of variation in monthly attendance. This reflects the fact that both village-to-marketplace *regatones* and *propios* are 'peasants' within a simple commodity form of production.

[12] In Ocotlan, many Magdalenans are accustomed to finishing or painting their metates in the marketplace sales area. Sometimes metates are sold either unfinished or unpainted or both, and the buyer will wait in the sales area until the *metatero* completes the finishing or painting.

[13] Graph A, which is derived from a larger sample than Graph B, indicates that sellers dominate negotiations only in January.

[14] In this analysis of price determination and bargaining I have profited considerably from the original discussion and analysis by Raymond Firth in his classic study of the *Malay Fishermen* (1966:193-204). The reader is invited to compare Firth's analysis with mine to discern the similarities and differences between bargaining and price determination among the Malayans and the Oaxacans. I also profited from the essay by Cassady (1968) which is summarized, with special emphasis on its relevancy to the Oaxaca marketing situation, by Beals (1975:Ch. 9).

[15] In a lengthy interview with a Magdalena *metatero* (May 8, 1968) about costs and earnings, the topic of the various incidental costs arose and I asked him how he kept track of these so that he could then estimate whether or not the negotiated selling price fully covered them. He replied: "Well, what comes out as surplus or debit is what one calculates (*lo que salga sobrando o faltando es lo que uno calcula*); this is how one calculates so as to sell a metate to cover one's expenditures. For example, the metate that I sold the other day, I took out all those expenditures and a 'profit' (". . .*saqué todos esos gastos y la ganacia*"). The metate in question was standard size and was sold for 50 pesos.

Haggling over the price of <u>manos</u> in Tlacolula and of a
metate in Ocotlán.

294

CHAPTER 7. VALUE, PRICE AND INCOME IN THE METATE INDUSTRY

Introductory Comments

In Chapter 5 we focussed upon the forces and social relations of metate production, that is, upon its physical and technological organization and the necessary social relations that _metateros_ establish among themselves and with others to participate in the labor process; and in Chapter 6 our focus was on the structural and behavioral aspects of the circulation of _metates_ from producers to consumers. It is now appropriate to reintegrate these two dimensions through an analysis of value, price and income in the industry. Starting with the empirically measurable results of the labor process (i.e., output), we will analyze the latter in terms of market prices and further examine the relationship between these and value conceived in terms of socially average labor cost. The assumption underlying this analysis is that our understanding of the production and circulation of metates will be enhanced by considering both the quantitative and qualitative dimensions and implications of this process, and by juxtaposing a Neoclassical analysis of supply and demand with a Marxist analysis of the role of labor in social production.

The Time Series Data

The time series data presented in Figures 10 and 11 represent the total quantity of metates traded and the average trading prices for all metates sold by San Sebastian Teitipac sellers in the Oaxaca City marketplace over a 23-month (101-week) period from August 1966 to July 1968. The data presented in Figures 12-14 pertain to the Magdalena sellers in the Ocotlan marketplace and encompass a 10-month period in 1967/68 (including in some categories partial supplementary data for an 8-month period in 1966/67). These data include: (1) the total number of new metates entering the marketplace, (2) the number of metates retained or held over in the marketplace between trading days, and (3) the total number and the average prices for all metates sold in the marketplace.[1] In the ensuing analysis of output and price variability in the San Sebastian and Magdalena segments of the

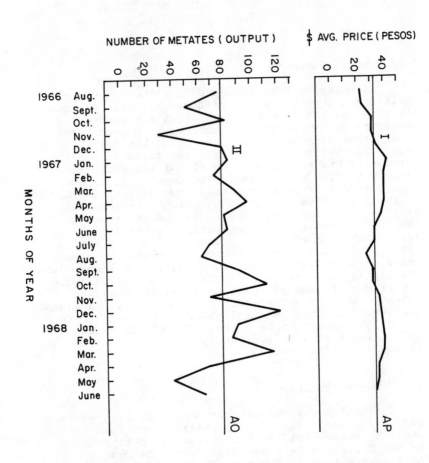

FIGURE 10. Aggregate monthly metate output and average monthly selling prices of metates in the Oaxaca City marketplace for the San Sebastian Teitipac metate industry over a 23-month period, 1966-1968.

Curve I represents the average monthly price per metate sold by San Sebastian sellers in the Oaxaca City marketplace during each of the 23 months in 1966-68; Curve II represents the total monthly metate output of the San Sebastian producers sold in the Oaxaca City marketplace over the 23-month period (1820 metates). Straight line AP represents the mean of the monthly metate sale price averages for the 23-month period; straight line AO represents average monthly metate output by the San Sebastian industry for the 23-month period.

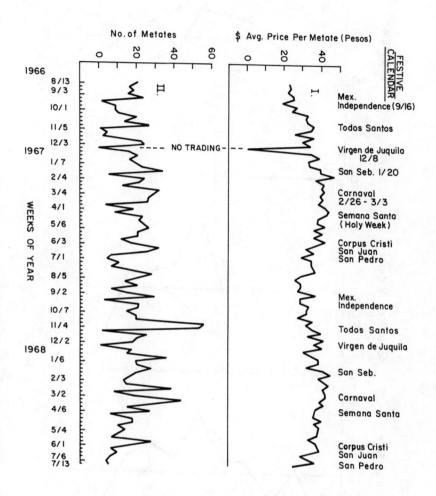

FIGURE 11.   Aggregate weekly metate output and average weekly
selling prices in the Oaxaca City marketplace for the
San Sebastian Teitipac metate industry over a
101-week period (August 1966–July 1968).

Curve I represents the average weekly price per metate sold by
San Sebastian sellers in the Oaxaca City marketplace during each of
101 weeks.   Curve II represents the total weekly metate output of
the San Sebastian industry sold in the Oaxaca City marketplace over
the 101-week period (1820 metates).   The 'festive calendar' lists
the names and dates of the major celebrations in the annual fiesta
cycle of San Sebastian.

297

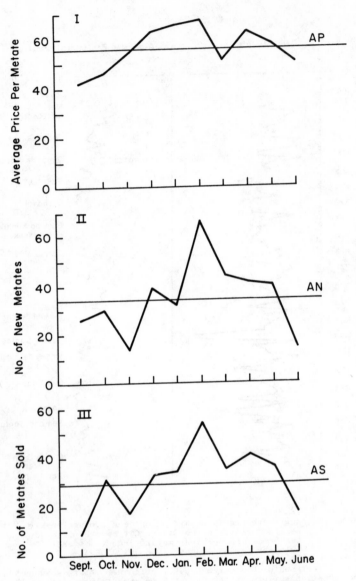

FIGURE 12. Magdalena sellers in the Ocotlan marketplace over a ten-month period in 1967-68 (I--average price per metate; II--number of new metates entering marketplace; III--number of metates sold).

298

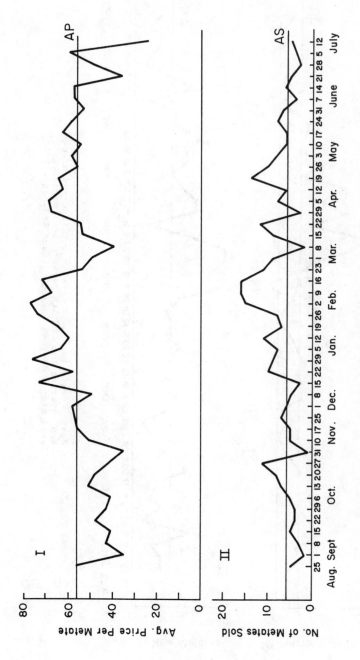

FIGURE 13. Aggregate weekly metate output and average weekly selling
prices in the Ocotlan Marketplace for the Magdalena
industry over a 47-week period (August 1967–July 1968).

299

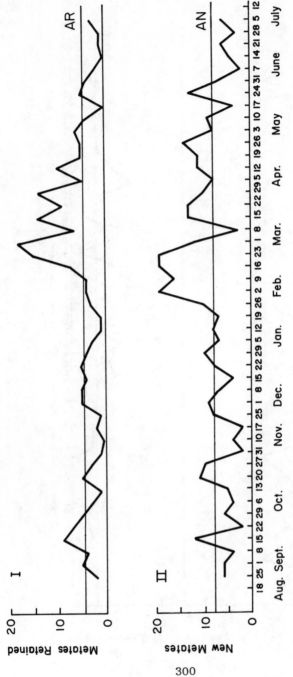

FIGURE 14. Aggregate weekly totals of metates retained and of new metates entering the Ocotlan marketplace (Magdalena sellers) over a 47-week period (August 1967–July 1968).

300

Oaxaca Valley metate industry, it will be necessary to alternate attention between these five figures since the market situation they represent is complex and can only be rendered intelligible by examining the data from different perspectives. To facilitate comparison monthly fluctuations are shown in Figures 11, 13, and 14.[2]

A cursory examination of the graphs in Figures 10 and 11 gives a prima facie impression of capricious and unpatterned fluctuation of the price and output curves. A closer scrutiny of, for example, Figure 10 suggests that this initial impression was mistaken. A significant relationship between price and output does emerge from this figure: the two most prolonged and unbroken periods of high average metate output (March-June 1967 and December 1967-March 1968) are closely associated with the two periods of high average price (January-May 1967 and November 1967-May 1968). Moreover, it will be noted that the month of highest metate output during the first year (April 1967) is also one of the two months of highest average price. Conversely, it will be noted that the months of lowest output (September and November 1966, August 1967, and May 1968) are also months of low average price. Finally, it will be noted that in the period from December 1966-April 1967 and in the period from November 1967-March 1968 general upswings in the output curve are accompanied by upswings in the average price curve; and conversely, in the period from April-September 1967 a sustained decline in output is accompanied by a decline in price, whereas in the period March-June 1968 a downward trend in total output is accompanied by a downward trend in price.

In this preliminary survey of the San Sebastian data we have isolated a series of apparently conjunctive movements in the price and output series. These movements suggest the possibility of a patterned relationship between the supply of metates and their average selling price, namely, that the supply of metates increases as the average price at which they are sold increases. We should also observe that the Curve 1 profiles in Figures 10 and 11 show a symmetrical undulating movement characterized by periodicity in calendar time. More specifically, in Figure 10 the upper portion of the first wave falls between December 1966 and June 1967, while the second wave lies between November 1967 and June 1968; in Figure 11 the profile of the weekly price series in Curve 1 follows a parallel course with its monthly counterpart--a gradual steady rise in the level of average prices beginning in September culminates in weekly peaks in February and March and then recedes gradually to weekly troughs in July and August.

As with the San Sebastian/Oaxaca City data, an examination of the Magdalena/Ocotlan data in Figures 12-15 gives an initial impression of capricious and unpatterned fluctuations which slowly yields to the discovery of significant patterned relationships between variables. Thus, it is clear from Figures 12 and 13 that the price and output curves follow a seasonal pattern of movement similar to that identified in the previous case: the period of high average metate sales and output (December-February) corresponds to the period of high average price. Likewise, the month of highest metate sales and output (February) corresponds to the month of highest average price per metate sold (see Figure 12). Finally, it should be noted that in the period from November 1967-February 1968 a progressive upswing in sales and output curves is accompanied by a corresponding upswing in the average price curve (see Figure 12); and, conversely, in the period from February-June a downward trend in price--the February highs contrasting sharply with the June lows. Again, the months of upward swings and intensification of trade are in the post harvest dry season, whereas the months of downward trends and trade decline are at the tail end of the dry season and into the rainy season when agricultural labor demand increases and agricultural surpluses diminish. In short, underlying these conjunctive oscillations in the price-quantity series are seasonal transitions coupled with changes in the agricultural work cycle--a situation which must be examined in some detail before we can proceed with the graphical analysis.

The Agricultural Work Cycle, Metate Production and Marketing

The reader will recall from previous chapters that in Oaxaca the calendar period from October-May corresponds with the 'dry season'--a period of almost no precipitation, whereas the calendar period from May-September corresponds with the 'rainy season.' The principal food crops cultivated in the region are, of course, maize, beans and squash; the planting and maturation cycle for these crops, in the absence of widespread irrigation and the limited availability of permanent water resources, is directly dependent upon

302

precipitation patterns. Thus, the rainy season corresponds with the planting and maturation phase of the major crop cycle; the harvest of the seasonal crops occurs early in the dry season, usually in September, October, and November; and the remainder of the dry season (December-March) corresponds with the land clearing and preparation phase of the seasonal (temporal) crop tilling cycle, a phase during which labor demand is dispersed more or less evenly throughout the period, rather than concentrated at particular times within it. Precisely how are these exogenous conditions relevant to the metate market situation?

From the supply side they are relevant in determining the amount of labor-time and -power available for and allocated to metate production. The majority of metateros, as discussed in Chapter 4, consider metate making a secondary occupation, second to farming in priority as a source of subsistence and livelihood. Even in terms of occupational self-image they consider themselves peasant-cultivators (campesinos) first and metateros second; even those metateros who are landless define 'wealth' as cultivable land and livestock and want to obtain them. In those years without major crop failures it is by working the land that the typical metatero acquires his basic supply of food and fodder. In these 'normal' years the manufacture and sale of metates (and manos) provides him with a cash supplement to his agricultural income. This cash supplement enables him to retain a larger portion of his harvest to satisfy (at least partially) the consumption demands of his family and livestock, rather than selling it on a piecemeal basis to raise cash. So, in Figure 10, the sharp decline in metate output shown on Curve II between April and August 1967 and between April and June 1968, and the equally sharp decline shown on Curves II and III between April and June 1968, reflects the movement of metateros from the quarries and into the fields as the planting season arrives and the demand for agricultural labor intensifies.

Given these conditions, many metateros will abandon the quarries completely until the rainy season passes--especially in Magdalena where many of the quarries fill with water and become unworkable--and the harvest is in, while others will simply spend less time in the quarries and more time in the fields during the rainy season. And, of course, this entire process works in reverse after the harvest is in and the demand for agricultural labor diminishes. Thus, from December

303

until the onset of the rainy season in April or May, there is a substantial increase in total metate output reflecting the movement of some workers from the fields back to the quarries and of reallocation of labor time from agricultural production to metate production by others.

This is not to imply, however, that all fluctuations in metate supply are attributable to the changing demand for labor associated with the agricultural cycle. A case in point is the month of March 1968 in the Magdalena/Ocotlan situation--a month of most marked decline in price, output and sales. The explanation of this March decline exposes one of the significant differences between the San Sebastian/Oaxaca City market situation and that in Magdalena/Ocotlan, namely, the problem of marketplace holdover and storage of metates which does not occur among the San Sebastian sellers mainly because of continued purchases by big- and small-lot merchants. In Figure 14 Curve 1 portrays a steady build-up of holdover metate inventory in the Ocotlan marketplace which peaks on March 1 (17 metates). It is the steady increase of this inventory, beginning on January 19 and increasing cumulatively until the March 1 peak, which is the crucial factor underlying the March decline in metate output (see Figure 14, Curve II). This hold-over inventory is symptomatic of the unpredictability and saturability (inelasticity?) of demand in the metate market, and provides the producer-seller with information that temporarily discourages him from allocating his labor to metate manufacture.

A glance at the weekly price curves (Figure 13, Curve I) indicates that price information received by the sellers reinforced their decision to reallocate their labor time. February 2 enjoyed the highest average price, not only for the month of February but for the entire 10-month period; the price level dropped markedly afterwards until reaching the seasonal low on March 8. On the other hand, the generally high price, brisk sales period beginning in mid-December and continuing into early February was conducive to the conditions of oversupply which made the March decline inevitable. Under such conditions a "buyers' market" prevails as reflected in the March decline of the average price level (Figure 13, Curve I). My records indicate that over 50% of the total metate inventory in the Ocotlan marketplace during March 1968 was in the holdover category (exceeded only by the 65% estimate for September). It is worth observing that

304

after the March decline the flow of new metates into
the Ocotlan marketplace never regains its February
volume--even though the average price level does re-
cover from its March doldrums, peaks again in early
April and then enters a seasonal downtrend to its July
lowpoint (Figure 13, Curve I). By June, in normal
years, the rainy season is well underway, and output
and sales bottom out (Figure 13, Curve II; Figure 14,
Curve II).

The _Metatero_ Program for Economic Action

The individual producer-seller is not swept
among impassively with the tide of these fundamental
ups and downs in economic activity. On the contrary,
he plans and evaluates his production and sales activities in accordance with a seasonally-adjusted program which he has formulated on the basis of work and
marketing experiences. Returning for a moment to the
'March decline' in the Magdalena/Ocotlan market, the
following excerpt from my field notes on March 15, 1968,
indicates that the 'decline' was anticipated by the
metateros:

> There was heavier buyer traffic today than
> on previous _plazas_ this month (this is the
> 3rd Friday of Lent); however, supply still
> outruns demand and there is generally a
> buyers' market. With few exceptions metate
> sellers are either making lower initial
> quotations or are giving ground from high
> initial quotations more readily than they
> did in January or February. This behavior
> seems to reflect 'seasonal programming' as
> much as it does the 'oversupply' situation.
> The metate sellers tell me that they ex-
> pect sales to slump during Lent--or, at
> least, they recognize it as a relatively
> low price season. According to their
> 'seasonal program' sales are best during
> the '_fandango_ season' (_temporada de fan-
> dangos_) between Christmas and Lent. After
> Lent, according to them, prices and sales
> pick up again until the rains begin.

The essential contours of this program are confirmed
by a Magdalena seller who, when asked by me if he
thought the value of a metate is stable or unstable,

responded as follows:

> It's not fixed because metates don't have
> the same price every month--they begin to
> have a value of 60 or 65 pesos from Novem-
> ber through February--four months only.
> In March the price lowers and by the 15-20
> of April it rises again.

The time series data seem to generally support the accuracy of the seasonal program of market expectations
summarized above: late December (Christmas) to early
March (beginning of Lent) boom--a Lent decline--
a short post-Lent upswing--a rainy season slump (note:
in 1968, Lent began on March 1 and culminated on April
14, Easter Sunday). Also, metateros responses to the
question, "When during the year do you manufacture
metates?" were strongly supportive of the existence of
such a program of expectations regarding market
activity.

My observations during the fieldwork period
tended to confirm the view that the metateros' responses
to short-term fluctuations are not made without considering the set of expectations derived from their
knowledge of the seasonal program of their economy,
expectations that suggest the future course of relevant
events in their economic field of action. Among the
expectations that are most significant to them are
those pertaining to the levels and directions of price
changes; more specifically, those established over the
time span for which the metateros plan the allocation
of their labor time and effort (usually not less than
a week or more than a season). It should be noted,
however, that it is only when they interpret price
movements (or expansions or contractions in demand) as
the beginning of a trend that they will alter the
conduct of their future production activity.[4]

We are justified in concluding from this discussion that the wavelike movements in price shown in
Figures 10-13 are not mere chance occurrences nor fig-
ments of the investigator's imagination; they are
profiles of actual and fundamental economic processes
that are understood and adapted to by the producer/sel-
lers and buyers of metates. The 'high price/low price'
periods for metates are annually recurring in the experience of the observer and the actor. There is some
variation from year to year as to when these periods

occur, the specific patterns of price movements within them, and the specific nature and intensity of buyer and seller reactions to them. But none of my informants can remember a year when such changes in market conditions failed to occur on a seasonal basis. It seems that these wavelike fluctuations do represent the basic structure of the metate market cycle. Only additional empirical investigation of markets for other commodities will enable us to determine to what extent the metate market cycle is representative of other commodity cycles in the regional economy.

On the Variability of Demand

Having examined the cyclical movement in metate marketing from the supply side, what can be said about it from the demand side? It is clear that the velocity and volume of circulation of metates into the marketplace is basically a function of the changing demand for labor associated with the agricultural cycle--and only secondarily reflects forces and factors exogeneous to the village economies of the _metateros_. They do remain sensitive to these and have their own ideas as to why the marketing situation is so variable. On the whole, consumer demand, month after month, dovetails nicely with the _metatero_ supply program; when _metatero_ labor is available to produce metates, consumers have cash available to purchase them. Is this correspondence of supply and demand coincidental? Can it be attributed to the pricing mechanism? Or are there more fundamental processes at work that determine supply, demand and price interaction in the metate market?

The data (which are, unfortunately, not as complete for demand as for supply) encourage me to give an affirmative answer to this latter question. The quest for a more basic understanding here points to the purely instrumental nature of money and to the fact that, in some fundamental sense, the supply of some products creates a demand for others. In the rural economy of Oaxaca, the supply of corn (and other crops) is the critical determinant of effective social demand. It is only after harvest that the average peasant can make large cash expenditures without borrowing cash or liquidating assets to acquire it. After harvest (at least in years without serious crop failures) the peasants' crop supply is, in effect, their fund for subsistence, ceremonial, rent, and replacement purposes (Wolf 1966). It follows, then, that the ability to pay for the products of rural non-agricultural industry is directly proportionate to the volume of the crop harvest.

The metateros obviously have thought about the causes of instability or variability on the demand side if their market and, consequently, are able to ascertain what they consider to be some of the underlying causes. One informant in telling me why he thought the sale of metates in the plaza was so variable said:

> People are interested in metates in September, November, December, January, March, and April. Because from November the fandangos begin and people have their harvest in. In November everyone has their harvest to sell--maize, that is--to buy metates, manos. Everyone says, 'We need this so let's go and buy it.' They sell maize in order to buy. And those who accept ritual kinship obligations--there are a lot of fandangos during that season. But from April to May, well, there are no fandango obligations and everyone is destitute. No one has money because their maize is scarce as is fodder for animals--and they are obliged to work a lot so as to be able to plant again. And so it is that they can't buy anything because they don't have the means to do so. And we sellers, now (May 20), can't sell metates because there's no one to buy them.

Another informant responded to the same question in a similar vein:

> Because there's a time when there's money and people buy metates and there are seasons when people don't look for metates because they aren't giving gifts (allusion to the custom of metate gifting by ritual kinsmen). So when there's maize, as from December to February, there's money to make purchases. And in July through August, when there's neither maize nor money, metates are cheap and people aren't enthusiastic about buying; our work doesn't pay

308

off. To sell, one can sell all the time, but not always at a worthwhile price.

So, to reiterate the previous argument, in the several dry season months after the harvest and before the next planting season, the Oaxaca peasant is best situated financially to make large purchases and to convert his consumer preferences and needs into effective demand. "Products are given in exchange for products," observed Say in elaborating his theory of markets, "once the exchange has been effected it is immediately discovered that products pay for products" (Gide and Rist 1947:130). Accordingly the Oaxaca peasant's supply of corn constitutes a demand for the metatero's metates. True, Say's statements simply expressed an idea that was familiar to the Physiocrats and to Adam Smith (later formalized in Marx's circulation formula C - M - C), namely, that money is an intermediary that is acquired in the sale of a product only to be passed on in exchange for another product. But in the regional peasant economy of Oaxaca it is the substantive magnitude of the peasants' harvest, and their subsequent acquisition of money, that directly provides them with purchasing power and the ability to employ it in converting their consumer preferences and needs into effective demand.

There are other factors that directly influence aggregate consumer demand for metates in Oaxaca. One is that metates wear out and must be periodically replaced, probably on the average of once every fifteen to twenty years in the typical household. A large portion of all metate sales each year are to meet this replacement generated demand. A second major source of demand for metates arises from a combination of demographic and cultural factors. Malinowski and De la Fuente in their study of the Oaxaca Valley economy explain this source as follows: "The change in the seasons is connected with the ritual custom of giving to the bride, at the time of her marriage, a metate painted and decorated with brilliant colors, which explains why these are more abundant (in the marketplace). . .between January and May" (1957:154). The marriage season in Oaxaca (which the metateros refer to as "la temporada de fandangos") falls between the end of the Fall harvest and the beginning of the next season's planting after the rains begin; this is a period when, as I already emphasized, the peasant household is relatively well situated to mobilize cash for consumer purchases. By no means all marriages nor all sales of gift metates occur during this season; but a majority do and it is clear that, in the absence of this ceremonially generated demand for gift metates, sales during the post-harvest, pre-planting months of the dry season would, other things remaining equal, inevitably decline.

The Festive Cycle and the Metate Market

A careful examination of Figure 11 isolates yet another factor that influences the variability of the metate market, namely, the festive calendar or, more precisely, the expenditures entailed by the celebration of mayordomías and other traditional religious and civic festivals. Curve II provides a convincing illustration of the relationship between metate output and the festival calendar. The hallmark of this relationship in terms of the series profile is the jagged peak followed by an abrupt drop to an equally jagged trough, a phenomenon that occurs throughout the series and produces a cyclical zigzag pattern of oscillation. During 1966/67 the most abrupt fluctuations in marketplace inventory occurred between the following dates: September 10-17, October 29-November 5, December 3-10, January 21-28, March 18-25, and June 10-July 1. It is significant that a similar pattern of movement is repeated during the 1967/68 period, a correspondence indicating that the fluctuations are seasonal in nature. It is apparent that the rhythm of the cycle follows that of the festive calendar, the principal celebrations being listed chronologically above Curve I to correspond with the appropriate dates on the horizontal time axis. In short, the time series data demonstrate that with few exceptions, metate inventories (output) peak on the market days preceding the major festive celebrations and plunge to their lowest levels on the market days immediately following the celebrations.

How is this production/marketing cycle to be explained in terms of the economic situation of the metatero household? As discussed above in chapter 3 all these festive occasions generate demands upon the household budgets of the metateros to make customary purchases of ceremonial goods and services and/or to provide material support to those villagers who are sponsoring mayordomias through the guelaguetza system. These expenditures are in considerable excess of those required to meet normal daily and weekly provisioning needs. For example, my detailed budget data

310

from Magdalena indicate that metatero households will spend 2 - 3 times more than the usual amount of special foodstuffs and other items for major festivals like Todos Santos/Dia de Los Muertos (All Saints/Day of the Dead). Only during the planting season and toward the end of the rainy season as harvest approaches do these households spend more. Given the range and intensity of these ceremonial demands, the peasant-metatero, even when festive occasions arise in periods of substantial agricultural work activity, will defer his agricultural tasks for a few hours each day or for a few days each week prior to the festive occasion so as to enable him to devote his time and effort to metate production. From the metatero perspective, it is not so much a question of which line of work yields greater material benefits in the long run but which provides the short-run opportunity to acquire needed cash.

A comparison of Curves I and II in Figures 10 and 11 shows that the prices prevailing in the metate market on trading days preceding the major celebrations are generally conducive to the peasant-metatero decisions to allocate scarce labor time and effort to the production of metates. Thus, December, January, and March--the months of the most important and expensive celebrations (with the exception of Todos Santos/Dia de Los Muertos at the end of October)--are, in reality and in the metatero program, 'high price-brisk sales' months in which market conditions are expected to favor the seller and generally do. This market situation alone, without the added burden of having to make festive expenditures from cash raised from metate sales, would be conducive to the metatero decision to allocate labor time and effort to metate production.

Again, this market situation is a two-sided affair; it favors the seller only because of a considerable increase in demand that is generated by the ceremonial cycle as it operates on a regional basis. As noted above, the festive season corresponds with the post-harvest, pre-planting months in the temporal crop cycle (corn, beans, squash dependent on rainfall); this is a period when agricultural returns for the year are in hand so as to provide peasant consumers with the ability to pay (thus, increasing effective demand). Buyer activity in the marketplace expands considerably on trading days immediately preceding festive celebrations as a reflection of the need of the Oaxaca peasant to provision his household with ceremonial goods. It is not surprising that some of this expanded activity has a direct impact upon metate sales when

311

one considers that worn-out metates must be replaced
in anticipation of heavy use during the festive period
(when extra tortillas are prepared). So, once again,
the conjunction of economic and cultural conditions
determines the course of supply, demand and price interaction in the metate market.

Sources of Interannual Variability in Supply
and Demand

Looking again at Curve II in Figure 10 we see
that the level of output was significantly higher during 1967/68 than it was during the corresponding period in 1966/67. How can this output increase be explained? One plausible approach is to interpret it
as a consequence of the poor harvest in 1967 which
resulted from inadequate rainfall during the May-August
growing season. A survey of my informants in San
Sebastian yielded a general consensus that the 1967
harvest averaged about one-half of the 1966 harvest in
terms of volume of unhusked corn per plot of cultivated land--1966 being widely considered as a normal
rainfall/harvest year. Because of this abnormally
meager 1967 harvest many San Sebastianos who work only
occasionally as metateros (even during the slack season in agriculture) apparently turned toward metate
production in an attempt to partially offset their
crop losses. Under bad harvest conditions, the peasant
head of household is forced to buy corn on the market
to meet his household provisioning needs. Metateros
often find themselves in this position even in relatively good harvest years but in bad years they must resort to this much earlier in the year (e.g., in January or February rather than in May or June). Their
only other viable alternative is to find work as day
laborers or as contract agricultual workers, a decision
that often results in their having to leave the village
for extended periods of time, as documented in Chapter 4. Consequently, it appears that the 1967/68 increase in San Sebastian metate output is attributable
to an increase in the total active metatero work force,
as a concomitant of crop failure, and not to an increase in per capita output by members of the incumbent work force. The disguised or shifting nature
of the metate industry labor supply reflects the fact
that many metateros are really peasant-cultivators
with metatero skills which they employ only when their
agricultural income falls below their minimal requirements.[6]

One difficulty with this explanation is that it seems to be contradicted by the data from Magdalena which also suffered a bad harvest in 1967. While I have a record of only 14 Ocotlan marketplace inventories over an 8-month period in 1966-67, nine of these include a larger number of metates than the corresponding trading day in 1967-68 (three of these, Dec. 29, Jan. 12 and Jan. 26 involve a total of 24 more metates than the corresponding dates in 1967/68). In other words, more metates entered the marketplace in the non-drought year than during the drought year, which is the opposite of the San Sebastian/Oaxaca City pattern. Of course, if the data were more complete (including records of hold-over inventory) they might, in fact, present a different picture. Also, it is likely that the nature and effects of the drought would differ between San Sebastian and Magdalena, and would possibly have a different impact on the household budget and labor situation. But if the data are accurate, then two separate _meta-tero_ populations apparently reacted differently to a sub-standard harvest.

What about the demand situation in 1966/67 compared to that in 1967/68--especially in the San Sebastian/Oaxaca City market? Given the substantial increase in supply from the first period to the second, which seems to be caused by factors external to the market, we might expect a decline in price (assuming that demand remains constant from period 1 to period 2). Yet the graphs show no significant change in the price level from period 1, which means that there was a substantial increase in demand to absorb the increase in supply (i.e., some buyers were willing to purchase more metates in 1967/68 at essentially the same schedule of prices that prevailed in 1966/67). The explanation here may lie in the dominant role of big-lot buyers in the San Sebastian/Oaxaca City metate market who, as was described in the last chapter, supply extensive market-areas in various regions of the state of Oaxaca on both a wholesale and retail basis.

On the Stable Element in Metate Output

In emphasizing the variability of metate output and the conditions that engender it, we must not overlook the small persevering groups of relatively landless _metateros_ who account for the stable core of the industry's output from month to month. Variability aside, the output data also show that metate production

313

is, with few exceptions, a continuous year-round activity. From week to week, month to month and from one year to the next, regardless of seasonal or market conditions, some metateros produce and sell metates. Even in the seasons of peak demand for agricultural labor there are always a few metateros who never totally abandon metate production. Likewise, in periods of generally low and stagnant price there are always some metateros who manufacture and sell metates.

What motivations or conditions are operative here? In essence, the aim of the persevering metateros is not to make profits nor to maximize their earnings but, simply, to convert their labor power into cash to enable them to acquire foodstuffs and other products and services which are required to meet the provisioning demands of their households. Ask a persevering metatero why he makes metates year round and he is apt to respond as did one of my informants: "Because there one earns a little money and money's always needed-- if only 50 or 60 pesos to buy a little corn or chickpeas for the week" ("Porque allí sale un poco de dinero y siempre hace falta dinero--mas sea 50 o 60 para compra maizito, garbanzo para la semana"). Metate manufacture not only provides metateros with a relatively stable cash income but also allows them a good deal of flexibility in planning and performing non-occupational work tasks that yield no direct cash remuneration. Many such tasks are necessary to the maintenance of their households and cost to have performed by someone outside the household (e.g., tending animals, cutting firewood, repairing buildings or tools, etc.). Only when metate earnings decline markedly or are totally cut off (e.g., through absence of buyer activity, shortage of stone in the quarries, etc.) do the persevering metateros seek employment in other lines of work. In their situation, to reiterate, it's the total cessation or marked diminution of cash earnings from metate sales, not a temporary or minor reduction of prices, that ultimately determines how they will allocate their labor time and effort.

Levels of Income

In this section we will be concerned with the market value of the output of the metate industry in San Sebastian and Magdalena, with calculating the magnitude and distribution of earnings on an industry-wide and per capita basis and, finally, with analyzing

314

these data comparatively for the two industrial units and relating them back to the annual production cycle.

The total output of the San Sebastian unit over a 23-month (101-week) period of study was 1820 metates and 6262 manos which yielded aggregate earnings of 65,922 pesos ($5,274 dollars) and 33,030 pesos ($2,642 dollars) respectively. The total average income per plaza day (99 during the 23-month period) for all sellers was 666 pesos ($53 dollars) for metates and 334 pesos ($27 dollars) for manos, a combined aggregate gross income of 1,000 pesos ($80 dollars). The average combined income (including both metate and mano sales) per seller per plaza day was 100 pesos ($8 dollars); since the average seller made ten trips to the plaza every 12 months, his total combined income for a year amounted to approximately 1,000 pesos ($80 dollars). By contrast, the total output of the Magdalena Ocotlan unit over a 10-month period (9/67-6/68) was 330 metates and 491 manos which yielded aggregate earnings of 18,660 pesos ($1,493 dollars) and 4,039 pesos ($323 dollars) respectively. The total average income per plaza day (44 during the 10-month period) for all sellers was 424 pesos ($34 dollars) for metates and 92 pesos ($7.34 dollars) for manos, a combined aggregate income of 516 pesos ($41.28 dollars). The average weekly income from metate sales was 76 pesos ($6.06 dollars) per seller over the 10-month period; this means that the average 10-month income from metate sales was 1,140 pesos ($91 dollars) per seller, given the fact that the average seller made 15 successful sales trips to the plaza over the 10-month period.

Figure 15 shows the monthly fluctuations in aggregate income for the San Sebastian metateros over the 23-month period in 1966-68; Figure 16 shows fluctuations for the Magdalena metateros over a 10-month period in 1967-68. A comparison of these curves with those shown in Figures 10 and 12 demonstrates the expected positive correlation between aggregate metate output (Figure 10, Curve II; Figure 12, Curve II) and aggregate income (Figure 15, Curve II; Figure 16, Curve II). Over the 10-month period from 9/67-6/68 the major difference in the income curve profiles for the San Sebastian and Magdalena units is found in March which is a month of continuing high output, price and income for the San Sebastianos but a month of sharp decline in these variables for the Magdalenans. As suggested above, this situation in Magdalena reflects the impact of a steady inventory build-up resulting in a short-term overproduction crisis. A comparable

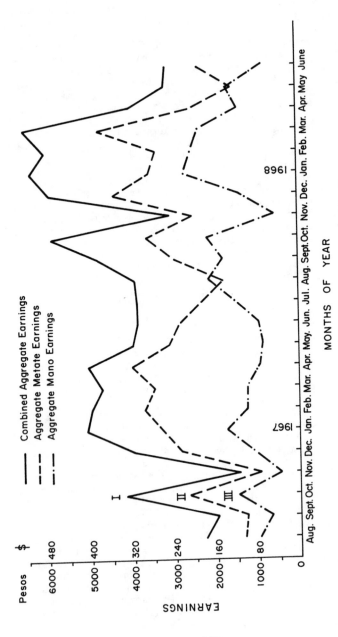

FIGURE 15. Aggregate monthly earnings of the San Sebastian Teitipac metate industry over a 23-month period (August 1966-June 1968).

Curve I represents combined earnings from both metate and mano sales; Curve II represents aggregate earnings from metate sales and Curve III represents aggregate earnings from mano sales.

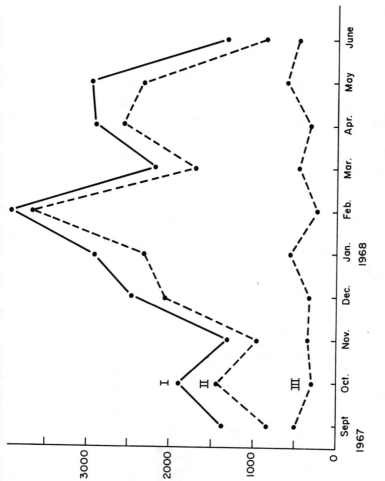

FIGURE 16. Aggregate monthly earnings of the Magdalena Ocotlan metate industry over a ten-month period from September 1967-June 1968.

317

situation does not occur in the San Sebastian case because of the sustained demand from big-lot buyers in the Oaxaca market.

This explanation should not be construed as a negation of the role of exogenous or 'non-market' conditions in generating fluctuations in market activity. While it is obvious that output and income are maximized in the metate industry when market prices are high, this coincidence of variables itself reflects a series of propitious non-market conditions (e.g., only after the harvest season ends does the metate market situation improve--effective demand increases, supply responds, and prices and income rise concomitantly). A good example of the role of exogenous factors is provided by the case of November which, as the figures show, is either a month of lowest (San Sebastian) or low (Magdalena) combined aggregate income. November is characterized by rising prices, reflecting increased effective demand facilitated by October harvests, but low output. Given the high demand for agricultural labor during this peak harvest month in both communities, it is not possible for metateros to increase their labor-time commitment to metate production. Nor would such a commitment be compatible with their household provisioning strategy which places maximum priority on the direct production of food and fodder for their domestic economy. In short, the constraints placed upon them by the agricultural regime and the domestic economy prevent the metateros from responding positively to metate market incentives.

Since Figures 14 and 15 present complete plaza inventories for the metate sellers in aggregate, differences between sellers are not discernible. Figures 17 and 18, on the other hand, are designed to highlight these differences and display the range of incomes among the 15 most active sellers in San Sebastian (12 propios, 3 regatones) and Magdalena (14 propios, 1 regatón) respectively. The range between the highest and lowest monthly incomes (200+ pesos in the case of Crispina vs. Cresencio in San Sebastian and in the case of Atanasio vs. Victorino in Magdalena) is reduced considerably when measured in terms of the number of plaza trips per seller during the period in question. Thus, the difference between Crispina with 30 trips and Cresencio with only 9 is reduced to less than 5 pesos, and the difference between Atanasio with 38 trips and Victorino with 10 is reduced to about 25 pesos. With a few exceptions (e.g., Pedro and Agustín in San Sebastian; German in Magdalena), however, metate

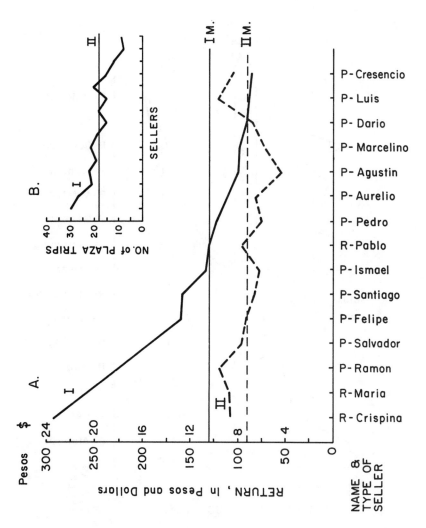

FIGURE 17. Average gross monthly returns for fifteen San Sebastian Teitipac metate sellers (producers and traders) over the period from September 1966 to July 1967.

Curve A.I. places the metate sellers in descending order of average monthly cash returns over the period; Curve A.II. follows the same order but gives the average returns per trip to the weekly <u>plaza</u> in each case. Straight line I.m. indicates the mean of the average monthly returns; straight line II.m. indicates the mean of the average returns per <u>plaza</u> trip. Curve B.I. indicates the number of plaza trips per seller over the entire period; B.II. indicates the average number of trips per seller.

319

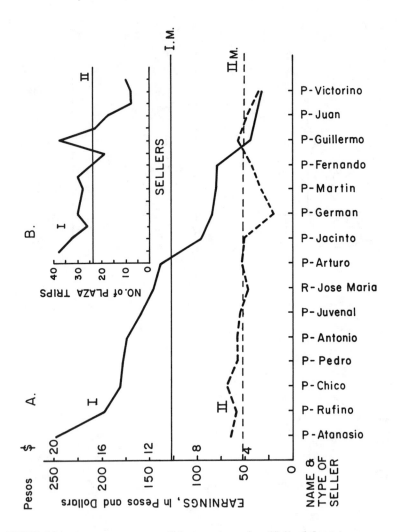

FIGURE 18. Average gross monthly earnings for 15 Magdalena
Ocotlan metate sellers over a ten-month period
September 1967–June 1968.

Curve A.I. places the sellers in descending order of average monthly
earnings over the period; A.II. follows the same order but gives the
average earnings per trip. Straight line I.m. indicates the mean of
the average monthly earnings; II.m. indicates the mean of the average
earnings per plaza trip. Curve B.I. shows the number of plaza trips
made by each seller over the period; straight line B.II. shows the
average number of trips per seller.

320

sellers with above average monthly incomes are also those who made more than an average number of sales trips to the plaza. Moreover, there are only two notable exceptions to a general correspondence between the trajectories of the average income curves (A.I and A.II) in both figures, namely, the case of Luís in San Sebastian and Germán in Magdalena. Luís is representative of the best metate craftsmen who gear their production to coincide with high price periods in the marketing cycle and who are astute bargainers in the marketplace. Germán, on the other hand, represents those metateros who produce more or less regularly--regardless of prevailing market conditions--and whose bargaining behavior is more reflective of their need for cash than of haggling skill.

Another interesting comparison that can be made on the basis of the data presented in these figures is the apparent difference in income accruing to traders as opposed to propios. In terms of gross income the San Sebastian traders occupy positions 1, 2, & 8 in the rank order whereas the only Magdalena trader ranks 7th. However, considering the fact that short-term money costs are higher for traders than for direct producers--primarily reflecting the cash outlay for acquiring the product (a factor which is only partially offset by the higher annual fixed costs incurred by direct producers, e.g., tool upkeep, fuse and blasting powder, etc.), the net cash incomes of traders are, more or less, on a par with those of the direct producers (assuming that the money equivalent of the labor-power embodied in a metate approximates the trader's purchase price). Over the long run the trader does appear to be in a better position than the direct producer to exploit price fluctuations in the metate market (i.e., buy cheap and sell dear); this gives the traders a potential edge vis-a-vis the direct producers regarding income maximization.

The data presented in Table 17, showing price and income levels in the Magdalena Ocotlan industry for two corresponding periods in 1967/68 and 1978, demonstrate vividly the impact of runaway inflation in the national and regional economy as well as a significant expansion in the scale of that industry (as reflected in the increase in the number of sellers and in the number of metates sold). The amazing six- to eight-fold increase in the average price of metates in the Ocotlan market between 1967-68 and 1978 reflects a conscious policy on the part of the metateros to adjust the prices of their products to the prices of products

321

and services which they must buy. An examination of
the data presented in Table 18 which compares the total
monthly expenditures of the same metatero household in
Magdalena (which has experienced a turnover in membership but still maintains the same size and ratio of
adults to children, 2:3) over a 4-month period from
June-September in 1968 and 1978 shows, however, that
expenditures have not increased at a rate directly proportional to the rise in the level of metate prices.
Nevertheless, the prices of the following random selection of products which were purchased by this household
in both years do show rates of increase comparable to
that for metates/manos:

Product	1968 Price (Pesos)	1978 Price (Pesos)
dry beans	3.20 kilo	15.00 kilo
shelled corn	1.25 kilo	3.80 kilo
sugar	1.80 kilo	6.00 kilo
salt	.60 kilo	2.00 kilo
coffee	10.00 kilo	48.00 kilo
fresh beef	16.00 kilo	60-80 kilo
soft drinks	.50 bottle	2.50 bottle
cigarettes	.40 pack	2.20 pack

In explaining increases in the prices of their products
over the 10-year period metateros are also quick to
point out that the value of labor-power has risen from
15-20 pesos for a day's wage in 1968 to 50-70 pesos in
1978, and that they must adjust the selling prices of
their metates to cover rising production costs in man-
days of labor. In essence, then, the upward shifts
in metate prices and metatero incomes over the ten-
year period are necessary concomitants of the upward
shift in the cost of the reproduction of labor-power.

It is precisely this finding which suggests the
possibility of an alternative analysis of output and
price behavior in the metate industry, namely, one
which seeks to understand these movements in terms of
the labor process and the reproduction of labor-power.
Before proceeding with such an analysis, however, it
will be necessary to contrast the neoclassical and
marxist approaches to the value/price problematic with
a view toward explaining the latter approach.

TABLE 17. Comparison of Price and Income Levels in
           Magdalena Ocotlan Metate Industry between
           Periods in 1967/68 and 1978.**

Period	No. of Sellers	No. of Metates Sold	Avg. Selling Price (pesos)	Total Sales Revenue (pesos)	Avg. Revenue Per Seller Per Plaza Day (pesos)
June 7-July 12, 1968	20	24	50 ($4.00 U.S.)	1185 ($94.80 U.S.)	60 ($4.80 U.S.)
June 2-July 14, 1978	29	35	308 ($13.68 U.S.)	10770 ($478.66 U.S.)	370 ($16.44 U.S.)
Sept. 22-Nov. 10, 1967	40	47	46 ($3.68 U.S.)	2146 ($171.68 U.S.)	54 ($4.32 U.S.)
Sept. 22-Nov. 10, 1978	52	61	372 ($16.53 U.S.)	22675 ($1077.77 U.S.)	436 ($19.37 U.S.)

**To properly interpret the figures in this table the reader
should keep in mind the devaluation of the Mexican peso vis-a-
vis the U.S. dollar which occurred between 1968 and 1978. At
the beginning of this decade the exchange rate from pesos to
dollars was 12.50 to 1, whereas in 1978 the exchange rate
(pesos to dollars) was 22.50 to 1. In other words, roughly
twice as many pesos were required to buy a U.S. dollar in 1978
than were required in 1968.

TABLE 18.   Total Monthly Expenditures of a <u>Metatero</u>
Household in Magdalena Ocotlan between
June 2 and September 30 in 1968 and 1978.

Year/Month		Expenditure	
		pesos	dollars
1968 June		397.55	31.80
July		466.51	37.32
August		780.80	62.46
September		403.55	32.38
	Total	2048.41	163.87
1978 June		1704.70	75.76
July		1430.40	63.57
August		1255.85	55.82
September		1146.50	50.96
	Total	5537.45	246.11

Neoclassical vs. Marxist Approaches to the
Value/Price Problematic Under Simple Commodity Production

What should be the relative roles of the Neoclassical and Marxist approaches in an analysis of
value and price under simple commodity production?
Are these approaches supplementary, complementary, mutually negating, or not comparable because they reflect different theoretical priorities and objectives?
While Marx did not deny the usefulness of supply and
demand analysis for dealing with relative prices and
their interrelationships, nor the role of supply and
demand forces in determining these (e.g., Marx 1935:
24-26, 1973:279-281; Godelier 1972:60-77), he was highly
critical of the bourgeois economists for their inability
to penetrate beneath the surface of observable economic
events. The Marxist method considers material categories as reflections of production relations among
people and is critical of bourgeois economists for
their failure to understand "that the process of 'per-
sonification of things' can only be understood as a
result of the process of 'reification of production
relations among people.'" The cause of this "commodity
fetishism" is their failure to consider value, money,
capital, etc. as expressions of human relations bound
to things, but "as the direct characteristics of the
things themselves, characteristics which are 'directly
interwined' with the natural-technical characteristics
of the things" (Rubin 1972:27). For example, whereas
bourgeois economics confuses the source of the 'value'
of commodities with their price as determined in the
market through supply-demand interaction, the Marxist
labor theory of value "is not based on an analysis of
exchange trasactions as such in their material form,
but on the analysis of those social production relations
expressed in the transaction" (ibid. p. 62).

More specifically, Rubin argues that "Marx's
theory analyzes the phenomena related to value from
qualitative and quantitative (my italics) points of
view" (ibid. p. 73) which he explains as follows:

> Marx's theory of value is built on two basic
> foundations: 1) the theory of the form of
> value as a material expression of abstract
> labor which in turn presupposes the exist-
> ence of social production relations among
> autonomous commodity producers, and 2) the

theory of the <u>distribution of social la-</u>
<u>bor</u> and the dependence of the <u>magnitude of</u>
<u>value</u> on the quantity of abstract labor
which, in turn, depends on the level of
<u>productivity of labor</u>. These are two sides
of the same process: the theory of value
analyzes the social form of value, the
form in which the process of distribution
of labor is performed in the commodity. . .
economy (original italics, ibid.).

What are the implications of this approach for supply
and demand analysis? "Supply and demand," said Marx,
"regulate nothing but the temporary <u>fluctuations</u> of
market prices" and ". . .explain. . .why the market
price of a commodity rises above or sinks below its
<u>value</u>, but they can never account for that value it-
self" (original italics, 1935:26). In other words, for
Marx, relative values (market prices) are the phenomenal
form of an underlying substratum or base in absolute
labor value (cf. Gordon 1968) but in a qualitative
sense are only understandable as reflections of the prevailing process and relations of production.

As a commodity which is produced and exchanged
in a monetized market economy, the metate can most
easily be transformed into other commodities through
money pricing. This is accomplished in the marketplace
by negotiation between seller and buyer. To restrict
this analysis of metate circulation to the pricing
process, however, would imply that the 'value' of
these commodities is exclusively and fundamentally a
function of supply and demand, whereas, in reality,
the meaning of the market exchange of metates lies in
its implications for social production in the regional
economy. While I have shown in Chapter 6 that pricing
processes reflect how supply and demand operate in the
metate market (see Cook 1970), I will argue here that
the true significance of metate valuation is to be
found in what it implies about the labor process and
the social relations of production in the regional
economy.

To return to the quantitative aspect of the value
problem, Marx argued that the price of any commodity
must be seen as nothing more than the money name of
the value embodied in it (1930:78), with the magnitude
of its value being reducible to the amount of socially
necessary labor required to produce it. The upshot of
his position is that the price of a commodity, as

determined in the market, may not correspond to its value as determined in the labor process. In Marx's words:

> The magnitude of the value of commodities. . .expresses a relation of social production; it expresses the necessary connection between a certain article and the amount of social labor time needed to produce it. As soon as magnitude of value is transformed into price, this necessary relation assumes the form of a more or less accidental exchange ratio between one commodity and another, the latter being the money commodity. But the exchange ratio may serve to express, either the real magnitude of the value of the commodity, or the more or less for which, in given circumstances, it may be parted with. Thus the possibility of a quantitative incongruity between price. . .and magnitude of value. . ., the possibility of a divergence of price from magnitude of value, is inherent in the price form. This is not a defect, for, on the contrary, it admirably adapts the price form to a method of production whose inherent laws can only secure expression as the average results of apparently lawless irregularities that compensate one another (1930:79).

Marx has discovered here a fundamental aspect of the functioning of any commodity economy, namely, that it is a "system of constantly disturbed equilibrium" (Rubin 1972:64). In a commodity economy like that of the 'Central Valleys' of Oaxaca, no individual or group controls the distribution of labor among the various village- and household-based branches of production. No metatero, for example, knows how many metates are needed by the regional population at a given time nor how many metates are produced (or are available) at any given time in all metatero (and regatón) households in his and other communities. Consequently, as we saw above, the production of metates fluctuates so as to either exceed demand (over-production, high inventory retention) or lags behind it (under-production). In other words, the amount of social labor which is embodied in metates is either too large or not large enough, and equilibrium between metate production and other branches of production in the regional economy is constantly disturbed.

The question arises that if this is true how does the regional economy continue to exist as a totality of different complementary branches of production? "The commodity economy can exist," says Rubin, "only because each disturbance of equilibrium provokes a tendency for its reestablishment" (1972:64). And he continues:

> This tendency to reestablish equilibrium is brought about by means of the market mechanism and market prices. In the commodity economy no commodity producer can direct another to expand or contract his production. Through their actions in relation to things some people affect the working activity of other people and induce them to expand or contract production (though they themselves are not aware of this) (ibid. p. 65).

Thus, other things remaining equal, the overproduction of metates and the resulting fall of average prices at or below MARs induces the metateros to contract production; the inverse is true in the case of underproduction. In short, the "deviation of market prices from values is the mechanism by means of which the overproduction and underproduction is removed and the tendency toward the reestablishment of equilibrium among the given branches of production of the (regional) economy is set up" (ibid.).

In an economy like that of the 'Central Valleys' region the "price form" implies, among other things, (1) that a commodity is exchangeable for money, and (2) the necessity for such an exchange if its value is to be realized (Marx 1930:80). Since wage-labor is widespread in this economy labor-power itself has a money price, and the latter serves to express (through an 'opportunity cost' type calculation by primary producers) the quantity of labor-time embodied in commodities like metates. But this by no means solves the riddle of the value/price relationship because, as any renegade from the study of Neoclassical price theory knows better than anyone else, the "price form" is a source of mystification of social reality in any commodity economy for actors and analysts alike. "This money form," says Marx, "is the very thing which veils instead of disclosing the social character of private and individual labor, and therewith hides the social relations between the individual producers" (1930:49). This "fetishism" of the "price form" would apparently be less characteristic (though by no means eliminated) of simple commodity economies than of capitalism because, according to Marx, as we move away from the latter toward simple commodity production, the determination of value by labor-time becomes increasingly visible on the surface of commodity exchange.

This argument was developed in more detail by Engels who wrote that ". . .the Marxian law of value holds generally, as far as economic laws are valid at all, for the whole period of simple commodity-production, that is, up to the time when the latter suffers a modification through the appearance of the capitalist form of production" (1967:900). "Up to that time," Engels continues, "prices gravitate towards the values fixed according to the Marxian law and oscillate around these values, so that the more fully simple commodity-production develops, the more the average prices over long periods. . .coincide with values within a negligible margin" (ibid.; cf. Rubin 1972:64). Accordingly, haggling between producer-sellers in a simple commodity economy is interpreted by Engels as an effort to obtain ". . .the full compensation for their labor-time expended on a product" (1967:899). The rationale for this explicit correspondence between value and price in such an economy is that, given the relatively limited range of products produced and the community-organized basis for the division of labor, peasant-artisan producers are likely to be familiar with the amount of labor time required for the manufacture of products obtained through exchange (cf. Engels 1967:897).

An innovative interpretation of the classic Marxist position by R.L. Meek (1956:198-200) is useful in analyzing value and price relationships in the metate industry. He argues that the Marx-Engels position (i.e., that during the whole period of precapitalist commodity production prices gravitate towards the values fixed by socially necessary labor equivalents and oscillate around these) is misleading if 'prices' refer to 'actual market prices' as seems to be the case. This is so because we cannot assume 'perfect competition' to prevail under simple commodity production owing, for example, to the prevalence of various forms of monopoly and a low degree of factor mobility.

Given these conditions Meek thinks that the classical position can be strengthened by interpreting 'prices' to mean "supply prices," that is, prices producers must receive for their commodities if they are to continue producing them. As he expresses it:

> Broadly speaking, there are two main types of supply price to be found in the history of commodity exchange--first, that of the producer who thinks of his net receipts as a reward for his labor, and second, that of the producer who thinks of his net receipts as a profit on his capital. It seems to me quite reasonable to assume that supply prices of the first type will tend to be proportionate to quantities of embodied labor, and that such supply prices are typical of commodity exchanges in pre-capitalist societies. Thus, even if the barriers standing in the way of an automatic adaptation of market prices to supply prices in pre-capitalist societies are too important to be assumed away. . .it can at least be said that the supply prices themselves "gravitate towards the values fixed by the Marxian law." What Marx did, in effect, was to assume that the first type of supply price was characteristic of commodity exchanges in pre-capitalist society and to demonstrate how the introduction of capitalism brought about the transformation of the first type of supply price into the second type (1966: 199-200).

Reformulated to incorporate Meek's contribution, the value/price problem before us can be expressed as follows: in the metate market (1) what is the relationship between relative market prices (i.e., those determined by marketplace negotiation) and "supply prices" (i.e., those which metate producer-sellers must receive for their metates if they are to continue producing them), and (2) what is the relationship between the latter and the social average labor time embodied in the standard (size and quality) metate?[8]

These are empirical questions which are not easy to resolve and, indeed, we must be cautious in our attempt to answer them in order not to lose sight of the dual nature of the value/price problem.

Rubin perceptively warned against a "one-sided understanding of the theory of value as an explanation of
exclusively quantitative proportions of exchange in
a simple commodity economy, to a total neglect of the
qualitative side. . ." which, he argued, was the same
in simple commodity and capitalist economies, unlike
the quantitative side (1972:93). Moreover, the general axiom 'value represents labor' is difficult to
operationalize because it makes no specific assumption
regarding the value/price relationship (cf. G. D. H.
Cole 1957:xviii-xxv), but in the context of simple
commodity production Marxism does present us with a
testable proposition. This, as outlined above, holds
that there is a tendency for the embodied labor ratios
of commodities to approximate their market prices (or,
at least their "supply prices"). Presumably, then, we
can demonstrate, by arguments derived from an empirical
analysis of actual costs and prices, that 'values' do
or do not depend upon the socially necessary amounts
of labor embodied in comodities like metates. Regret-
tably, my attempt to do this remains tentative if
only because, for the metate industry, the empirical
corpus of actual price data is set against a series of
gaps and ambiguities in the empirical record of production costs. Fortunately, these are not of sufficient magnitude to preclude analysis.

Given this background discussion of the fundamental principles of the Marxist approach to the value/
price problematic under simple commodity production,
I can now legitimately turn to the following analysis
of the metate industry data. Nonetheless, it is important to reiterate, before proceeding, the 'infra-
capitalist' nature of the Oaxaca economy and its petty
commodity sector within which the metate industry is
inserted. The reader should keep in mind the fact
that I am applying principles from that branch of the
Marxist labor theory of value which were specifically
formulated to be applied to a 'pure' petty commodity
economy rather than to such an economy made 'impure'
through its subsumption by capital. It is my contention that, despite this, the metate industry itself
remains effectively non-capitalist, even as its workers
have been partially proletarianized outside of the industry. The proceeding analysis will attempt to take
account of these complicating factors.

A Re-examination of the Value/Price Data

Some specific caveats should be added to those mentioned above. Previous analysis has shown that in the metate industry market prices do not automatically adapt to "supply prices" in the short-run (i.e., on any given trading day and intraseasonally); yet, such an adjustment does appear to occur over the long-run (i.e., interseasonally or over the complete annual cycle). Indeed, this would seem to be the necessary, if not a sufficient condition, to keep metateros in the quarries and the supply of metates in the marketplace from season to season and year to year. My data do tend to support (at least from the metate sellers' viewpoint) Engels' contention that haggling between producer-sellers in a simple commodity economy reflects an effort to obtain ". . .the full compensation for their labor-time expended on a product;" and also support Meek's suggestion that such producer-sellers think of their "net receipts" as a reward to their labor (though the data do show that they tend also to think of their gross returns in this way). Predictably, I did have trouble in my attempt to accurately estimate the amount of socially average labor-time that is embodied in the standard metate. One complication was that while a majority of the metateros do generally conceive of their products as embodiments of their labor, and view their gross returns as a money-form of that labor, they don't systematize their calculations and, consequently, operate with only rough estimates of the actual exchange (labor) value of their metates.

There were also certain metate industry-specific problems of measurement and statistical computation which I approached in common-sense terms rather than with scientific sophistication. For example, as pointed out in Chapter 5, a given metatero may spend several man-days of work in a quarry without extracting any stone suitable for manufacturing metates; this makes accurate per metate cost accounting difficult for metatero and anthropologist alike. On the other hand, when such stone is available (e.g., after a successful blast) it is relatively uncomplicated to record the amount of work-time required to manufacture a semi-finished metate (metate barreteado); but it is more difficult to arrive at an accurate estimate of the 'social average' because of the individualized and dispersed nature of production during the manufacturing stage. Also, since 'finishing' (la labrada) is usually done in the privacy of the village residence lot at irregular hours and by various family members, it is difficult to arrive at a precise estimate of the socially necessary labor-time expended during the finishing stage of production.

Given these complications how does my estimate of the socially necessary labor time embodied in the standard metate relate to the average market price of the metates sold by the metateros? The time series presented and discussed above show that over a 23-month period in 1966-68 in the Oaxaca City marketplace, the San Sebastian sellers sold 1820 metates; the mean of the monthly sale price averages was 34 pesos, with the highest monthly average price at 43 pesos and the low at 23 pesos over the 23-month period. Based on an average going wage for local day labor of 12 pesos per diem during this same period, the 17-1/4 hour estimate of the socially average amount of labor time for one standard metate (see Chapter 5) is equivalent in money terms to about 26 pesos*--or some 8 pesos less than the average monthly market price. When we take into consideration the additional costs that the metateros must meet if they are to continue to produce metates for sale on a regular basis (e.g., tool maintenance and replacement, powder and fuse, village-to-marketplace transport costs, marketplace surcharge, paint), it appears that the resulting average 'cost of production' would closely approximate the 'average market price.' Nevertheless, given the significant fluctuations which characterize prices monthly and seasonally, the difference between average price and socially average labor cost in the short-run can, perhaps, best be explained in terms of Neoclassical supply and demand analysis.

Neoclassicists will no doubt exploit this latter admission as representing the achilles heel of Marxist analysis and argue, ipso facto, that the average market price of metates cannot be explained as proportional to labor cost, and in the short- and long-run is determined by the law of supply and demand. In terms of Neoclassical accounting 'market prices' of commodities are roughly equivalent to 'total costs'--computed by aggregating the costs of labor, of other factor inputs, and of marketing (incl. transport)--plus a profit on invested 'capital' (tools, powder, fuse, etc.). This might enable the Neoclassicist to make a convincing prima facie case against the proposition that in the

*This assumes an 8-hour work day.

metate industry 'value = labor' but would still leave us without an explanation of why 'value' represents 'labor.' In other words, it would not provide us with an understanding of the unique social role played by marketing in the   regional economy in realizing value created through the discrete household-based and community-organized labor process.[9]

Before we draw any conclusions about the Marxist analysis of the metate industry situation, it is appropriate to consider more closely some of the subjective and objective conditions of metate production and circulation. It is axiomatic that in any commodity economy pricing does not occur unless the "labor process" yields products destined for use by people other than those who produced them. The metatero can make metates for exchange only because, in so doing, he is satisfying a definite social demand in an inter-community division of labor. As a general rule, his labor-power can meet the wants of his own household only to the extent that it is exchangeable for the labor-power of other regional producers (in his own or other communities). In other words, the market system in the Valley of Oaxaca serves as a mechanism for the equalization of different kinds of labor (e.g., of the metatero, the potter, the weaver, the basketmaker, the peasant cultivator, etc.). Through the medium of money pricing it reduces these to 'abstract human labor' and facilitates exchange because of this implicit abstraction (cf. Rubin 1972:66). In the marketplace, the metateros' metates, which have no use-value for them, become their 'exchange-value' by enabling them to obtain, through the medium of money, other materialized forms of labor-power (e.g., a sarape, pottery, bread, maize, etc.) whose use-value they do want to actualize. In essence, the 'labor equalization' function in this simple commodity economy must be realized through concrete acts of market exchange (cf. Rubin 1972:70 and Chapter 9). Here lies the central meaning of the proposition 'value represents labor,' i.e., social labor can only be realized through value (as 'price form').[10]

It will be instructive at this point in our discussion to follow Marx in employing the hypothetical method for expository purposes and assume, for the moment, that a metate is animate and endowed with the human capacity for speech; this anthropomorphized commodity would explain its circulatory situation as follows (cf. Marx 1930:58):

My use-value may interest you human beings; but it is not an attribute of mine, as a thing; my attribute as a thing is the human labor power I embody--therein lies my value. My interrelations with other commodities in the Valley of Oaxaca economy, with sarapes, pottery, baskets, maize, mescal, etc., prove this: we are related only as exchange values. From my point of view I consider these and all other commodities which interest you metateros to be nothing more than the fundamental form of my own value. When, for example, you exchange me and transform me into money, you don't endow me with value (which I already embody in the form of your own labor); you simply give my value a specific form. And, when you transport me to the marketplace because you want something that is not me--it is only by exchanging me for a bundle of money, i.e., realizing my exchange value by seeking another individual who wishes to realize my use-value.

I'm not being at all facetious when I say that this hypothetical metate's view of itself closely approximates reality in the Valley of Oaxaca economy: the metates' actual values are realized only through a sequence of marketplace exchanges which, given the regional structure of production and inter-community division of labor, socially relate a series of producer-sellers.

When we say, for example, that a metate has a value of, say 200 pesos we are saying, in effect, that the metate is a commodity, that it is produced for the market, that the metatero is related to other members of regional society by production relations among commodity owners, that the regional economy has a determined social form, namely that of commodity economy (cf. Rubin 1972:69). As Rubin so perceptively expresses it:

We do not learn anything about the technical aspects of the production or about the thing itself, but we learn something about the social form of the production and about the people who take part in it. This means that "value" does not characterize things,

335

but human relations in which things are
produced. It is not a property of things
but a social form acquired by things due
to the fact that people enter into determined production relations with each other
through things. Value is a "social relation taken as a thing," a production relation among people which takes the form of
a property of things. Work relations among
commodity producers or social labor are
"materialized" and "crystallized" in the
value of a product of labor. This means
that a determined social form of organization of labor is consistent with a particular social form of product of labor
(original italics, ibid.).

The social relationship between producers as
buyer-sellers in regional Oaxaca marketplaces emerges
not because of some instinctive urge on their part to
trade or because of some innate propensity to monetize,
to perceive and evaluate things and events like a trader
as some writers have suggested (e.g., Parsons 1936:12-
13, 445; Malinowski and De La Fuente 1957:23; Leslie
1960:67-71; cf. Beals 1975:186-187). It exists, I
would argue, because of the relationship between these
peasant-artisan producers and their products. The
bargaining situation is one of reciprocal alienation
rooted in the fact that producers are producing what
they don't need and need what they don't produce. Or,
expressed differently, in the simple commodity sector
those products which are 'useful' to each producer are,
more often than not, of alien manufacture (cf. Marx
1930:63). All other aspects of the marketing situation
are subordinate to this fundamental reality. The market exchanges engaged in by the metateros are, then,
necessary consequences of the internal structure of
their regional society; they are part and parcel of
the social process of production (cf. Rubin 1972:62).

Let me reiterate that the metatero, like other
peasant-artisans in the Valley of Oaxaca (Beals 1975:
Ch. 4), does not live exclusively on the products of
his own labor. Indeed, his participation in a regional
marketing system emphasizes the fact that he can only
live if he gets rid of his own products (cf. Mandel
1970:58). As a part-time cultivator he does produce
some of his own use-values but, most importantly, he
produces commodities which are converted into use-values for others through the market mechanism; and, then,

336

through the medium of money, first into exchange-values and, finally, into use-values for himself and his household. Thus, when the <u>metatero</u> appears in the market-place, he does not want to realize the use-values which, in turn, will enable him to acquire needed complementary goods and services. The <u>metatero</u>, when he goes to the marketplace, must encounter a holder of money, M, who is willing to realize the exchange-value of the metate, C.* Also, this money-holder must be prepared to hand over his or her money if he or she wants to realize the use-value of the metate (as a buyer for private use) or if he or she wants to profit from its exchange-value (as <u>regatón</u> or <u>regatona</u>). Therefore, the sale of the metate, C - M occurs at the mutual convenience of the transactors. The value of M is determined by negotiation (<u>regateo</u>) and is variable as shown in the preceding chapter (cf. Beals 1975:188-197). In short, the <u>metateros</u> produce exclusively to transform their metates into money, and concomitantly convert their private and concrete labor into social and abstract labor.

Since the <u>metatero</u> sells his metate to acquire other products, for example, a woven blanket (sarape) for home use, he takes the cash pocketed from the metate sale and looks for a <u>sarape</u> seller in the marketplace. When he locates one and initiates negotiations with him, the transaction M - C' can occur. When these two successive operations of sale and purchase are completed (usually on the same trading day) the <u>metatero</u> has a commodity (the <u>sarape</u>) which is of use to him rather than one (the metate) for which he has no direct use.** And his labor has been socially realized as such vis-a-vis that of the <u>sarapero</u>. A Magdalena <u>metatero</u> expressed these relationships clearly with emphasis on his basic need for maize:

> Since one needs money, well, one sells a metate cheaply to get it. . . . I sell because I need money to buy maize and because I <u>understand that I can do some-thing with money and not with the metate</u> (com-<u>prendo que puedo hacer algo con el dinero y no con el metate</u>). For example, if I don't have any maize this week and I sell a metate, it's certain that I'm going to buy

*C = Commodity; M = Money
**The complete series of transactions is symbolized as C - M - C'.

maize and other items. But, if I calculate
that my metate is worth 80 pesos, and a buyer
offers me 80 pesos, I'll sell; and if not
I'll sell it the following week. I understand that I have maize, I have a source of
pennies, since I can sell my metate at a
good price. But assuming there's maize at
home! When there's no maize at home and
someone offers me 50 pesos for my metate,
of course, I'll have to sell it--because
50 pesos is something. Let's suppose that
when maize is worth 4 pesos per almud . . .
I buy some 6 or 7 almudes and have something left over from the 50 pesos for other
items. There you are. And if I don't sell
the metate, where am I going to get money
to buy maize and the other items? That's
the way things are. When there's maize at
home one doesn't worry and when there's no
maize one worries. One is looking here and
there for a way to maintain his family.

This informant has given a vivid illustration of the
Mexican counterpart of what Galeski (1972:17), referring
to Poland, aptly labels a "'hunger' type of commodity
production." It is only occasionally, under conditions
of a household provisioning crisis that a metatero may
be compelled to sell a metate for less than his minimum
acceptable return (MAR).

One important issue which is implicit in the
above statement is that of how the metateros themselves
view value and price relationships. In their responses
to my question about how they calculated the value of
the metates they manufactured, the metateros emphasized
that their primary consideration was to obtain a price
that adequately compensated them for their work which
they estimated in money terms on the basis of the going
jornalero wage rate (10-15 pesos daily in 1967). Their
answers indicate that they bring their metates to plaza
to convert them into a cash equivalent of the labor
(and other incidental costs) expended in manufacturing
them. This negotiated cash 'equivalent' may or may not
yield a 'surplus' above the estimated cost (this depends on general market conditions). The metatero
does not negotiate with the intent of persuading the
potential buyer to agree on a price which exceeds
estimated cost; if successful he refers to the 'excess'
as a ganancia which he considers to be a sort of "superior wage" for his own labor rather than as 'profit'

on capital invested (Meek 1956:23, 26). Ultimately, the metateros' concern is not to maximize ganancia but to convert their metates (embodied labor) into cash at a level which minimally covers labor and other incidental costs. Since the costs of metate manufacture are more or less constant throughout the year, the metateros' minimum acceptable return (MAR) varies little for metates of the same size and quality. However, as argued above, their minimum expected return (MER) varies seasonally in accordance with fluctuations in demand and average price levels. My field observations confirm that metateros haggle to maximize the difference between MARs and MERs but, on any given trading day (día de plaza), they are ultimately willing to accept bids which, at least, equal their MARs. Over the long run, however, the average "supply price" appears to approximate a mid-point between MAR and MER.

In short, the metatero enters the marketplace to trade but does so with a producer's orientation; he comes not to sell a product but his product in which his own labor-power is embodied. "I sell what is mine, not what is someone else's; I sell my own work" ("Yo vendo lo que es mio, no vendo el ajeno; yo vendo mi propio trabajo") are the words one of my informants used to express this.[11]

Recapitulation and Conclusions

At the microanalytical level the variability of metate industry output should be approached from the perspective of the total economic situation of the metatero's household unit. This situation is rooted in the inescapable need to satisfy, at some minimal level, the daily material requirements of simple reproduction through the allocation of available labor-power into production for own-use and for exchange (either directly via wage-labor or indirectly via the sale of metates or other commodities); and it varies in accordance with the necessary labor/surplus labor ratio within the household unit which, in turn, depends upon the size, composition, means of production endowment, occupational mix, and other socioeconomic factors internal to each unit. As a broad generalization, and taking into consideration the varying mix of external and internal conditions and forces which impinge upon and shape the allocational process within each household, the metateros can be characterized as versatile actors in a provisioning-oriented, market-integrated economy who plan, act, react, and improvise in allocating limited productive means and labor-power in agriculture and craft production. The overriding purpose of these calculations and actions is to reproduce the labor-power in and maintain the economic viability of their household units--from day to day, week to week, month to month, season to season, and year to year. They may conduct themselves in the marketplace as entrepreneurs and outside of the marketplace as kinsmen or, as 'worker-owners' who occasionally engage the labor-power of others, they may appear to be petty capitalists. But, for the most part, they remain domestic provisioners and bearers of labor-power who, when they can't earn a living, make it--and, often, with different and uncertain material outcomes.[12]

The results of the macro-analysis of the quantitative and qualitative data on value and price show that the allocation of labor-power to metate production and the weekly flow of metates into the marketplace are processes that are determined by a complex series of mutually interrelated factors including: (1) the prevailing price level of metates, (2) buyer outlay or demand patterns, (3) producer expectations about market conditions, (4) the provisioning requirements of the ceremonial or festive cycle, (5) the labor requirements of the agricultural cycle, (6) the availability and other conditions of alternative employment opportunities for the metateros, and (7) the volume of the annual corn harvest.

The aggregate time series data display periodicities as well as regularities, cycles as well as patterns. Metate output, sales and income fluctuate periodically in time to the calendar of agricultural operations, to the festive calendar, and to the marriage calendar; these fluctuations are patterned cyclically or seasonally on a more or less coordinate basis. Finally, the data (reinforced by informant statements and my own observations) suggest that, other things remaining equal, metate output increases when price and demand conditions create or reinforce an expectation of relatively high earnings, and decreases when price and demand conditions do not create or reinforce such an expectation.

This analysis is compatible with the assumption that 'value' is a property of commodities like metates; that it is something that attaches itself to them like 'utility' and is reflected in their market price and in the socially necessary labor-time embodied in them.

However, I have also attempted to emphasize certain qualitative aspects of 'value' in the macro-analysis of the metate industry data. In particular, I have argued that the labor-value embodied in metates is realized through exchange in the marketplace where, in effect, the inter-village division of labor is regulated to meet social demand and integrated to facilitate social reproduction.

More specifically, it has been shown that meta-teros (propios) and petty traders (regatones) alike adjust their bargaining strategies to the seasonal fluctuations of the market. This reflects the fact that the marketing system in the regional economy adjusts prices over the long run to maintain rough equivalences between the value of labor embodied in various types of commodities. For example, following the harvest in September-November there is a general rise in the metate price level which correlates with the increased availability of corn and cash, as well as an intensified velocity of circulation of money (i.e., increased effective demand). As the average market price of metates rises vis-a-vis those of other commodities (especially food crops like maize and beans), the value of the metateros' labor increases vis-a-vis that of other producers (e.g., peasant cultivators who grow corn and beans). This suggests that, over the annual cycle (other things remaining equal), the market functions to 'equalize' the labor of various commodity producers in the regional economy. Needless to say, we are only beginning to understand, in the most general and tenuous way, how this might happen. Many crucial questions remain unanswered and I will attempt to identify these and to discuss several of them in an exploratory fashion in the next (and concluding) chapter.[13]

[1] Between August 1967 and July 1968 I conducted field work in the municipio of Magdalena Ocotlan and in the marketplace of the district town or cabecera Ocotlan de Morelos. The relative smallness of the metate industry in Magdalena and the lack of congestion in the metate sales area of the Ocotlan marketplace (compared to Oaxaca City) enabled me to collect more precise data than was possible in the San Sebastian-Oaxaca City market study; the data include records of more than 100 separate seller-buyer negotiations for a total of 35 separate trading days. Since 1968 I have visited Oaxaca several times and have been able to monitor the metate marketing situation in Ocotlan.

[2] A "time series" may be defined simply as "a series of data observed successively in time" (Davis 1941:1) or, more precisely, as "a succession of statistics of production, prices, sales, etc. for a sequence of periods such as a day, week, month or year" (Seldon and Pennance 1965:418). The study of economic time series, especially those that relate to the price and production of the same commodity, has yielded important insights into the nature of the relationships between supply and demand (Davis 1941:8). And in the field of econometrics, one expert observes that the "real . . . problems begin when we study whole series of observations, in particular series indicating the course of a certain magnitude in time, the so-called time series" (Tinbergen 1951:53).

Time series have been utilized by economists as a point of departure in their analyses of trade cycles (for an excellent review of these analyses see Tintner et al., 1968). According to one of the pioneers of this type of analysis, Wesley Clair Mitchell:

> Business cycles are a species of fluctuations in the economic activities of organized communities. The adjective business restricts the concept to fluctuations in activities which are systematically conducted on a commercial basis. The noun "cycles" bars out fluctuations which do not occur

with a measure of regularity [1927:469].

Many economists who study business cycles deny that the scope of their study includes the phenomenon of periodicity with respect to calendar time (Brandis 1964:62). This reflects their general aversion to the external theories (i.e., those that seek causes outside of the economic system for economic behavior) and they habitually make statistical corrections for seasonal variation as a preliminary to time series analysis. As Samuelson bluntly expresses it: "First . . . we must remove from our statistical data irrelevant, disturbing factors such as seasonal patterns. . . ." (1955:323).

Economic anthropologists need not emulate the purism of economists in order to profit from the latter's knowledge of time series phenomena in economic life, nor to benefit from their rigorous guidelines for pattern determination in time series. One economist has outlined these criteria as follows:

> In the analysis of empirical data in any
> branch of science, the search is necessarily
> for relations which may exist between two or
> more of the measurable quantities which are
> the object of investigation. These relation-
> ships, if they exist and are to be recog-
> nized as valid, must exhibit themselves in
> more or less well-defined patterns. But
> this is not enough to give them general
> recognition. The patterns must persist.
> If they are discovered in one set of [ob-
> servations], then they must also be dis-
> covered in a second and independent set . . .
> under identical conditions. In the case
> of time series, the patterns discovered
> in one period must again exhibit themselves
> in another, or else valid reasons will be
> advanced for their effacement. But even
> this criterion of continuity is not suf-
> ficient to establish laws of science. The
> final stage is to give a priori arguments
> for the existence of the patterns . . . to
> explain the nature of the phenomena which
> have been discovered from the data. It
> is probably needless to add that in emer-
> ging sciences . . . it is not always pos-
> sible to give full validity to the rela-

tionships discovered or suspected [Davis 1941:24-25].

In my analysis of the time series data for the Valley of Oaxaca metate industry, I will attempt to adhere to the spirit, if not the letter, of this economist's program. However, in my analysis factors that economists arbitrarily dismiss as irrelevant and disturbing, while they may be found to be disturbing, will not be discarded as irrelevant.

[3]There is a need for more intensive study of the ecological aspects of the precipitation cycle in Oaxaca since the existing literature (e.g., Lorenzo 1960; Schmieder 1930; Flannery et al., 1967) is not definitive. It is apparent, however, that changing weather conditions from one season to the next significantly affect activities in a wide range of industries in the peasant-artisan economy of Oaxaca. Moreover, it is obvious that differences from year to year in the intensity of precipitation and other weather conditions within each season introduce an irregular movement in the course of economic fluctuations.

[4]This is not to imply that the metate marketer does not act in accordance with an "extremum principle" that operates in most market economies (i.e., maximizing money receipts as a seller and minimizing money expenditures as a buyer--Lowe 1965:36-37); it simply implies that his decisions must ultimately be a function of expectations engendered by his total cognitive orientation. The issue as to what extent his choices follow the "extremum principle" is a problem that requires "working out the relationships among the relevant functions, and . . . defining, or at least specifying the general characteristics of the relevant functions" (LcClair and Schneider 1968:459). In my preliminary analysis of the metate sales data I have found that it is much more difficult to work out these relationships quantitatively in the case of producer-sellers than it is in the case of middlemen traders who, of course, do have a money cost basis for calculating profit margins and to serve as a point of departure for marketplace negotiations. In contrast, the producer-seller is limited to an "opportunity cost-plus" formula in negotiating and calculating returns, a formula that lacks the quantitative precision of the trader's money cost formula.

[5]J. B. Say (1767-1832) was a French political

economist who popularized Adam Smith's ideas in Europe and who developed many original ideas of his own that influenced the subsequent history of economic thought. For a summary of his life and thought consult Gide and Rist (1947:122-133).

[6]A. V. Chayanov (1966:106-109), the Russian agricultural economist, explained a similar series of relationships among pre-Bolshevik peasant-artisan groups in his country. In support of this general line of argument my data indicate a close association between the individual metatero's land holdings and the degree to which his work as a metatero is either seasonally variable or varies in reaction to economic crises (e.g., a crop failure). Thus, the metateros who spend the most labor time in metate production from month to month are those with the least amount of land to cultivate. Conversely, those metateros who work only seasonally, for a few months during the post-harvest dry season each year or as a consequence of economic crisis, usually have access to more cultivable land than do their more active colleagues.

[7]This section is a somewhat revised portion of my 1976 article. I wish to express my appreciation once again to the following persons who kindly offered substantive comments and suggestions on the original article: Ralph Beals, Pedro Carrasco, Martin Diskin, Maurice Godelier, Ronald Meek, Richard Salisbury, and Harold Schneider. Prof. Sutti Ortiz has made available to me her recently published essay (1979) which contains many useful comments on my article in the course of her stimulating contribution to the problematic. None of these colleagues is to be held responsible for how his or her comments might be reflected in the present chapter.

[8]Morishima and Catephores (1975) raise some significant questions regarding Meek's "supply price" interpretation of the labor theory. They point to the fact that the latter implies a subjective concern with labor, whereas Marx dealt with labor 'objectively' (i.e., not as the "disutility of 'toil and trouble' implicit in the notion of 'exertion'" but as "the expenditure of a quantifiable force residing within human beings and measured in hours of work" (op. cit. p. 317). They also point out that recasting the idea of "supply price" in terms of cost price (I have attempted to juxtapose these rather than recast the former in terms of the latter) to permit 'objective determination' would lead the investigator of a pre-capitalist (or

simple) commodity economy into an obstacle, namely, that a "clear conception of value, and hence of cost as determined by labour, was not arrived at in precapitalist economies" (ibid.). They make a parallel point about the idea of abstract (vs. concrete) labor (i.e., "the expenditure of human labour power in production without regard to the special kind of useful object produced") arguing that this idea can emerge only within a capitalist mode of production.

These are issues which, unfortunately, can no longer be resolved by economic anthropologists in the context of autonomous precapitalist tribal economies given the demise of these latter or their incorporation into advanced commodity economies. However, they can be approached in the context of the subsumed simple commodity sectors where the effects of monetization, wage-labor, etc. have presumably created the subjective conditions which Morishima and Catephores postulate as necessary for the objective operation of the Marxian law of value.

[9]Rubin (1972) in his discussion of the "false impression of the complete identity between labor and value" (i.e., that labor is value) notes that "Marx's well-known statement that value is 'congealed' or 'crystallized' labor is usually interpreted" to reinforce this false identity (1972:111). He argues, on the contrary, that the proposition 'value represents labor' must not be understood to mean 'value = labor' but that "value is a representation or expression of labor" (ibid.). This understanding would, of course, be faithful to the meaning of Marx's criticism of classical political economy that "it has never once asked the question why labor is represented by the value of its product and labor time by the magnitude of that value" (1967, I:80) which, in turn, rests on his distinction between 'value-form' and 'value-magnitude.'

[10]Rubin (1972) warned against the distortion of Marx's thought which arises from the reduction of the labor theory of value to the axiom 'value = materialized labor.' Early in his discussion he points out that "It is more accurate to express the theory of value inversely: in the commodity-capitalist economy, production-work relations among people necessarily acquire the form of the value of things, and can appear only in this material form; social labor can only be expressed in value" (p. 62). Elsewhere he argues that "Labor cannot be identified with value in the full

346

sense of the word, labor as the substance of value
must be treated in its inseparable connection with the
social 'value form' (Wertform)" (p. 112); he further
elaborates on Marx's analysis of value in terms of its
form, substance and magnitude or in its <u>qualitative</u>
and <u>quantitative</u> aspects (cf. Marx 1967, I:47-83).

[11]The general proposition that a worker becomes
the owner of a product in which his labor is embodied
(or of a resource like land on which work was performed)
is widespread among the <u>metateros</u> but they have little
difficulty in reconciling this notion with that of
ownership by purchase. In the following interview with
a <u>metatero</u> informant, which followed up a complete inventory of his material possessions, his distinction
between "<u>dueño por trabajo</u>" (owner by work) and "<u>dueño
por dinero</u>" (owner by money) illustrates this:

Q: What do you understand by the term
    '<u>propio</u>'?

R: It's the same as owner (<u>dueño</u>).
    '<u>Propio</u>' means that one is owner also.

Q: Then according to you, you are 'owner'
    of all these things in the inventory;
    and also of the quarry and of the
    plots of land that you cultivate?

R: Well, almost owner because I have
    work in those things ("<u>tengo trabajo
    sobre esas cosas</u>"). They cost us
    work.

Q: For example, the metates that you
    bring home from the quarry are in the
    same category with the material property
    in your house?

R: That's right. We are 'owners' (<u>propios</u>)
    of the metates because we've put our
    work into them.

Q: And what happens when a <u>regatón</u> gives
    you money for your metate? Who is
    the owner then?

R: Well, the owner of the metate then is
    the one who 'turns loose the bread'
    (<u>Es él que suelta la lana</u>).

347

Q: But is he an 'owner' in the same sense as was the metatero?

R: The metate belongs to the metatero when he hasn't sold it; but when he sells it he's no longer its owner. Then he's an owner of money. And the one who gave money for the metate is owner of the metate. So when one comes home from the quarry with a metate and he hasn't sold it, then, he's its owner because he made it. Then, when a regatón arrives and gives money or pays the price, he becomes owner of the metate. And the metatero who owned the metate before now owns the money. He no longer owns the metate. . . . The money that paid for the metate paid for the work of the metatero (El dinero que pagó por el metate pagó por el trabajo del metatero). The regatón is owner of the metate because he bought it. He doesn't know how to make a metate but he knows how to make money to buy a metate, and he knows how to trade metates. The metatero, on the other hand, can't make money but he can make metates, and from metates comes money. . . . Then one is "owner by money" ("dueño por dinero") because he 'turned loose the bread' ("soltó la lana") or paid the price of a thing. He became 'owner by money' (se hizo dueño por dinero).

[12]This summary characterization of the metateros should be evaluated in the context of my discussion in Chapter 2 of the crucial economic role of women in the domestic unit, and should not be construed by the reader to imply that I consider the metateros to be 'supermen' who are the exclusive reproducers of labor-power (their own and others') in their domestic units. Both women and children (especially the former) contribute indispensably, if with varying degrees of productivity, to the process of labor reproduction in metatero households. For the record I hereby acknowledge my failure to systematically examine women's roles in metatero households during my earlier research, even though I recognized from the beginning the significance (if not the full implications) of women's involvement in the various levels of the social division of labor (see

Ch. 2 above). Among other factors, this failure reflected my tendency to reify the metateros' activities
and to allow my interest in and admiration for the
physically demanding nature of the metate industry's
labor process and the uniquely male or 'macho' superstructure associated with it, to monopolize my time and
thought. Moreover, I was then of the belief, through
my admiration for Raymond and Rosemary Firth's remarkable studies in rural Malaya, that 'householding' merit-
ed separate and extensive attention, preferably by a
female researcher. While my most recent research in
Oaxaca (1977-1980) has proven that male researchers can
study women's work with some degree of success, I still
remain unconvinced that intensive research on domestic
work and householding, which primarily but not exclusively or necessarily involves females, can best be
studied by female researchers--given the structure of
the sexual division of labor and its ideological matrix
in rural Oaxaca. Nevertheless, my future work on the
Oaxaca rural economy will not be as deficient as my
earlier work was with regard to the economic role of
women.

[13]An anonymous reviewer of an earlier version of
this manuscript focused the brunt of his attack on the
second half of the present chapter as follows:

> What would be the most interesting chapter
> from a Marxist perspective is simply
> wrongheaded--the wrong question is asked and
> the wrong data are brought to bear on it.
> The question Cook asks is whether or not
> stonecutters valorize their product in terms
> of the labor embodied in it. His answer
> is that they do, inasmuch as the "average"
> price of their product works out to be
> more or less equivalent to the going price
> of unskilled labor in the region. If
> there ever was a basic misconception of
> Marx's (or Ricardo's) labor theory of
> value, this is it. A Marxist has no reason
> ever to expect price to reflect labor
> value--quite the opposite in fact. Price
> reflects advantage in the market--some
> prices will be higher and others lower than
> labor value because of unequal advantage
> in the market (or over the means of pro-
> duction)--though all prices of all products
> will reflect average labor value in the
> entire market economy. . . .

As the study stands now, however, there is
nothing interesting about the finding or
the author's treatment of it. More significantly the author does not seem to
understand the whole "transformation" problem between value and price . . . the
author describes the Neoclassical approach
to price, which he contrasts with the
Marxist approach, but in fact what he represents as the Neoclassical approach is
the Marxist approach, and what he describes
as Marxist is vulgar Ricardianism.

I will spare the reader the discomfort of having to
digest additional excerpts from this 'review' but I
hope that you will bear with me as I put myself on
record in specific rebuttal.

Suffice it to say that this is one of those
performances which reveals much more about the perform-
er than it does about the object of the performance.
Thus we can immediately infer that this anonymous
critic (1) has read the manuscript very superficially,
at best, and with no comprehension, (2) is ignorant
of the pertinent Marxist literature, and (3) suffers
from a one-sided 'capital-centrism' which sees capitalism as ubiquitous and conceives of Marxist problem-
atics and theory entirely in its image. Let me elaborate my rebuttal on three specific points.

First, the question I asked is to what extent
the labor theory of value provided a better explanation
of metate circulation than the supply and demand approach; the metateros' labor-centered valorization of
their commodities [which was the original basis for my
interest in the topic] was presented as data, not posed
as a question. Second, our masked critic inexplicably
overlooked the fact that the value/price problematic
at issue here is focused on simple commodity production
and not on the capitalist mode of production. His
presumptuous assertion that, "A Marxist has no reason
ever to expect price to reflect labor value . . ." not
only confirms his adherence to a doctrinaire 'capital-
centrism' but violates a basic Marxist principle that
relativizes its laws to historically specific forms of
social production so as to avoid imposing, for example,
the logic of advanced commodity production upon the
simple commodity form. To make matters worse, the reviewer chooses to ignore the lengthy quote from Marx
[and my discussion of same] which suggests that he

350

isolated a fundamental aspect of the functioning of any commodity economy, namely, that it is a system of constantly disturbed equilibrium in which the possibility of a divergence of price from magnitude of value is inherent in the price form. The question of which law of value operates and how (i.e., vis-a-vis the transformation of value into market price [SCMP] or 'prices of production' [CMP] in a petty commodity sector of a capitalist formation like Mexico is an important one of high priority for continuing investigation. Expressed differently this question becomes: Which is operative, the system of value accounting outlined by Marx in Capital v. I where he argues that prices gravitate around labor-value, or the system outlined in Capital v. III where he argues that prices deviate from the direct and indirect labor ingredients of commodities (cf. Morishima and Catephores 1975:310; Emmanuel 1972:390-391)? In essence, as Howard and King (1975:143) persuasively argue: ". . . the transformation problem arises only when capitalism is sufficiently well-developed for competition, and the resulting mobility of capital actually gives rise to a tendency for the equalization of the rate of profit in different sectors of the economy. In earlier stages of capitalism, and even in pre-capitalist societies, the problem is wholly irrelevant." And, of course, we know enough about the rural Oaxaca economy to realize that there are structural limits on the movement of labor and capital between and within productive sectors.

Lastly, our phantom critic completely misses the central argument of the chapter which seeks to demystify or defetishize our approach to the market in a simple commodity economy—first, by distinguishing between the quantitative and qualitative dimensions of the problem and, then, by following the circulation of commodities into the social division of labor and production relations which comprise its matrix. In short, what our anonymous pseudo-critic flaunts as the correct Marxist approach dissolves into a crude caricature of Marxism and is empiricist, economistic, and—worst of all—painfully misinformed.

Magdalena woman holding child and decorating a metate in the Ocotlán marketplace.

CHAPTER 8. CAPITAL AND SIMPLE COMMODITY
PRODUCTION IN OAXACA: THE CURRENT SITUATION
IN THEORY AND ANALYSIS

Preliminary Statement

In the preceding chapter I sought to integrate the concepts of production and circulation in an analysis of the value/price/income relationship in the metate industry. And, in doing so, I proposed that this relationship could only be explained in the total context of social production (i.e., the division of labor) in the regional economy; in other words, the metateros were considered as but one group of specialized commodity producers among many others enmeshed in a regional web of interdependency. This was, of course, a simplified view of the real economy which is a complex field encompassing many extra-regional and advanced-commodity relations and processes. As indicated in Chapter 1 and in subsequent chapters, the Oaxaca economy--though by no means completely capitalist--is, nevertheless, pervaded by advanced commodity relations which extend into the national and international division of labor. In this concluding chapter I will attempt to insert the metate industry and its participating households into this wider matrix of commodity and class relations, and to characterize and analyze the relational process between non-capitalist and capitalist spheres of production and circulation in the contemporary Oaxaca economy. Necessarily, then, the metateros will be joined by many other small producers many of whom, as will be discussed, are much more directly or extensively engaged in relations with capital or in capitalist development than are the metateros and their industry. Before proceeding with this analysis, however, it will be useful to formulate a theoretical framework which will enable us to present and evaluate the data in terms of some general questions and concepts.

On Value and Its Distribution in the Regional
Economy

A Preliminary Analysis

The Production-Reproduction Circuits. One of the
principal manifestations of the subordination of small
production to the interests of capitalist accumulation
is said to be a net transfer of exchange-value from
rural direct producers to capital through its local and
regional operators or representatives (cf. Stavenhagen
1976:19). It has long been argued by Marxist scholars
that the transition to or imposition of capitalism in a
non-capitalist economy results in an "exchange of values between large-scale and petty production under
which the latter gives more to the former than it receives" (Preobrazhensky 1968:88). Some of the mechanisms which are believed to facilitate this unequal exchange (or exploitation) have been specified for the
Mexican economy in general (Stavenhagen 1976:20-21) and
for the Oaxaca economy in particular (Cook and Diskin,
eds., 1976:272-275), but we lack a systematic analysis
of how these operate and of the nature and volume of
transfers accruing over given periods of time.[1]

The diagram on the following page is presented
as a heuristic device to facilitate an exploratory discussion of this difficult issue of value transfers. In
an economy like that of the 'Central Valleys' region,
the transfer of value from non-capitalist to capitalist
circuits occurs to a significant degree through the
intervention of merchant capital in the circulation
process. This is shown on the diagram in the circuit
C - (M - C - M') - C' where the price (D) that the
merchant pays to the direct producer for a given non-
agricultural commodity (C) is a sort of 'inferior wage'
which is viable as such only because the PADUs (Peasant-
Artisan Domestic Units), in effect, subsidize the reproduction of their labor-power, thus depriving themselves of a portion of the exchange value they produce.
In the Mexican economy where many commodities are produced by capitalist as well as by non-capitalist units,
prices tend to be determined by the former since they
apparently produce these commodities (e.g., corn or
wheat) more efficiently and at a lower cost than do
non-capitalist (i.e., PADU) units. Consequently, the
socially necessary cost for a given commodity (e.g.,
corn or wheat) tends to be less for capitalist firms
than it is for PADUs. However, in the case of commodities which are produced exclusively by non-capitalist
units as in the case of metates, the socially necessary

354

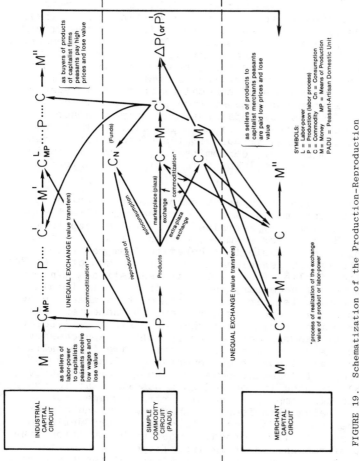

FIGURE 19. Schematization of the Production-Reproduction
Circuits and the Process of Unequal Exchange
between Small Production and Capital in the
Central Valleys Region of Oaxaca, Mexico.

355

cost is set by a non-capitalist dynamic. The price which merchant capital pays to intervene in the circulation of such commodites (i.e., purchases for resale purposes) tends to fluctuate around this non-capitalist socially necessary cost and approximates the subsidized 'inferior wage' referred to above.

One of the ways in which PADUs may cope with this situation is to increase the working day of their laborers without increasing proportionately the prices they charge for their products. This means, in essence, that rural direct producers through self-exploitation 'give away' some of their labor-power to the buyers of their products. These producers continue to participate in this process of unequal exchange, not because they are stupid nor because they are forced to do so by mandate of the state apparatus, but simply to survive through the maintenance of the viability of their domestic units. They produce to transform their commodities into money and, concomitantly, to convert their private and concrete labor into social and abstract labor.

It is important in this context to caution against making the assumption that peasant direct producers transfer only 'surplus labor' to the capitalist sector. Bartra, for example, contends that "it is the bourgeoisie as a whole that benefits from peasant surplus-labor which is 'given as a gift' to society" (1974: 82). This implies that PADUs have satisfied a minimum requirement of necessary labor prior to their involvement in capitalist circuits, a proposition which is by no means axiomatic and is erroneous to the extent that it ignores the crucial fact that many PADUs sell their products or labor-power to capitalists as a necessary means to assure physical reproduction (i.e., to satisfy the 'necessary labor' requirement) (cf. Roseberry 1976). The concept of "remnant peasant labor-power" (Szekely 1977:58) has been introduced as a possible way to avoid the misleading implications of Bartra's usage, the "remnant" being comprised of labor-power which either cannot be absorbed by the PADUs means of production or is unproductive if absorbed. Under such conditions the product of peasant labor is insufficient to meet their vital needs; peasants sell only a part of their excess capacity, either directly as wage-labor or indirectly in their products, and do so for a price equivalent to an 'inferior wage.'[2]

Several remaining points should be made with regard to merchant capital. First, petty traders (_rega-_

<u>tones</u>) are involved in the circulation of almost every
type of commodity produced in the regional economy for
local consumption, and it would be a mistake to overlook or underestimate the possibilities inherent in
this activity for capital accumulation on a scale sufficient to underwrite the expansion of trading operations. Second, I think that it is safe to generalize
that a majority of petty traders in the regional economy never escape from the necessity of converting a
substantial part of their earnings (M') directly into
use values to provision their domestic units. Some
portion of their earnings must be earmarked to replace
inventory or meet other necessary costs but usually in
a way which precludes an expansion of the scale of
trading or of intervention in the labor process. Finally, it must be reiterated that merchant capital in
Oaxaca is not simply a servant of industrial capital.
As the circuit represented in the lower part of the
diagram shows, merchant capital is involved in a quest
for incremental profits or for "value in process" (Marx
1967, I:154-155) on the basis of its transactions with
the non-capitalist sector (cf. Kay 1975:66). In the
'Central Valleys' economy this movement of merchant
capital has, as argued earlier, proceeded from indirect
control over producers to more direct control through
the spread of the putting-out system and to the establishment of workshops and small manufactories (e.g.,
in the weaving industry in Ocotlan de Morelos, Oaxaca
City, and in the Tlacolula district).

    With regard to the direct transfer of value from
PADUs to the industrial capital circuit two possibilities are presented in the diagram. First is the 'commoditization' of peasant-artisan labor-power which often occurs through periodic or seasonal wage work in
industries like construction, mescal and <u>panela</u> (caked
brown sugar) production, or on farms or plantations
(especially in coffee, tropical fruit, or sugar cane
producing regions). A 'net transfer' occurs here because peasant-artisan labor-power is employed for an
'inferior wage' (i.e., below its minimum cost of reproduction). As argued above, PADUs are essentially collectively subsidizing the labor reproduction process
for the capitalist sector by producing foodstuffs for
a peasantry which, paradoxically, could not survive
in the absence of periodic wage-work. The key to un-
ravelling this paradox is that the inferior-wage worker, as member of a PADU, does not calculate the cost
of the agricultural products produced by the PADU
through autoexploitation and destined only for auto-
consumption. The implication here is that if these

357

production costs were accurately calculated they would be found to exceed those of capitalist farms and would force PADU workers to reallocate their labor-time to more remunerative pursuits outside of agriculture and to buy their foodstuffs.

A second mechanism by which industrial capital extracts value from PADUs is the sale of consumer goods to or the purchase of raw or semi-finished materials from them. In the first instance, PADUs are obliged to pay high prices for commodities produced by capitalist firms and, in the second, they must accept low prices for the raw materials or semi-finished products they produce. What this double bind of the 'price scissors' frequently engenders is the circulation of peasant-artisans into the migratory labor stream or their permanent migration from rural to urban areas. Although we lack empirical studies at the local, regional or state level of the scale and impact of seasonal and permanent rural-to-urban migration in Oaxaca one set of statistics which suggests that this was sizeable between 1960 and 1970 is that whereas the total state population grew some 16.8% during this decade, the economically active population (EAP) declined by 16% and the agricultural population dropped by 27% (from 507,905 in 1960 to 372,950 in 1970) (S.P.P., 1979, Sector Agropecuario, pp. 26-27). Migrant laborers, of course, remain as seasonal participants in PADUs in which they contribute directly to the production of their own means of reproduction, a burden which overwise would have to be absorbed by the capitalist sector (e.g., via more jobs or increased wages). When laborers emigrate permanently from the region, on the other hand, the regional economy loses the social reproductive costs incurred up to the time of emigration.[3]

Industrial Capital in the State and Regional Economy. A painful fact of life for those who equate economic development in the state of Oaxaca with capitalist industrialization, and who consider the latter to be the only viable route toward raising the material standards of living of a majority of Oaxacans, is that its 'industry' is preponderantly of a labor-intensive variety where 'capital' is operative on a small-scale, at best, or is of a highly intensive, enclavist variety which is disarticulated with the regional economy and where the benefits of accumulation are siphoned out of the state. It is paradoxical, given this situation, that small-scale, labor-intensive industry remains, with few exceptions, beyond the pale of substantive consideration by the data-gathering, policy-making, and administrative offices of state and federal government. Accordingly, in the latest and most comprehensive series of background reports dealing with Oaxaca--compiled by the federal agency charged with the planning, budgeting and programming of economic development (i.e., PIDER or Programa para Inversiones para el Desarrollo Rural of the Secretaría de Programación y Presupuesto)--the most recent data (1978) is based only on a partial census of "principal" industries (of the 151 enterprises surveyed, 113 were classified as small, 24 as medium, and 14 as large), and there is no data at all for thousands of "small enterprises that operate at the family level" (S.P.P., 1979b:1).* To cite a specific example, data on the clothing and textile industry pertains to two cotton gins and four textile plants, with no data on the manufacture of 'ropa tipica' which employs thousands of Oaxacans in domestic, workshop, and manufactory type enterprises and which, among other things, is a locus of substantial capital accumulation. This contradictory and haphazard treatment of labor-intensive forms of production results in a series of errors ranging from the statistical misrepresentation of the "productivity" of Oaxaca "industry" (i.e., underestimating the state's PIB or Producto Interno Bruto--see S.P.P 1979b:49) and the structure of its labor force (e.g., assigning 75% of the PEA to the 'sector agropecuario' and only 6% to the 'sector industrial' so as to bury artisan and other small-scale non-agricultural production in the first category, underestimate its presence in the second, or ignore it altogether--ibid. p. 56), to a failure to develop adequate programs or institutional support to diagnose and remedy the multiple economic needs (e.g., credit, technical assistance, marketing analysis) of the domestic and other small-scale enterprises.

Having documented these deficiencies in the official approach to labor-intensive industry in Oaxaca, it is now appropriate to summarize some of the salient

---

*'Industry' as defined for purposes of these government reports is synonymous with 'branches of production' with the principal ones being agriculture, animal husbandry, forestry, petrochemicals, chemicals and pharmaceuticals, construction materials, textiles and clothing and energy.

points from the official literature dealing with the
'industrial' sector of the state economy. According to
the 1975 Federal Industrial Census there were 3840 "industrial enterprises" in Oaxaca of which 3800 small
units represented an aggregate investment of 241,662,000
pesos (13% of the total industrial investment) and had
8,376 employees (2.2 per enterprise), in comparison
with a total capital investment of 1,149,345,000 (62%
of the total) and 5,018 employees (717 per enterprise)
for the seven large enterprises. Regarding the location
of industrial units by region, the small-scale enterprises were concentrated in the 'Central Valleys'
region (1467 units), with the remainder being distributed among the seven remaining regions (from 142 to
523 units per region); medium-sized enterprises were
dispersed among six regions with from 2 to 8 enterprises per region (except for the 'Cañada' and the
'Mixteca' where neither medium nor large enterprises
were reported); and the seven large enterprises were
divided between only two regions: the 'Isthmus' and
'Tuxtepec.' In a more recent (1978) survey by the state
government (Dirección General de Desarrollo Económico)
this picture changes only with respect to large enterprises with a total of 14 being identified, only one
of which was located in the 'Central Valleys' region
(i.e., Triplay de Oaxaca, a plywood factory in Oaxaca
City), five in the Tuxtepec region, and the remainder
in the Isthmus. Only 389 'industrial enterprises'
were included in this 1978 survey; these were estimated
to have a gross product worth 4,640,502,000 pesos (205,
730,000 dollars) and to employ 9,874 persons. Although
the 'Central Valleys' region had 72% of these enterprises, they accounted for only 23% of the gross product
and for only 28% of the industrially employed population
(S.P.P 1979a:21-22).

While these government reports are deficient in
their handling of the small enterprise sector in the
state economy, they present a more accurate portrayal
of the role of larger enterprises. What they document,
in a nutshell, is a classic situation of 'enclavism'
in which large enterprises in Oaxaca are capital-intensive (e.g., the paper products industry in the Tuxtepec
region and the petroleum refining and petrochemical
industry in the Isthmus) and, therefore, provide relatively few permanent jobs for Oaxacans and produce commodities destined primarily for markets in other areas
of Mexico or in foreign countries (also the case for
medium-size enterprises). Table 19 on the following
page presents specific information of selected principal
industrial enterprises in Oaxaca. Incidentally, a

TABLE 19. Selected Principal Industrial Enterprises in Oaxaca and Their Markets
(S.P.P. 1979b)

Branch of Production	Name, Size, and Location of Enterprise	Size and Location of Markets
Canning (pineapple)	COFRINSA, large, Loma Bonita (Tuxtepec)	80% export to U.S., Spain, Argentina
Sugar Refining	(various mills), large, Tuxtepec/ Isthmus	122,000 tons to national market; 37,000 tons to U.S.--annually
Pharma-ceuticals	PROQUIVEMEX, large, Tuxtepec Also medium-sized firms in Tuxtepec and Isthmus	20% to U.S.; 80% to national market
Plywood	NOVOPAN & TRIPLAY, large, Oaxaca City	90% national market; 10% export
Cellulose and Paper	CELOX, large, Cosolapa/Tuxtepec	70,000 tons of newsprint 34,000 tons of cellulose (annually)--national market
Shrimp Processing	Productos Pesque-ros de Salina Cruz, large, Isthmus	1,500 tons annually-- 100% to U.S.
Gasoline Refining	PEMEX, large, Salina Cruz (Isthmus)	62 million barrels an-nually and climbing; to Mexican Pacific coast (90+%) and export (climbing)
Cement	Cooperative CRUZ AZUL, large, Isthmus	480,000 tons annually; most to petroleum region of Veracruz and Tabasco; some to Oaxaca
Drydock--construction and repair of ships	Astillero No. 8, large, Salina Cruz (Isthmus)	Mexican Navy and PEMEX; shrimp boats to India and England

comparable situation prevails in agriculture where since 1970 huge investments have been made by the federal government in large-scale irrigation projects, encompassing some 58,000 hectares in the Isthmus region alone (S.P.P. 1979d:125). Thus, the state finds itself in the paradoxical position of having to import an estimated 70,000 tons of maize annually (distributed through the federal government's CONASUPO network) to meet the consumption needs of its population, which 'underproduces' this crucial subsistence crop, but being a major producer at the national level of cash crops like rice, sugar cane, peanuts, coffee, cotton, castor beans, pineapple, limes, and coconuts which are destined for export mostly as raw or semi-processed products (Noticias, October 7, 1979:p. 1).

In addition to the industries listed in Table 19 there are several others in which medium-sized enterprises predominate, and which produce and market their products as follows (S.P.P. 1979b).

Mescal--	8 million liters annually produced in the districts of Tlacolula, Yautepec, and Ejutla--and in San Augustin de las Juntas (Centro); mostly for local and national markets
Rubber--	1650 tons of laminated rubber annually--100% to D.F.
Pine Resin--	2208 tons annually--100% to D.F., Guadalajara, and Monterrey
Soap--	432 tons annually, 100% to D.F.
Vegetable and fruit oil--	75 tons annually of oil of lime essence, 100% to U.S.; 1200 tons annually of castor oil to D.F., Guadalajara, and Monterrey for further processing
Lumber--	273,000 cubic meters annually, 90% to D.F. and Puebla, 10% to Oaxaca
Soft-drinks--	13 million cases annually, 75% to Oaxaca, 25% to southeast Mexico

Candles--   1344 tons annually to Oaxaca
                 and other southeastern Mexican
                 markets

Lime (cal)--   75000 tons annually--to Oxaca

Plastic   1260 tons annually--Oaxaca and
containers--   southeastern Mexico

This list demonstrates that only in the case of soft
drinks, candles, lime, and plastic containers is a
significant proportion of production destined for Oaxaca
markets. This also appears to be the case for mescal
where approximately 65% of the output of the major production center, Santiago Matatlan (Tlacolula), for any
given month is destined for consumption within the state
(Díaz Móntes 1979:76). The remainder of the industries
listed export products to markets in the urban-industrial areas of central and northern Mexico or to the
United States. A similar pattern also characterizes
the mineral products industry which has some 30 active
small private and communal enterprises engaged in
mining graphite, iron, antimony, gold, silver, lead,
copper, zinc, asbestos, feldspar, silica, mica, marble,
limestone, onyx, and salt.

Unfortunately, comparable data are not yet available for a whole range of village-based industries,
with either domestic or other small-scale types of enterprises, which produce a diverse array of products
such as baskets, mats, rope and other hard-fiber products, pottery, bricks, woven goods (wool, cotton, and
synthetics), and traditional clothing. Metates are representative of one extreme, namely, that of products
destined almost exclusively for use in Oaxaca by peasant-
artisan or proletarian households (characteristic also
of unglazed, nondecorative pottery, rope and hard-fiber
products, and palm mats among other products), whereas
wool tapestries, many other wool and cotton woven products, and most embroidered products represent another
extreme in being destined principally for national
and international 'tourist' or urban middle-class markets.

Regarding the industrial employment situation,
data are harder to come by. Table 20 presents an overview of the employment statistics available for the 151
enterprises surveyed in 1978 by the state government.
It is apparent from these figures that most employment
is in the agro-industrial sub-sector (which includes

363

TABLE 20. Jobs Generated in the Industrial
Sector of the Oaxaca Economy as of
1978 (S.P.P. 1979b)

Industrial Sub-sector	Number of Enterprises	Type of Employees	
		Direct*	Indirect**
I. Agroindustries	131	20,274	47,360
II. Capital goods, petro-chemical, chemical and construction materials	14	4,158	6,000
III. Clothing and textiles	6	558	712
TOTAL	151	24,990	54,072

*direct jobs--generated and provided directly by the
enterprise surveyed

**indirect jobs--refer principally to workers engaged
in the production of raw materials
like sugar-cane and cotton, or service jobs

lumbering and fishing). Indeed, as it turns out, some
84% of employment in the so-called "industrial" sector
is generated by only five branches of sub-sectors I
and II, as follows: 14,000 in forest products (I),
2000 in pineapple processing (I), 1900 in sugar refin-
ing(I), 1755 in drydock and shipbuilding (II), and 1500
in the PEMEX refinery (II) at Salina Cruz where the
number of employees is expected to double in 1980 as
construction progresses to increase the capacity of
the refinery. And, to reiterate, literally thousands
of men, women, and children in Oaxaca, who work in
domestic and other small-scale enterprises producing a
variety of craft and other products, are precluded from
the ranks of the 'employed' simply because of the arbitrary and biased survey and statistical procedures

364

utilized by state and federal agencies.

Those persons and groups who equate 'economic development' and 'industrial growth' in Oaxaca with the appearance and spread of medium- and large-scale, capital-intensive enterprises must concede that these processes have been slow to occur and unevenly dispersed sectorally and regionally. This judgment is supported by official statistics which show that there were 2,229 'industrial enterprises' operating in the state in 1960 with a total capital investment of 544 million pesos, and that by 1975 the number of enterprises had increased to only 3839 with an investment of 1865 million pesos. This translates into a factoral increase in investment of only 3.4 and a net employment increase of only 1739 persons over the 15-year period (S.P.P. 1979b:1). The most recent official estimate gives an increase of 10,394 jobs in the industrial sector between 1960 and 1978; 28,000 persons are listed as being employed in the industrial sector in 1978 which, considering that this includes employeees in molinos de nixtamal and bakeries, remains miniscule in comparison with the estimated 600,000 persons in the EAP (op. cit.). When it is considered that an overwhelming proportion of the enterprises surveyed in 1975 and 1978 were classified as small, and that tens of thousands of household- and workshop-level commodity-producing units were not surveyed, the pessimism and frustration prevalent among private and governmental spokesmen for the 'developmentalist' movement in Oaxaca appears to be justified.

The industrial sub-sectors which are the most likely arenas for conflicts of interest between small labor-intensive and large capital-intensive enterprises are the agroindustrial, mining, and clothing and textiles sectors. A variety of conditions and factors peculiar to each branch of production within these subsectors will probably be decisive in determining the shape, course, and outcome of antagonistic relations between small and large enterprises. However, it must be admitted that forces or conditions external to a particular branch of production, especially policy decisions made within the financial sector, may in the last analysis prove decisive. Our knowledge here is uneven but it seems that the displacement of small by large enterprises is not inevitable in all branches of production. Moreover, given certain characteristics in the structure of production (e.g., widely dispersed or scattered raw material sources, restricted labor supply, limitations on technological inputs or mechaniza-

365

tion) or circulation (e.g., market constraints), it is not feasible according to the cost-benefit logic of advanced commodity production for large enterprises to enter certain branches of production. This is clearly the case in the metate industry, for a combination of factors inherent in the production and circulation of its products which were analyzed in preceding chapters, as well as in other craft industries where the persistence of labor-intensive forms reflect production conditions (e.g., nature of the labor process) or market conditions (e.g., the quality of being 'handmade' is the source of use-value).

There are cases, however, which are complicated by unique circumstances. The mezcal industry in the 'Central Valleys' region is illustrative. The predominant form of production in this industry is the medium-sized enterprise where a worker-owner supplements family labor with hired help. This production form depends upon a more costly and sophisticated technology (centered on the 'alambique' or large copper kettle and copper tubing for the still) than the more primitive traditional form (wooden and clay containers and reed or other tubing) which is found in some isolated communities, but is less costly and productive than the more capital-intensive (and rationalized) labor-process in the only modern distillery operating in the region (San Agustín de las Juntas, Centro). The alambique process has an average monthly output of between 2-3,000 liters (per alambique) compared to a 48,000 liter output for the modern distillation process in the factory (Díaz Móntes 1979:47). Nevertheless, the aggregate output statistics indicate the continuing dominance of the 'copper kettle-still' form (though several alambiques may be owned or controlled by one person or enterprise): the total monthly output of mezcal from 270 alambiques (distributed among 5 districts in the 'Central Valleys'), all of which are owned or controlled by small- or medium-sized enterprises, is about 640,000 liters or more than 13 times larger than the output of the modern distillery. One condition which seems to favor the smaller enterprise in the mezcal industry is the dispersal of maguey (agave) plantations (the maguey plant provides the 'piña' or 'pineapple' from which liquid is extracted to distill mezcal) and the relative difficulty of its procurement; it is grown as a cash crop on marginal lands by private proprietors, ejidatarios, or comuneros throughout the 'Central Valleys' and adjacent regions—but especially in the districts of Tlacolula and Yautepec (Díaz Móntes 1979:34-42; Beals 1975:61). Maguey is, in turn, marketed through a complex network linking growers, intermediaries, and mezcal producers--any one of whom may own or rent trucks to haul piñas; the maguey trade completely bypasses the regional system of rotating marketplaces or 'plazas.'

Another factor which may ultimately determine the fate of the mezcal industry is the role of the government, first through its tax policies and second through its policies of agricultural development with regard to maguey cultivation and of industrial development regarding its possible entry (through the establishment of a parastate enterprise) into mezcal production or its provision of credit assistance to producers. The mezcal producers are subject to local, state, and federal taxes and confront a labyrinth of bureaucratic red tape and corruption. Bribes and payoffs are a necessary cost of doing business in this industry (Díaz Móntes 1979:119-126). This situation became so intolerable in late 1979 that complaints by the mezcal producers made the national press under sensational headings like "Denuncian Extorsión por un Millón de Pesos Unos Productores de Mezcal" (Excelsior, Dec. 2, 1979:p. 26-A), and armed violence was reported to have erupted in Matatlan between those mezcal producers who supported the anti-extortion campaign and others who favored continued 'cooperation' with the extortioners (El Imparcial, Jan. 17, 1980:1). Finally, the federal and state governments have also collaborated in a program to expand maguey cultivation through the extension of credit to growers (also under public attack for mismanagement); and rumours are circulating to the effect that a government-backed distillery is being planned. Given this series of conditions it appears that the future of the family-owned or operated mezcal distillery (palenque) is in some jeopardy.

Before shifting this discussion to an unrelated industry, it is appropriate to mention, as yet another symptom of the dependent status of the Oaxaca economy, that the leaves (pencas) of the maguey mescalero which are processed by hand into ixtle fiber for household use in most communities of the region are not employed as the basic raw material in the regional fiber products (jarciería) industry in Tlacolula district (except in the villages of Santo Domingo and Santa Catarina Albarradas). A small decorticating plant to process ixtle fiber from the maguey mescalero did operate for a time in Tlacolula de Matamoros but failed for a number of reasons including the poor quality of its fiber. The local artisans, who make rope and a

367

variety of related products, now purchase _ixtle_ at premium prices through a network which leads from
Tlacolula to a Oaxaca City merchant and, finally, to a
decorticating plant in Ciudad Victoria, Tamaulipas.
The state government has been made aware of this situation and has tentative plans to establish a new decorticating plant in the Tlacolula-Yautepec area to
produce _ixtle_ from the _maguey mescalero_. Until this
project materializes, however, the regional fiber products industry will continue to depend on distant
sources (i.e., Tamaulipas or Yucatan) and to pay premium prices for its raw material.

   The clothing/textiles sub-sector encompasses a
variety of industries which also display unique conditions of production and circulation that influence the
nature and trajectory of its development. Confining
my comments to the 'Central Valleys' region, it can be
asserted that with the single exception of two highly
mechanized but archaic cotton thread and cloth factories in the district of Etla, this sub-sector is characterized by a diversified labor process in which the
domestic unit of production predominates but, as in the
case of embroidery, usually as an outwork unit employed on a piecework basis by merchant capital. The
workshop and small manufactory are also present in this
regional industry. The future development of this sub-
sector will by no means reflect the free, competitive
struggle for hegemony between these different production forms because of the dominance already exercised
by regional merchants and by national monopoly capital
in most of its component industries.[4]

   Raw cotton is grown in Oaxaca, especially along
the Pacific coastal plains, but it is sold almost exclusively to textile industries in other areas of
Mexico (e.g., Puebla, Mexico City, Saltillo). Ironically, the two cotton thread and fabric mills in Etla
spin thread only for the cloth they manufacture for
flour and grain sacks, all of which are sold exclusively to Mexico City buyers. Some raw cotton is hand-
spun by backstrap loom weavers in areas like the
district of Jamiltepec (e.g., in Pinotepa de Don Luis,
San Jan Colorado, Huazolotitlan) but even these industrious artisans buy large quantities of factory-made
thread as do all of the weavers and needleworkers in
the 'Central Valleys' region. As is the case with most
manufactured articles, the marketing of factory-made
cloth and thread (cotton, wool, or synthetic) is controlled by an oligopoly of exclusive factory agents or
distributors in Oaxaca City and their network of mer-

chants and commission agents in the towns and villages of the hinterland. This results in a permanently unfavorable market situation for direct producers who are obliged to pay premium prices for factory-made raw materials. The following experience of some weavers from Xaagá, Tlacolula, is illustrative. They use substantial amounts of cotton thread per loom each week and, constantly confronted with cash scarcity because many of the Mitla intermediaries who buy their products often defer payment, they make several trips weekly (on foot or bicycle) to Mitla to buy just enough thread from local merchants to keep their looms working. Periodically, when cash is available, they travel by bus to Oaxaca City to purchase several weeks' supply of thread at prices which are more reasonable than those in Mitla. Their entrepreneurial logic told them that it would be worth their while to 'save up' for a trip to the thread factories in the Tlaxcala-Puebla area for the purpose of purchasing a several months' supply at factory prices. Such a trip was made by two weavers at considerable expense in time and money but proved to be unrewarding: the factories either refused to deal with them or refused out-right to sell thread on the pretext that the quantities solicited were too small. The disappointed weavers were referred by the factories to their distributors back in Oaxaca City. Thus the weavers of Xaagá, who are aware of the supposed advantages of the wholesale purchase of raw materials and are disposed to organize themselves to realize these advantages, continue to buy thread as before at prices which continue to rise capriciously. The vicious circle closes as the logic of monopoly capital prevails.

Merchant and Commercial Capital in the State and Regional Economy. The available data do not enable us to make a definitive statement of the position of merchant capital relative to that of industrial capital in the state or regional economy, nor do they provide us with any indication of its relationship to the labor process which, as we've discussed in the case of needlework and textiles, is quite significant. For example, if we examine the relative input of the commercial and industrial sectors to the Gross Internal Product of the state economy in 1970, we find that 38% of the total derives from commerce and tourism, whereas only 25% derives from industry proper (S.P.P. 1979b:48). Moreover, in 1970 there were a total of 11,225 commercial enterprises with 20,209 employees compared to only 3,483 industrial enterprises with 16,132 employees--with an equal degree of exclusion of

369

domestic enterprises in both sectors (S.P.P. 1979c, p. 33, Cuadro C-4; S.P.P. 1979b, p. 130, Cuadro I-8). Yet in terms of salaries or wages, the industrial sector in 1970 paid 164,312,000 pesos compared to only 60,581,000 paid in the commercial sector (ibid.). Similarly, a look at net capital investment in 1970 shows that the industrial sector invested 1,132,780,000 pesos (325,000 pesos or 13,000 dollars per enterprise) compared to only 722,923,000 pesos (64,000 pesos or 2560 dollars per enterprise) invested in the commercial sector. The tendency, displayed in the last two sets of statistics, for the industrial sector to 'outperform' the commercial sector in quantitative terms at the state level, appears to prevail as well in the 'Central Valleys' region where, in 1970, 55.9% of the total economically active population corresponded to the Agricultural (and other 'primary' activities) sector, 16.2% to the Services sector, 14.6% to the Industrial sector, and only 6.6% to the Commercial sector (S.P.P. 1979a: 10).

Unfortunately, these comparisons must be tempered by the fact that the official statistical record suffers from multiple deficiencies such as the differential availability of statistics (e.g., statistics for the industrial sector are available for 1975 and 1978 but only 1970 statistics are available for the commercial sector), lack of standardized categories or criteria of measurement (e.g., some tabulations employ scale of enterprise, others use type of activity), imprecision and inconsistency regarding concepts and procedures employed for computing measurements, and a uniform tendency to 'under count' small-scale, domestic-level activity especially in the countryside. Consequently, it would be misleading to rely upon official statistics alone as a source for analyzing or evaluating the role of the industrial, commercial or any other sector in the state and regional economy. But it would be equally reprehensible to ignore them because of their deficiencies.

Regardless of how we interpret the official statistical record, given the importance of the marketing and merchandising of industrial commodities produced outside the state as well as of commodities produced internally to the daily economic life of Oaxaca, the role of the commercial or mercantile sector is undeniably crucial. The large capitalist firms of Central and Northern Mexico are not, for the most part, directly involved in the sale of their products in Oaxaca, just as relatively few of the small-scale, labor-intensive industries in Oaxaca directly market their products outside the regional economy. In other words, the flow of products from producer to consumer in Oaxaca is controlled by a plethora of intermediaries, ranging from various types of traders and peddlers operating in villages and regional marketplaces to a wide-array of town- and city-based traders and commercial operators engaged in various combinations, types, and scales of wholesale and retail activities (see Beals 1975:286-87 for a relevant classification).

A survey of the type of commercial enterprises operating in Oaxaca shows the predominance of those handling processed food products (67.7% of the total)--a category which includes everything from small village stores to large grocery warehouses in Oaxaca City; following in order of importance are those specializing in clothing products (7.8%), unprocessed agricultural products (7.6%), fresh meat and fish products (5.9%), and sundry articles of personal use (3.2%) (S.P.P. 1979c:3). Collectively, these commercial enterprises account for 80% of the employees in this sector. With regard to net sales, processed foods occupy first place with 27% of the total, followed in order by transport equipment (including parts and accessories) with 15%, combustibles and lubricants with 11%, beverages with 10%, and unprocessed agricultural products with 7%. These five types of enterprises accounted for 70% of total net sales within the commercial sector in 1970 (S.P.P. 1979c:4).

The large number and wide variety of commercial enterprises in the Oaxaca economy mask a tendency toward the monopolization of many key materials and products. For example, a recent public protest by an organization of bakers (Cámara de la Industria de la Panificación en Oaxaca) alleges that one Oaxaca City merchant has exclusive distribution rights throughout the state for 4 different brands of yeast, that another merchant controls the sale of sugar, and that a handful of merchants control the distribution of flour (Panorama Oct. 10, 1979:3). The bakers' protest is symptomatic of conditions which confront all types of small rural and urban producers. Thus, potters of the village of Atzompa find the supply of glaze controlled by one Oaxaca City merchant who represents a factory in Monterrey; needleworkers and weavers find the supply of factory-made cotton, wool and synthetic thread, cloth, and dyestuffs controlled by two or three large dealers in Oaxaca City. Many other examples could be cited, all having the same outcome: arbitrary price-gouging and profiteering by merchants and skyrocketing production costs for direct producers, most of whom find their ability to pass on increased costs to buyers restricted or constrained by the peculiar structure of the markets they supply.

Last but not least it should be reiterated here that the role of merchant or commercial capital in the regional economy, and more particularly its relationship to small production, is by no means restricted to its control over the marketing of commodities produced by absentee capitalist firms. As mentioned in the preceding section, merchant capital intervenes in the labor process in several rural cottage industries, especially those which produce craft products and most notably in the embroidery industry which is dispersed throughout several districts of the 'Central Valleys' region but is centered in the district of Ocotlan. Its importance in this district is underlined by the fact that only three or four of its twenty municipios have little or no embroidery; eleven of the twelve communities surveyed by my project in 1978-79 had a significant incidence of families engaged in this work ranging from 100% of the families censused (40% random sample) in San Isidro Zegache to a low of 16% in Santa Lucia (38% random sample) with the average incidence being 56% of all families censused (467) in the eleven communities. Regarding the distribution of value in this industry our data indicate that embroiderers earn the equivalent of an hourly wage of 1-2 pesos with intermediaries earning substantially more. Preliminary computations, based on survey data from 24 intermediaries in four separate communities (San Martin Tilcajete, Ocotlan de Morelos, San Juan Chilateca, and San Antonio) yield a total gross annual income from sales of embroidered products of 2,671,594 pesos or an average annual per capita gross income among these 24 intermediaries went from a high of 1,129,550 pesos ($49,980 U.S.) for a San Antonino merchant to a low of 6699 pesos ($292 U.S.) for another merchant in the same community. With regard to the number of outworkers per merchant, the range was from 400 to 2; however, only four of the 24 intermediaries interviewed admitted to having more than 150 outworkers with the rest claiming to employ between two and twelve. It is difficult to judge the reliability of these data but my inclination is to belive that most informants underestimated the value of annual sales (which is supported by one opportunity I had during the summer of 1979 to observe a transaction between a village intermediary and a Mexico buyer involving 97 embroidered dresses

372

and blouses for 27,300 pesos). Intermediaries pay outworkers (1978-79) between 80-100 pesos for a standard embroidered (floral design) blouse and sell finished blouses for 200-250 pesos each, but must deduct the costs of material and, if applicable, of additional labor to arrive at a net profit (not considering overhead or fixed capital costs). It appears, with no systematic data at this point to back up this generalization, that the highest profits in the embroidery industry accrue to those intermediaries (usually non-Oaxacans and often non-Mexicans) who are twice or further removed from the labor process; mark-ups from 50 to 100% above the original cost appear to be the rule at this stage in the marketing process which takes place in retail shops specializing in 'Mexican handicrafts' located in Mexico City or tourist centers in Mexico, in the surburban U.S., and throughout Europe. Surely, one of the priorities for current and future research on the status of the small production of craft commodities and its workers must be to systematize our knowledge of the distribution of value and to expose and analyze, from a critical perspective, the conditions which sustain it.[5]

> The Government Apparatus and Financial Capital in the State and Regional Economy.[6] Even the most casual student of Oaxaca cannot help but recognize the pervasive and dominant role of the state and federal governmental apparatus in its economic life. Whether one looks at the production sector with reference to agricultural or industrial development, at marketing with respect to the supply of essential foodstuffs or commodity pricing, or at distribution and the determination of wage levels and taxation--or almost any other aspect of economic life--some agency of the state and especially of the federal government will be found to play an important or dominant role. The programmatic scope and financial magnitude of this role can be best appreciated by examing the evolution and current structure of public finance in the state and region.

A scrutiny of the official statistical record pertaining to the origin of the financial resources of the public sector in Oaxaca and to the evolution of its budget structure over a period from 1970-1978 discloses two salient trends: first, the rapid and progressive growth in the magnitude of monies available for public expendutures and, second, the shifting and progressively larger role of federal monies in the public sector's budget. These two trends may be demonstrated as follows: in 1970, 86% of the state government's budget was internally generated (71 million pesos) with only 14% being derived from federal transfer funds (11 million pesos), whereas this was dramatically reversed in 1978 so that only 28% (272 million pesos) of the state government's budget was internally generated and 72% (699 million pesos) derived from funds injected into the state treasury by the federal government. Moreover, in 1978 alone the federal government spent an additional 7,760,000,000 pesos ($343,862,000 dollars) through its various dependencies in the state of Oaxaca, an amount more than 28 times larger than the internally generated portion of the state budget.

In essence, the statistical record documents in startling and unequivocal fashion a massive 'federalization' of the public sector budget in Oaxaca between 1970 and 1978, a financial phenomenon which has had profound economic, social, and political repercussions in provincial life. This is especially true in light of the fact that this trend has gone hand-in-hand with a nationwide policy of 'bureaucratic decentralization' enacted by the López Portillo regime which has resulted in the establishment and staffing in Oaxaca City of southeastern regional offices for most of the major dependencies of the federal government.

A closer scrutiny of the origin of the monies spent annually by the state government is instructive. In 1977 and 1978, 35% and 34%, respectively, of the internally generated income of the state derived from the 'Central Valleys' region, with the Isthmus occupying a distant second place (14% and 15% and the Cañada in last place (5% and 6%). It is not surprising to learn that a major share of the state's internally-generated income (67% in 1978) is collected as tax revenues. In 1978, 32% of the state's income came from the agricultural and forest products sector, a whopping 83% of this representing tax receipts from coffee producers. Ironically, it has been the mezcal producers rather than the coffee growers who have been the most demonstrative and publicly outspoken critics of tax abuses. Indeed, the situation deteriorated in this industry during 1979-80 to a point where outbreaks of feuding between producers were occurring in the leading mezcal-producing village (Matatlan, Tlacolula) due to differences among them as to how to deal with dishonest government tax agents. According to newspaper reports, several tax agents were suspended pending the outcome of official investigations on charges of bribery, extortion, and corruption. One report alleges that three tax agents extorted 94,000 pesos ($41,000 dollars) monthly from Matatlán producers over a period of 2 1/2 years (Noticias, Feb. 2, 1980:1). On the heels of the mezcal producers' protest another important group of small producers in the regional economy, the brickmakers (ladrilleros) of San Agustín Yatareni (Centro), also initiated a taxpayers' rebellion to protest an announced increase in their monthly state tax from 100-200 pesos to 750 pesos (El Imparcial, Feb. 7, 1980:1 & 7b). The government, in this instance, was forced to suspend the proposed tax and to postpone any subsequent increases pending the outcome of an economic study of productivity and income levels in the industry. Subsequently, a new tax structure requiring monthly payments of 174 to 270 pesos per producer in accordance with productivity and income was instituted for this industry (ibid.).

A quite small percentage of state revenues derives from rural land taxes reflecting, among other factors, a continuing low rate of registration of privately owned agricultural land. Our survey of land tax rolls in the district of Ocotlán for 11 villages with a combined total of 1839 heads of household yielded a combined total of only 90 registered taxpayers, most of whom registered only one parcel of land each. Similarly, only 4% of state revenues were obtained from the industrial sector which, in any case, is mostly comprised of small labor-intensive enterprises located in rural communities where state and federal taxes are, for the most part, ill-conceived, capriciously administered and widely evaded. The case of one of the largest textile-producing villages in the district of Tlacolula is typical: out of a population with several hundred weaving households and many large workshops only nine weavers were listed on the 1978 state government tax rolls. Most of the listed taxpayers in this community, as is the case almost everywhere, were owners of commercial establishments (e.g., stores, grinding mills, catinas). In view of this situation the commercial sector contributed almost four times as much to state tax revenues as did the industrial sector.

Regarding the regional and sectoral allocation of state government expenditures (including federal transfer funds), 23% went to programs in the 'Central Valleys' region in 1977 and 25% in 1978. In this same two-year period, the Mixtec region was the recipient of the second largest allotment of state funds (17.4 and 19.6%). Whereas the Isthmus received only

14% and 11% of state expenditures in these two years, its relative share of federal funds spent in Oaxaca has probably been much higher. Moreover, every indication is that its relative share of the public sector's budget--especially of authorized federal expenditures--will be substantially increased over the next several years. For example, in the Governor's Annual Report of October 31, 1979, twenty-four pages were devoted exclusively to a status report on an ambitious government-backed development program in this region encompassing projects in agriculture (e.g., 26,526 hectares cleared and brought under cultivation to date at a cost of 210 million pesos), agroindustry (e.g., 1,900 million pesos or 84+ million dollars invested to date in a sugar mill in Juchitan), petroleum (e.g., 8,000 million pesos or 350+ million dollars earmarked in 1979-80 for the 2nd stage of construction of the PEMEX oil refinery, which will reportedly make it Mexico's largest), fishing (12 million 500 thousand pesos spent in 1978 on various projects in the fishing industry), and cement (2 billion pesos or 89+ million dollars invested in the CRUZ AZUL plant in Juchitan by 1979). In short, when these figures are considered together with additional massive public investments in housing (INFONAVIT, PEMEX, INDECO), transportation (e.g., 'Plan Alfa Omega' of the Secretaría de Comunicaciones y Transportes) to construct a 'land bridge' between the port of Coatzacoalcos, Veracruz, on the Gulf of Mexico and Salina Cruz on the Pacific for transporting containerized cargos by railway has a total projected cost of 170 million pesos in Oaxaca of which 17 million was spent in 1979, and other related areas of 'infrastructure,' it is clear that the Isthmus has been targeted as Oaxaca's 'growth pole' of capital-intensive industrial development.

Table 21 compares the relative amounts expended by the state and federal government during 1978 in the four sectors where both allocated funds. In addition to these areas of joint expenditure, the federal public expenditure in Oaxaca covered six other sectors in the following proportions: industrial (72%), agriculture and forestry (7.5%), commerce (2.9%), tourism (.4%), fishing (.35%), and administration and defense (.09%). The priorities of expenditures by the public sector are unmistakable from these figures. The state government in 1978 was able to collect internal revenues amounting to only 272 million pesos, with the remainder of its 971 million pesos budget derived entirely from federal transfer payments. By comparison the total federal public expenditure in Oaxaca in 1978 exceeded

TABLE 21. Comparison of State and Federal
Expenditures in Oaxaca in Four
Sectors During 1978.

| Sector | Expenditures (thousands of pesos) | |
	Federal	State
Communications and transport	804,200 (10%)	163,000 (54.5%)
Education, Culture, Science and Technology	243,000 (3%)	73,000 (24.4%)
Health and Social Security	96,200 (1.2%)	26,000 (8.7%)
Human Settlements	114,000 (1.5%)	37,000 (12.4%)
TOTAL	1,257,400	299,000

7,760 million pesos ($343,362,000 dollars), with approx-
imately 4% of this amount earmarked for rural development through programs administered or coordinated by
PIDER (i.e., Programa de Inversiones para el Desarrollo
Rural), a dependency of the Secretaría de Programación
y Presupuesto. This percentage remained essentially
unchanged in 1979 with a slightly increased allocation
of 500 million pesos (22+ million dollars) (El Imparcial), Jan. 23, 1980:1). All told, these figures
dramatically attest to the overwhelming federal presence
in Oaxaca's economic life, to the ultra-high priority
status of industrialization schemes, and to the relatively low priority status of rural development and
social welfare programs.

A possibly significant caveat is in order at
this point which may alter somewhat the prioritization
of public expenditures summarized above. Given the
way in which data on public expenditures is presented
in official documents, combined with the fact that the
budgets of many significant agencies or programs are

not included and are not readily available, it is next
to impossible to pinpoint their absolute and relative
impact on rural small-scale production. It is likely
that this is larger than the above interpretation leads
us to believe but how much larger is difficult to estimate. We do know, for example, that BANCRISA (Banco
del Crédito Rural del Istmo), a major public financial
institution affiliated with the BANRURAL group, extended 1,313 million pesos (58 million dollars) in credit
to small agriculturalists in Oaxaca during 1979 (incidentally only 44.5 million pesos or 1.96 million dollars of which went to the 'Central Valleys' region);
it is beyond the scope of the present inquiry to determine what the indirect impact of these loans may
have been on non-agricultural production. No credit
program of comparable scale for small-scale non-agricultural producers within this or any other major public
or private banking institution has come to my attention.
A federal dependency like INI-COPLAMAR (Instituto
Nacional Indigenista-Coordinación General del Plan Nacional de Zonas Deprimidas y Grupos Marginados) which
does have an extensive program designed to assist "marginal indigenous communities" in a variety of areas
(e.g., agricultural mechanization, establishment of
small-scale industries) operates with a relatively
small budget (32 million pesos or 1.4 million dollars
in 1979 for all of its programs in Oaxaca) (V. Informe
de Gobierno, Jiménez Ruíz, Oct. 1979:4). Likewise,
FONART (Fondo Nacional para el Fomento de las Artesanías), an agency which operates selectively to promote
the production and commercialization of craft products,
had only a 3 million pesos (133,000 dollars) budget
in 1977 to purchase craft products in 89 separate communities in Oaxaca; 38% of this budget was spent in 24
communities within the 'Central Valleys' region.

In conclusion, and keeping in mind the caveat
mentioned above, although the impact of federal monies
and the federal control over Oaxaca's economic affairs
which this implies is wide-ranging and decisive, it is
selective, variable, contradictory and underfunded vis-
a-vis the sector of small-scale, labor-intensive production. The official record indicates that a major
proportion of public expenditures earmarked for 'economic development' in Oaxaca is programmed to flow into
capital-intensive projects with immediate accumulation
potential.[7]

378

Class Formation, Political Struggle, and the
Economy in the 'Central Valleys' Region

Class or Ethnicity? There are many social scientists who prefer to investigate the rural Mexican
social structure with an emphasis on 'ethnicity' rather
than on 'class.' From this 'indigenista' perspective,
which was largely unchallenged in the social anthropological literature until the publication of the sem-
inal critique by Pozas and Pozas (1973), the majority
of rural direct producers in states like Oaxaca were
automatically classified as 'indígenas' who suffer
economic deprivation and social subordination due to
a quasi-colonial system of ethnic discrimination, a
situation that would diminish as a consequence of the
elimination of civil rights violations and the 'inte-
gration' of the indígenas into the mainstream of national life. In other words, the solution to the 'problema
indígena' according to the indigenista argument, is the
incorporation of ethnic minorities into the national
capitalist class structure (from which they putatively
remain excluded) thereby permanently extricating them
from their low caste position in a historically-deter-
mined structure of ethnic relations. Expressed differently, the so-called "internal colonial situation"
(González Casanova 1965) found in "refuge regions"
(Aguirre Beltrán 1967), especially in southern Mexico,
is seen to be a vestige of a previous epoch which has
no integral relationship to contemporary Mexican capitalism; accordingly, underdevelopment in regions
heavily populated by indigenous peoples is, by implication, a precapitalist phenomenon. In Oaxaca studies
this view has been most notably argued by Nolasco (1972:
9-13, 289-295, et passim).

In sharp contrast to this indigenista view is
the clasista approach which emphasizes the 'peasant'
or 'proletarian' (as opposed to the 'Indian') status
of rural direct producers in Oaxaca and similar areas;
it has several variant forms which differ in their conception of 'social class' and disagree about precisely
how the class position of rural direct producers should
be analyzed. Despite the theoretical differences among
them, the proponents of this approach (e.g., Pozas and
Pozas 1973; Bartra 1974; Warman 1974; Reyes et al.,
1974) agree that it is more accurate and analytically
fruitful to consider rural direct producers as 'peasants' or 'proletarians' first and as 'ethnics' second,

and to conceive of their status as primarily a problem
of class exploitation rather than of ethnic discrimination. This approach emphasizes that an overwhelming
majority of Mexico's rural direct producers, despite
appearing to be culturally separated or socially isolated, are integrated within the Mexican capitalist
economy as (1) sources of cheap labor power, (2) sources
of cheap agricultural and craft products, and (3) as
a demand group for consumer products of capitalist industry. They do not reject the significance of the
ethnic factor but simply contend that it is secondary
to 'role in the production process' in contributing
to an understanding of the status of rural direct producers in regional and national life (see Artis-Mercadet and Coello Hernández 1977 for a clasista critique
of the indigenista position).

The analytical concerns of Mexican clasistas
are essentially Leninist. Consequently, their analysis
of rural social structure aims at exposing the "basic
social forces operating, i.e., those groups or col-
lectivities whose activity could be recognized as fundamental in determining the course, and even the feasi-
bility, of programs for the transformation of production
relations and, above all, of the process and outcome
of the struggle for power" (Galeski 1972:101-102).
Differences arise among them, however, over such crucial
issues as the composition of the class of rural direct
producers, its capacity for independent political action, and the nature and implications of the encounter
between petty commodity production and capitalist production.

Pozas and Pozas, for example, reject any notion
of the peasantry as a separate class within the Mexican
rural social structure and prefer to consider it as
divided between various levels of the bourgeoisie or
proletariat (1973:115-155). Roger Bartra, by contrast,
considers the peasantry to comprise a sort of hybrid
'transitional class' which is simultaneously proletarian
and petty bourgeois but which is undergoing decomposition; depeasantization, for Bartra, is synonymous with
proletarization and he considers this process to be
relatively advanced in contemporary Mexico to the extent that the ". . .rural masses today have an essentially proletarian, not a peasant, character" (1974:
171; cf. pp. 152-162). Arturo Warman defines the peasantry broadly as rural agricultural workers who may
own, rent, hold in usufruct or otherwise cultivate the
soil at a level of simple reproduction (i.e., without
accumulation). As he expresses it: "The peasantry is

the social segment which through a productive relationship with the land succeeds in subsisting without accumulating" (1974:118). In marked contrast to Bartra's
strict Leninist posture, Warman manifests populist tendencies and asserts unequivocally that the "peasantry
is the majority sector of our (Mexican) society" (1974:
129). Finally, Reyes, Stavenhagen, et al. (1974)
conceive not of one but several 'peasant classes' in
the rural Mexican social structure which are seen as
categories of the agricultural population established
primarily on the basis of their specific relationship
to the land. Four such classes are identified as follows: (1) the ejidatarios, (2) the private minifun-
distas, (3) the medium landed proprietors (propietarios
medianos), and (4) agricultural day-laborers (jornaleros agricolas--ibid., pp. 413-429). Most of category
1, all of 2, and all of 4 considered collectively constitute in the word of these authors the "oppressed
classes of the countryside" (ibid., p. 429) [See
Harris 1978 for a more comprehensive review and critique of the 'clasista' Literature.]

   In the study of Oaxaca society, given the in-
terregional cultural diversity of its population, it
is neither possible nor desirable to adopt an inflex-
ible position in the indigenista vs. clasista controversy. The ethnic factor is clearly less relevant in
the study of the 'Central Valleys' region than it is,
for example, in the study of an area like the district
of Jamiltepec where ethnic boundaries between mestizos,
blacks, and Mixtec-speaking peoples are still maintained (see Flanet 1977) or a sub-region of the Isthmus
like the districts of Tehuantepec and Juchitan where
mestizo, Zapotec and Huave populations are still significantly differentiated in terms of language, community membership, and identity (see Signorini 1979)
in an area of rapidly intensifying capitalist development. Several other regions and sub-regions in Oaxaca
could be mentioned in which ethnicity does play a significant role in social process. Nevertheless, at this
conjuncture in Oaxaca's history an undiluted indigenista
posture is as anachronistic as it is analytically sterile. The still widespread tendency among anthropologists and others to persist in delimiting discrete
population zones along ethnic lines is more reflective
of careerist strategies for securing niches in the lab-
yrinthine Mexican governmental apparatus than it is
of the social reality of Oaxaca. In my view, admittedly
based on a 'Central Valleys' bias in terms of research
experience, there is not an area in Oaxaca in 1980
where 'ethnicity' (and its implicit subordinate con-

concepts) is an adequate tool for describing, analyzing or explaining social reality; capitalist accumulation and its concomitant forces and processes, which are by no means uniform in their trajectory or impact, have everywhere either emasculated or subsumed the ethnic factor in economic, political and ideological dimensions of social life.[8]

On the Dynamics of Class Formation. As the preceding discussion implies, there are many operational difficulties in the use of the concept of social class and the various concepts implicit in and subordinate to it (e.g., class situation, class position, class interest, class consciousness--Harnecker 1974), yet it remains an indispensable analytical tool if only because it enables us to expose and examine a series of relevant questions. Lenin's definition of class (1967: 213-214) which emphasizes the relationship between peoples' roles in the process of social production or their positions vis-a-vis the means of production remains the best departure point for analysis. One set of questions which is of particular importance to the study of social process in areas like Oaxaca relates to the issue of the impact of commodity production and wage labor on the composition of the class of rural direct producers. What, for example, is the 'class position' of landless craft workers? Do they have a 'class interest' separate from that of peasant cultivators? Does, in fact, the insertion of peasant cultivators into commodity production or wage labor promote the formation of class fractions, the formation of a single class, or are there conditions under which it does not lead to either of these developments? Does the wage labor involvement have a different impact on class formation than commodity production by non-waged workers? In which situations do rural direct producers in regional society tend to act as a class, and in which situations does it appear that differences between discrete groups of direct producers are decisive?

While not contributing directly to the systematic analysis of these and other related questions, several recent occurrences in Oaxaca City and its surrounding hinterland are indicative of class formation and underlying class conflict. The most notable and complex of these was the political turmoil which surfaced during 1976 and continued into the Spring of 1977 following the resignation of the incumbent governor Manuel Zarate Aquino and his replacement by General Eliseo Jiménez Ruíz who served as interim governor for several months until being 'elected' to serve out a term through 1980. The struggle behind these events involved a polarization of social forces: a leftist, populist coalition movement (COCEO or Coalición de Obreros, Campesinos y Estudiantes de Oaxaca) mainly comprised of university and preparatory school students together with certain worker and peasant groups and political parties represented one pole, and various conservative elements in the public and private sectors, spearheaded by business organizations and the state bureaucracy, represented the other. For several months during 1977 Oaxaca was, in effect, under a modified form of martial law which saw the popular movement subjected to a systematic campaign of repression and subversion the most notorious example of which was the forced resignation and exile from the state of Felipe Martínez Soriano, the rector of the state university and most prominent spokesman of the popular movement (see Bustamante et al. 1978 for a detailed analysis of this period and its recent historical background).

Apart from a series of strikes and public demonstrations by the dissidents in Oaxaca City, Juchitan and other urban centers--and with more ominous social and political implications--were several developments in the countryside. These can be traced back, at least, to October 28, 1974, during the governorship of Zárate Aquino when a group of peasants in the community of El Trapiche (Zimatlan) 'invaded' 97 hectares of agricultural land owned by an absentee landlord family, after several year of frustrated efforts to buy it through the federal government (Departamento de Asuntos Agrarios y Colonización, and the Banco Ejidal). The peasant activists, with the support of the Bufete Popular Universitario, an organization of lawyers and law students in Oaxaca City sympathetic to their cause, proceeded to consolidate their successful invasion by establishing collectivist programs which, despite both internal and external opposition, continue to operate (see Avilés 1979, Oct. 21:1 and 6). Subsequent to the coming to power of the Jiménez Ruíz regime in 1977, the collectivist program in El Trapiche was subjected to various repressive and subversive measures by opposition elements in the private sector and the state government, most notably a 'reverse land invasion' organized and carried out by the so-called Confederación Campesina Oaxaqueña (CONCAOAX) built around a nucleus of 27 dissidents from El Trapiche with the encouragement (and possible funding) of the state government and two wealthy Oaxaca City families with large landholdings in the Zimatlan district. This abortive event, which took place on April 30, 1979, but involved several prior incidents, involved a fight between the original 'collectivists' and some 50 armed intruders (allegedly including professional agitators or 'porros'), resulting in the deaths of two of the latter, and culminating in the intervention of the army and state police and the arrest of several 'collectivists' (see Avilés 1979 for further details). Although the CONCAOAX reinvasion failed its member, who claimed to represent all of the El Trapiche peasants opposed to the continuing collectivist organization and who seek to work the land as individual pequeños propietarios, persist in their opposition; thus in March 1980 they met with the Governor and with the head of the Comisión Agraria Mixta, which is charged with resolving the dispute, and let it be known that they intend to resort to armed force once again if their rights are not promptly recognized (Noticias, March 27, 1980:1 & 12). In the community of Santa Gertrudis, also in the district of Zimatlan, during the early part of 1977 a large group of peasants invaded land belonging to one of the same Oaxaca City-based landlord families that supported CONCAOAX and the 're-invasion' movement in El Trapiche, and proceeded to establish a collectivist program similar to that operating in the latter community. The Santa Gertrudis peasants subsequently experienced several crises similar to those in El Trapiche (see Paz Paredes and Moguel 1979 for a brief history of this movement and testimonials by the principal activists and the contending landlord).

Whereas both of these collectivist agrarian movements and their programs have managed to survive into the 1980s, albeit with internal and external opposition, it would be erroneous to infer from them that the regional peasantry is pervaded by class consciousness and is on the verge of initiating a social-ist revolution in the Oaxaca countryside. There are factors which set the communities of El Trapiche and Santa Gertrudis apart from the majority of rural communities in the 'Central Valleys.' First, they share a unique historical relationship with large haciendas and, in the post-Revolutionary period, both populations suffered the consequences of a successful attempt by powerful Oaxaca City-based families to maintain large-scale landholdings in their communities. Second, they are located in the district of Zimatlan which has a relatively high percentage of first-class agricultural land (i.e., de riego and de humedad), a relatively high rate of investment per hectare of arable land, and a social division of labor with no significant craft or other non-agricultural industries. In other

384

words, it seems fair to generalize that neither the historical experiences of the populations of these two communities nor the economic characteristics of the district of Zimatlan itself (see Appendix II) are typical of the region. This does not mean that the recent history of these communities should be discounted as aberrant; on the contrary, what has occurred there may be a harbinger of future social and political upheaval to the degree that they are genuinely symptomatic of an intensification of contradictions within the Oaxaca social order which is a concomitant of accelerated, if selective, capitalist development.

In the period 1978-80, with a renewed effort by the state and federal governments to industrialize and modernize Oaxaca including an ambitious fiscal reform program, we saw, on the one hand, the emergence of several organizations representing certain traditional, small-scale rural industries which operated through public and private channels to protest governmental programs or policies judged to be directly detrimental to their interests and, on the other, the founding of an association in Oaxaca City to promote industrial growth in the state. The mescal producers of Matatlan (Tlacolula) and the brick producers of Yatareni (Centro) are among those whose interests were represented by independent producers' organizations. Selected details of their activities have been outlined in Section II. Suffice it to say here that what distinguishes these two industries from others like the metate industry and, perhaps, partially explains their organized activism is the relatively more capital-intensive nature of their labor process and the larger volume of their production and revenues, coupled with the fact that both face direct competition from even more highly capitalized and rationalized enterprises, as well as aggressive taxation policies by the government.

A parallel development of considerable interest was the appearance in 1978-79 of a well-publicized and ambitious promotional campaign for industrialization in Oaxaca, spearheaded in the public sector by the Industrial Promotion Office within the Dirección General De Desarrollo Económico of the state government and in the private sector by the Asociación Para La Industrialización del Estado de Oaxaca which was founded and is headed by the president of the Oaxaca branch of CANACINTRA (Cámara Nacional de las Industrias de Transformación). In a press conference held to inaugurate the program of this Association, its president blamed the lack of 'industry' in Oaxaca on the conservatism and lack of confidence of its "industrialists of yesteryear" and he promised a new approach to the problem by his Association which represented "young investors better prepared than the old entrepreneurs of Oaxaca because they have studied in Monterrey, Mexico City and in foreign countries" (Panorama Oaxaqueño, Oct. 15, 1978:1). In a later statement this same spokesman ironically appealed for unity among Oaxaca's industrialists and emphasized that "labor and natural resources exist in sufficient quantity to exploit (sic), what is lacking are those who will invest in the state which occupies first place in emigration due to the lack of sources of employment" (Panorama Oaxaqueño, Feb. 17, 1979:1 & 8).

Industrialization in Oaxaca has been supported financially as documented above but it should also be noted that its promotional arm has received significant programmatic and institutional support. For example, in 1974 the federal government took the initiative in creating the Centro de Investigaciones y Asistencia Tecnológica de Oaxaca (CIATO) to follow-up a 1972 policy of the Echeverría regime to decentralize industries concentrated in or around Mexico City. The director of CIATO, in a 1978 statement, admitted to the failure of the 1972 policy to attract industry to Oxaca and blamed the indifference of the entrepreneurial sector to CIATO to the mistaken belief that it was just another niche for bureaucrats created by the government (Panorama Oaxaqueño, Oct. 10, 1978:1 & 5). He went on to disclose that CIATO is jointly funded by the Consejo Nacional de Ciencia y Tecnología (CONACYT), the Laboratorios Nacionales de Fomento Industrial, and the Comité Promotor para el Desarrollo Económico del Estado de Oaxaca (COPRODEO), has an annual budget of 2 million pesos, and a staff that includes seven engineers and 3 laboratory technicians. Given the types of services offered by CIATO (which include the development of new technology, supervision of quality control of raw materials and finished products, distribution, replacement and withdrawal of machinery, and control and improvement of production process), it is not unreasonable to conclude that what its frustrated director refers to as "apathy" may in fact be a 'paucity' of enterprises in Oaxaca which could benefit from its services. Perhaps more in line with actual conditions and needs was a recent conference on "Perspectives of Industrial Development for the State of Oaxaca" jointly sponsored by the state and federal governments and the Mexican Institute of Chemical Engineers. It was billed as a step toward initiating an important stage of industrial

development in Oaxaca and focussed its proceedings on
the possibilities for installing 11 new industries including a sugar-cane by-products industry, a tomato
processing plant, a plant for extracting oil from castor
beans, and a plant to decorticate the pencas or leaves
of the maguey mescalero most of which presently go to
waste in the region (Panorama, Oct. 5, 1979:1).

These organizations and ideological developments,
among others which could be cited, go hand-in-hand with
the trend in public finance and investment during the
decade of the 1970s, namely, the ascendancy of industrial capital to a position of quasi-hegemony in Oaxaca's
political economy.

What is the posture of merchants in the commercial sector to the apparent ascendancy of industrial
capital in the state's economic life? In a survey conducted during 1978 by my project of 15 business proprietors in Oaxaca City engaged in the buying and selling
of regional craft products on a retail and/or wholesale basis, with reported annual sales from 50 thousand to 7 million pesos, there was not a single unfavorable response to an open-ended question which asked
whether the respondent considered that the Pro-Industrialization Association and its program would benefit
the commercial sector. None of these respondents, all
of whom were members of a section of the local Chamber
of Commerce for craft products (i.e., Comerciantes de
Artesanías de Oaxaca or CAO), admitted to any conflict
of interest between the commercial and industrial sectors or expressed any reservations about the possible
impact of outside industrial capital on craft production; on the contrary, a few of them specifically stated
that industrialization was the best solution for regional unemployment. The owner of the second most prosperous craft products business in the City, while not formally a member of the Pro-Industrialization Association,
spoke of the need for all business people to organize
so as to overcome their individualism; and, in observing that he had studied at the Monterrey Institute of
Technology (Mexico's M.I.T.) with the son of the founder
of the Association, he implied sharing a positive attitude toward industrialization and its impact. In short,
at this conjuncture in the development of capitalism
in Oaxaca there would appear to be no perceived conflict between the embryonic industrial sector and, at
least one branch of the commercial sector of the regional capitalist class.

Most of the negative attitudes expressed by these 15 merchants were directed at the role of government enterprises, agencies, and functionaries engaged in the buying and selling of craft products. These views ranged from the extreme of accusing the government of unfair competition and of responsibility for the declining quality of artisan products to that of hyper-bureaucratization, impersonality in dealing with the public, corruption, and inefficiency. A large majority of these respondents emphasized the virtues of private enterprises managed by individual proprietors whose income is determined by their business performance in comparison with the defects of public enterprises managed by salaried employees whose incomes are not tied to business performance. Essentially, these 15 business proprietors saw no conflict of interest between their own activities and those of industrialists but did view their interests and activities to be incompatible with those of managers of government enterprises and of government functionaries in general. Rather than reflecting resentment by these merchants over the major role of the government in the program to industrialize the Oaxaca economy, this negative posture was probably more reflective of the active role of various government enterprises or dependencies in the marketing of craft products in direct competition with private enterprises.

Some Concluding Propositions

Several concluding theses derived from my study of the metate industry and from my continuing research in Oaxaca can now be proposed. It is my hope that despite their tentativeness they will be suggestive to others who are seeking to understand and explain the structure, functioning, and evolution of labor-intensive commodity production which is regionally located in the Mexican or other developing capitalist formations in Latin America or elsewhere.

First, a specific craft industry like the metate industry must be analyzed in the context of a social division of labor which, in turn, is inserted in a total economy. Given the present historical conjuncture of the Mexican social formation its economy is dominated by a dependent form of State monopoly capitalism (Semo 1978:127-136) but its regional branches display a differing mix of capitals (e.g., industrial vs. merchant) and of small commodity forms, with these latter, nevertheless, always subsumed by the former. It is through the social division of labor

that a regional economy discloses the prevailing configuration of the capitalist/noncapitalist relations
internal to it. In the 'Central Valleys' region of
Oaxaca, for example, it is clear that a social division
of labor based upon an inter-community system of production specializations, which has its origins in the
precolonial and colonial period, is still visible, and
that commodities circulate between different groups
of regional direct producers/consumers through a complementary system of periodic markets or _plazas_ where
exchange rates still respond to non-capitalist forces.
But it is equally clear that the regional economy is
inserted into a social division of labor of national
and international scope whose rationale is that of advanced forms of industrial, commercial, and financial
capital. Given this situation, I would argue that the
precise impact of the capitalist/noncapitalist relational process in the regional economy upon discrete labor-
intensive commodity-producing industries, as well as
the specific nature of their insertion into the complex social division of labor, must remain a subject
for empirical determination, as must the problem of
ascertaining the ways in which the production and circulation of commodities is or is not expressive or diagnostic of the subsumption of simple commodity forms.
For example, the fact that metates are produced almost
exclusively by non-wage workers who own or possess the
means of production indicates that this industry is
not capitalist. However there are complicating factors.
Since the wage system and labor markets are operative
in the agricultural and other sectors of the regional
economy, the _metateros_ do experience wage labor in other
productive roles; this is inevitably reflected in the
pricing of metate industry products where the _metateros_
consider the labor power they expend in manufacturing
their products to be a production cost. This suggests
that the metate industry is, indirectly at least, pen-
etrated by capitalism.

We are now led to a second point that merits emphasis, namely, that the relational process between
capitalist and noncapitalist production is not necessarily one of externality between two separate and discrete structural forms (i.e., the capitalist mode of
production and the simple commodity or 'peasant' mode)
or between two separate and distinct sets of agents
(i.e., capitalists and peasants) as proposed in general
terms by Díaz Polanco (1977:88-90) and specifically for
Oaxaca by Alcalá and Reyes (1977:2-13). Likewise, it
should not be assumed that this process always leads
to a crystallization of social relations in a particular

small-scale industry. For example, elements like private control over the means of production and production for exchange are internal to both the capitalist and simple commodity forms, as are price-determining markets and the accumulation of exchange value, the crucial difference being that in advanced capitalism this is a reproductive necessity whereas in the simple commodity form it is, more often than not, an unrealized possibility. The worker-owner in a simple commodity producing unit, to the extent that he may be said to pay himself a wage or to accumulate exchange-value (appropriated by marketing his commodities) for the purpose of expanding the commodity-producing (and exchange-value accumulating) capacity of his 'enterprise,' can be viewed as a 'double agent': petty capitalist, on the one hand, and direct producer/worker, on the other. It is quite possible, of course, to encounter a combination of capitalist and non-capitalist relations of production in a single craft industry, a situation which obtains to a limited degree in the metate industry but is much more prevalent, for example, in the weaving industry. As argued above, however, the real significance of wage-labor in the metate industry lies in product pricing and valorization and not in the relations of production. And, to reiterate, this instance of capitalist/noncapitalist articulation derives from the metateros' experiences outside of their industry in productive roles associated with other branches of regional production.

A third thesis which appears to be supported by the metate industry data is that the relational process between capitalist and small commodity production in the regional economy is not unidirectional. It does not lead inevitably to the demise of simple commodity production, either as a result of the predatory, expansionist tendencies of capitalism or of the realization of tendencies toward advanced development (e.g., accumulation, social differentiation) inherent in small commodity production. Two aspects of this thesis require further discussion. First, and related directly to point two above, the process of the subsumption of small commodity production to the laws of functioning of capitalist production involves the internalization of noncapitalist forms within the dominant capitalist form. This occurs, for example, when merchant capital subordinates independent peasant-artisan domestic units to its direct control through the extension of credit (e.g., regatones to metateros in the metate industry or empleadoras to tejedoras de petates in the palm-weaving industry) or the putting-out of materials (e.g.,

390

intermediaries to embroiderers in the embroidery industry). In both cases, but especially in the latter, the payment received by the direct producer for his/her products may be considered as a de facto 'inferior wage.' Nevertheless, in the example of the metate and palm-weaving industries, the producers remain in control of the means of production, while in the embroidery case the most important means of production (cloth and thread) are supplied to the producers but remain the property of the supplier. What does sometimes occur, however, is that outworkers--once they acquire sufficient skill and access to the necessary means of production--break with their employer, become independent producers for a time and, then, establish their own network of outworkers. Indeed, this 'hiving off' process appears to be important in the expansion of the regional embroidery industry.

A second aspect of the thesis of the non-unidirectionality of the relational process between capitalist and small commodity production is that the latter can lose its agents to the former via two routes: (1) proletarianization or depeasantization, and (2) mercantilization or accumulation (i.e., the entrepreneurialization of direct producers or petty traders). In the first instance, the small producer loses control of his means of production and is pushed into the ranks of the rural or urban proletariat. In the second instance, the worker-owner (or petty trader) accumulates exchange value and, in the process of investing this in the expansion of the commodity-producing (or value-yielding) capacity of his/her 'enterprise,' is pulled into the lower ranks of the capitalist class. My Oaxaca data suggest that neither movement is irreversible. On the contrary, it appears that, given the maintenance of the corporate community/domestic group in the structure of production (which presents the temporarily proletarianized peasant-artisan with the possibility of 'repeasantization' via the acquisition of land by inheritance, agrarian reform, purchase, etc., and the fallen entrepreneur with the refuge of simple reproduction) the small commodity regime can be reproduced indefinitely.

A fourth concluding proposition is that any generalization about the destiny of small commodity production within a national or regional economy must be taken cum grano salis. This is so not only because of the dialectical complexities at the economic level of capitalist/noncapitalist relations but also because of the very real differences that exist between separate branches of production or industries regarding the possible substantive impact and outcome of these relations. It may be that in one branch of production the labor process itself, or the type of product it produces to satisfy social demand, places strict limits on an industry's capacity to absorb capital inputs (e.g., via mechanization). Capital may penetrate a small industry at the level of circulation or, if it intervenes at the level of production, it may do so without necessarily acquiring direct ownership of the means of production or altering the small-scale, technologically simple, and non-waged configuration of the labor process. Therefore, industries like the metate industry, with their traditional product-types and market structures, will probably never develop beyond the level of the small workshop or support a large-scale marketing operation.

Finally, it is clear that the destiny of small commodity production is inextricably tied to the "periodization" of the reproduction of capitalist relations, a process whose arena is international in scope but which becomes directly operational at the level of the nation-state and its internal formations (Poulantzas 1978:part I, esp. pp. 134-135; cf. Semo 1978:139-160). This implies the need for a totalizing approach which incorporates methodological and conceptual instruments for considering the economic process as but one sphere of an historical stream in which the main class agents are structurally fractionalized and, therefore, constrained ideologically and politically in their economically-determined conflict for State hegemony (cf. Poulantzas 1973:137-141 et passim). In other words, the capitalist/noncapitalist relational process in a given capitalist formation should be approximated by focussing on the class struggle in a framework of dialectical relationships with and between economic structure, State structure, and State policies or interventions in national and regional life (cf. Wright 1978: ch. 1). Small commodity producers, because of the fundamental contradiction transecting their economic structure, are situated on the periphery of the central class struggle between the proletariat and the bourgeoisie which permeates every capitalist formation. Given this contradictory class location, they tend to be ideologically confused and politically disorganized and, consequently, are vulnerable to manipulation by those classes (or class fractions) which have (or are in contention for) hegemony. In short, the economic destiny of small commodity production in developing capitalist formations like Mexico will ultimately be resolved in the political arena of the class struggle which has in-

ternational dimensions, and will be tied to the career
in that arena of peasants and artisans whose ambivalent
status as either 'petty bourgeoisie' or 'semi-proletar-
iat' mirrors the contradictions of their transitional
class situation.[9]

[1]Perhaps more than any other single problem which confronts economic anthropologists in their attempt to formulate a Marxist research agenda for a regional economic study, that of 'value, price, and unequal exchange' is the most complex. It clearly lies within the field of political economy proper (i.e., the political economy of capitalism). This was true to a lesser degree of the value/price relationship dealt with in Chapter 7 because these were restricted to simple commodity production. Most experts agree with Marx and Engels that a separate and less complicated law of value operates under conditions of simple commodity production than under those of capitalism (cf. Emmanuel 1972:389-90). However, in this final Chapter we have ventured into terrain where capitalist dominance thrusts upon us the full repertory of conceptual and methodological tools known to the science of political economy. This is an intimidating experience for an anthropologist. I have relied heavily on Kay (1975), and to a lesser extent on sections of Marx's Capital v. 2, in formulating this tentative schematic framework for operationalizing the problem. My consultation of sources like Emmanuel (1972) has convinced me that any further elaboration of this framework to encompass a wider range of capitalist/noncapitalist relations, including the international dimension, will require a much more sophisticated, full-blown political economic treatment.

[2]Alcalá and Reyes (1977:9) recognize that PADUs may produce for exchange either actual surplus-product or a portion of their necessary product; nevertheless, they erroneously characterize the "peasant economy" as self-sufficient at the level of production and, consequently, as one in which production is predominantly for use and autoconsumption rather than for exchange (1977:12). Unfortunately, this theoretical posture carries over into their concluding characterization of the Mixteca Baja economy as one "of infrasubsistence . . . with few possibilities for accumulation and condemned to reproduce their conditions of functioning cycle by cycle . . . since it doesn't generate a sufficient quantity of surplus to permit accumulation" (1977:122--my rough translation). I suspect, however, that had their theoretical point of departure conceived of the "peasant economy" as characterized by small com-

modity production, which contains internally the seeds for accumulation and differentiation, their conclusions would have had a different emphasis (and with statistical support).

[3]In a brief published report based partially on an unpublished study by the late Jorge Martinez Rios, a Oaxaca sociologist affiliated with the Instituto de Investigaciones Sociales of U.N.A.M., it is estimated that 1,511,000 Oaxacans between the ages of 15 and 65 have emigrated from the state in search of employment since 1960, as follows: 1960-1965: 104,000 emigrants; 1965-1970: 260,000 emigrants; 1970-1975: 440,000 emigrants; and 1975-1980: 707,000 emigrants. Concerning internal migration no figures are given but it is argued that the most important flow is from the 'Central Valleys' to the 'Isthmus' and to the 'Costa Chica,' followed in order by that from the 'Mixteca' to the 'Costa Chica' and the 'Isthmus' and, finally, by that from the 'Sierra Júarez' to the lowlands of Choapam, the Mixe and Tuxtepec (Aguilar 1980:1 & 12).

A good example of the type of background study, using available census data, which must precede any first-hand empirical study of migration at the regional level is provided by Alcalá and Reyes 1977.

[4]That the development of capitalism in Oaxaca does not follow a one-way linear trajectory but, rather, has run a capricious, fluctuating course, is illustrated by Young's retrieval of the fact that a British firm built a textile factory in a Sierra Júarez community some 15 kilometers from Ixtlán on the Oaxaca City-Ixtlán road in 1873 which was supplied with raw cotton from plantations in Choapam and Veracruz (1976:243). That this now defunct factory was no fly-by-night operation is indicated by the fact that it produced some 25,000 lbs. of yarn and 15,000 lengths of cloth annually for regional markets. We also learn that an active role by the governmnent in facilitating capitalist operations in Oaxaca is no recent phenomenon; Young notes that the state government built a graded dirt road from Oaxaca City to the factory-site, with an extension to the mines near Ixtlán, to facilitate the marketing of the cotton cloth and yarn (ibid.).

[5]In March 1980 newspaper reports (Noticias, March 12:1 & 4 and March 23:7) indicate that six small assembly plants (maquiladoras), employing initially some 120 women (mostly ambulatory peddlers from the city marketplaces and ex-prostitutes displaced by the clo-

sure of the red-light district), will soon be established in Oaxaca City. These 'maquiladoras' will sew together clothing articles sent in pre-cut patterns from various commercial houses in Mexico City. More specifically, according to one of these reports, "se trata unicamente de unir las piezas que se envien, presumiendose que Oaxaca será el punto clave para la realización del maquilado a los almacenes de Mexico y otros del Norte del pais" (Noticias, Mar. 12, 1980:4). This imminent insertion of external commercial capital into clothing production in Oaxaca City is ironically occurring at a time when the role of local merchant capital in the traditional mantelerías is declining (PESPIDEO files).

[6]Unless otherwise specified the discussion in this section is based on various published and unpublished documents obtained from offices of the state (Dirección General de Desarrollo Económico) and federal (Programa de Inversiones para el Desarrollo Rural of the Secretaría de Programación y Presupuesto) government in Oaxaca City. The principal published document consulted was the Quinto Informe de Gobierno presented by Governor Eliseo Jimenez Ruiz on October 31, 1979; the complete text of the governor's speech was published as a ten-page supplement in local newspapers. However, the complete Informe comprises several volumes which have been published by the state government press. Much of the statistical material in this section was extracted from Apendice II, Desarrollo Económico y Producción of the Quinto Informe de Gobierno which is a separate volume.

[7]Unfortunately, at the time of this writing I have not had time to research the role of the private and public banking sector in rural development and other aspects of economic life in Oaxaca. There are some 15 banking institutions in Oaxaca City including Mexico's largest private (e.g., BANAMEX, BANCOMER, BANCA SERFIN, MULTIBANCO COMERMEX) and semi-private or public (Banco del Pequeno Comercio, Banco Agropecuario del Sur, Banco Nacional de Fomento Cooperativo) institutions. Many of these institutions, especially BANCOMER and BANAMEX, have established regional and sub-regional offices particularly in the 'Central Valleys', the Isthmus, and Tuxtepec. Until the role of these banks is analyzed our understanding of the Oaxaca economy will be deficient.

[8]In what is presented as a "new interpretation" of class and ethnicity in Mexican studies Lomnitz-Adler

superimposes a series of computer-correlated pairs of variables extrapolated from the 1970 federal General Population Census (e.g., "empresarios" and "trabajadores por su cuenta," "obrerosempleados" and "peonesjornaleros") on a spatial grid encompassing the state of Morelos. This exercise yields specific conclusions like ". . . la diferenciación tradicional entre los altos y el valle de Morelos . . . se refleja en la estructura de clases" (P. 455) and general conclusions such as, "Ni la estructura de clases ni el aislamiento geográfico o la marginalidad económica constituyen explicaciones que . . . pudieran predecir los fenómenos de las relaciones étnicas en el México contempraneo" and "es necesario analizar la evolución histórica del concepto de indianidad, el significado de ser indio, para poder analizar adecuadamente los diversos factores . . . que inciden en el manejo de los símbolos étnicos por la población" (1979:471). What this "new interpretation" lacks, even as a preliminary inquiry, is a clarification of the concept of 'social class' and a formulation of the author's approach to its operationalization. What it most convincingly illustrates is the inadequacy or irrelevancy of variables extracted from the Mexican national census to 'class analysis' and, consequently, the need for theoretically-informed, carefully designed, firsthand empirical research.

[9]For further relevant discussion of issues like class alliances, hegemony, and counter-hegemonic strategies in Mexican state capitalism see two important works by Roger Bartra, a book in Spanish (1978) and an article in English (1975); incidentally, the latter is part of an excellent collection of essays by various scholars entitled Mexico: The Limits of State Capitalism, Latin American Perspectives II, 2 (1975) which contains another outstanding contribution by Leal.

One discontinuity emerges in the general literature between the metropolitan (e.g., Poulantzas, Wright, Miliband, Therborn) and Third World (e.g., Bartra, Leal) contributors: the former persist in viewing the Bonapartist state as an 'exceptional' form of capitalist state, whereas the latter (in this instance departing from Latin American realities) see nothing exceptional about it. The neo-Bonapartist state, in fact, appears to be the rule, not the exception, under the conditions of neocolonial capitalism. This discontinuity raises a whole host of important issues in method, theory and analysis which will certainly be the object of future inquiry and debate.

A Magdalena metatero leaning on his barreta
during a rest break in the quarry.

APPENDIX I. Socioeconomic Data from the General Census of 1970 for the nine districts within the "Central Valleys" of Oaxaca. [1]

Districts Within Region	Total EAP*	Total Population	Surface (km²)	Population Density	Average Members in Families	% Families with Annual Income < $1000 (pesos)	% Families with Annual Income > $1500 (pesos)	% of Total EAP in Agriculture or in Transformation Industry
Centro	42,748	158,497	643	246.5	4.88	77.1	.61	38.5
Ejutla	10,114	35,984	1,146	31.4	4.66	97.8	.09	86.1
Etla	15,841	61,761	1,750	35.3	4.74	94.5	.39	81.3
Miahuatlan	19,879	71,947	3,752	19.2	4.65	97.2	.29	90.2
Ocotlan	12,414	46,295	1,008	45.9	4.58	96.8	.40	84.2
Sola de Vega	11,108	41,311	3,719	11.1	4.65	97.9	.31	89.6
Tlacolula	19,076	76,638	2,922	25.2	4.62	96.2	.84	84.5
Zaachila	4,009	19,574	504	38.8	4.95	96.5	.92	80.9
Zimatlan	10,323	40,553	790	57.4	4.67	96.2	.28	86.7
Total	102,812	549,560	16,234					
Regional Average				56.08	4.71	94.5	.46	80.2
State of Oaxaca	521,385	2,015,424	95,364	21.13	4.76	92.6	.51	80.3
Mexican Nation	12,955,057	48,225,238	1,967,183	24.51	5.22	68.7	.70	56.1

*EAP - Economically Active Population

[1] From IX Censo General De Población por Entidades Federativas, 1970. No. 20, Oaxaca. Mexico, D.F.: Dirección General de Estadística, 1972b.

APPENDIX I., Continued

Districts Within Region	% of EAP in Agricultural Activities	% of EAP that Works in Agricultural Occupations	% of EAP in Agricultural Occupations that are "jornaleros/peons"	% of EAP in Agricultural Occupations that are Self-Employed	% of EAP in Agricultural Occupations that are "ejidatario"	% of EAP in Agriculture or Transformation Industry Who Earn < $500 Monthly
Centro	23.07	22.7	45.9	32.3	7.9	71.2
Ejutla	76.05	75.3	40.9	34.8	7.9	96.4
Etla	70.7	69.8	35.6	51.1	4.5	90.0
Miahuatlan	83.8	82.8	35.2	48.3	1.2	94.5
Ocotlan	77.4	75.7	35.9	39.4	14.7	94.1
Sola de Vega	87.09	85.2	21.8	63.4	2.5	97.6
Tlacolula	75.08	72.5	35.0	49.2	2.5	95.4
Zaachila	75.3	72.0	27.2	53.8	8.9	94.3
Zimatlan	80.7	79.3	39.9	41.2	5.1	90.4
Regional Average	72.21	70.6	35.3	45.9	6.1	91.5
State of Oaxaca		69.5	34.2	46.5	7.6	78.9
Mexican Nation		38.2	17.3	8.8	6.3	58.6

400

APPENDIX I., Continued

Districts Within Region	% of EAP in Agricultural Occupations that Earn < $500 Monthly	% of EAP that Work as "jornalero/peon" that Earn < $1000 Monthly	% of Households that Do Not Consume: Eggs	Meat	% of Dwellings Not Owned	% of EAP in Agriculture that Works 6 Months or Less
Centro	87.1	87.0	20.3	13.2	38.9	6.4
Ejutla	97.0	99.1	40.6	35.4	11.5	6.2
Etla	92.5	96.3	23.7	19.5	13.8	9.1
Miahuatlan	94.9	97.6	26.9	29.8	9.5	11.4
Ocotlan	95.5	97.9	28.6	20.9	13.5	6.7
Sola de Vega	97.4	98.2	36.3	43.3	9.2	4.7
Tlacolula	97.3	98.6	30.1	22.2	9.4	5.6
Zaachila	96.3	97.3	43.0	36.5	6.1	7.5
Zimatlan	93.0	97.2	32.3	16.5	13.2	11.9
Regional Average	94.5	96.6	31.3	26.4	13.9	7.7
State of Oaxaca	93.9	96.7	27.6	24.9	15.1	8.3
Mexican Nation	77.0	93.7				14.7

APPENDIX I., Continued

Districts Within Region	% of EAP in Transformation Industry that Works 6 Months or Less	% of EAP in Agriculture that Works 10-12 Months	% of EAP in Transformation Industries that Work 10-12 Months
Centro	6.0	89.6	90.01
Ejutla	4.9	84.6	92.02
Etla	7.4	86.2	88.64
Miahuatlan	17.1	80.45	73.15
Ocotlan	7.8	85.2	87.2
Sola de Vega	8.9	91.6	87.1
Tlacolula	5.2	90.3	87.98
Zaachila	2.7	91.19	95.04
Zimatlan	10.9	83.9	85.3
Regional Average	7.8	87.0	87.4
State of Oaxaca	7.8	85.6	87.9
Mexican Nation	10.8	76.97	83.9

APPENDIX II. Agricultural Data from the V Agricultural Livestock Census of 1970 for the nine districts within the 'Central Valleys' of Oaxaca.[1]

Districts Within Region	% of cultivated land within the total area censused	% of TAC* unsuited for agriculture	% of uncultivated TAC which is arable	% of private production units of 5 has. or less	% of land seasonally cultivated	% of producer owned production units
Centro	54.3	13.5	1.5	93.5	87.4	94.4
Ejutla	25.4	14.7	.07	93.3	95.3	96.5
Etla	13.3	21.6	2.1	96.8	78.3	92.8
Miahuatlan	37.9	33.4	4.6	83.4	88.2	96.0
Ocotlan	26.1	31.3	.12	92.1	95.9	87.2
Sola de Vega	7.4	35.8	3.9	85.2	96.8	80.1
Tlacolula	13.5	24.6	2.4	93.8	74.7	93.7
Zaachila	18.2	26.7	.007	96.2	98.8	99.4
Zimatlan	21.7	4.8	1.3	73.8	94.6	94.4
Region	24.2	22.9	1.8	89.8	92.2	92.7
State of Oaxaca	19.0	18.9	3.6	82.8	87.9	92.9
Mexican Nation	18.3	14.4	4.3	59.6	80.2	93.4

*TAC - Total Area Censused

[1]From V Census Agricola-Ganadero por Entidad Federativa, Oaxaca. Mexico, D.F.: Direccion General de Estadística, 1975.

APPENDIX II, Continued

Districts Within Region	% of rented production units	% of private units that use animal energy	% of private units that use mechanical energy	Total annual expenditures for all units (thousands of pesos)	Expenditure per avg. unit of production	Total value of agricultural production (thousands of pesos)
Centro	5.4	66.7	3.2	6,026	2,177.02	17,623
Ejutla	1.4	98.4	1.6	2,514	2,070.84	15,652
Etla	1.7	57.3	7.0	4,823	864.80	17,771
Miahuatlan	.92	98.3	.70	3,723	513.52	25,081
Ocotlan	12.1	83.5	2.1	1,776	381.03	17,418
Sola de Vega	19.6	98.6	.53	984	809.81	26,729
Tlacolula	6.1	65.8	4.3	3,278	655.73	19,078
Zaachila	.51	73.5	1.9	1,158	605.65	6,794
Zimatlan	3.2	37.6	3.3	4,443	1,517.42	22,468
Region	5.6	75.5	2.7	28,725	824.32	168,634
State of Oaxaca	3.1	85.8	2.8	264,476	288.52	972,500
Mexican Nation	5.3	79.4	10.7	14,083,183	1,380.68	31,912,795

APPENDIX II, Continued

Districts Within Region	Capital invested in all units of production	Avg. invested capital per unit	Avg. value of agric. output per unit larger than 5 has.	Avg. value of agric. output per unit smaller than 5 has.	Avg. invested capital per unit of prod. larger than 5 has.	Avg. invested capital per unit of prod. less than 5 has.
Centro	114,716	41,443	22,059	943	145,843	8,326
Ejutla	70,342	56,636	11,581	1,295	46,890	4,848
Etla	174,327	31,256	13,705	1,090	27,604	6,909
Miahuatlan	113,178	15,582	7,153	1,509	18,639	4,715
Ocotlan	98,723	21,180	10,764	1,506	35,735	7,012
Sola de Vega	769,188	633,076	8,727	1,905	71,284	11,610
Tlacolula	100,858	20,175	14,537	1,717	26,927	4,334
Zaachila	61,894	32,371	10,716	1,271	59,250	9,302
Zimatlan	256,353	87,552	12,824	2,397	63,367	18,023
Region	1,75,579	104,363	12,451	1,514	55,059	8,342
State of Oaxaca	6,108,245	72,500	13,168	1,283	73,002	7,475
Mexican Nation	169,779,770	166,448	25,409	1,460	193,555	20,430

405

APPENDIX II, Continued

Districts Within Region	Avg. invested capital in ejidos or agrarian communities	Avg. value of agric. output in ejido or agrarian communities	Avg. returns for prod. units larger than 5 has.	Avg. returns for prod. units smaller than 5 has.	Avg. returns for ejidos or agrarian communities
Centro	1,523,818	153,590	17,492	720	120,954
Ejutla	1,421,214	399,892	10,272	1,003	304,750
Etla	2,246,000	69,567	10,532	807	56,108
Miahuatlan	1,898,733	274,266	5,984	1,006	246,866
Ocotlan	1,054,424	166,393	8,401	1,197	125,636
Sola de Vega	32,556,500	753,181	6,525	1,449	571,636
Tlacolula	892,257	111,085	11,068	1,286	89,771
Zaachila	2,667,750	204,166	8,700	938	173,083
Zimatlan	7,030,285	246,761	11,546	2,335	136,523
Region	5,698.989	237,938	10,057	1,193	202,814
State of Oaxaca	3,349,788	446,101	11,499	996	367,363
Mexican Nation	3,048,870	499,168	22,419	1,183	430,432

REFERENCES CITED

Adams, R.N.
1970   Crucifixion by Power. Austin: University
        of Texas Press.

Aguilar, Silvio
1980   "Millón y medio de Oaxaqueños han emigrado
        en veinte años." Noticias, Año III, no.
        1187, March 27:1 & 12.

Aguirre Beltrán, Gonzalo
1967   Regiones de Refugio. México, D.F.: Insti-
        tuto Interamericano Indigenista.

Alavi, Hamza
1975   "India and the colonial mode of production."
        Economic and Political Weekly (August):
        1235-1262.

Alcalá Delgado, Elio and Reyes, Teófilo
1977   La Economía Campesina En La Mixteca Baja.
        Departamento de Etnología y Antropologia
        Social, I.N.A.H., Cuadernos de Trabajo no.
        21, México, D.F.

Andrianov, B.V. and L.F. Monogarova
1976   "Lenin's doctrine of concurrent socioeconomic
        systems and its significance for ethnography."
        Soviet Anthropology and Archaeology, Spring,
        pp. 3-26.

Arroyo, E.
1961   Los Dominicos, Forjadores de la Civilización
        Oajaqueña. Vol. 2: Los Conventos. Oaxaca,
        Mexico.

Artis-Mercadet, G. and M. Coello-Hernández
1977   "Indigenismo sin indigenistas?" El Día, 12
        de septiembre, p. 9.

Assadourian, C.S. et al.
1973   Modos de Producción en América Latina.
        Córdoba, Argentina: Cuadernos de Pasado y
        Presente 40.

Avilés, Jaime
1979 "El Trapiche, una comunidad ejemplar." Uno
Mas Uno, Oct. 21-24.

Banaji, Jairus
1972 "For a theory of colonial modes of production." Economic and Political Weekly, Dec.
23, pp. 2498-2503.
1975 "India and the colonial mode of production."
Economic and Political Weekly, Dec. 6, pp.
1887-1892.
1976 "Summary of selected parts of Kautsky's The
Agrarian Question." Economy and Society 5,
1:1-49.
1977 "Modes of production in a materialist conception of history." Capital and Class, no.
3:1-43.

Bartra, Roger
1973 Breve Diccionario de Sociología Marxista.
México, D.F.: Editorial Grijalbo.
1974 Estructura Agraria y Clases Sociales en
México. Mexico, D.F.: Serie Popular Era.
1975 "Sobre la articulación de modos de producción
en América Latina." Historia y Sociedad 5:
5-19.
1978 El Poder Despótico Burgués. México, D.F.:
Serie Popular Era.

Beals, Ralph L.
1967 "The structure of the Oaxaca market system."
Revista Mexicana de Estudios Antropológicos
21:333-342.
1970 "Gifting, reciprocity, savings, and credit
in peasant Oaxaca." Southwestern Journal
of Anthropology 26:231-41.
1975 The Peasant Marketing System of Oaxaca,
Mexico. Berkeley and Los Angeles: University of California Press.

Belshaw, C.S.
1969 The Conditions of Social Performance.
London: Routledge and Kegan Paul.

Bernstein, H.
1979 "Concepts for the analysis of contemporary
peasantries." Journal of Peasant studies
6,4:421-444.

Blanton, Richard E.
1978 Monte Albán. New York: Academic Press.

1980   "Cultural ecology reconsidered." American
        Antiquity 45,1:145-151.

Boege, E.
    1980   Desarrollo del Capitalismo y Transformación
            de la Estructura de Poder en la Región de
            Tuxtepec, Oaxaca. Cuadernos de Investigación
            I, Vol. I. Mexico: SEP-INAH.

Bradby, Barbara
    1975   "The destruction of natural economy."
            Economy and Society 4,2:127-161.

Brandis, R.
    1964   "Business cycles and business fluctuations."
            In Dictionary of the Social Sciences, pp.
            62-63, Gould and Kolb, eds. New York: Free
            Press.

Burgoa, Fr. Francisco de
    1934   Geográfica Descripción. México, D.F.:
            Talleres Gráficos de la Nación.

Bustamante, R. et. al.
    1978   Oaxaca, Una Lucha Reciente: 1960-1978.
            México: Ediciones Nueva Sociología.

Cancian, Frank
    1967   "Political and religious organizations." In
            Handbook of Middle American Indians, Vol. 6:
            Social Anthropology, M. Nash (ed.), pp. 283-
            298. Austin: University of Texas Press.

Cardoso, C.F.S.
    1975   "On the colonial modes of production of the
            Americas." Critique of Anthropology 4 & 5
            (Autumn):1-36.

Carrasco, Pedro
    1951   "Las culturas indígenas de Oaxaca, México.:
            Américan Indígena 11:99-114.
    1961   "The civil-religious hierarchy in Meso-
            American communities . . ." American
            Anthropologist 63:483-97

Cassady, R.
    1968   "Negotiated price-making in Mexican tradi-
            tional markets: a conceptual analysis."
            America Indigena 28:51-78.

Chance, John K.
    1978   Race and Class in Colonial Oaxaca. Stanford,
            Calif: Stanford Univ. Press.

Chapple, E.D. and C. Coon
    1942   Principles of Anthropology. New York: Holt.

Chayanov, A.V.
    1966   The Theory of Peasant Economy. Homewood,
            Ill.: Irwin.

Clammer, J. (Ed.)
    1978   The New Economic Anthropology. New York:
            St. Martin's.

Coello, M.
    1975   "Caracterización de la pequeña producción
            mercantil campesina." Historia y Sociedad
            8:3-19.

Cole, G.D.H.
    1930   "Introduction." In K. Marx, Capital, Vol.
            1, part 1. New York: Dutton (Everyman's
            Library).

Cook, Scott
    1968   Teitipac and Its Metateros. Unpublished
            doctoral dissertation, University of
            Pittsburgh.
    1969   "The 'anti-market' mentality re-examined: a
            further critique of the substantive approach
            to economic anthropology." Southwestern
            Journal of Anthropology 25:378-406.
    1970   "Price and output variability in a peasant-
            artisan stoneworking industry in Oaxaca,
            Mexico . . ." American Anthropologist 72:
            776-801.
    1973a   "Production, ecology and economic anthro-
            pology: notes toward an intergrated frame
            of reference." Social Science Information
            XII, 1:25-52.
    1973b   "Stone tools for steel-age Mexicans? Aspects
            of production in a Zapotec stoneworking in-
            dustry." American Anthropologist 75:1485-
            1503.
    1974   "Economic anthropology: problems in theory,
            method, and analysis." In Handbook of
            Social and Cultural Anthropology, J.J.
            Honigmann, ed., pp. 795-860. Chicago: Rand
            McNally.

1976 "Value, price, and simple commodity production: the case of the Zapotec stoneworkers." Journal of Peasant Studies 3,4:395-427.

1977 "Beyond the Formen: towards a revised Marxist theory of precapitalist formations and the transition to capitalism." Journal of Peasant Studies 4,4:360-389.

1978 "Petty commodity production and capitalist development in the 'Central Valleys' region of Oaxaca, Mexico." Nova Americana I: Mercato, mercati e mercanti. Torino: Einaudi, pp. 285-332.

Cook, S. and M. Diskin (eds.)
1978 Markets in Oaxaca. Austin: University of Texas Press.

Contreras, A. J.
1976 "Economía pequeño-mercantil y mercado capitalista." Historia y Sociedad 12:66-77.

Dahlgren de Jordan, B.
1963 Nocheztli, la Grana Cochinilla. Nueva Biblioteca de Obras Historicas 1. Mexico, D.F.

Dalton, George
1969 "Theoretical issues in economic anthropology." Current Anthropology 10:63-102.

Davis, H. T.
1941 The Analysis of Economic Time Series. Bloomington, Indiana: The Principia Press.

Dennis, P. A.
1976 Conflictos Por Tierras en el Valle de Oaxaca. Mexico, D.F.: SEP-INI.

Desai, M.
1974 Marxian Economic Theory. London: Gray-Mills Publishing Ltd.

DeWalt, Billie R.
1974 "Cambios en los sistemas de cargos de Mesoamerica." América Indígena XXXIV, 2: 531-550.

Diaz, May
    1966 Tonalá. Berkeley: Universit of California
          Press

Díaz Móntes, Fausto
    1979 El Impacto de la Agroindustria del Mezcal
          en la Estructura Social de Una Comunidad.
          Unpublished licenciatura thesis, Programa
          para la Formacion de Profesores e Investiga-
          dores en Ciencias Sociales, Univerdidad
          Autónoma 'Benito Juárez' de Oaxaca.

Díaz Polanco, Hector
    1977 Teoría Marxista De La Economía Campesina.
          México, D.F.: Juan Pablos Editor.

Dirección General de Estadística (DGE)
    1972a IX Censo General de Población, 1970. Resúmen
          General Abreviado. Mexico, D.F.
    1972b IX Censo General De Población por Entidades
          Federativas, 1970. No. 20, Oaxaca. 2 vols.
          Mexico, D.F.
    1975 V Censos Agrícola-Ganadero por Entidad
          Federativa. Oaxaca. Mexico, D.F.

Diskin, Martin
    1969 "Estudio estructural del sistema de plazas
          en el valle de Oaxaca." América Indígena
          29:1077-1099.

Dobb, Maurice
    1963 Studies in the Development of Capitalism.
          New York: International Publishers.
    1976 "From feudalism to capitalism." In The
          Transition from Feudalism to Capitalism.
          London: New Left Books.

Dorfman, R.
    1964 The Price System. Englewood Cliffs, N.J.:
          Prentice-Hall.

Emmanuel, Arghiri
    1972 Unequal Exchange. New York: Monthly
          Review Press.

Engels, Frederick
    1967 "Supplement to Capital, Volume Three."
          In K. Marx, Capital, Vol. 3, pp. 889-910.
          New York: International Publishers

Ennew, J., P. Hirst and K. Tribe
   1977   "'Peasantry' as an economic category."
           Journal of Peasant Studies 4,4:295-322.

Fernandez, R.A.
   1977   The United States-Mexico Border. Notre Dame:
           Notre Dame University Press.

Firth, Raymond
   1965   Primitive Polynesian Economy, 2nd edition.
           London: Routledge and Kegan Paul.
   1966   Malay Fishermen: Their Peasant Economy,
           2nd edition.   London Routledge and Kegan
           Paul.
   1967   "Themes in economic anthropology: a general
           comment."   In Themes in Economic Anthro-
           pology, ed. by Raymond Firth, pp. 1-28.

Firth, Rosemary
   1966   Housekeeping Among Malay Peasants, 2nd
           Edition. London: Athlone Press.

Flanet, Veronique
   1977   Viviré Si Dios Quiere, Un Estudio de la
           Violencia en la Mixteca de la Costa.   Mexico,
           D.F.:   Instituto Nacional Indigenista.

Flannery, Kent, et. al.
   1968   "Farming systems and political growth in
           ancient Oaxaca."   Science 158:445-454.

Foster-Carter, Aidan
   1978   "The modes of production controversy."
           New Left Review 107:47-78.

Foster, G.
   1942   A Primitive Mexican Economy.   New York:
           American Ethnological Society.
   1948   "The folk economy of rural Mexico with
           special reference to marketing."   Journal
           of Marketing 13:153-162.
   1967   Tzintzuntzan: Mexican Peasants in a
           Changing World: Boston: Little, Brown.

Frazer, L.M.
   1947   Economic Thought and Language.   London:
           Black.

Friedman, H.
   1980   "Household production and the national
           economy: concepts for the analysis of

413

  agrarian formations." Journal of Peasant
  Studies 7,2:158-184.

Galeski, B.
  1972 Basic Concepts in Rural Sociology.
        Manchester: Manchester University Press.

Gamio, Manuel
  1971 Mexican Immigration to the U.S. New York:
        Dover (re-issue of 1930 edition).

Gide, C. and C. Rist
  1947 A History of Economic Doctrines. New York;
        D.C. Heath.

Godelier, Maurice
  1971 "Salt currency and the circulation of
        commodities among the Baruya of New Guinea."
        In G. Dalton, ed., Studies in Economic
        Anthropology, pp. 52-73. Anthropological
        Studies no. 7. Washington, D.C.: American
        Anthropological Association.
  1972 Rationality and Irrationality in Economics.
        New York: Monthly Review Press.

González Casanova, Pablo
  1965 La Democracia en México. México, D.F.:
        Serie Popular Era.

Gordon, D.F.
  1968 "Labor theory of value." In Sills, ed.,
        International Encyclopedia of the Social
        Sciences. New York: Free Press/Macmillan.

Guzmán, Alejandro
  1977 Artesanos de la Sierra Norte de Puebla.
        Estudios de Folklore y de Arte Popular 4.
        Mexico: Secretaría de Educación Pública.

Hammett, B.
  1971 Politics and Trade in Southern Mexico.
        Cambridge: Cambridge University Press.

Harnecker, Marta
  1974 Los Conceptos Elementales del Materialismo
        Histórico. México: Siglo XXI.

Harris, R.L.
  1978 "Marxism and the agrarian question in Latin
        America." Latin American Perspectives,
        Issue 19,Vol.V, no.4:2-26.

Herskovits, M.J.
1952   Economic Anthropology. New York: Knopf.

Hindess, B. and P.Q. Hirst
1975   Pre-Capitalist Modes of Production. London: Routledge and Kegan Paul.

Holmes, W.H.
1895   Archaeological Studies Among the Ancient Cities of Mexico. Chicago: Field Museum Publication No. 8.

Howard, M.C. and J.E. King
1975   The Political Economy of Marx. Essex: Longman.

Isaac, Barry L.
1965   "'Rational' and 'Irrational' factors in southern Mexican Indian capitalism." América Indígena 25:427-36.

Jiménez Ruíz, Eliseo
1979   Quinto Informe de Gobierno. Oaxaca, Mexico.

Kautsky, K.
1974   La Cuestión Agraria. Mexico: Ediciones de Cultura Popular.

Kay, G.
1975   Development and Underdevelopment: a Marxist Analysis. New York: St. Martin's Press.

Kirkby, Anne
1973   The Use of Land and Water Resources in the Past and Present Valley of Oaxaca, Mexico. Memoirs of the Museum of Anthropology, no. 5. Ann Arbor: University of Michigan.

Kosik, Karel
1967   Dialéctica de lo Concreto. México, D.F.: Editorial Grijalbo.

Kowalewski, Stephen A.
1980   "Population--Resource Balances in period I of Oaxaca, Mexico." American Antiquity 45, 1:151-165.

Krader, L.
1975   The Asiatic Mode of Production. Assen, Netherlands: Van Gorcum.

Kula, W.
1976   An Economic Theory of the Feudal System.
       London: New Left Books.

Laclau, E.
1971   "Feudalism and capitalism in Latin America."
       New Left Review 67 (May-June).
1977   Politics and Ideology in Marxist Theory.
       London: New Left Books.

Landes, K.K. and R.C. Hussey
1948   Geology and Man. Englewood Cliffs, N.J.:
       Prentice-Hall.

Leal, J.F.
1975   "The Mexican state: 1915-1973. An histor-
       ical interpretation." Latin American
       Perspectives, Issue 5, Vol. II, no. 2:48-63.

LeClair, E.E., Jr.
1959   "A minimal frame of reference for economic
       anthropology (revised)." Troy, N.Y.:
       Rensselaer Polytechnic Institute (mimeo-
       graph).
1962   "Economic theory and economic anthropology."
       American Anthropologist 64:1179-1203.

LeClair, E.E., Jr. and H.K. Schneider (eds.)
1967   Economic Anthropology: Readings in Theory
       and Analysis. New York: Holt, Rinehart &
       Winston.

Lees, S.H.
1973   Socio-Political Aspects of Canal Irrigation
       in the Valley of Oaxaca, Mexico. Memoirs
       of the Museum of Anthropology, no. 6. Ann
       Arbor: University of Michigan.

Lenin, V.I.
1964   The Development of Capitalism in Russia.
       Moscow: Progress Publishers.
1967   Selected Works, Vol. III. New York: In-
       ternational Publishers.
1974   "What the 'Friends of the People' are and
       how they fight the social democrats." In
       Marx, K. Engels, F. and Lenin, V.I., On
       Historical Materialism. New York: Inter-
       national Publishers.

Leslie, C.M.
1960 Now We Are Civilized. Detroit: Wayne
State University Press.

Lewis, Oscar
1949 "Aspects of land tenure and economics in a
Mexican village." Middle American Research
Records I,13:195-209.

Ley Federal de Reforma Agraria, 1974. Mexico, D.F.:
Editorial Porrua.

Littlefield, Alice
1976 La Industria de las Hamacas en Yucatán,
México. Serie de Antropológia Social no.
52. México, D.F.: SEP-INI.

Lorenzo, J.L.
1960 "Aspects físicos del valle de Oaxaca."
Revista Mexicana de Estudios Antropológicos
16:49-63.

Lowe, A.
1965 On Economic Knowledge. New York: Harper
and Row.

Lomnitz-Adler, Claudio
1979 "Clase y etnicidad en Morelos: una nueva
interpretación." Américan Indígena XXXIX,
3:439-475.

Lukacs, George
1971 History and Class Consciousness. Cambridge,
Mass.: M.I.T. Press.
1972 "Labour as a model of social practice." The
New Hungarian Quarterly XIII, 47:5-43.

Luxemburg, Rosa
1968 The Accumulation of Capital. New York:
Monthly Review Press.

Malinowski, B. and Julio de la Fuente
1957 La Economía de un Sistema de Mercados en
México. Acta Anthropológica, Epoca 2, Vol.
1, no. 2. México: Escuela Nacional de
Antropológia, Sociedad de Alumnos.

Mandel, E.
1970 Marxist Economic Theory. Vol. 1. New
York: Monthly Review Press.

1971   The Formation of the Economic Thought of
        Karl Marx. New York: Monthly Review
        Press.

Marroquín, A.
    1957   La Ciudad Mercado: Tlaxiaco. Mexico, D.F.:
        Imprenta Universitaria.

Martínez-Alier, Juan
    1977   Haciendas, Plantations and Collective Farms.
        London: Cass.

Marx, Karl
    1904   Critique of Political Economy. Chicago:
        Kerr.
    1930   Capital, Vol. 1. London: Dent (Everyman's
        library edition).
    1935   Value, Price and Profit. New York: In-
        ternational Publishers.
    1963   Theories of Surplus Value, Part I. Moscow:
        Progress.
    1965   Precapitalist Economic Formations. New
        York: International Publishers.
    1967   Capital, 3 Vols. New York: International
        Publishers.
    1973   Grundrisse. London: Penguin Books.

Mauss, Marcel
    1954   The Gift. London: Cohen and West.

McBryde, F.W.
    1945   Cultural and Historical Geography of South-
        western Guatemala. Institute of Social
        Anthropology, publication no. 4. Washington,
        D.C.: Smithsonian Institution.

Medina, A. and N. Quezada
    1975   Panorama De Las Artesanías Otomies Del
        Valle Del Mezquital. Mexico, D.F.: UNAM,
        Instituto de Investigaciones Antropologicas.

Meek, R.L.
    1956   Studies in the Labour Theory of Value.
        London: Lawrence and Weshart.

Meillasoux, C.
    1972   "From reproduction to production." Economy
        and Society 1, 1:93-105.

Mendieta y Nuñez, Lucio (ed.)
    1949   Los Zapotecos.   Mexico: Imprenta Universi-
           taria.

Mitchell, W.C.
    1927   Business Cycles, the Problem and Its
           Setting.   New York: National Bureau of
           Economic Research.

Moguel, Reyna
    1979   Regionalizaciones Para El Estado De Oaxaca,
           Análisis Comparativo.   Oaxaca: Centro de
           Sociologia de la U.A.B.J.O.

Morishima, M. and G. Catephores
    1975   "Is there an 'historical transformation
           problem'?"   The Economic Journal 85,338:
           309-328.

Murdock, G.P.
    1949   Social Structure.   New York: Macmillan.

Nash, Manning
    1961   "The social context of economic choice in
           a small society."   Man 219:186-191.
    1966   Primitive and Peasant Economic Systems.
           San Francisco: Chandler.

Nolasco, Margarita
    1972   Oaxaca Indígena.   Mexico, D.F.:   Secretaría
           de Educación Pública.

Novelo, Victoria
    1976   Artesanías y Capitalismo en México.   México:
           SEP-INAH.

O'Laughlin, Bridget
    1975   "Marxist approaches in anthropology."
           In Siegel, B.J. (ed.) Biennial Review of
           Anthropology.   Stanford, Calif.:   Stanford
           University Press.

Ortiz, Sutti
    1979   "The estimation of work: labour and value
           among Paez farmers."   In Wollman, Sandra
           (ed.), Social Anthropology of Work, pp.
           207-228.   New York: Academic Press.

Ossowski, S.
1963   Class Structure in the Social Conscious-
       ness. New York: Free Press.

Padilla Aragón, E.
1969   México, Desarrollo con Pobreza. Mexico:
       Siglo XXI.

Palerm, Angel
1980   Antropología y Marxismo. Mexico: Editorial
       Nueva Imagen.

Parsons, E. C.
1936   Mitla, Town of the Souls. Chicago: Uni-
       versity of Chicago Press.

Paso y Troncoso, Francisco del (ed.)
1905   Papeles de Nueva España. Tomo IV, Relaci-
       ones Geográficas de la Diocesis de Oaxaca.
       Madrid.

Paz Paredes, Lorena and Julio Moguel
1979   Santa Gertrudis: Testimonios de una Lucha
       Campesina. México, D.F.:   Serie Popular
       Era.
Poulantzas, Nicos
1973   Political Power and Social Classes. London:
       New Left Books.
1978   Classes in Contemporary Capitalism. London:
       Verso Editions.

Pozas, R. and I. de Pozas
1973   Los Indios en las Clases Sociales de México.
       México, D.F.:   Siglo XXI.

Preobrazhesky, E.
1965   The New Economics. London: Clarendon
       Press.

Ravicz, R. S.
1967   Organización Social de los Mixtecos.
       Colección de Antropología Social no. 5.
       México, D.F.:   Instituto Nacional Indi-
       genista.

Reichert, J. S.
1981   "The migrant syndrome: seasonal U.S. wage
       labor and rural development in central
       Mexico." Human Organization 40, 1:56-66.

Rey, P. P.
    1976 Las Alianzas de Clases. Mexico, D.F.:
          Siglo XXI.

Reyes, Osorio, S., R. Stavenhagen, et. al.
    1974 Estructura Agraria y Desarrollo Agricola en
          Mexico. Mexico, D.F.: Fondo de Cultura
          Economica.

Roseberry, W.
    1976 "Rent, differentiation, and the development
          of capitalism among peasants." American
          Anthropologist 78:45-58.

Rubin, I. I.
    1972 Stone Age Economics. Chicago: Aldine.

Samuelson, P. A.
    1955 Economics: An Introductory Analysis. New
          York: McGraw-Hill.

Sanders, W. T.
    1972 "Population, agricultural history, and
          societal evolution in Mesoamerica." In
          Population Growth: Anthropological Implica-
          tions, ed. by B. Spooner, pp. 101-153.
          Cambridge, Mass.: M.I.T. Press.

Seddon, D. (ed.)
    1978 Relations of Production. London: Frank Cass.

Seldon, A. and Pennance, F. G.
    1965 Everyman's Dictionary of Economics. London:
          Dent.

Schmeider, O.
    1930 The Settlements of the Tzapotec and Mije
          Indians: State of Oaxaca, Mexico. Univ-
          ersity of California Publications in Geog-
          raphy no. 4, Berkeley: University of
          California Press.

Schneider, H. K.
    1974 Economic Man. New York: Free Press.

Secretaria de Programacion y Presupuesto (S.P.P.),
Programa de Inversiones para el Desarrollo Rural
(P.I.C.E.R.), Delegacion de Oaxaca

    1979a Oaxaca, Plan Estatal de Desarrollo: Sub-
          Region De Los Valles Centrales. Mimeo-
          graph.
    1979b Oaxaca, Plan Estatal De Desarrollo, Sector
          Industrial. Mimeograph.

1979c Oaxaca, Plan Estatal De Desarrollo, Sector
       Comercial. Mimeograph.
1979d Oaxaca, Plan Estatal De Desarrollo, Sector
       Agropecuario. Mimeograph.
1979e Oaxaca, Plan Estatal De Desarrollo, Sub-
       Región del Istmo. Mimeograph.

Semenov, Yu. I.
1974   "Theoretical problems of 'economic anthro-
       pology.'" Philosophy of the Social Sciences
       4:201-231.

Semo, E.
1974   "Tres aspectos de la estructura económica
       del México actual." Historia y Sociedad,
       2nda epoca, 1:5-22.
1978   Historia Mexicana, Economía y Lucha de
       Clases. México: Serie Popular Era.

Shanin, T.
1972   The Awkward Class. London: Oxford Univ-
       ersity Press.

Signorini, Italo
1979   Los Huaves de San Mateo del Mar, Ideología
       e Instituciones Sociales. México, D.F.:
       Instituto Nacional Indigenista.

Spores, R.
1965   "The Zapotec and Mixtec at Spanish Con-
       tact." In Archaeology of Southern Meso-
       america: part Two, ed. by G. R. Willey,
       pp. 962-987. Handbook of Middle American
       Indians, Vol. 3, R. Wauchope (ed.). Austin:
       University of Texas Press.

Stavenhagen, Rodolfo
1969   Las Clases Sociales en las Sociedades
       Agrarias. México, D.F.: Siglo XXI.
1970   "Social aspects of agrarian structure in
       Mexico." In Agrarian Problems and Peasant
       Movements in Latin America. R. Stavenhagen,
       ed., pp. 225-270. New York: Doubleday-
       Anchor.
1976   "Capitalismo y campesinado en México."
       In Capitalismo y Campesinado en México,
       R. Stavenhagen, ed., pp. 11-27. México,
       D.F.: SEP-INAH.

Sweezy, P. M., et al.
1967 The Transition from Feudalism to Capitalism.
      New York: Science and Society.

Swetnam, J.
1973 "Oligopolistic prices in a free market--
      Antigua, Guatemala." American Anthropolo-
      gist 75, 5:1504-1510.

Szekely, E. M.
1977 "Funcionamiento y perspectivas de la
      economía campesina." Naxí-Nantá, Revista
      de Economía Campesina, marzo:50-64.

Takahashi, H. K.
1967 "A contribution to the discussion." In
      The Transition from Feudalism to Capitalism,
      P. M. Sweezy, M. Dobb, et al., pp. 30-35.
      New York: Science and Society.

Tax, Sol
1953 Penny Capitalism: A Guatemalan Indian
      Economy. Washington, D.C.: Smithsonian
      Institution, Institute of Social Anthropol-
      ogy Publication no. 16.

Taylor, W. B.
1972 Landlord and Peasant in Colonial Oaxaca.
      Stanford: Stanford University Press.

Thompson, E. P.
1966 The Making of the English Working Class.
      New York: Vintage Books.

Tinbergen, J.
1951 Econometrics. New York: Blakiston.

Tintner, G., et al.
1968 "Time series." In The International Ency-
      clopedia of the Social Sciences, Vol. 16:
      47-87, D. L. Sills, ed. New York: Free
      Press/Macmillan.

Udy, S. H., Jr.
1959 Organization of Work. New Haven: HRAF
      Press.

Van Ginneken, W.
1980 Socio-economic Groups and Income Distribu-
      tion in Mexico. New York: St. Martin's
      Press.

Wagner, P. A.
 1960   The Human Use of the Earth. New York:
        Free Press.

Warman, Arturo
 1974   Los Campesinos, Hijos Predilectos del
        Régimen. México, D.F.: Editorial Nuestro
        Tiempo.
 1976   Y Venimos a Contradecir. México, D.F.:
        SEP-INAH.

Waterbury, R.
 1970   "Urbanization and a traditional market
        system." In The Social Anthropology of
        Latin America. W. Goldschmidt, ed., pp.
        126-156. Los Angeles: Latin American
        Center, UCLA.

Waterbury, R. and Carole Turkenik
 1976   "The marketplace traders of San Antonino:
        a quantitative analysis." In Markets in
        Oaxaca, S. Cook and M. Diskin, eds.,
        pp. 209-230. Austin: University of Texas
        Press.

Weber, Max
 1961   General Economic History. New York:
        Collier Books.

Welte, C. R.
 1976   "Appendix: Maps and Demographic Tables."
        In Markets in Oaxaca, Cook and Diskin, eds.,
        pp. 283-285. Austin: University of Texas
        Press.
Whitecotton, Joseph W.
 1977   The Zapotecs: Princes, Priests and Peas-
        ants. Norman: University of Oklahoma
        Press.

Williams, H. and R. F. Heizer
 1965   Geological Notes on the Ruins of Mitla and
        Other Oaxacan Sites, Mexico. Sources of
        Stone Used in Prehistoric Mesoamerican
        Sites. Contributions to the University of
        California Archaeological Research Facility,
        no. 1. Berkeley: Department of Anthro-
        pology.

Wittfogel, K.
   1957   Oriental Despotism. New Haven: Yale
          University Press.

Wolf, Eric
   1955   "Types of Latin American peasantry: a
          preliminary discussion." American Anthro-
          pologist 57:452-471.
   1966   Peasants. Englewood Cliffs, N. J.:   Pren-
          tice-Hall.
   1967   "The Valley of Oaxaca and its Zapotec-
          speaking hinterland." In Handbook of
          Middle American Indians, vol. 6, Social
          Anthropology, M. Nash, ed., pp. 301-308.
          Austin: University of Texas Press.

Wolpe, H.
   1972   "Capitalism and cheap labour-power in South
          Africa: from segregation to apartheid."
          Economy and Society 1,4:425-456.

Wright, Eric Olin
   1978   Class, Crisis and the State.   London: New
          Left Books.

Young, C. M.
   1976   The Social Setting of Migration: Factors
          Affecting Migration from a Sierra Zapotec
          Village in Oaxaca, Mexico.   Unpublished
          doctoral thesis, University of London.

A gift metate decorated (<u>bordado</u>) by the
'bas relief' technique in which the metatero
uses the small hammer and chisels shown (San
Juan Teitipac).

INDEX

Advanced commodity production. See Capitalism; Capital; Capital-intensive
Agriculture, 6-8, 10, 23, 38-39, 60, 66-68, 76-80, 105-107, 129-137, 140-141, 201-202, 307, 311, 312, 318, 358, 362, 376, 384
Agricultural means of production, 129-133
Animal husbandry, 6, 40-41, 57, 117-118, 134, 144
Articulation of modes of production, 24-25, 353-358, 388-393
Artisans, 10, 23, 100-101, 137-139, 367, 368, 393. See also Crafts; Craft production; Small industry
Banks, 136, 285, 378, 396
Bargaining, 261-266, 267-282, 329, 339
Barter, 25, 96, 118, 124, 255-256
Blacksmithing, 100-101
Brick industry, 375, 385
Broom production, 37, 38, 105
Campesino. See Peasant
Capital(-ist), 1, 3, 6, 7, 9, 14, 15, 22, 23, 24, 25, 44, 46, 55, 57, 81, 116, 156, 331, 346, 350-351, 353-393
Capital accumulation, 2, 14, 25, 114-115, 118, 119-120, 138-139, 285-286, 339, 357, 358, 359, 378, 382, 390, 391
Capital-intensive, 358, 360, 365, 366, 376, 378, 385
Capitalism, 2, 13, 14, 23, 24, 25, 53, 54, 394, 395, 397
Cash advances, 64, 137, 250, 255, 281, 286, 290
Caveat emptor, 257-261
Central valleys region of Oaxaca, 1, 7, 8, 10, 13, 16, 20, 22, 23
Circulationism, 3-4, 288
Civil-religious hierarchy, 82-84, 88
Class analysis, 378-380, 382-388, 397
Class relations, 6, 53, 70-72, 225, 290, 379-393
Class struggle, 87, 382-385, 392-393
Commodity, 241, 325-328, 330, 331, 334-335, 353, 354, 355, 356, 357, 358, 365, 370, 373, 382, 388, 389, 390, 391
Commodity economy, 289, 327-331, 345-346, 350-351
Commodity fetishism, 288, 289, 325, 328-329, 351
Commoditization, 23, 53, 54, 120, 124, 355, 357
Communal relations, 6, 69-70, 223-228, 235-236
Compadrazgo. See Fictive kinship

431

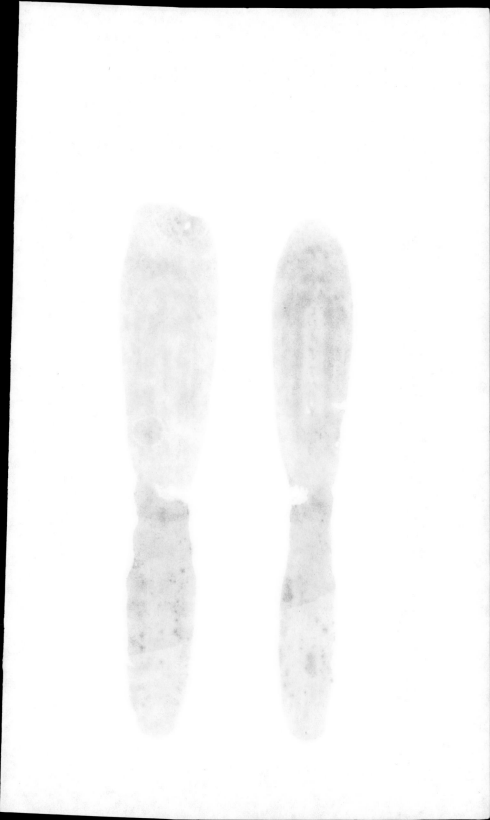

DATE DUE
